5th International Natural Language Generation Conference 2008

(INLG 2008)

Salt Fork, Ohio, USA
12-14 June 2008

ISBN: 978-1-61738-547-6

Printed from e-media with permission by:

Curran Associates, Inc.
57 Morehouse Lane
Red Hook, NY 12571

Some format issues inherent in the e-media version may also appear in this print version.

Printed by Curran Associates, Inc. (2010)

For permission requests, please contact the Association for Computational Linguistics at the address below.

Association for Computational Linguistics
209 N. Eighth Street
Stroudsburg, Pennsylvania 18360

Phone: 1-570-476-8006
Fax: 1-570-476-0860

acl@aclweb.org

Additional copies of this publication are available from:

Curran Associates, Inc.
57 Morehouse Lane
Red Hook, NY 12571 USA
Phone: 845-758-0400
Fax: 845-758-2634
Email: curran@proceedings.com
Web: www.proceedings.com

Table of Contents

Session 3: Psycholinguistics and Affect

Session 4: Realization

Session 5: Embodied Conversational Agents

Session 6: Content and Text Planning

Session 7: Evaluation

INLG Posters

Referring Expression Generation Challenge Papers & Posters

GREC

TUNA Shared Tasks

TUNA Open Track

Preface

We are pleased to introduce the technical program of the Fifth International Natural Language Generation Conference (INLG 2008), the Biennial Meeting of SIGGEN, the ACL Special Interest Group in Natural Language Generation. INLG is the leading international conference on research into natural language generation. It has been held in Sydney (Australia) in 2006, at Brockenhurst (UK) in 2004, in Harriman (New York, USA) in 2002, and in Mitzpe Ramon (Israel) in 2000. Prior to 2000, the INLG meetings were International Workshops, running every other year since 1984. The INLG conference provides a forum for the discussion, dissemination and archiving of research topics and results in the field of text generation. This year, INLG is being held immediately prior to the main ACL-08:HLT conference, on June 12–14, 2008, in southeastern Ohio, USA, at the Salt Fork Resort and Conference Center.

The INLG program consists of substantial, original, and previously unpublished results on all topics related to natural language generation. This year, as in previous years, each submission was reviewed by at least three members of an international program committee of leading researchers in the field, listed on the next page. We received 35 submissions (both full papers and poster papers) from all over the world, from which we accepted 17 as full papers and 7 as posters. One poster was subsequently retracted as unfortunately the authors could not find sponsorship to attend the conference.

This year, the program includes two invited talks, one by Kiwako Ito and Shari Speer (The Ohio State University, USA), entitled "Prominence and Phrasing in Spoken Discourse Processing," and one by Matthew Stone (Rutgers University, USA), entitled "Language, Embodiment and Social Intelligence." We are also excited to host a special session devoted to the Referring Expression Generation Challenge 2008, organized by Anja Belz (University of Brighton, UK) and Albert Gatt (University of Aberdeen, UK).

Our sincere thanks go to our invited speakers, the Referring Expression Generation Challenge organizers, all who submitted papers to INLG 2008, and to our program committee for their hard work. We would also like to thank the the SIGGEN board for their support and advice; Priscilla Rasmussen, the ACL Business manager, and Claudia Morettini, OSU Linguistics, for administrative support; Jody Croley Jones and Miles Oldenburg, OSU College of Humanities Web Services, for their help with the design and implementation of the web site; and the Salt Fork team, who have been very flexible in accommodating the event to our liking. Finally, we gratefully acknowledge the Ohio State Department of Linguistics for sponsoring two student volunteers, Emily Jamison and Dennis Mehay.

We welcome you to the conference and hope you will find it to be an enjoyable and productive experience!

Michael White, Crystal Nakatsu and David McDonald
INLG 2008 Organizers

Conference Organization

Program Chairs

Michael White, The Ohio State University, USA
Crystal Nakatsu, The Ohio State University, USA
David McDonald, BBN Technologies, USA

Referring Expression Generation Challenge Chairs

Anja Belz, University of Brighton, UK
Albert Gatt, University of Aberdeen, UK

Program Committee

John Bateman, Universität Bremen, Germany
Anja Belz, University of Brighton, UK
Kalina Bontcheva, University of Sheffield, UK
Stephan Busemann, DFKI, Germany
Charles Callaway, University of Edinburgh, UK
Giuseppe Carenini, University of British Columbia, Canada
Nathalie Colineau, CSIRO, Australia
Robert Dale, University of Macquarie, Australia
Hercules Dalianis, Stockholm University, Sweden
Laurence Danlos, Université Paris 7, France
Barbara Di Eugenio, University of Illinois at Chicago, USA
Philip Edmonds, Sharp Laboratories of Europe, UK
Noemie Elhadad, Columbia University, USA
Roger Evans, University of Brighton, UK
Claire Gardent, CNRS/LORIA, France
Michel Généreux, LIPN, France
Nancy Green, University of North Carolina Greensboro, USA
Markus Guhe, University of Edinburgh, UK
John Kelleher, Dublin Insitute of Technology, Ireland
Ivana Kruijff-Korbayova, Universität des Saarlandes, Germany
James Lester, North Carolina State University, US
Chris Mellish, University of Aberdeen, UK
Jon Oberlander, University of Edinburgh, UK
Stephan Oepen, University of Oslo, Norway
Cécile Paris, CSIRO ICT Centre, Australia
Paul Piwek, The Open University, UK
Rashmi Prasad, University of Pennsylvania, USA
David Reitter, University of Edinburgh, UK
Graeme Ritchie, University of Aberdeen, UK
James Shaw, The Thomson Corporation, USA
Amanda Stent, Stony Brook University, USA
Matthew Stone, Rutgers, USA
Mariet Theune, University of Twente, The Netherlands
Takenobu Tokunaga, Tokyo Institute of Technology, Japan

Kees van Deemter, University of Aberdeen, UK
Ielka van der Sluis, University of Aberdeen, UK
Sebastian Varges, University of Trento, Italy
Sandra Williams, The Open University, UK
Michael Zock, CNRS/LIF, France

Invited Speakers

Shari R. Speer, The Ohio State University, USA
Kiwako Ito, The Ohio State University, USA
Matthew Stone, Rutgers, USA

Conference Program

Thursday, June 12, 2008

12:00–1:15 Registration and Lunch

1:15–1:30 Opening Remarks

Session 1: Summarization

1:30–2:00 Generating Textual Summaries of Bar Charts
Seniz Demir, Sandra Carberry, Kathleen McCoy

2:00–2:30 Using Spatial Reference Frames to Generate Grounded Textual Summaries of Georeferenced Data
Ross Turner, Somayajulu Sripada, Ehud Reiter, Ian Davy

2:30–3:00 Dependency Tree Based Sentence Compression
Katja Filippova, Michael Strube

3:00–3:30 Extractive vs. NLG-based Abstractive Summarization of Evaluative Text: The Effect of Corpus Controversiality
Giuseppe Carenini, Jackie C. K. Cheung

3:30–4:00 Break

Session 2: Referring Expressions

4:00–4:30 Referring Expressions as Formulas of Description Logic
Carlos Areces, Alexander Koller, Kristina Striegnitz

4:30–5:00 Attribute Selection for Referring Expression Generation: New Algorithms and Evaluation Methods
Albert Gatt, Anja Belz

5:00–5:30 The Use of Spatial Relations in Referring Expression Generation
Jette Viethen, Robert Dale

6:15–7:45 Banquet

Friday, June 13, 2008

7:00–9:00	Breakfast
	Session 3: Psycholinguistics and Affect
9:00–10:00	Prominence and Phrasing in Spoken Discourse Processing *(Invited Talk)* *Shari R. Speer, Kiwako Ito*
10:00–10:30	Using Tactical NLG to Induce Affective States: Empirical Investigations *Ielka van der Sluis, Chris Mellish*
10:30–11:00	Break
	Session 4: Realization
11:00–11:30	Practical Grammar-Based NLG from Examples *David DeVault, David Traum, Ron Artstein*
11:30–12:00	Accurate and Robust LFG-Based Generation for Chinese *Yuqing Guo, Haifeng Wang, Josef van Genabith*
12:00–1:00	Lunch
1:00–4:30	Activity Break
	Referring Expression Generation Challenge
4:30–5:30	The GREC Challenge 2008: Overview and Evaluation Results *Anja Belz, Eric Kow, Jette Viethen and Albert Gatt*
	The TUNA Challenge 2008: Overview and Evaluation Results *Albert Gatt, Anja Belz and Eric Kow*
	Poster Session
5:30–7:00	INLG Posters
	REG Challenge Posters
7:00–8:30	Dinner

Saturday, June 14, 2008

7:00–9:00	Breakfast
	Session 5: Embodied Conversational Agents
9:00–10:00	Language, Embodiment and Social Intelligence *(Invited Talk)* *Matthew Stone*
10:00–10:30	Automated Metrics That Agree With Human Judgements On Generated Output for an Embodied Conversational Agent *Mary Ellen Foster*
10:30–11:00	Break
	Session 6: Content and Text Planning
11:00–11:30	Simple but effective feedback generation to tutor abstract problem solving *Xin Lu, Barbara Di Eugenio, Stellan Ohlsson, Davide Fossati*
11:30–12:00	What's In a Message? Interpreting Geo-referenced Data for the Visually-impaired *Kavita Thomas, Yaji Sripada*
12:00–12:30	Evolving Questions in Text Planning *Mick O'Donnell*
12:30–1:30	Lunch
	Session 7: Evaluation
1:30–2:00	Generation of Output Style Variation in the SAMMIE Dialogue System *Ivana Kruijff-Korbayová, Ciprian Gerstenberger, Olga Kukina, Jan Schehl*
2:00–2:30	Evaluating an Ontology-Driven WYSIWYM Interface *Feikje Hielkema, Chris Mellish, Peter Edwards*
2:30–3:00	The Importance of Narrative and Other Lessons from an Evaluation of an NLG System that Summarises Clinical Data *Ehud Reiter, Albert Gatt, Francois Portet, Marian van der Meulen*

Prominence and Phrasing in Spoken Discourse Processing

Shari R. Speer
Department of Linguistics
Ohio State University
Columbus, Ohio, USA
speer@ling.osu.edu

Kiwako Ito
Department of Linguistics
Ohio State University
Columbus, Ohio, USA
ito@ling.osu.edu

Abstract

We review psycholinguistic research on the use of intonation in dialogue, focusing on our own recent work. In experiments using complex real-world tasks and naïve speakers and listeners, we show that speakers reliably specific prosodic cues to signal their intensions, and that listeners use these cues to recognize syntactic and pragmatic aspects of discourse meaning.

1 Introduction

The intonation of an utterance conveys a great deal of information about a speaker's intended message. Recent research has addressed whether, when, and how speakers use intonation to transmit linguistic and paralinguistic meaning. Speakers use intonation for a broad range of functions in communication, such as: to mark the difference between immediately relevant vs. background information; to express contrast, contradiction, and correction; and to indicate the intended syntax of ambiguous utterances.

In this paper, we will review recent experimental studies of naïve speakers' and listeners' use of intonation during production and comprehension. We focus primarily on our own work, where we have used naturalistic, relatively complex real-world tasks to elicit speakers' intonation in dialogue, and to examine listeners' ability to use intonation during comprehension.

1.1 Structure of the Review

The review includes a very brief overview of the ToBI (Tone and Break Indices: Beckman, Hirshberg & Shattuck Hufnagel, 2005; Brugos, Shattuck Hufnagel, & Veilleux, 2006), a system widely used to annotate the locations and types of intonational entities present in speech. We then turn to the correspondence between intonational phrasing and syntactic constituency, examining whether and how speakers use the location and size of prosodic breaks as they produce syntactic structure, and testing listeners' ability to use this correspondence. Next, we will discuss the role of intonational prominence in discourse structuring. In particular, we will examine the production and comprehension of accentual prominence to express referential contrast. Our experimental findings suggest that both phrasing and prominence cues are robust for understanding spoken messages, and infelicitous use of those prosodic cues may mislead the listener's comprehension processes. The closing discussion emphasizes the contribution of intonation to spoken language processing, and its essential role in discourse modeling.

2 Prosodic phrasing and syntactic structure

Production experiments investigating the correspondence of prosodic and syntactic phrasing in language production were conducted using a partially-scripted two-player board game task (Speer, Warren, & Schafer, 2003, Schafer, Speer, & Warren, 2005). The game was constructed to elicit particular syntactic contrasts as the players spoke to each other to exchange information and move game pieces from start to goal, avoiding hazards and collecting bonuses. Speakers were required to use a fixed set of sentence frames and game piece names to construct instructions, requests and acknowledgements. Board layouts were carefully constructed to create situational contexts for the resulting dialogues produced by the speakers, so that potentially syntactically ambiguous utterances sometimes remained ambiguous given the game context, but sometimes were contextually disambiguated. The task allowed recording of multiple renditions of a sentence from the same speaker, as well as across speakers.

Phonetic analyses and phonological transcription of speech from the game task experiments demonstrates that speakers reliably used prosodic cues to signal syntactic structure, and to convey the intended meaning of syntactically ambiguous sentences. Although speakers produced a wide variety of prosodic patterns for the same sentence, they consistently placed the strongest prosodic break in the syntactic location that indicated their intended meaning. This effect held for different syntactic types, and was robust across various types of potentially disambiguating situational contexts.

Companion comprehension experiments used the naïve speakers' productions from the game task as stimuli in forced-choice experiments. Results show that listeners make reliable use of prosodic regularities to accurately recover the speakers' intended meanings.

3 Intonational prominence and contrast

To investigate naïve speakers' use of intonational prominence to mark contrast, Ito, Speer & Beckman (2004; Ito & Speer, 2006) elicited unscripted speech using a holiday tree decoration task. Naïve speakers were asked to be 'directors,' giving instructions about how to hang ornaments on a tree to a confederate 'decorator.' Photos of ornaments and the tree were used to give 'directors' the sequence of ornaments and their intended locations on the tree. By using a set of common color terms and object names for the ornaments, we collected multiple spontaneous productions of target adjective-noun pairs (e.g. "*green bell*") in a natural conversational setting. The sequence of decoration was constructed to create contrastive discourse contexts (green bell -> blue bell). Prosodic annotation of the spontaneous speech and supporting phonetic measurements indicated that speakers used prominent pitch accent more frequently when the decoration sequence was contrastive than when it was not (e.g. "green bell.... → Now, find a BLUE bell": where the adjective 'blue' is accented and the repeated noun 'bell' is deaccented).

To test how prominent accent guides referential resolution during comprehension, a set of experiments was conducted using eye movement monitoring technique (Ito & Speer, 2008). Spoken stimuli modeled on the productions from the previous production study were recorded by a trained phonetician. This time, naïve listeners followed instructions to locate ornaments and hang them as specified on a small tree.

Results showed the immediate use of intonational cues by the listeners. For example, when a prominent accent felicitously marked contrast on a color adjective ("First hang the red ball. → Next, hang the BLUE ball"), fixation proportions to target cells increased more quickly than when intonation did not cue the contrast ("Hang the red ball. → Next, hang the blue ball."). The timing of fixations indicates that listeners moved their eyes to the correct ornament before processing the segmental information of the noun. In addition, prominent accent misled listeners when the decoration sequence did not prompt contrast (blue ball → GREEN drum: here, participants looked at balls before they redirected fixations to the drum). These incorrect fixations increased toward the end of the adjective and continued to rise halfway into the noun with conflicting segmental information. Thus, listeners were executing their initial visual search based on the intonational information of the adjective, demonstrating the use of prosody for making predictions during comprehension of running speech.

Acknowledgments

To our colleagues and co-investigators, especially Ping Bai, Mary Beckman and Laurie Maynell, and to NSF BCS-0617609 & REU-0617609 and NIH DC007090.

References

Beckman, M.E., Hirschberg, J., & Shattuck-Huffnagel, S. (2005). The original ToBI system and the evolution of the ToBI framework. In Sun-Ah Jun (ed.), *Prosodic models and transcription: Towards prosodic typology*. Oxford University Press.

Brugos, A., Shattuck-Hufnagel, S., & Vielleux, N. (2006). *Transcribing Prosodic Structure of Spoken Utterances with ToBI.*, MIT Open Courseware, `http://ocw.mit.edu/OcwWeb/Electrical-Engineering-and-Computer-Science/6-911January--IAP--2006`.

Ito & Speer, S.R. (2006). Using interactive tasks to elicit natural dialogue. In P. Augurzky & D. Lenertova (Eds.), *Methods in Empirical Prosody Research*, Mouton de Gruyter.

Ito, K., & Speer, S.R. (2008). Anticipatory effects of intonation: Eye movements during instructed visual search. *Journal of Memory and Language, Special issue on Language-Vision interaction.*

Ito, K., Speer, S.R., & Beckman, M. (2004). Informational status and pitch accent distribution in spontaneous dialogues in English. *Proceedings of the International Conference on Speech Prosody*. Nara, Japan.

Schafer, A.J., Speer, S.R., & Warren, P. (2005). Prosodic influences on the production and comprehension of syntactic ambiguity in a game-based conversation task. In M. Tanenhaus & J. Trueswell (Eds.) *Approaches to Studying World Situated Language Use: Psycholinguistic, Linguistic and Computational Perspectives on Bridging the Product and Action Tradition*, Cambridge: MIT Press.

Speer, S.R., Warren, P., & Schafer, A.J. (2003). Intonation and sentence processing. Proceedings of the Fifteenth International Congress of Phonetic Sciences, Barcelona, Spain.

Language, Embodiment and Social Intelligence

Matthew Stone
Computer Science and Cognitive Science
Rutgers, The State University of New Jersey
110 Frelinghuysen Road, Piscataway NJ 08854-8019
Matthew.Stone@Rutgers.EDU

Abstract

It is an honor to have this chance to tie together themes from my recent research, and to sketch some challenges and opportunities for NLG in face-to-face conversational interaction.

Communication reflects our general involvement in one anothers' lives. Through the choices we manifest with one another, we share our thoughts and feelings, strengthen our relationships and further our joint projects. We rely not only on words to articulate our perspectives, but also on a heterogeneous array of accompanying efforts: embodied deixis, expressive movement, presentation of iconic imagery and instrumental action in the world. Words showcase the distinctive linguistic knowledge which human communication exploits. But people's diverse choices in conversation in fact come together to reveal multifaceted, interrelated meanings, in which all our actions, verbal and nonverbal, fit the situation and further social purposes. In the best case, they let interlocutors understand not just each other's words, but each other.

As NLG researchers, I argue, we have good reason to work towards models of social cognition that embrace the breadth of conversation. Scientifically, it connects us to an emerging consensus in favor of a general human pragmatic competence, rooted in capacities for engagement, coordination, shared intentionality and extended relationships. Technically, it lets us position ourselves as part of an emerging revolution in integrative Artificial Intelligence, characterized by research challenges like human–robot interaction and the design of virtual humans, and applications in assistive and educational technology and interactive entertainment.

Researchers are already hard at work to place our accounts of embodied action in conversation in contact with pragmatic theories derived from text discourse and spoken dialogue. In my own experience, such work proves both illuminating and exciting. For example, it challenges us to support and refine theories of discourse coherence by accounting for the discourse relations and default inference that determine the joint interpretation of coverbal gesture and its accompanying speech (Lascarides and Stone, 2008). And it challenges us to show how speakers work across modalities to engage with, disambiguate, and (on acceptance) recapitulate each others' communicative actions, to ground their meanings (Lascarides and Stone, In Preparation). The closer we look at conversation, the more we can fit all its behaviors into a unitary framework—inviting us to implement behavioral control for embodied social agents through a pervasive analogy to NLG.

We can already pursue such implementations easily. Computationally, motion is just sequence data, and we can manipulate it in parallel ways to the speech data we already use in spoken language generation (Stone et al., 2004). At a higher level, we can represent an embodied performance through a matrix of discrete actions selected and synchronized to an abstract time-line, as in our RUTH system (DeCarlo et al., 2004; Stone and Oh, 2008). This lets us use any NLG method that manipulates structured selections of discrete actions as an architecture for the production of embodied behavior. Templates, as in (Stone and DeCarlo, 2003; Stone et al., 2004), offer a good illustration.

Nevertheless, face-to-face dialogue does demand qualitatively new capabilities. In fact, people's choices and meanings in interactive conversation are profoundly informed by their social settings. We are a long way from general models that could allow NLG systems to recognize and exploit these connections in the words and other behaviors they use. In my experience, even the simplest social practices, such as interlocutors' cooperation on an ongoing practical task, require new models of linguistic meaning and discourse context. For example, systems must be creative to evoke the distinctions that matter for their ongoing task, and use meanings that are not programmed or learned but invented on the fly (DeVault and Stone, 2004). They must count on their interlocutors to recognize the background knowledge they presuppose by general inference from the logic of their behavior as a cooperative contribution to the task (Thomason et al., 2006). Such reasoning becomes particularly important in problematic cases, such as when systems must fine-tune the form and meaning of a clarification request so that the response is more likely to resolve a pending task ambiguity (DeVault and Stone, 2007). I expect many further exciting developments in our understanding of meaning and interpretation as we enrich the social intelligence of NLG.

Modeling efforts will remain crucial to the exploration of these new capabilities. When we build and assemble models of actions and interpretations, we get systems that can plan their own behavior simply by exploiting what they know about communication. These systems give new evidence about the information and problem-solving that's involved. The challenge is that these models must describe semantics and pragmatics, as well as syntax and behavior. My own slow progress (Cassell et al., 2000; Stone et al., 2003; Koller and Stone, 2007) shows that there's still lots of hard work needed to develop suitable techniques. I keep going because of the methodological payoffs I see on the horizon. Modeling lets us take social intelligence seriously as a general implementation principle, and thus to aim for systems whose multimodal behavior matches the flexibility and coordination that distinguishes our own embodied meanings. More generally, modeling replaces programming with data fitting, and a good model of action and interpretation in particular would let an agent's own experience in conversational interaction determine the repertoire of behaviors and meanings it uses to make itself understood.

Acknowledgments

To colleagues and coauthors, especially David DeVault and the organizers of INLG 2008, and to NSF IGERT 0549115, CCF 0541185 and HSD 0624191.

References

J. Cassell, M. Stone, and H. Yan. 2000. Coordination and context-dependence in the generation of embodied conversation. In *INLG*, pages 171–178.

D. DeCarlo, M. Stone, C. Revilla, and J. J. Venditti. 2004. Specifying and animating facial signals for discourse in embodied conversational agents. *Computer Animation and Virtual Worlds*, 15(1):27–38.

D. DeVault and M. Stone. 2004. Interpreting vague utterances in context. In *COLING*, pages 1247–1253.

D. DeVault and M. Stone. 2007. Managing ambiguities across utterances in dialogue. In *DECALOG: Workshop on the Semantics and Pragmatics of Dialogue*.

A. Koller and M. Stone. 2007. Sentence generation as a planning problem. In *ACL*, pages 336–343.

A. Lascarides and M. Stone. 2008. Discourse coherence and gesture interpretation. *Ms, Edinburgh–Rutgers*.

A. Lascarides and M. Stone. In Preparation. Grounding and gesture. *Ms, Edinburgh–Rutgers*.

M. Stone and D. DeCarlo. 2003. Crafting the illusion of meaning: Template-based generation of embodied conversational behavior. In *Computer Animation and Social Agents (CASA)*, pages 11–16.

M. Stone and I. Oh. 2008. Modeling facial expression of uncertainty in conversational animation. In I. Wachsmuth and G. Knoblich, editors, *Modeling Communication with Robots and Virtual Humans*, pages 57–76. Springer.

M. Stone, C. Doran, B. Webber, T. Bleam, and M. Palmer. 2003. Microplanning with communicative intentions: The SPUD system. *Computational Intelligence*, 19(4):311–381.

M. Stone, D. DeCarlo, I. Oh, C. Rodriguez, A. Stere, A. Lees, and C. Bregler. 2004. Speaking with hands: Creating animated conversational characters from recordings of human performance. *ACM Transactions on Graphics*, 23(3):506–513.

R. Thomason, M. Stone, and D. DeVault. 2006. Enlightened update: a computational architecture for presupposition accommodation. *Ms, Michigan–Rutgers*.

Generating Textual Summaries of Bar Charts

Seniz Demir Sandra Carberry Kathleen F. McCoy
Department of Computer Science
University of Delaware
Newark, DE 19716
{demir, carberry, mccoy}@cis.udel.edu

Abstract

Information graphics, such as bar charts and line graphs, play an important role in multimodal documents. This paper presents a novel approach to producing a brief textual summary of a simple bar chart. It outlines our approach to augmenting the core message of the graphic to produce a brief summary. Our method simultaneously constructs both the discourse and sentence structures of the textual summary using a bottom-up approach. The result is then realized in natural language. An evaluation study validates our generation methodology.

1 Introduction

Information graphics, such as bar charts and line graphs, are an important component of a multimodal document. However, summarization has focused primarily on the text of a document. But as shown in (Carberry et al., 2006), information graphics in magazine and newspaper articles often convey a message that is not repeated in the article's text. Thus information graphics cannot be ignored.

Individuals with sight impairments can access the text of an electronic document via text to speech systems. But such individuals are stymied when they encounter information graphics. The SIGHT system (Elzer et al., 2007) has the goal of providing the user with the message and knowledge that one would gain from viewing the graphic, rather than providing alternative access to what the graphic looks like. In the current Bayesian network implementation, the system uses the communicative signals present in the graphic to recognize one of the twelve message categories that can be conveyed by a bar chart and produces a logical representation of what we will refer to as the **core message** conveyed by the graphic; this representation is translated into natural language via templates. For example, the system determines that the core message of the graphic in Figure 1 is that the bar for the United States has the maximum value of the entities listed, and the system produces Maximum(First_Bar) as the logical representation of that message. However, this is insufficient as a summary of the graphic since it doesn't convey the particularly significant features of the graphic such as the fact that the number of hacker attacks in the United States is far greater than in the other countries listed.

In this paper, we explore the generation of an effective initial summary of a bar chart within the SIGHT system. Input to our system is a logical representation of the graphic's core message (as produced by SIGHT) and the XML representation of the graphic which specifies the components of the graphic such as the number of bars and the heights of each bar. Our goal is to generate a succinct coherent summary of a graphic that captures its core message and the most important and significant features. At the same time, the summary need not include all information that could be extracted from the graphic since future work on SIGHT includes a mechanism for responding to follow-up questions from the user.

Our work is unique in that it generates a summary of the content of a bar chart with no domain restriction and constructs a high-quality but brief summary by incorporating the graphic's core mes-

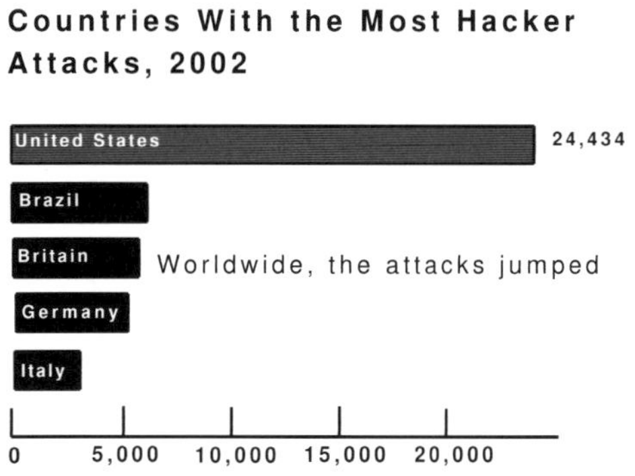

Figure 1: Graphic conveying a maximum bar.

sage and the most important and significant features of the graphic. Our system produces a coherent organization of the content of the summary that we hypothesize lends itself to follow-up questions, applies the notion of syntactic complexity in choosing how to aggregate information into sentence-sized pieces, utilizes a sentence realizer to convey the output in natural language, and applies heuristics for constructing referents for graphical elements. Thus, our work addresses several generation problems.

Section 2 discusses related work in the area of graph summarization. Section 3 presents our methodology for identifying the content of initial summaries. Section 4 describes our approach for organizing the summaries. Section 5 presents some issues that we addressed in realizing the summaries and a few example summaries generated by our system. Section 6 discusses the results of an evaluation study that validates our methodology.

2 Related Work

Graph summarization has received some attention. The SumTime project uses pattern recognition techniques to generate textual summaries of automatically generated time-series data; different systems have been designed in three domains, such as SumTime-Turbine (Yu et al., 2007) for data from gas turbine engines. However, each of these systems is domain-dependent. We view this as a very different problem from the one that we address in this paper, since we are working on domain independent graphical representations. The iGRAPH-Lite system (Ferres et al., 2007), whose main objective is to make the information in a graphic accessible to blind users via keyboard commands, uses templates to provide a short textual summary of what the graphic looks like, but their summary is not concerned with the higher level knowledge conveyed by the graphic. The goal of Futrelle's project (Futrelle, 1999) is to produce a summary graphic that captures the content of one or more graphics. However, the end result is itself a graphic, not text.

3 Informational Content of the Summaries

In (McCoy et al., 2001), we reported an informal experiment in which human subjects were asked to write a brief summary of a series of line graphs with the same high-level intention. This experiment led to three observations:

- the intended message of the graphic was contained in all summaries.
- summaries of the same graphic by different subjects were similar.
- summaries of different graphics in the same message category (such as Rising_Trend) varied in the information provided.

Subjects included more than the core message of the graphic in their summaries. The extra information could be explained as capturing features of the graphic that were visually salient. It was hypothesized that what is taken as visually salient in a graphic relates to the overall message of the graphic. For example, in the line graphs analyzed, if the overall message of the graphic is an increasing trend and the variance in that trend is large, then the variance is salient. The fact that the summaries only included the core message and the visually salient features, correlates with Grice's Maxim of Quantity (Grice, 1975) which states that one's discourse contribution should be as informative as necessary for the purposes of the current exchange but not more so.

To extend these observations to other kinds of information graphics, particulary to simple bar charts, we needed to identify the kinds of features that were salient with respect to the graphic's overall message. For this purpose, we conducted a set of formal experiments with human subjects. Our goal was a set of rules that took into account the message category (such as Rising_Trend or Rank_of_Entity) and the visual features of the graphic to specify what propositions should be included in the initial summary.

3.1 Experimental Setup

Based on our experience with summarizing graphics, we first identified the set of all propositions (PROP_ALL) that reflect information that we envisioned someone might ask about a simple bar chart. Twenty graduate students from a variety of departments participated in the experiments. Each subject was given an information graphic along with a sentence conveying the intended message of the graphic (as identified by the SIGHT system) and a subset of PROP_ALL, and was asked to classify these additional propositions into one of three classes according to how important they felt it was to include that proposition in the initial summary: **essential**, **possible**, and **not important**. Subjects were told to assume that the graphic was part of an article that the user is reading and that he would be able to ask follow-up questions after receiving the summary.

Twenty-one graphics were used in the experiments and each participant was given six graphics to view. The graphics were either selected from articles in popular media or constructed from scratch to present a number of different salient features within the same graphic. Eight different message categories were tested in the experiments[1] and the graphics from the same message category reflected different salient features that had been observed in a corpus of collected graphics.

3.2 Computationalizing Proposition Selection

To analyze the experiment's results, we assigned a numeric score to each category (essential=3, possible=1, not important=0) indicating the level of importance assigned by the subjects. We computed an importance level **(IL)** for each proposition that might be included in a summary of a graphic, estimating how important it is to be included in the initial summary. The **IL** of a proposition is computed based on the average of the importance assigned by each subject. We classify a proposition as a highly-rated proposition in a graphic (and therefore worthy of being included in the initial summary) if its importance level is equal to or above the importance level that would be obtained if at least half of the subjects had classified the proposition as essential. The particular assignments of values to categories shown above was used in order to emphasize instances in which subjects placed a proposition in the essential category.

For each message category, we analyzed the sets of highly-rated propositions identified for the graphics associated with that message category and hand constructed a set of content identification rules specifying whether a proposition should be included in the initial summary. If a proposition was classified as highly-rated for all graphics in a particular message category, the content identification rule stated that the proposition should be included in the initial summary for every graphic whose core message fell into that message category. For the other highly-rated propositions for a message category, we identified a feature that was visually salient only in the graphics where the proposition was marked as essential, and our content identification rule used the presence of this feature in the graphic as a condition for the proposition to be included in the initial summary. Thirty content identification rules were defined in the system.

Besides the propositions capturing salient features of the graphic, we observed that the subjects selected propositions whose absence might lead the user to draw false conclusions by default (for example, the propositions indicating that the trend starting from 1997 does not cover the full range of bar labels in the graphic in Figure 2). We constructed rules to add such content. This correlates with the maxim in (Joshi et al., 1984) which states that a system should not only produce correct information but should also prevent the user from drawing false inferences.

The following are glosses of two representative content identification rules applicable to a graphic whose core message is an increasing trend:

- If (message_category **equals** 'increasing_trend') then **include**(propositions conveying the rate of increase of the trend)
- If (message_category **equals** 'increasing_trend') and (coverage(graphic) **not equal** coverage(trend)) then **include**(propositions indicating that the trend does not cover the full range of bar labels)

To see how our rules might affect the generated

[1] We did not test message categories that are the opposite of categories used in the experiments, such as *Minimum* which is the opposite of *Maximum* and thus can be modeled similarly.

summary, consider the graphic in Figure 2. The SIGHT system recognizes the core message as an increasing trend from 1997 to 2002. The content identification rules defined for increasing trend select the following pieces of additional information to include in the initial summary of the graphic:

- The overall rate of increase of the trend, which is moderate
- The range of the bar values in the trend: $480,000 to $1,230,000
- The fact that there is an unusually steep rise between 2000 and 2001
- The period that the graphic covers, which is from 1996 to 2002

4 Organizing Coherent Summaries

At this point in the processing, the system has identified the informational content to be conveyed in the initial summary, which consists of the core message and the set of propositions identified by the content identification rules. We need to represent and organize the information to be communicated, determine how the content should be aggregated into sentence-sized pieces, and make decisions about referring expressions (Reiter and Dale, 1997).

To represent and help organize the propositions that should be included in the initial summary, we use two kinds of predicates. Relative predicates, such as *differs*, are used to express relations between the graphical elements. For example, **differs(bar(A),maximum_bar,50%)** shows that the percentage difference between the values of bar(A) and the maximum bar is 50%. Attributive predicates, such as *has_attribute*, are used to elaborate the graphical elements. For example, **has_attribute(trend,"type","increasing")** shows that the trend observed in the graphic is an increasing trend. We refer to the first argument of a predicate as its **main entity** and the others as **secondary entities**.

Since a top-down planning approach does not guarantee that all propositions will be covered by the final text plan (Marcu, 1997), we use a bottom-up planner for structuring the initial summaries. The propositions selected for inclusion in the initial summaries can be classified as **message_related, specific, or computational** based on the type of information they convey. The core message of the graphic is captured by the message_related propositions. Specific propositions focus on specific pieces of information in the graphic such as the propositions conveying the unusually large rise between 2000 and 2001 in the graphic in Figure 2. On the other hand, computational propositions require computations or abstractions over the whole graphic, such as the propositions conveying the rate of increase in the graphic in Figure 2. Once the propositions to be included in the summary are identified, we assign them to one of these three classes.

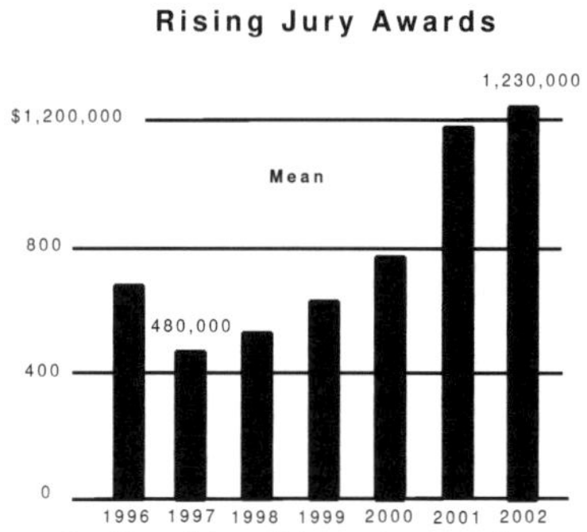

Figure 2: Graphic with an increasing trend.

We hypothesize that the message-related class of propositions should be presented first since this places emphasis on the core message of the graphic. We anticipate that the user will ask follow-up questions after receiving the initial summary. Therefore, it is appropriate to close the initial summary with propositions from the computational class so that the whole graphic is in the user's focus of attention (Grosz and Sidner, 1986). Thus we hypothesize that a good ordering of propositions in the initial summary is the message-related class, the specific class, and finally the computational class. This produces a partial ordering of the propositions to be included in the summary.

Each proposition can be realized as a single sentence. For example, **shows(graphic,trend)** can be realized as "The graphic shows a trend" or "There is a trend in the graphic". Consequently, a set of propositions can be viewed as a set of single sentences. Figure 3 shows the propositions in the message_related class for the graphic in Figure 2, along with a possible realization for each.

Although each proposition could be conveyed as a single sentence, the result is unnatural and not very

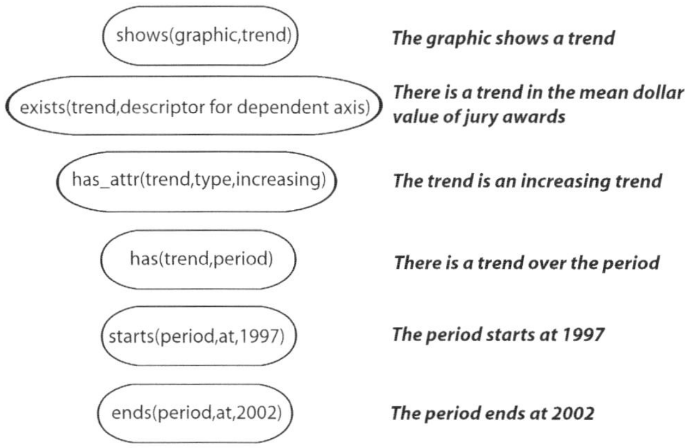

Figure 3: Propositions in Message_related Class.

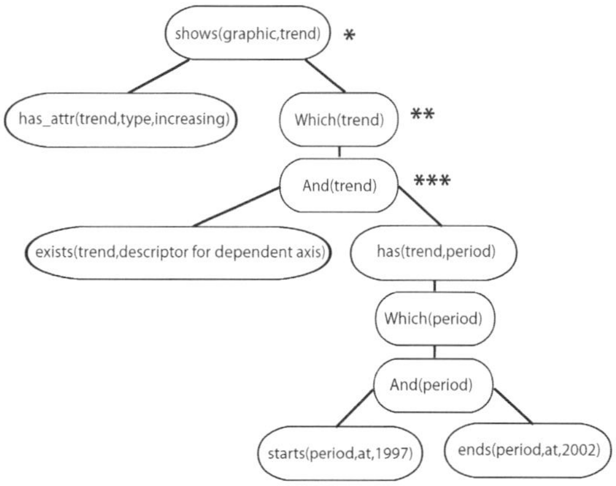

Figure 4: Best Structure of Message_related Class.

coherent. Thus, we define operators to relate propositions and explore aggregating them. The operators work on trees; initially, each proposition is the root of a single node tree. Each tree represents one or more propositions that can be realized as a single sentence, and operators combine individual trees in a class into more complex trees. The following are two such operators which work on relative predicates:

- **And_Operator:** This operator combines two trees if their root propositions share the same main entity. An And_predicate with the same main entity forms the root of the new tree, and the trees that are combined form the descendents of this root.
- **Which_Operator:** This operator attaches one tree as a descendent of another tree, connected by a Which_predicate, if the main entity of the proposition at the root of the first tree is a secondary entity in the proposition at the root of the second tree. That particular entity forms the main entity of the Which_predicate.

One possible result of applying our operators to the set of propositions (single node trees) in Figure 3 produces the single but more complex tree shown in Figure 4. The And_predicate (***) in Figure 4 is produced by the And_Operator and the resultant subtree is attached to the predicate **shows** by the Which_Operator.

4.1 Evaluating Structures

Different combinations of operators produce different sets of trees, each of which represents a different text structure and consequently leads to different realized text. These structures must be evaluated to determine which one is the best. We don't want a structure where each proposition is realized as a single sentence nor a structure where groups of propositions are realized with sentences that are too complex. Our objective is to find a structure which stands at a mediatory point between these extremes.

Each tree in a structure represents a set of propositions that can be realized as a single sentence. The most straightforward way of realizing a tree would be conjoining the realizations of subtrees rooted by an And_predicate, embedding the realization of a subtree rooted by a Which_predicate as a relative clause, and realizing a subtree that consists solely of an attributive predicate as an adjective or a prepositional phrase. However, care must be taken that the sentence realization of a tree is not too complex.

Research has used a number of different measures to assess syntactic complexity of written text and spoken language samples (Roark et al., 2007). We apply the notion of syntactic complexity to evaluate the semantic units (predicates) that will be realized. The revised D-level sentence complexity scale (Covington et al., 2006) forms the core of our syntactic complexity measure. The D-Level scale measures the complexity of a sentence according to the sequence in which children acquire the ability to use different types of sentences. The sentence types with the lowest score are those that children acquire first and therefore are the simplest types. Among the seven levels defined in the revised D-Level scale, the levels of interest in our work are (in order of increasing complexity): simple sentences, conjoined sentences, sentences with a rela-

Message_Related:
The graphic shows an increasing trend in the mean dollar value of jury awards over the period from 1997 to 2002.
Specific:
The value of these awards ranges from 480,000 dollars to 1,230,000 dollars. The graphic covers a period from 1996 to 2002. Between 2000 and 2001, an unusually steep rise is observed in the value of these awards.
Computational:
Moderate increases are observed every year during the period from 1997 to 2002 in the value of these awards.

Table 1: Realization of the Initial Overall Structure.

Message_Related:
Although the graphic covers a period from 1996 to 2002, the graphic shows an increasing trend in the mean dollar value of jury awards over the period from 1997 to 2002.
Specific:
The value of these awards ranges from 480,000 dollars to 1,230,000 dollars.
Computational:
Except for a steep rise between 2000 and 2001, moderate increases are observed every year in the value of these awards.

Table 2: Realization of the Final Overall Structure.

tive clause, and sentences with more than one level of embedding. However, the definition of sentence types at each level is too general. Therefore, we use a finer distinction between sentence types within each D-level, such as a simple sentence with more than one preposition has a higher complexity than a simple sentence with a single preposition.

To measure the complexity of sentences that will realize a structure, we define a number of complexity estimators. A tree consisting of a single node is identified as having the lowest syntactic complexity. We use And_predicate and Which_predicate estimators to estimate the complexity of the sentences used to realize more complex trees. To do this, estimators look for realization opportunities that would produce lower complexity values than what the most straightforward realization would produce. For instance, the And_predicate estimators check whether or not the realizations of two subtrees rooted by an And_predicate can be combined into a single sentence which is not a compound sentence consisting of two independent sentences. These estimators have similar considerations to the clause-combining operations used by Walker et.al (2002) in the SPoT sentence planner. For example, one of the And_predicate estimators can successfully determine that the realizations *"There is a trend in the mean dollar value of jury awards"* and *"There is a trend over the period from 1997 to 2002"*[2] can be combined into *"There is a trend in the mean dollar value of jury awards over the period from 1997 to 2002"* for the tree in Figure 4. This results in a complexity score which is lower than the score of a compound sentence consisting of two conjoined independent sentences. The Which_predicate estimators check whether a tree rooted by a Which_predicate can be realized as an adjunct to the modified entity rather than as a more complex relative clause. For example, one of the Which_predicate estimators can identify that * and the subtree rooted at ** in Figure 4 can be realized as *"The graphic shows a trend in the mean dollar value of jury awards over the period from 1997 to 2002"*.

Center-embedded relative clauses are more difficult to comprehend than corresponding right-branching clauses (Kidd and Bavin, 2002). Our complexity metric for evaluating the complexity of a tree penalizes Which_predicates that will be realized as a relative clause in the middle of a sentence more than one that appears at the end. Once the complexity metric has evaluated the complexity of each tree in a candidate structure, the complexities of the trees are summed to get the complexity of the structure. Our metric for selecting the best structure balances the number of sentences and their complexity.

The initial overall structure of the summary consists of the best structures for the message_related, specific, and computational classes. As a final step, we check whether we can improve the evaluation of the overall structure of the summary by moving trees or subtrees between the best structures for the three classes. For example, the best structure for the specific class might contain a tree that conveys information about an entity introduced by a proposition

[2]Assume that the subtree in Figure 4 rooted by Which(period) can be realized as "from 1997 to 2002".

in the message_related class. Moving this tree to the message-related class and using the Which operator to combine it with the tree introducing the entity (thereby realizing it as a relative clause) might improve the evaluation of the overall structure of the summary. To be consistent with the motivation behind the initial groupings of the propositions, we do not allow movements from the message_related class or any movement that will empty the computational class. Table 1 presents the summary that our system generates for the graphic in Figure 2 before the movements between classes, and Table 2 presents the summary after the movements.

5 Realizing Summaries

To realize the summaries in natural language, we use the FUF/SURGE surface realizer (Elhadad and Robin, 1996) with some changes made to address a few problems encountered with respect to the use of conjunctions and subject-ellipsises. Different strategies are defined in the system for aggregating the realizations of trees that are linked with operators. The strategy selected by the system is based on the relation (such as concession) that holds between the propositions at the root of the trees and the syntactic forms of their realization opportunities. For example, the system uses different strategies for aggregating the trees rooted by the And_predicates in Figure 4, where the tree rooted by And(period) is realized as a combination of prepositional phrases and the tree rooted by And(trend) is realized as a full sentence containing a set of prepositional phrases.

5.1 A Descriptor for the Dependent Axis

The dependent axis of an information graphic is often not labelled with a full descriptor of what is being measured and therefore a mechanism for extracting an appropriate descriptor had to be developed. We undertook a corpus analysis and implemented a system to realize the descriptors (Demir et al., 2007). Our corpus analysis found that the full descriptor often must be built from pieces of text extracted from different places in the graphic. We identified seven text levels (text components) which form a hierarchy (the top being the Overall_Caption and the bottom being the Dependent_Axis_Label), and we observed that the texts at the lower levels are more

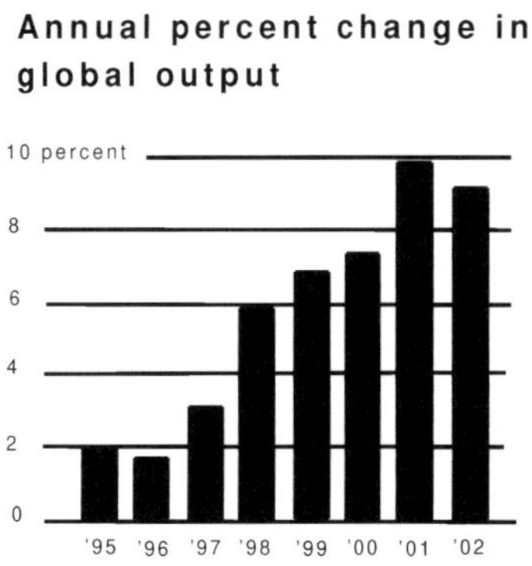

Figure 5: Graphic conveying a contrast change.

likely to contribute to the descriptor than the texts at the higher levels. We developed a set of heuristics and augmentation rules for constructing the descriptor for the dependent axis and validated them on a previously unseen corpus of graphics.

5.2 Referent Generation

The descriptor that our system constructs is always a noun phrase, but it may be quite long. Our referring expression generator uses the full descriptor when the dependent axis is first referenced in the text, but only the head noun for subsequent references. To relate the head noun to the descriptor in the text, the demonstratives "this" or "these" is added to the front of the head noun unless it follows a comparison such as "more". This simple mechanism appears to work well for our initial summaries.

5.3 Example Summaries

For the graphic in Figure 1, the SIGHT system posits that the graphic's core message is that the bar for the United States has the maximum value among the bars listed. Our system adds additional propositions and produces the following summary:
"The graphic shows that United States with 24,434 has the highest number of hacker attacks among the countries[3] *Brazil, Britain, Germany, Italy, and United States. United States has 4.9 times more attacks than the average of other countries."*

For the graphic in Figure 5, the SIGHT system posits that the core message is that the change at the last bar is in contrast with the previous increasing trend. Our system generates the following summary:

[3]Our system has a module which identifies the ontological category of the bar labels (Demir et al., 2007).

"The graphic shows a small drop in 2002 in contrast with the increasing trend in annual percent change in global output over the period from 1995 to 2001. Except for a small drop in 1996, varying increases are observed every year during the period from 1995 to 2001 in this change, which shows an overall increase of 485.4 percent and shows a decrease of 8.7 percent between 2001 and 2002."

6 Evaluation

The work presented in this paper consists of several different components, all of which we claim contribute to the quality of the graphical summary. Our evaluation focused on three of these and evaluated whether or not our decisions with respect to these components contributed to the perceived quality of the summary: the organization and ordering of the informational content **(O)**, the aggregation of the information into more complex structures **(A)**, and the metric used to evaluate the structures that represent different possible aggregations of the informational content **(E)**. We conducted an experiment with fifteen participants where they were presented with four different summaries of twelve graphics from a variety of domains. We focused on increasing and decreasing trend graphics since they have the greatest variety of possible summaries. For each of the graphics, the participants were asked to rank randomly ordered summaries in terms of their quality in conveying the informational content. The summaries varied according to the test parameters:

- **S_O+A+E+:** A summary that uses the ordering rules, the aggregation rules, and is rated highest by the evaluation metric. This is the summary produced by our system.
- **S_O+A+E-:** A summary that uses the ordering and aggregation rules, but was not rated highest by the evaluation metric.
- **S_O-A+E+:** A summary where the propositions are randomly ordered, but aggregation takes place, and the aggregation is rated best by the evaluation metric.
- **S_O-A-E-:** A summary consisting of single sentences that are randomly ordered.

The results of the experiment are presented in Table 3. It is particularly noteworthy that the summary generated by our system was most often (65.6% of the time) rated as the best summary and overwhelmingly (92.2% of the time) rated as one of the top two summaries. The table shows that omitting the evaluation metric (S_O+A+E-) or omitting ordering of propositions (S_O-A+E+) results in summaries that are substantially less preferred by the subjects. We gained insights into improving the system's performance by looking at the comments made by the subjects when our summary was not selected as the best. For example, it appears that the subjects did not like summaries where exceptions were fronted on the core message with an "although" clause rather than following the core message (S_O+A+E-). We hypothesize that fronting the exception detracted from the core message. This is easily remedied in our evaluation metric. Overall, the results shown in Table 3 support our methodology for generating summaries. In the future, we will test the summaries with blind individuals to determine their effectiveness in providing alternative access to graphics.

Summary_type	**Best**	**2nd**	**3rd**	**4th**
S_O+A+E+	**65.6%**	26.6%	6.7%	1.1%
S_O+A+E-	16.7%	**32.2%**	33.3%	17.8%
S_O-A+E+	16.7%	30%	**40%**	13.3%
S_O-A-E-	1%	11.2%	20%	**67.8%**

Table 3: Ranking of Summary Types.

7 Conclusion

This paper has presented our methodology for generating brief and coherent summaries of simple bar charts. Our work is the first to address the problem of summarizing the content of bar charts. We have presented our approach for identifying the appropriate content of an initial summary, ordering and aggregating the included propositions, and evaluating the resultant summary structures to select the best one. Overall, the results of an evaluation study validate our ordering, aggregation, and evaluation methodology.

Acknowledgements

We would like to thank Dr. Stephanie Elzer for her advice, help, and implementation of the SIGHT system upon which this work is built and Dr. Charles Callaway for his valuable help in addressing the problems encountered with the realizer.

References

Sandra Carberry, Stephanie Elzer, and Seniz Demir. 2006. Information graphics: an untapped resource for digital libraries. In *Proc. of SIGIR'2006*.

Michael A. Covington, Congzhou He, Cati Brown, Lorina Naci, and John Brown 2006. How complex is that sentence? A proposed revision of the Rosenberg and Abbeduto D-Level scale. *Research Report, AI Center, University of Georgia*.

Seniz Demir, Sandra Carberry, and Stephanie Elzer. 2007. Effectively realizing the inferred message of an information graphic. In *Proc. of RANLP'2007*.

Michael Elhadad and Jacques Robin. 1996. An overview of SURGE: a re-usable comprehensive syntactic realization component. In *Proc. of INLG'1996*.

Stephanie Elzer, Edward Schwartz, Sandra Carberry, Daniel Chester, Seniz Demir, and Peng Wu. 2007. A browser extension for providing visually impaired users access to the content of bar charts on the web. In *Proc. of WEBIST'2007*.

Leo Ferres, Petro Verkhogliad, Gitte Lindgaard, Louis Boucher, Antoine Chretien, and Martin Lachance. 2007. Improving accessibility to statistical graphs: the iGraph-Lite system. In *Proc. of ASSETS'2007*.

Robert Futrelle. 1999. Summarization of diagrams in documents. In *Advances in Automated Text Summarization*. MIT Press, pp. 403-421.

Paul Grice. 1975. Logic and conversation. In *Syntax and Semantics, Speech Acts*, 3:41-58.

Barbara Grosz and Candace Sidner. 1986. Attention, intentions, and the structure of discourse. In *Computational Linguistics*, 12(3):175–204.

Aravind Joshi, Bonnie Webber, and Ralph Weischedel. 1984. Living up to expectations: computing expert responses. In *Proc. of NCAI'1984*.

Evan Kidd and Edith Bavin. 2002. English-speaking childrens comprehension of relative clauses: evidence for general-cognitive and language-specific constraints on development. In *Journal of Psycholinguistic Research*, 31(6):599-617.

Daniel Marcu. 1997. The rhetorical parsing, summarization, and generation of natural language texts. *PhD thesis, Department of Computer Science, University of Toronto*.

Kathleen F. McCoy, Sandra Carberry, Tom Roper, and Nancy Green. 2001. Towards generating textual summaries of graphs. In *Proc. of HCI'2001*.

Ehud Reiter and Robert Dale. 1997. Building applied natural language generation systems. In *Natural Language Engineering*, 3(1):57–87.

Brian Roark, Margaret Mitchell, and Kristy Hollingshead. 2007. Syntactic complexity measures for detecting mild cognitive impairment. In *Proc. of BioNLP'2007*.

Marilyn Walker, Owen Rambow, and Monica Rogati. 2002. Training a sentence planner for spoken dialogue using boosting. In *Computer Speech and Language: Special Issue on Spoken Language Generation*, 16(3-4):409-433.

Jin Yu, Ehud Reiter, Jim Hunter, and Chris Mellish. 2007. Choosing the content of textual summaries of large time-series data sets. In *Natural Language Engineering*,13(1):25–49.

Using Spatial Reference Frames to Generate Grounded Textual Summaries of Georeferenced Data

Ross Turner, Somayajulu Sripada and Ehud Reiter
Dept of Computing Science,
University of Aberdeen, UK
{rturner,ssripada,ereiter}@csd.abdn.ac.uk

Ian P Davy
Aerospace and Marine Intl.,
Banchory, Aberdeenshire, UK
idavy@weather3000.com

Abstract

Summarising georeferenced (can be identified according to it's location) data in natural language is challenging because it requires linking events describing its non-geographic attributes to their underlying geography. This mapping is not straightforward as often the only explicit geographic information such data contains is latitude and longitude. In this paper we present an approach to generating textual summaries of georeferenced data based on spatial reference frames. This approach has been implemented in a data-to-text system we have deployed in the weather forecasting domain.

1 Introduction

Data-to-text systems are NLG systems that generate texts from raw input data. Many examples of such systems have been reported in the literature, which have been applied in a number of domains and to different types of input. For example, BabyTalk (Portet et al., 2007) generates medical reports from sensors monitoring a baby in a Neonatal Intensive Care Unit, while (Hallett and Scott, 2005) describe a system for generating reports from events in medical records. SumTime (Reiter et al., 2005), (Coch, 1998) and Fog (Goldberg et al., 1994) generate weather forecasts from the output of weather computer simulation models, while (Iordanskaja et al., 1992) and (Rösner, 1987) both generate summaries from employment statistics.

As the above examples show most work in data-to-text up to now has concentrated almost exclusively on time series data. Work on generating text from spatial data has been reported in Coral (Dale et al., 2005), which generates route descriptions of a path constructed from Geographical Information Systems (GIS) datasets. Unlike the input to Coral however, most georeferenced data contains only limited spatial information(in many cases, only latitude and longitude).

As (Roy and Reiter, 2005) point out, connecting language to the non-linguistic world is an important issue in Cognitive Science and Aritificial Intelligence; moreover, geographic data is becoming increasingly ubiquitous as the availability of low cost locational devices such as GPS increases, and GIS become more user friendly. Therefore, we believe exploring the issue of generating textual reports grounded in real world geographical data is an important challenge. On a more practical level, it is also a natural next step in the application of data-to-text technology to apply it to geographically referenced data.

In the RoadSafe project described in the following section, we have been investigating this issue in a data-to-text system that generates road ice weather forecasts. The subsequent focus of this paper is the adaption of NLG techniques to the task of summarising georeferenced data. In particular, the incorporation of spatial reference frames to generate grounded (from external GIS data sources) spatial references.

2 Background

Weather forecasting has been one of the most successful and widely researched application domains for NLG systems. The main novel aspect that sets RoadSafe apart from other weather forecast generators and indeed, other data-to-text systems, is it's application to spatio-temporal data. The input to RoadSafe is generated by a road ice simulation model, which outputs a large (in order of Megabytes) multivariate data set, shown in Figure 1.

The output of the model contains predicted measurements of 9 meteorological parameters for 1000's of points across a road network, each measured at 20 minute intervals during a 24 hour forecast period. A map of such a network, belonging to a local council in the UK, is shown in Figure 2. This model forms the basis of a road ice forecasting ser-

ID	Latitude	Longitude
UKHA001000000	50.7695	-1.6433
UKHA001000001	50.7591	-1.6258
UKHA001000002	50.7491	-1.5545
....	....	....

ID	Parameter	1200	1220	1240	1300	1320	1340	1400	.....
UKHA001000000	T	4.7	4.8	4.9	5	5.1	5.2	5.2	.....
	W	-2.5	-2.5	-2.6	-2.7	-2.7	-2.8	-2.9	.....
	R	9.5	9.4	9.3	9.2	9.1	9	8.9	.....
	C	0	0	0	0	0	0	0	.....
	D	354	354	355	355	355	355	355	.....
	V	19	19	19	19	19	19	18	.....
	G	28	28	28.1	28.1	28.1	28	26.5	.....
	S	90.4	91.6	91.7	90.9	89.5	87.7	86	.....
	P	0	0	0	0	0	0	0	.....
UKHA001000001	T	4.7	4.9	5	5.1	5.2	5.2	5.3	.....
	W	2.4	-2.5	-2.5	-2.6	-2.7	-2.7	-2.8	.....
	R	9.2	9.1	9	8.9	8.7	8.6	8.5	.....
	C	0	0	0	0	0	0	0	.....
	D	354	354	355	354	355	355	355	.....
	V	19	19	18	18	18	18	18	.....
	G	28.7	28.7	27.2	27.2	27.2	27.2	27.2	.....
	S	90.4	91.6	91.7	90.9	89.5	87.7	86	.....
	P	0	0	0	0	0	0	0	.....
UKHA001000002	T	5	5.1	5.2	5.3	5.4	5.4	5.4	.....
	W	1.9	-1.9	-2	-2.1	-2.2	-2.3	-2.4	.....
	R	9.9	9.8	9.7	9.7	9.6	9.5	9.3	.....
	C	61	61	61	61	61	61	61	.....
	D	354	354	354	354	354	354	354	.....
	V	20	19	19	19	19	19	19	.....
	G	29.8	28.4	28.4	28.4	28.4	28.4	28.3	.....
	S	91.2	92	92.5	93	93.4	93.7	94.2	.....
	P	0	0	0	0	0.1	0.1	0.1	.....
....	....	.....	.....	.....	.....	.....	.....	.....	.....

Figure 1: Part of a RoadSafe input data set showing corresponding spatial and non-spatial attribute tables; T=Air Temperature (Deg C), W=Dew Point (Deg C), R=Road Surface Temperature (Deg C), C=Weather Code, D=Wind direction (Degrees), V=Mean wind Speed (knots), G=Wind Gust (knots),S=Sky Cover (%), P=Precipitation Water Equivalent (mm).

vice provided by Aerospace and Marine International (AMI), which is delivered to local councils via an online Road Weather Information System (RWIS). This service provides road engineers with up to the minute weather information using graphs, graphics and textual reports that allows them to base their road maintenance operations on during the winter months. In RoadSafe we have been working on generating the textual reports, such as the one shown in Figure 3, automatically from the model data.

The communicative goal of the textual reports is to complement detailed tabular and graphical presentations of the model data with a more general overview of the weather conditions. In the context of our work this presents a number of challenges:

1. The input data has to be analysed, this is non-trivial due to the complexity and size of the input data.

2. Our system is required to achieve a huge data/text compression ratio (Human authored texts are short and concise summaries). Therefore, content selection is a serious issue for our system.

3. Describing the effect of the underlying geography on weather conditions, such as 'possible gale force gusts on higher ground', is an integral part of the communicative goal of the text. Information containing such relationships is not explicit in the input data and therefore must be grounded.

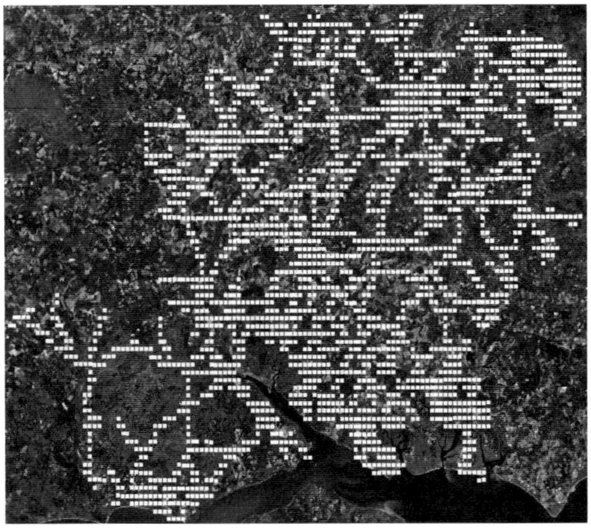

Figure 2: Road Ice Model Data Points Map

'Another night with all routes quickly falling below zero this evening. Only isolated urban spots in the south will only drop to around zero. Freezing fog patches will become more widespread during the night but thin a little tomorrow morning especially in the south.'

Figure 3: Example Human Authored Corpus Text

3 Architecture

As noted in the previous section, the input data to our system contains only limited spatial information: a point identifier that ties the measurement site to a particular route and a latitude longitude coordinate. Therefore it is necessary for our system to perform additional spatial reasoning to characterise the input in terms of its underlying geography. The architecture of our system shown in Figure 4, extends

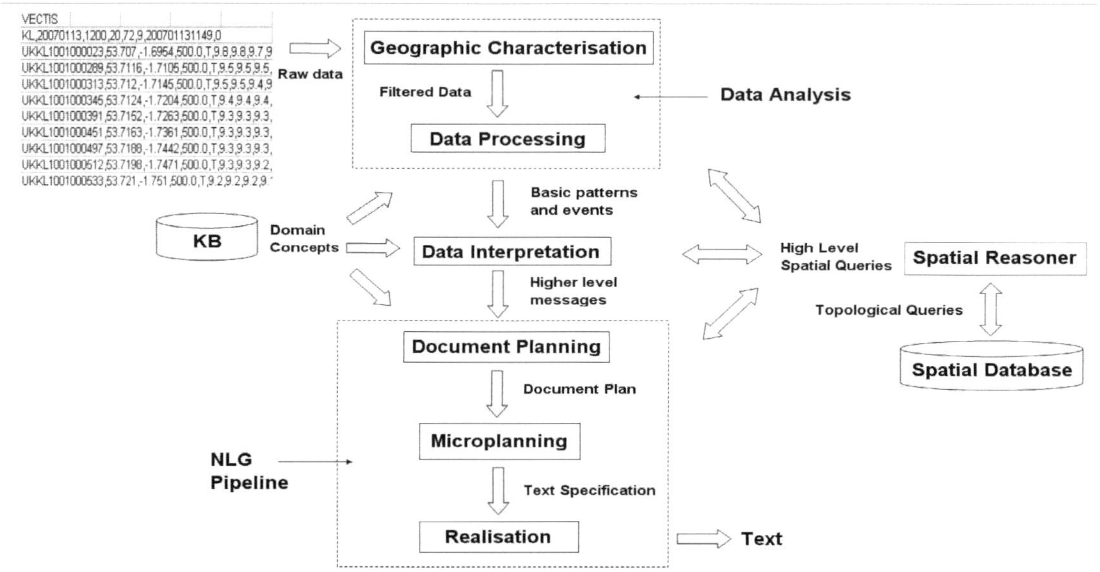

Figure 4: RoadSafe System Architecture

the architecture for data-to-text systems proposed in (Reiter, 2007) to include this additional processing. In Section 3.1 we explain some of the rationale behind these design decisions based on observations from our knowledge acquisition(KA) Studies. In Sections 3.2 and 3.3 we explain the additional modules we have introduced in more detail.

3.1 Observations from Knowledge Acquisition Studies

We have been working closely with experts at AMI for a number of winters now in the development of RoadSafe. During this time we have found that two interrelated aspects in particular have influenced the architecture of our system, which we describe next.

Spatial Reference Frames Frames of reference in this context are a particular perspective in which the domain can be observed. More precisely, they are sets of related geographical features (such as elevated areas) which partition the domain into meaningful sub areas for descriptive purposes. In Levinson's terminology (Levinson, 2003), they are absolute reference systems as they employ fixed bearings. In the RoadSafe domain we have identified 4 main spatial frames of reference used by experts in our corpus described in (Turner et al., 2008):

1. Altitude e.g. 'rain turning to snow on higher ground'.
2. Absolute Direction e.g. 'some heavier bursts in the north'.
3. Coastal Proximity e.g. 'strong winds along the coast'.
4. Population e.g. e.g. 'Roads through the Urban areas holding just above freezing'.

Communicative Purpose of Spatial Descriptions From our studies we have found that experts generally follow 4 steps when writing road ice forecasts:

1. Build frames of reference to geographical features that may affect general weather conditions.
2. Build an overview of the general weather pattern.
3. Select important features to communicate from the pattern.
4. Communicate the summary.

Building frames of reference to geographical features is important for a human forecaster to be able to take into account how the geography of the region influences the general weather conditions. Understanding the weathers interaction with the terrain enables them to make reliable meteorological inferences. For example a spatial description such as 'rain turning to snow in rural areas' may be geographically accurate, but does not make sense meteorologically as it is purely by chance that this event is occurring at that location.

From a NLG system perspective it is important to take into account the communicative purpose of spatial descriptions in this context, which are expressing causality (the effect of geographical features on weather conditions) rather than being purely locative. For example, changes in precipitation type are more commonly seen in higher elevation areas where the air temperature is generally lower, so a spatial description describing such an event should make use of a reference frame that reflects this interaction. Similarly, road surface temperatures are generally higher in urban areas where there is a general population effect. For a referring expression generation (REG) strategy this means that this requires not only adequate spatial representation and reasoning capabilities about an objects location, but also additional information about an objects function in space. This is a problem which has been acknowledged in the psycholinguistic literature e.g. (Coventry and Garrod, 2004).

3.2 Geographic Characterisation

Geographic Characterisation is responsible for grounding the location of the data by making the relationship between it's underlying geography explicit. As the first stage of data analysis it assigns additional spatial properties to each data point by intersecting the point with external GIS data sources representing the frames of reference we have identified. For example after characterisation, the first point in the spatial attribute table shown in Figure 1 is assigned values [0m,SSW,Urban,Coastal] to represent elevation, absolute compass direction, population density of its immediate area and its proximity to the coast respectively. This process is more commonly known as a form of data enrichment in the Spatial Data Mining community (Miller and Han, 2001). In the scope of our work it is important for two reasons: most importantly, it provides a set of properties that are used by the REG module to generate spatial descriptions; secondly, these properties can be taken into account by our analysis method during the initial segmentation of the data.

3.3 Spatial Reasoner and Spatial Database

The spatial database provides a repository of geographic information. Frames of reference are stored as thematic layers from various GIS data sources consisting of sets of boundary objects. For example, altitude is represented as sets of polygons representing altitude contours at a given resolution and population is a set of town boundary polygons. The spatial reasoning module provides a high level interface between the spatial database and the rest of the system. It is responsible for performing geographic characterisation and providing spatial query functionality to the rest of the system.

4 Text Generation

In Section 2 we outlined 3 main challenges that our system must address. Our approach to the first, analysis of the input data, is described in (Turner et al., 2007). In the following Sections 4.1 and 4.2, we describe the approach taken by our text generator to the former two: content selection and generating spatial references.

4.1 Content Selection

The input to the document planning module of our system is a series of meteorological events (such as rises in temperature) describing each parameter over specific periods of time and locations. The basic events are generated by data analysis which are then abstracted into higher level concepts by data interpretation. As it is impossible to include all these events in such a short summary our system also generates a table as well as text shown in Figure 5.

In our KA studies we have found experts use a qualitative overview of weather conditions when writing forecasts to perform this task, confirming similar observations reported in (Sripada et al., 2001). We take the same approach as experts in our system by including the internal information of the table (generated by the data analysis module) as input to document planning. This serves as the overview for content selection and allows construction of an initial document plan consisting of overview event leaf nodes. An example of this structure for the system output shown in Figure 5 is given in Figure 6. Each overview event corresponds to a column (or columns in the case of snow and rain) in the table if the column indicates a significant threshold for the parameter it describes (i.e. yes for ice).

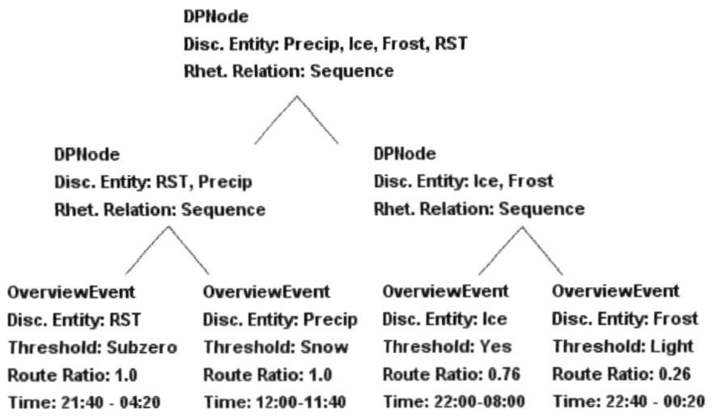

Figure 6: Overview event tree for the text output in Figure 5

Issued by Aerospace & Marine International:- Valid from noon on 11/03/2008

24 Hour Forecast for Kirklees										
Confidence/Comments	This initial analysis is carried out by the advanced RoadSafe system and is computer generated.									
All Routes	Min RST	Time <= 0c	Ice	Hoar Frost	Snow	Fog	MaxGusts	Rain	TS	
Worst/Best	-2.4/0	21:40/ 04:20	YES /NO	LIGHT /NO	HEAVY/HEAVY	NO/NO	82/69	HEAVY/MODERATE	NO	
Overview	Road surface temperatures will fall below zero on all routes during the late evening and tonight except in areas below 100M.									
Wind (mph)	SW 10-25 gusts 45-50 this afternoon in southwestern areas, veering WSW and increasing 15-35 after midnight, gusts 55-60 during the evening and tonight except in areas above 500M, increasing 20-45 then veering W by early morning, gusts 70-75 tomorrow morning in most southern and central places.									
Weather	Wintry precipitation will affect most routes at first, falling as snow flurries in some places above 300M at first. Snow spreading throughout the forecast period to all areas and persisting in some places above 300M until end of period. Ice will affect most routes from the late evening until early morning except in areas below 100M. Hoar frost will affect some routes during the late evening until around midnight. Road surface temperatures will fall slowly during the mid afternoon until tonight, reaching zero in some places above 500M by 22:00.									
Route	All routes summary worst/best									
1	-0.3 /0.5	00:40 /NA	YES /NO	NO/NO	HEAVY/HEAVY	NO/NO	71/65	MODERATE/MODERATE	NO	
2	0.0 /1.1	04:00 /NA	NO /NO	NO/NO	HEAVY/HEAVY	NO/NO	70/57	MODERATE/MODERATE	NO	
3	-0.2 /0.8	01:00 /NA	YES /NO	NO/NO	HEAVY/HEAVY	NO/NO	71/53	MODERATE/MODERATE	NO	
4	-0.2 /0.8	01:00 /NA	YES /NO	NO/NO	HEAVY/HEAVY	NO/NO	70/64	MODERATE/MODERATE	NO	
5	-0.1 /0.7	01:20 /NA	YES /NO	NO/NO	HEAVY/HEAVY	NO/NO	70/52	MODERATE/MODERATE	NO	
6	0.0 /1.1	01:40 /NA	NO /NO	NO/NO	HEAVY/HEAVY	NO/NO	70/63	MODERATE/MODERATE	NO	
7	0.0 /0.9	04:00 /NA	NO /NO	NO/NO	HEAVY/HEAVY	NO/NO	70/53	MODERATE/MODERATE	NO	
8	0.0 /0.8	03:40 /NA	NO /NO	NO/NO	HEAVY/HEAVY	NO/NO	70 /49	MODERATE/MODERATE	NO	
9	0.0 /1.0	04:00 /NA	NO /NO	NO/NO	HEAVY/HEAVY	NO/NO	69/53	MODERATE/MODERATE	NO	
10	0.0 /1.0	02:00 /NA	NO /NO	NO/NO	HEAVY/HEAVY	NO/NO	69 /49	MODERATE/MODERATE	NO	
11	-0.3 /0.9	00:40 /NA	YES /NO	NO/NO	HEAVY/HEAVY	NO/NO	71/59	MODERATE/MODERATE	NO	
12	-1.4 /0.3	23:20 /NA	YES /NO	LIGHT /NO	HEAVY/HEAVY	NO/NO	81/64	MODERATE/LIGHT	NO	
......	......	......	......	......	....	......	......	....	......	

Figure 5: Example system output with text and partial table

The next stage is to construct messages from the leaf nodes of the document plan. This is done in a top down fashion by further annotating the tree with events from the input list. Additional events are selected by using the information from the overview events to retrieve them from the list. This has the benefit of keeping the content of both text and table consistent. The final tree comprises the input to the microplanner where messages are realised as sentences in the final text and typically contain two events per message (as observed in our corpus). For example the overview event describing Precip in Figure 6 is realised as two sentences in Figure 5: Wintry precipitation will affect most routes throughout the forecast period at first [overview event], falling as snow flurries in some places above 300M at first [event]. Snow spreading throughout the forecast period to all areas [event] and persisting in some places above 300M until end of period [event].

4.2 Generating Spatial References to Geographic Areas

Approaches to REG to date have concentrated on distinguishing descriptions (e.g. (Gatt and van Deemter, 2007),(van Deemter, 2006),(Horacek, 2006),(Krahmer et al., 2003),(Dale and Reiter, 1995); more specifically that is given a domain, they look to generate a description of a target object that uniquely distinguishes it from all other objects within that domain. In a large geographic environment such as a road network consisting of 1000's of points, where the task is to refer to an event occurring at a small subset of those points, it is impractical (generated descriptions may be long and complex) and prohibitively expensive (large numbers of spatial relations between objects may have to be computed) to take this approach. A more practical approach is to generate spatial descriptions in terms of regions that are not strictly distinguishing (i.e. urban areas, high ground) rather than in terms of the points contained within that region. Indeed, this is the strategy employed by human authors in our corpus. Therefore, in a description such as 'road surface temperatures will fall below zero in some places in the south west', distractors can be defined as the set of points within the south western boundary that do not satisfy this premise.

The relaxation of the requirement to generate a distinguishing description simplifies the REG task in this context as a single referring expression may be deemed acceptable to refer to a wide range of situations. For example, 'in some places in the south west' could be used to refer to a large number of possible subsets of points that fall within the south western boundary of the network. A simple REG strategy is to find the set of properties to use in a description that introduce the least number of distractors. However, as mentioned previously in Section 3.1, an added constraint is that a spatial description should use an appropriate frame of reference in the context of the event it is describing. For example, describing a change in precipitation type using population as a frame of reference (i.e ‘rain turning snow in some rural places’) is not a sound meteorological inference because population density does not affect precipitation. This could cause a reader to infer false implicatures (Grice, 1975), and consequently lead to unnecessary treatment of part of the road network so should be avoided. To account for this, following (Dale and Reiter, 1995) we include a preference set of reference frames for each type of event that must be described. Absence from the set signifies that the specified frame of reference should not be used in that context.

Recall from Section 3.2 that properties in this case relate directly to sets of boundary objects within a frame of reference. Our content selection module takes as input a series of individual proportions describing the spatial distribution of each parameter within each frame of reference at a particular time point. A score is calculated for each set of properties by averaging over the sum of proportions for each frame of reference. An appropriate frame of reference is then selected by choosing the one with the highest score from the preference set for the given event. An example[1] of the input for the generated description ‘falling as snow flurries in some places above 300M at first’ in Figure 5 is shown in Figure 7.

Parameter:	Snow	
Class:	Flurries	
Time point:	12:00 {	
Reference Frame	Boundary	Proportion
Altitude		
	0m:	0.0
	100m:	0.0
	200m:	0.0
	300m:	0.07
	400m:	1.0
	500m:	1.0
Direction		
	CentralNE:	0.0
	CentralNW:	0.0
	CentralSE:	0.0
	CentralSW:	0.0
	EastNorthEast:	0.0
	EastSouthEast:	0.0
	SouthSouthEast:	0.0
	SouthSouthWest:	0.18
	TrueNorthEast:	0.0
	TrueSouthEast:	0.0
	TrueSouthWest:	0.56
	WestSouthWest:	0.23
Population		
	Rural:	0.02
	Urban:	0.0
}		

Figure 7: Example input to content selection for REG. Proportions are number of points affected by snow within given boundary at the specified time point. Scores by Reference Frame: Altitude = 0.35, Direction = 0.07, Population = 0.01

5 Evaluation

The system presented in this paper is in its first incarnation, RoadSafe is still actively under development in preparation for a full scale user evaluation. We have been evaluating the quality of the output of the current system using post edit techniques and feedback from expert meteorologists at AMI. Our prototype has been installed at AMI since the start of the year and is being used to generate draft road ice forecasts for one of their local council clients. One forecast is generated per day which is then post-edited by an on duty forecaster before it is sent to the client. While common in Machine Translation post-edit evaluations are still relatively rare in NLG. The only large scale post-edit evaluation of an NLG system to our knowledge has been reported in (Sripada et al., 2005).

Our current evaluation is small in comparison to that evaluation; SumTime-Mousam, the system being evaluated in that work was generating 150 draft forecasts per day. However, it does try to address some of the problems the authors encountered during that evaluation. The main issue outlined by (Sripada et al., 2005) was that their analysis was post-hoc and therefore not supported by authors or by an editing tool, which made it difficult to analyse why post-edits were made. We have accounted for this by including post-editing as part of our development process and making use of a simple online interface that allows the editor to select check boxes as they edit and insert any general comments they may have. Check boxes record edit reasons at a high level, for example content, sentence order, spatial description used etc. This is because it is not reasonable to expect a time-constrained forecaster to spend time recording every edit he makes.

Another important lesson pointed out by (Sripada et al., 2005) is the need for a pilot study to analyse the post-edit behaviour of individual authors to account for noisy data. This is certainly worthwhile, but is difficult to carry out in our domain where forecasters work in variable shift patterns and on variable forecasting tasks at different times. Instead, we

[1] N.B. this example is taken from route network that is land locked and therefore coastal proximity is not taken into account in this case.

have used feedback forms as a way to gain qualitative data on both the general quality of the texts and the post-editing process. We present our results in Section 5.1. In Section 5.2 we provide some discussion of the results and describe future work.

5.1 Results

Our post-edit corpus currently consists of 112 texts, 2 texts(1 generated,1 edited) for 56 forecast days. Of the 56 generated texts 54 have been edited before being released to the user. As a general evaluation criterion, our generated texts are generally too long with a mean word length of 72 (standard deviation of 21) compared to a mean word length of 53 (standard deviation of 17). The mean word count difference per forecast is 21 (standard deviation of 15). In general analysis of the corpus is difficult, as in some cases (18) texts have been basically rewritten. This is not reflecting the quality of the text as such, but the fact that the author has access to other information sources such as satellite maps, which can lead him to draw different inferences to those in the raw model data available to the system. Furthermore, (Hopwood, 2004) acknowledge as ice prediction models have become increasingly advanced, the primary added value provided by weather forecasters is to function as quality control and error mitigation for the model, using their insight and experience to make amendments particularly on marginal nights (where the road surface temperature may or may not fall below zero). Such cases can only be considered as noise for analysis purposes, and the fact that our system cannot account for this without the additional information has been acknowledged by all forecasters in their editing comments and feedback forms.

Focusing on 74 real post-edits (not attributed to model data) recorded in our corpus, they can be classified into the following broad error categories: content edits - 65% and microplanning edits 35%. One major problem we have identified with the current generated text is the way in which overview events described in 4.1 are realised. Deletions of whole sentences describing overview events such as the one highlighted in bold in Figure 8 constitute over half (52%) of content edits, which may help to explain the large descrepency in word counts. Essentially forecasters believe they can often communicate similar information as subsequent statements about the same parameter making the texts repetitive at times. Therefore they suggest they should either be omitted or be realised as more interpretative statements, such as ‘A marginal night for most routes’ for the omitted statement in Figure 8. Forecasters also often delete subsequent statements following overview sentences when they describe an event (such as rain turning heavy) occuring only at a small number of locations. So the spatial extent of an event and not only its meteorological importance should be considered during content selection. RoadSafe does not currently include much domain reasoning at the document planning level to be able to do this.

Generated Text:

‘**Road surface temperatures will reach near critical levels on some routes from the late evening until tomorrow morning.** Rain will affect all routes during the afternoon and evening. Road surface temperatures will fall slowly during the mid afternoon and evening, reaching near critical levels in areas above 500M by 21:00.’

Post-edited Text:

‘Rain will affect all routes during the afternoon and evening. Road surface temperatures will fall slowly during the mid afternoon and evening, reaching near critical levels in areas above 500M by 21:00.’

Figure 8: Content selection post-edit example (road surface temperature overview information removed)

Generated Text:

‘Road surface temperatures will reach near critical levels on some routes after midnight until tomorrow morning. Rain will affect all routes **throughout** the forecast period, **falling as snow in some places above 500M by 08:00. Snow clearing by 08:00.** Road surface temperatures will fall slowly during the late evening and tonight, reaching near critical levels in areas above 500M by 03:00.’

Post-edited Text:

‘Road surface temperatures will reach near critical levels on some routes after midnight until tomorrow morning. Rain will affect all routes **during** the forecast period, **this may fall as sleet later on highest ground before dying out.** Road surface temperatures will fall slowly during the late evening and tonight, reaching near critical levels in areas above 500M by 03:00.’

Figure 9: Microplanning post-edit example (lexicalisation and aggregation)

Microplanning edits, as highlighted in bold in Figure 9, are due to individual lexical choice or aggregation issues. In all questionnaires experts have commented that the generated texts are grammatically sound but could flow better. Aggregation is done in a fairly basic fashion in our system at present as is lexicalisation. There have been no edits to the frame of reference used in the generated spatial descriptions, which we have taken as indication that our REG strategy works well.

5.2 Discussion

The general feedback to our system has been encouraging. In terms of the exploitability of the system in its current form it has received mixed reviews from 4 forecasters: 1 forecaster rated the system as good for content and very poor on fluency; 1 rated it as ok for both; 1 forecaster rated it as poor for content and ok for fluency; 1 forecaster rated it as poor for both. Generally all forecasters believe the generated texts should tell a more fluent story about weather conditions with more causal linking between events. In terms of the techniques and approach outlined in this paper they have worked well, although as acknowledged in the previous section more sophisticated domain reasoning and aggregation techniques are required if the text is to function as a concise summary, and indeed reach the standard of human authored texts.

Making the required improvements highlighted in the previous section is the focus of current work. After these improvements have been made we plan to carry out an evaluation with users of the forecasts. We hope to also extend the functionality of the system by generating individual route forecasts, which can be accessed interactively through the table.

6 Conclusions

We have presented an approach to generating geographically grounded summaries of georeferenced data using spatial reference frames. This approach has been implemented in a data-to-text system for generating road ice forecasts. An important task in summarising georeferenced data is to describe the data in terms of its underlying geography it references. This presents an interesting challenge for conventional REG approaches as finding a distinguishing description for large numbers of objects in geographic space is not practical. We have found characterising the geography in terms of spatial reference frames provides a good solution as it provides a flexible representation to describe set of objects in terms of geographic areas.

We have also implemented a simple top down content selection approach based on the idea of overview, taken from how we have observed experts commonly performing the summarisation task. While this approach works well for content selection, a post-edit evaluation with experts has highlighted that realising the overview in the text can make texts verbose and have the effect of making subsequent statements describing related events in the discourse sound repetitive. This is important as experts require a short concise summary of weather conditions.

Acknowledgments

Many thanks to our collaborators at Aerospace and Marine International UK, especially Keith Thomson and the other Meteorologists, for their helpful feedback and comments. The RoadSafe project is supported jointly by Aerospace and Marine International UK, and the UK Engineering and Physical Sciences Research Council (EPSRC), under a CASE PhD studentship.

References

J. Coch. 1998. Multimeteo: multilingual production of weather forecasts. *ELRA Newsletter*, 3(2).

K. R. Coventry and S. C. Garrod. 2004. *Saying, Seeing and Acting: The Psychological Semantics of Spatial Prepositions*. Psychology Press.

R. Dale and E. Reiter. 1995. Computational interpretations of the gricean maxims in the generation of referring expressions. *Cognitive Science*, 19:233–263.

R Dale, S Geldof, and J-P Prost. 2005. Using natural language generation in automatic route description. *Journal of Research and Practice in Information Technology*, 37(1):89–105.

A. Gatt and K. van Deemter. 2007. Lexical choice and conceptual perspective in the generation of plural referring expressions. *Journal of Logic, Language and Information*, 16:423–443.

E. Goldberg, N. Driedger, and R. Kittredge. 1994. Using natural-language processing to produce weather forecasts. *IEEE Expert*, 9(2):45–53.

H. Grice. 1975. Logic and conversation. In P. Cole and J. Morgan, editors, *Syntax and Semantics*, volume 3, Speech Acts, pages 43–58. Academic Press: New York.

C. Hallett and D. Scott. 2005. Structural variation in generated health reports. In *Proceedings of the 3rd International Workshop on Paraphrasing (IWP2005)*, pages 33–40, Jeju Island, Republic of Korea.

Philip Hopwood. 2004. Improvements in road forecasting techniques & their applications. In *12th International Road Weather Conference*, Bingen, Germany.

Helmut Horacek. 2006. Generating references to parts of recursively structured objects. In *Proceedings of the 4th International Conference on Natural Language Generation*, pages 47–54.

Lidija Iordanskaja, Richard Kittredge, Benoit Lavoie, and Alain Polguère. 1992. Generation of extended bilingual statistical reports. *COLING-92*, pages 1019–1023.

Emiel Krahmer, Sebastiaan van Erk, and Andr Verleg. 2003. Graph-based generation of referring expressions. *Computational Linguistics*, 29(1):53–72.

Stephen C. Levinson. 2003. *Space in language and cognition: explorations in cognitive diversity*. Cambridge University Press, Cambridge.

Harvey J. Miller and Jiawei Han. 2001. Geographic data mining and knowledge discovery: An overview. In *Geographic Data Mining and Knowledge Discovery*, chapter 1, pages 1–32. Taylor & Francis.

F. Portet, E. Reiter, J. Hunter, and S. Sripada. 2007. Automatic generation of textual summaries from neonatal intensive care data. In *11th Conference on Artificial Intelligence in Medicine (AIME 07)*, pages 227–236.

E. Reiter, S. Sripada, J. Hunter, J. Yu, and I. Davy. 2005. Choosing words in computer-generated weather forecasts. In *Artificial Intelligence*, volume 67, pages 137–169.

E. Reiter. 2007. An architecture for data-to-text systems. In *ENLG07*, pages 97–104.

D. Rösner. 1987. The automated news agency: Semtex: A text generator for german. In *Natural Language Generation: New Results in Artificial Intelligence, Psychology, and Linguistics*. Nijhoff.

D. Roy and E. Reiter. 2005. Connecting language to the world. *Artificial Intelligence*, 167:1–12.

S. Sripada, E. Reiter, J. Hunter, and Jin Yu. 2001. A two-stage model for content determination. In *ENLG2001*, pages 3–10.

S Sripada, E Reiter, and L Hawizy. 2005. Evaluation of an nlg system using post-edit data: Lessons learnt. In *10th European Workshop on Natural Language Generation*.

R. Turner, S. Sripada, E. Reiter, and I. Davy. 2007. Selecting the content of textual descriptions of geographically located events in spatio-temporal weather data. In *Applications and Innovations in Intelligent Systems XV*, pages 75–88.

R. Turner, S. Sripada, E. Reiter, and I. Davy. 2008. Building a parallel spatio-temporal data-text corpus for summary generation. In *Proceedings of the LREC2008 Workshop on Methodologies and Resources for Processing Spatial Language*, Marrakech, Morocco.

K van Deemter. 2006. Generating referring expressions that involve gradable properties. *Computational Linguistics*, 32:195–222.

Dependency Tree Based Sentence Compression

Katja Filippova and **Michael Strube**
EML Research gGmbH
Schloß-Wolfsbrunnenweg 33
69118 Heidelberg, Germany
http://www.eml-research.de/nlp

Abstract

We present a novel unsupervised method for sentence compression which relies on a dependency tree representation and shortens sentences by removing subtrees. An automatic evaluation shows that our method obtains result comparable or superior to the state of the art. We demonstrate that the choice of the parser affects the performance of the system. We also apply the method to German and report the results of an evaluation with humans.

1 Introduction

Within the field of text-to-text generation, the sentence compression task can be defined as follows: given a sentence S, consisting of words $w_1 w_2 ... w_n$, what is a subset of the words of S, such that it is grammatical and preserves essential information from S? There are many applications which would benefit from a robust compression system, such as subtitle generation, compression for mobile devices with a limited screen size, or news digests. Given that to date most text and speech summarization systems are extractive, sentence compression techniques are a common way to deal with redundancy in their output.

In recent years, a number of approaches to sentence compression have been developed (Jing, 2001; Knight & Marcu, 2002; Gagnon & Da Sylva, 2005; Turner & Charniak, 2005; Clarke & Lapata, 2008, inter alia). Many explicitly rely on a language model, usually a trigram model, to produce grammatical output (Knight & Marcu, 2002; Hori & Furui, 2004; Turner & Charniak, 2005; Galley & McKeown, 2007). Testing the grammaticality of the output with a language model is justified when working with a language with rigid word order like English, and all but one approach mentioned have been applied to English data. However, compressing sentences in languages with less rigid word order needs a deeper analysis to test grammaticality. And even for languages with rigid word order the trigram model ignores the structure of the sentence and therefore may significantly distort the meaning of the source sentence. Approaches going beyond the word level either require a comprehensive lexicon (Jing, 2001), or manually devised rules (Gagnon & Da Sylva, 2005; Clarke & Lapata, 2008) to determine prunable constituents. A lexicon is not always available, whereas the hand-crafted rules may not cover all cases and are too general to be universally applicable (e.g. *PPs can be pruned*).

In this paper we present a novel unsupervised approach to sentence compression which is motivated by the belief that the grammaticality of the output can be better ensured by compressing trees. In particular, given a dependency tree, we want to prune subtrees which are neither obligatory syntactic arguments, nor contribute important information to the content of the sentence. A tree pruning approach does not generate new dependencies and is unlikely to produce a compression with a totally different meaning. Our approach is unsupervised and adaptable to other languages, the main requirement being that there are a dependency parser and a corpus available for the languages. We test our approach on English and German data sets and obtain results comparable or superior to the state of the art.

2 Related Work

Many existing compression systems use a noisy-channel approach and rely on a language model to test the grammaticality of the output (Knight & Marcu, 2002; Turner & Charniak, 2005; Galley & McKeown, 2007). Other ways to ensure grammaticality and to decide whether a constituent is obligatory or may be pruned are to utilize a subcategorization lexicon (Jing, 2001), or to define a set of generally prunable constituents. Gagnon & Da Sylva (2005) prune dependency trees by removing prepositional complements of the verb, subordinate clauses and noun appositions. Apparently, this does not guarantee grammaticality in all cases. It may also eliminate important information from the tree.

Most approaches are supervised and require training data to learn which words or constituents can be dropped from a sentence (Riezler et al., 2003; McDonald, 2006). However, it is difficult to obtain training data. Still, there are few unsupervised methods. For example, Hori & Furui (2004) introduce a scoring function which relies on such information sources as word significance score and language model. A compression of a given length which maximizes the scoring function is then found with dynamic programming. Clarke & Lapata (2008) present another unsupervised approach. They formulate the task as an optimization problem and solve it with integer linear programming. Two scores contribute to their objective function – a trigram language model score and a word significance score. Additionally, the grammaticality of the output is ensured by a handful of linguistic constraints, stating e.g. which arguments should be preserved.

In this paper we suggest an alternative to the popular language model basis for compression systems – a method which compresses dependency trees and not strings of words. We will argue that our formulation has the following advantages: firstly, the approach is unsupervised, the only requirement being that there is a sufficiently large corpus and a dependency parser available. Secondly, it requires neither a subcategorization lexicon nor hand-crafted rules to decide which arguments are obligatory. Thirdly, it finds a globally optimal compression by taking syntax and word importance into account.

3 Dependency Based Compression

Our method compresses sentences in that it removes dependency edges from the dependency tree of a sentence. The aim is to preserve dependencies which are either required for the output to be grammatical or have an important word as the dependent. The algorithm proceeds in three steps: tree transformation (Section 3.1), tree compression (Section 3.2) and tree linearization (Section 3.3).

3.1 Tree Transformation

Before a dependency tree is compressed, i.e. before some of the dependencies are removed, the tree is modified. We will demonstrate the effect of the transformations with the sentence below:

(1) He said that he lived in Paris and Berlin

The first transformation (ROOT) inserts an explicit rootnode (Fig. 1(a)). The result of the second transformation (VERB) is that every inflected verb in the tree gets an edge originating from the rootnode (Fig. 1(b)). All edges outgoing from the rootnode bear the *s* label. Apart from that we remove auxiliary edges and memorize such grammatical properties as voice, tense or negation for verbs.

The purpose of the remaining transformations is to make relations between open-class words more explicit. We want to decide on pruning an edge judging from two considerations: (i) how important for the head this argument is; (ii) how informative the dependent word is. As an example, consider a source sentence given in (2). Here, we want to decide whether one prepositional phrase (or both) can be pruned without making the resulting sentence ungrammatical.

(2) After some time, he moved to London.

It would not be very helpful to check whether an argument attached with the label *pp* is obligatory for the verb *move*. Looking at a particular preposition (*after* vs. *to*) would be more enlightening. This motivates the PREP transformation which removes prepositional nodes and places them as labels on the edge from their head to the respective noun (Fig. 1(c)). We also decompose a chain of conjoined elements (CONJ) and attach each of them to the head of the first element in the chain with the label the first

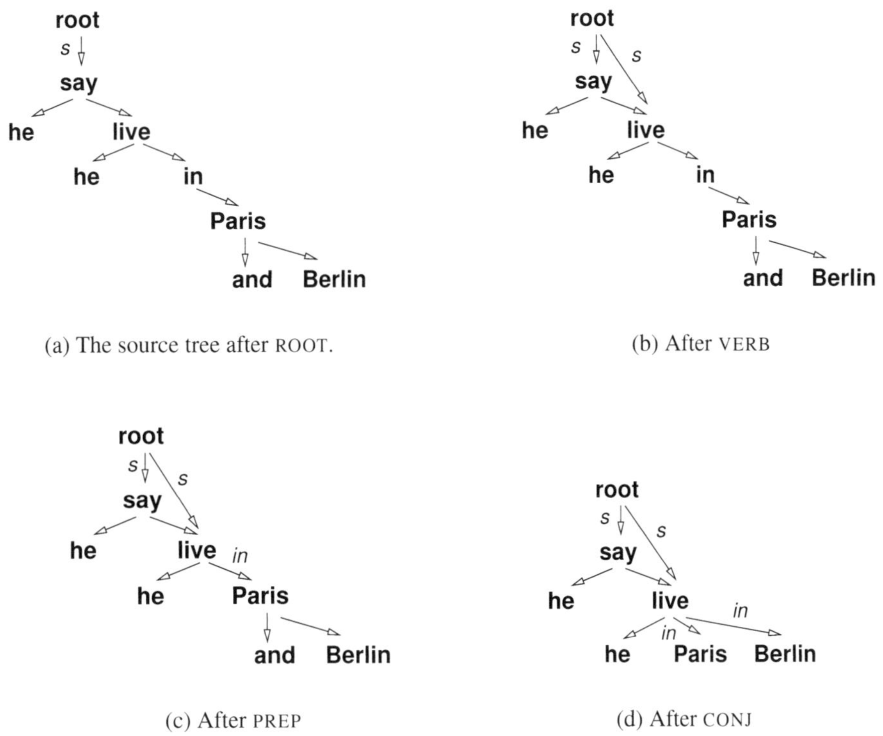

Figure 1: The dependency structure of *He said that he lived in Paris and Berlin* after the transformations

element attaches to its head with (Fig. 1(d)). This way we can retain any of the conjoined elements in the compression and do not have to preserve the whole sequence of them if we are interested in only one. This last transformation is not applied to verbs.

3.2 Tree Compression

We formulate the compression task as an optimization problem which we solve using integer linear programming[1]. Given a transformed dependency tree (a graph if new edges have been added), we decide which dependency edges to remove. For each directed dependency edge from head h to word w we thus introduce a binary variable $x^l_{h,w}$ where l stands for the edge's label:

$$x^l_{h,w} = \begin{cases} 1 & \text{if the dependency is preserved} \\ 0 & \text{otherwise} \end{cases} \quad (1)$$

The goal is to find a subtree which gets the highest score of the objective function (2) to which both the probability of dependencies ($P(l|h)$) and the importance of dependent words ($I(w)$) contribute:

$$f(X) = \sum_x x^l_{h,w} \cdot P(l|h) \cdot I(w) \quad (2)$$

Intuitively, the conditional probabilities prevent us from removing obligatory dependencies from the tree. For example, $P(subj|work)$ is higher than $P(with|work)$, and therefore the subject will be preserved whereas the prepositional label and thus the whole PP can be pruned. This way we do not have to create an additional constraint for every obligatory argument (e.g. subject or direct object). Neither do we require a subcategorization lexicon to look up which arguments are obligatory for a certain verb. Verb arguments are preserved because the dependency edges, with which they are attached to the head, get high scores. Table 1 presents the probabilities of a number of labels given that the head is *study*. Table 2 presents the probabilities for their German counterparts.

Note that if we would not apply the PREP transformation we would not be able to distinguish be-

[1]In our implementation we use lp_solve (`http://sourceforge.net/projects/lpsolve`).

subj	dobj	in	at	after	with	to
0.16	0.13	0.05	0.04	0.01	0.01	0.01

Table 1: Probabilities of *subj, d(irect)obj, in, at, after, with, to* given the verb *study*

subj	obja	in	an	nach	mit	zu
0.88	0.74	0.44	0.42	0.09	0.02	0.01

Table 2: Probabilities of *subj, obja(ccusative), in, at, after, with, to* given the verb *studieren*

tween different prepositions and could only calculate $P(pp|studieren)$ which would not be very informative. The probabilities for English are lower than those for German because we calculate the conditional probabilities given word lemma. In English, the part of speech information cannot be induced from the lemma and thus the set of possible labels of a node is on average larger than in German.

There are many ways in which word importance, $I(w)$ can be defined. Here, we use the formula introduced by Clarke & Lapata (2008) which is a modification of the significance score of Hori et al. (2003):

$$I(w_i) = \frac{l}{N} \cdot f_i \log \frac{F_A}{F_i} \quad (3)$$

w_i is the topic word (either noun or verb), f_i is the frequency of w_i in the document, F_i is the frequency of w_i in the corpus, and F_A is the sum of frequencies of all topic words in the corpus. l is the number of clause nodes above w and N is the maximum level of embedding of the sentence w belongs to.

The objective function is subject to constraints of two kinds. The constraints of the first kind are stuctural and ensure that the preserved dependencies result in a tree. (4) ensures that each word has one head at most. (5) ensures connectivity in the tree. (6) restricts the size of the resulting tree to α words.

$$\forall w \in W, \sum_{h,l} x^l_{h,w} \leq 1 \quad (4)$$

$$\forall w \in W, \sum_{h,l} x^l_{h,w} - \frac{1}{|W|} \sum_{u,l} x^l_{w,u} \geq 0 \quad (5)$$

$$\sum_{x} x^l_{h,w} \leq \alpha \quad (6)$$

α is a function of the length of the source sentence in open-class words. The function is not linear since the degree of compression increases with the length of the sentence. The compression rate of human-generated sentences is about 70% (Clarke & Lapata, 2008)[2]. To approximate this value, we set the proportion of deleted words to be 20% for short sentences (5-9 non-stop words), this value increases up to 50% for long sentences (30+ words).

The constraints of the second type ensure the syntactic validity of the output tree and explicitly state which edges should be preserved. These constraints can be general as well as conditional. The former ensure that an edge is preserved if its source node is retained in the output. Conditional syntactic constraints state that an edge has to be preserved if (and only if) a certain other edge is preserved. We have only one syntactic constraint which states that a subordinate conjunction (*sc*) should be preserved if and only if the clause it belongs to functions as a subordinate clause (*sub*) in the output. If it is taken as the main clause, the conjunction should be dropped. In terms of edges, this can be formulated as follows (7):

$$\forall x^{sc}_{w,u}, x^{sub}_{h,w} - x^{sc}_{w,u} = 0 \quad (7)$$

Due to the constraint (4), the compressed subtree is always rooted in the node added as a result of the first transformation. A compression of a sentence to an embedded clause is not possible unless one preserves the structure above the embedded clause. Often, however, main clauses are less important than an embedded clause. For example, given the sentence *He said they have to be held in Beirut* it is the embedded clause which is informative and to which the source sentence should be compressed. The purpose of the VERB modification is to amend exactly this problem. Having an edge from the rootnode to every inflected verb allows us to compress the source sentence to any clause.

3.3 Tree Linearization

A very simple but reasonable linearization technique is to present the words of a compressed sentence in the order they are found in the source sentence. This method has been applied before and this is how we

[2]Higher rates correspond to longer compressions.

linearize the trees obtained for the English data. Unfortunately, this method cannot be directly applied to German because of the constraints on word order in this language. One of the rules of German grammar states that in the main clause the inflected part of the verb occupies the second position, the first position being occupied by exactly one constituent. Therefore, if the sentence initial position in a source sentence is occupied by a constituent which got pruned off as a result of compression, the verb becomes the first element of the sentence which results in an undesirable output. There are linearization methods developed for German which find an optimal word order for a sentence (Ringger et al., 2004; Filippova & Strube, 2007). We use our recent method to linearize compressed trees.

4 Corpora and Annotation

We apply our method to sentences from two corpora in English and German. These are presented below.

English Compression Corpus: The English data we use is a document-based compression corpus from the British National Corpus and American News Text Corpus which consists of 82 news stories[3]. We parsed the corpus with RASP (Briscoe et al., 2006) and with the Stanford PCFG parser (Klein & Manning, 2003). The output of the former is a set of dependency relations whereas the latter provides an option for converting the output into dependency format (de Marneffe et al., 2006) which we use.

TüBa-D/Z: The German corpus we use is a collection of 1,000 newspaper articles (Telljohann et al., 2003)[4]. Sentence boundaries, morphology, dependency structure and anaphoric relations are manually annotated in this corpus.

RASP has been used by Clarke & Lapata (2008) whose state of the art results we compare with ours. We use not only RASP but also the Stanford parser for several reasons. Apart from being accurate, the latter has an elaborated set of dependency relations (48 vs. 15 of RASP) which is not overly large (compared with the 106 grammatical relations of the Link Parser). This is important for our system which relies on syntactic information when making pruning decisions. A comparison between the Stanford parser and two dependency parsers, MiniPar and Link Parser, showed a decent performance of the former (de Marneffe et al., 2006). It is also of interest to see to what extent the choice of the parser influences the results.

Apart from the corpora listed above, we use the Tipster corpus to calculate conditional probabilities of syntactic labels given head lemmas as well as word significance scores. The significance score is calculated from the total number of 128 million nouns and verbs. Conditional probabilities are calculated from a much smaller portion of Tipster (about 6 million tokens). The latter number is comparable to the size of the data set we use to compute the probabilities for German. There, we use a corpus of about 4,000 articles from the German Wikipedia to calculate conditional probabilities and significance scores. The corpus is parsed with the highly accurate CDG parser (Foth & Menzel, 2006) and has the same dependency format as TüBa-D/Z (Versley, 2005).

Although all corpora are annotated with dependency relations, there are considerable differences between the annotation of the English and German data sets. The phrase to dependency structure conversion done by the Stanford parser makes the semantic head of the constituent its syntactic head. For example, in the sentence *He is right* it is the adjective *right* which is the root of the tree. Unlike that, sentences from the German corpora always have a verb as the root. To unify the formats, we write a set of rules to make the verb the root of the tree in all cases.

5 Evaluation

We evaluate the results automatically as well as with human subjects. To assess the performance of the method on the English data, we calculate the F-measure on grammatical relations. Following Riezler et al. (2003), we calculate average precision and recall as the amount of grammatical relations shared between the output of our system and the gold stan-

[3]The corpus is available from `http://homepages.inf.ed.ac.uk/s0460084/data`.

[4]The corpus is available from `http://www.sfs.uni-tuebingen.de/en_tuebadz.shtml`.

dard variant divided over the total number of relations in the output and in the human-generated compression respectively. According to Clarke & Lapata (2006), this measure reliably correlates with human judgements. The results of our evaluation as well as the state of the art results reported by Clarke & Lapata (2008) (LM+SIG+CONSTR), whose system uses language model scoring (LM), word significance score (SIG), and linguistic constraints (CONSTR), are presented in Table 3. The F-measure reported by Clarke & Lapata (2008) is calculated with RASP which their system builds upon. For our system we present the results obtained on the data parsed with RASP as well as with the Stanford parser (SP). In both cases the F-measure is found with RASP in order to allow for a fair comparison between the three systems. We recalculate the compression rate for the gold standard ignoring punctuation. On the whole corpus the compression rate turns out to be slightly higher than that reported by Clarke & Lapata (2008) (70.3%).

	F-measure	*compr.rate*
LM+SIG+CONSTR	40.5	72.0%
DEP-BASED (RASP)	40.7	49.6%
DEP-BASED (SP)	49.3	69.3%
GOLD	-	72.1%

Table 3: Average results on the English corpus

As there are no human-generated compressions for German data, we evaluate the performance of the method in terms of *grammaticality* and *importance* by means of an experiment with native speakers. In the experiment, humans are presented with a source sentence and its compression which they are asked to evaluate on two five-point scales. Higher grades are given to better sentences. Importance represents the amount of relevant information from the source sentence retained in the compression. Since our method does not generate punctuation, the judges are asked to ignore errors due to missing commas. Five participants took part in the experiment and each rated the total of 25 sentences originating from a randomly chosen newspaper article. Their ratings as well as the ratings reported by Clarke & Lapata (2008) on English corpus are presented in Table 4.

	grammar	*importance*
LM+SIG+CONSTR	3.76	3.53
DEP-BASED (DE)	3.62	3.21

Table 4: Average results for the German data

6 Discussion

The results on the English data are comparable with or superior to the state of the art. These were obtained with a single linguistic constraint (7) and without any elaborated resources which makes our system adaptable to other languages. This suggests that tree compression is a better basis for sentence compression systems than language model-oriented word deletion.

In order to explain why the choice of parser significantly influences the performance of the method, we calculate the precision P defined as the number of dependencies shared by a human-generated compression (dep_c) and the source sentence (dep_s) divided over the total number of dependencies found in the compression:

$$P = \frac{|dep_c \cap dep_s|}{|dep_c|} \quad (8)$$

The intuition is that if a parser does not reach high precision on gold standard sentences, i.e. if it does not assign similar dependency structures to a source sentence and its compression, then it is hopeless to expect it to produce good compression with our dependency-based method. However, the precision does not have to be as high as 100% because of, e.g., changes within a chain of conjoined elements or appositions. The precision of the two parsers calculated over the compression corpus is presented in Table 5.

	RASP	Stanford parser
precision	79.6%	84.3%

Table 5: Precision of the parsers

The precision of the Stanford parser is about 5% higher than that of RASP. In our opinion, this partly explains why the use of the Stanford parser increases the F-measure by 9 points. Another possible reason for this improvement is that the Stanford parser identifies three times more dependency relations than

RASP and thus allows for finer distinctions between the arguments of different types.

Another point concerns the compression rates. The compressions generated with RASP are considerably shorter than those generated with the Stanford parser. This is mainly due to the fact that the structure output by RASP is not necessarily a tree or a connected graph. In such cases only the first subtree of the sentence is taken as input and compressed.

The results on the German set are not conclusive since the number of human judges is relatively small. Still, these preliminary results are comparable to those reported for English and thus give us some evidence that the method can be adapted to languages other than English. Interestingly, the importance score depends on the grammaticality of the sentence. A grammatical sentence can convey unimportant information but it was never the case that an ungrammatical sentence got a high rating on the importance scale. Some of the human judges told us that they had difficulties assigning the importance score to ungrammatical sentences.

7 Conclusions

We presented a new compression method which compresses dependency trees and does not rely on a language model to test grammaticality. The method is unsupervised and can be easily adapted to languages other than English. It does not require a subcategorization lexicon or elaborated hand-crafted rules to decide which arguments can be pruned and finds a globally optimal compression taking syntax and word importance into account. We demonstrated that the performance of the system depends on the parser and suggested a way to estimate how well a parser is suited for the compression task. The results indicate that the dependency-based approach is an alternative to the language model-based one which is worth pursuing.

Acknowledgements: This work has been funded by the Klaus Tschira Foundation, Heidelberg, Germany. The first author has been supported by a KTF grant (09.009.2004). We would like to thank Yannick Versley who helped us convert TüBa-D/Z in the CDG format and Elke Teich and the three anonymous reviewers for their useful comments.

References

Briscoe, Edward, John Carroll & Rebecca Watson (2006). The second release of the RASP system. In *Proceedings of the COLING-ACL Interactive Presentation Session,* Sydney, Australia, 2006, pp. 77–80.

Clarke, James & Mirella Lapata (2006). Models for sentence compression: A comparison across domains, training requirements and evaluation measures. In *Proceedings of the 21st International Conference on Computational Linguistics and 44th Annual Meeting of the Association for Computational Linguistics,* Sydney, Australia, 17–21 July 2006, pp. 377–385.

Clarke, James & Mirella Lapata (2008). Global inference for sentence compression: An integer linear programming approach. *Journal of Artificial Intelligence Research*, 31:399–429.

de Marneffe, Marie-Catherine, Bill MacCartney & Christopher D. Manning (2006). Generating typed dependency parses from phrase structure parses. In *Proceedings of the 5th International Conference on Language Resources and Evaluation,* Genoa, Italy, 22–28 May 2006, pp. 449–454.

Filippova, Katja & Michael Strube (2007). Generating constituent order in German clauses. In *Proceedings of the 45th Annual Meeting of the Association for Computational Linguistics,* Prague, Czech Republic, 23–30 June 2007, pp. 320–327.

Foth, Kilian & Wolfgang Menzel (2006). Hybrid parsing: Using probabilistic models as predictors for a symbolic parser. In *Proceedings of the 21st International Conference on Computational Linguistics and 44th Annual Meeting of the Association for Computational Linguistics,* Sydney, Australia, 17–21 July 2006, pp. 321–327.

Gagnon, Michel & Lyne Da Sylva (2005). Text summarization by sentence extraction and syntactic pruning. In *Proceedings of Computational Linguistics in the North East,* Gatineau, Québec, Canada, 26 August 2005.

Galley, Michel & Kathleen R. McKeown (2007). Lexicalized Markov grammars for sentence compression. In *Proceedings of Human Language Technologies 2007: The Conference of the North American Chapter of the Association for Computational Linguistics,* Rochester, N.Y., 22–27 April 2007, pp. 180–187.

Hori, Chiori & Sadaoki Furui (2004). Speech summarization: An approach through word extraction and a method for evaluation. *IEEE Transactions on Information and Systems*, E87-D(1):15–25.

Hori, Chiori, Sadaoki Furui, Rob Malkin, Hua Yu & Alex Waibel (2003). A statistical approach to automatic speech summarization. *EURASIP Journal on Applied Signal Processing*, 2:128–139.

Jing, Hongyan (2001). *Cut-and-Paste Text Summarization*, (Ph.D. thesis). Computer Science Department, Columbia University, New York, N.Y.

Klein, Dan & Christopher D. Manning (2003). Accurate unlexicalized parsing. In *Proceedings of the 41st Annual Meeting of the Association for Computational Linguistics,* Sapporo, Japan, 7–12 July 2003, pp. 423–430.

Knight, Kevin & Daniel Marcu (2002). Summarization beyond sentence extraction: A probabilistic approach to sentence compression. *Artificial Intelligence*, 139(1):91–107.

McDonald, Ryan (2006). Discriminative sentence compression with soft syntactic evidence. In *Proceedings of the 11th Conference of the European Chapter of the Association for Computational Linguistics,* Trento, Italy, 3–7 April 2006, pp. 297–304.

Riezler, Stefan, Tracy H. King, Richard Crouch & Annie Zaenen (2003). Statistical sentence condensation using ambiguity packing and stochastic disambiguation methods for Lexical-Functional Grammar. In *Proceedings of the Human Language Technology Conference of the North American Chapter of the Association for Computational Linguistics,* Edmonton, Alberta, Canada, 27 May –1 June 2003, pp. 118–125.

Ringger, Eric, Michael Gamon, Robert C. Moore, David Rojas, Martine Smets & Simon Corston-Oliver (2004). Linguistically informed statistical models of constituent structure for ordering in sentence realization. In *Proceedings of the 20th International Conference on Computational Linguistics,* Geneva, Switzerland, 23–27 August 2004, pp. 673–679.

Telljohann, Heike, Erhard W. Hinrichs & Sandra Kübler (2003). *Stylebook for the Tübingen treebank of written German (TüBa-D/Z).* Technical Report: Seminar für Sprachwissenschaft, Universität Tübingen, Tübingen, Germany.

Turner, Jenine & Eugene Charniak (2005). Supervised and unsupervised learning for sentence compression. In *Proceedings of the 43rd Annual Meeting of the Association for Computational Linguistics,* Ann Arbor, Mich., 25–30 June 2005, pp. 290–297.

Versley, Yannick (2005). Parser evaluation across text types. In *Proceedings of the 4th Workshop on Treebanks and Linguistic Theories,* Barcelona, Spain, 9-10 December 2005.

Extractive vs. NLG-based Abstractive Summarization of Evaluative Text: The Effect of Corpus Controversiality

Giuseppe Carenini and Jackie Chi Kit Cheung[1]
Department of Computer Science
University of British Columbia
Vancouver, B.C. V6T 1Z4, Canada
{carenini,cckitpw}@cs.ubc.ca

Abstract

Extractive summarization is the strategy of concatenating extracts taken from a corpus into a summary, while abstractive summarization involves paraphrasing the corpus using novel sentences. We define a novel measure of corpus controversiality of opinions contained in evaluative text, and report the results of a user study comparing extractive and NLG-based abstractive summarization at different levels of controversiality. While the abstractive summarizer performs better overall, the results suggest that the margin by which abstraction outperforms extraction is greater when controversiality is high, providing a context in which the need for generation-based methods is especially great.

1 Introduction

There are two main approaches to the task of summarization—extraction and abstraction (Hahn and Mani, 2000). Extraction involves concatenating extracts taken from the corpus into a summary, whereas abstraction involves generating novel sentences from information extracted from the corpus. It has been observed that in the context of multi-document summarization of news articles, extraction may be inappropriate because it may produce summaries which are overly verbose or biased towards some sources (Barzilay et al., 1999). However, there has been little work identifying specific factors which might affect the performance of each strategy in summarizing evaluative documents containing opinions and preferences, such as customer reviews or blogs. This work aims to address this gap by exploring one dimension along which the effectiveness of the two paradigms could vary; namely, the controversiality of the opinions contained in the corpus.

In this paper, we make the following contributions. Firstly, we define a measure of controversiality of opinions in the corpus based on information entropy. Secondly, we run a user study to test the hypothesis that a controversial corpus has greater need of abstractive methods and consequently of NLG techniques. Intuitively, extracting sentences from multiple users whose opinions are diverse and wide-ranging may not reflect the overall opinion, whereas it may be adequate content-wise if opinions are roughly the same across users. As a secondary contribution, we propose a method for structuring text when summarizing controversial corpora. This method is used in our study for generating abstractive summaries.

The results of the user study support our hypothesis that a NLG summarizer outperforms an extractive summarizer by more when the controversiality is high.

2 Related Work

There has been little work comparing extractive and abstractive multi-document summarization. A previous study on summarizing evaluative text (Carenini et. al, 2006) showed that extraction and abstraction performed about equally well, though for different reasons. The study, however, did not

[1]Authors are listed in alphabetical order.

look at the effect of the controversiality of the corpus on the relative performance of the two strategies.

To the best of our knowledge, the task of measuring the controversiality of opinions in a corpus has not been studied before. Some well known measures are related to this task, including variance, information entropy, and measures of interrater reliability. (e.g. Fleiss' Kappa (Fleiss, 1971), Krippendorff's Alpha (Krippendorff, 1980)). However, these existing measures do not satisfy certain properties that a sound measure of controversiality should possess, prompting us to develop our own based on information entropy.

Summary evaluation is a challenging open research area. Existing methods include soliciting human judgements, task-based approaches, and automatic approaches.

Task-based evaluation measures the effectiveness of a summarizer for its intended purpose. (e.g. (McKeown et al., 2005)) This approach, however, is less applicable in this work because we are interested in evaluating specific properties of the summary such as the grammaticality and the content, which may be difficult to evaluate with an overall task-based approach. Furthermore, the design of the task may intrinsically favour abstractive or extractive summarization. As an extreme example, asking for a list of specific comments from users would clearly favour extractive summarization.

Another method for summary evaluation is the Pyramid method (Nenkova and Passonneau, 2004), which takes into account the fact that human summaries with different content can be equally informative. Multiple human summaries are taken to be models, and chunks of meaning known as Summary Content Units (SCU) are manually identified. Peer summaries are evaluated based on how many SCUs they share with the model summaries, and the number of model summaries in which these SCUs are found. Although this method has been tested in DUC 2006 and DUC 2005 (Passonneau et al., 2006), (Passonneau et al., 2005) in the domain of news articles, it has not been tested for evaluative text. A pilot study that we conducted on a set of customer reviews on a product using the Pyramid method revealed several problems specific to the evaluative domain. For example, summaries which misrepresented the polarity of the evaluations for a certain feature were not penalized, and human summaries sometimes produced contradictory statements about the distribution of the opinions. In one case, one model summary claimed that a feature is positively rated, while another claimed the opposite, whereas the machine summary indicated that this feature drew mixed reviews. Clearly, only one of these positions should be regarded as correct. Further work is needed to resolve these problems.

There are also automatic methods for summary evaluation, such as ROUGE (Lin, 2004), which gives a score based on the similarity in the sequences of words between a human-written model summary and the machine summary. While ROUGE scores have been shown to often correlate quite well with human judgements (Nenkova et al., 2007), they do not provide insights into the specific strengths and weaknesses of the summary.

The method of summarization evaluation used in this work is to ask users to complete a questionnaire about summaries that they are presented with. The questionnaire consists of questions asking for Likert ratings and is adapted from the questionnaire in (Carenini et al., 2006).

3 Representative Systems

In our user study, we compare an abstractive and an extractive multi-document summarizer that are both developed specifically for the evaluative domain. These summarizers have been found to produce quantitatively similar results, and both significantly outperform a baseline summarizer, which is the MEAD summarization framework with all options set to the default (Radev et al., 2000).

Both summarizers rely on information extraction from the corpus. First, sentences with opinions need to be identified, along with the features of the entity that are evaluated, the strength, and polarity (positive or negative) of the evaluation. For instance, in a corpus of customer reviews, the sentence "Excellent picture quality - on par with my Pioneer, Panasonic, and JVC players." contains an opinion on the feature *picture quality* of a DVD player, and is a very positive evaluation (+3 on a scale from -3 to +3). We rely on methods from previous work for these tasks (Hu and Liu, 2004). Once these features, called Crude Features (CFs), are extracted, they are mapped onto a taxonomy of User Defined Features (UDFs), so named because they can be defined by the user. This mapping provides a better conceptual organization of the CFs by grouping together semantically similar CFs, such as *jpeg picture* and *jpeg slide show* under the UDF *JPEG*. For the purposes of our study, feature extraction, polarity/strength identification and the mapping from CFs to UDFs are not done automatically as in (Hu and Liu, 2004) and (Carenini et al, 2005). Instead, "gold standard" annotations by humans are used in order to focus on the effect of the summarization strategy.

3.1 Abstractive Summarizer: SEA

The abstractive summarizer is the Summarizer of Evaluative Arguments (SEA), adapted from GEA, a system for generating evaluative text tailored to the user's preferences (Carenini and Moore, 2006).

In SEA, units of content are organized by UDFs. The importance of each UDF is based on the number and strength of evaluations of CFs mapped to this UDF, as well as the importance of its children UDFs. Content selection consists of repeating the following two steps until the desired number of UDFs have been selected: (i) greedily selecting the most important UDF (ii) recalculating the measure of importance scores for the remaining UDFs.

The content structuring, microplanning, and realization stages of SEA are adapted from GEA. Each selected UDF is realized in the final summary by one clause, generated from a template pattern based on the number and distribution of polarity/strength evaluations of the UDF. For example, the UDF *video output* with an average polarity/strength of near -3 might be realized as "several customers found the video output to be terrible."

While experimenting with the SEA summarizer, we noticed that the document structuring of SEA summaries, which is adapted from GEA and is based on guidelines from argumentation theory (Carenini and Moore, 2000), sometimes sounded unnatural. We found that controversially rated UDF features (roughly balanced positive and negative evaluations) were treated as contrasts to those which were uncontroversially rated (either mostly positive, or mostly negative evaluations). In SEA, contrast relations between features are realized by cue phrases signalling contrast such as "however" and "although". These cue phrases appear to signal a contrast that is too strong for the relation between controversial and uncontroversial features. An example of a SEA summary suffering from this problem can be found in Figure 1.

> Customers had mixed opinions about the Apex AD2600. Although several customers found the video output to be poor and some customers disliked the user interface, customers had mixed opinions about the range of compatible disc formats. However, users did agree on some things. Some users found the extra features to be very good even though customers had mixed opinions about the supplied universal remote control.

Figure 1: SEA summary of a controversial corpus with a document structuring problem. Controversial and uncontroversial features are interwoven. See Figure 3 for an example of a summary structured with our alternative strategy.

To solve this problem, we devised an alternative content structure for controversial corpora, in which all controversial features appear first, followed by all positively and negatively evaluated features.

3.2 Extractive Summarizer: MEAD*

The extractive approach is represented by MEAD*, which is adapted from the open source summarization framework MEAD (Radev et al., 2000).

After information extraction, MEAD* orders CFs by the number of sentences evaluating that CF, and selects a sentence from each CF until the word limit has been reached. The sentence that is selected for each CF is the one with the highest sum of polarity/strength evaluations for any feature, so sentences that mention more CFs tend to be selected. The selected sentences are then ordered according to the UDF hierarchy by a depth-first traversal through the UDF tree so that more abstract features tend to precede more specific ones.

MEAD* does not have a special mechanism to deal with controversial features. It is not clear how overall controversiality of a feature can be effectively expressed with extraction, as each sentence conveys a specific and unique opinion. One could include two sentences of opposite polarity for each controversial feature. However, in several cases that we considered, this produced extremely incoherent text that did not seem to convey the gist of the overall controversiality of the feature.

3.3 Links to the Corpus

In common with the previous study on which this is based, both the SEA and MEAD* summaries contain "clickable footnotes" which are links back into an original user review, with a relevant sentence highlighted. These footnotes serve to provide details for the abstractive SEA summarizer, and context for the sentences chosen by the extractive MEAD* summarizer. They also aid the participants of the user study in checking the contents of the summary. The sample sentences for SEA are selected by a method similar to the MEAD* sentence selection algorithm. One of the questions in the questionnaire provided to users targets the effectiveness of the footnotes as an aid to the summary.

4 Measuring Controversiality

The opinion sentences in the corpus are annotated with the CF that they evaluate as well as the strength, from 1 to 3, and polarity, positive or negative, of the evaluation. It is natural then, to base a measure of controversiality on these annotations. To measure the controversiality of a corpus, we first measure the controversiality of each of the features in the corpus. We list two properties that a measure of feature controversiality should satisfy.

Strength-sensitivity: The measure should be sensitive to the strength of the evaluations. e.g. Polarity/strength (P/S) evaluations of -2 and +2 should be less controversial than -3 and +3

Polarity-sensitivity: The measure should be sensitive the polarity of the evaluations. e.g. P/S evaluations of -1 and +1 should be more controversial than +1 and +3.

The rationale for this property is that positive and negative evaluations are fundamentally different, and this distinction is more important than the difference in intensity. Thus, though a numerical scale would suggest that -1 and +1 are as distant as +1 and +3, a suitable controversiality measure should not treat them so.

In addition, the overall measure of corpus controversiality should also satisfy the following two features.

CF-weighting: CFs should be weighted by the number of evaluations they contain when calculating the overall value of controversiality for the corpus.

CF-independence: The controversiality of individual CFs should not affect each other.

An alternative is to calculate controversiality by UDFs instead of CFs. However, not all CFs mapped to the same UDF represent the same concept. For example, the CFs *picture clarity* and *color signal* are both mapped to the UDF *video output*.

4.1 Existing Measures of Variability

Since the problem of measuring the variability of a distribution has been well studied, we first examined existing metrics including variance, entropy, kappa, weighted kappa, Krippendorff's alpha, and information entropy. Each of these, however, is problematic in their canonical form, leading us to devise a new metric based on information entropy which satisfies the above properties. Existing metrics will now be examined in turn.

Variance: Variance does not satisfy polarity-sensitivity, as the statistic only takes into account the difference of each data point to the mean, and the sign of the data point plays no role.

Information Entropy: The canonical form of information entropy does not satisfy strength or polarity sensitivity, because the measure considers the discrete values of the distribution to be an unordered set.

Measures of Inter-rater Reliability: Many measures exist to assess inter-rater agreement or disagreement, which is the task of measuring how similarly two or more judges rate one or more subjects beyond chance (dis)agreement. Various versions of Kappa and Krippendorff's Alpha (Krippendorff, 1980), which have shown to be equivalent in their most generalized forms (Passonneau, 1997), can be modified to satisfy all the properties listed above. However, there are important differences between the tasks of measuring controversiality and measuring inter-rater reliability. Kappa and Krippendorff's Alpha correct for chance agreement between raters, which is appropriate in the context of inter-rater reliability calculations, because judges are asked to give their opinions on items that are given to them. In contrast, expressions of opinion are volunteered by users, and users self-select the features they comment on. Thus, it is reasonable to assume that they never randomly select an evaluation for a feature, and chance agreement does not exist.

4.2 Entropy-based Controversiality

We define here our novel measure of controversiality, which is based on information entropy because it can be more easily adapted to measure controversiality. As has been stated, entropy in its original form over the evaluations of a CF is not sensitive to strength or polarity. To correct this, we first aggregate the positive and negative evaluations for each CF separately, and then calculate the entropy based on the resultant Bernoulli distribution.

Let $ps(cf_j)$ be the set of polarity/strength evaluations for cf_j. Let the importance of a feature, $imp(cf_j)$, be the sum of the absolute values of the polarity/strength evaluations for cf_j.

$$imp(cf_j) = \sum_{ps_k \in ps(cf_j)} |ps_k|$$

Define:

$$imp\_pos(cf_j) = \sum_{ps_k \in ps(cf_j) \wedge ps_k > 0} |ps_k|$$

$$imp\_neg(cf_j) = \sum_{ps_k \in ps(cf_j) \wedge ps_k < 0} |ps_k|$$

Now, calculate the entropy of the Bernoulli distribution corresponding to the importance of the two polarities to satisfy polarity-sensitivity. That is, Bernoulli with parameter

$$\theta_j = imp\_pos(cf_j) / imp(cf_j)$$

$$H(\theta_j) = -\theta_j \log_2 \theta_j - (1 - \theta_j) \log_2 (1 - \theta_j)$$

Next, we scale this score by the importance of the evaluations divided by the maximum possible importance for this number of evaluations to satisfy strength-sensitivity. Since our scale is from -3 to +3, the maximum possible importance for a feature is three times the number of evaluations.

$$max\_imp(cf_j) = 3 \times |ps(cf_j)|$$

Then the controversiality of a feature is:

$$contro(cf_j) = \frac{imp(cf_j) \times H(\theta_j)}{max\_imp(cf_j)}$$

The case corresponding to the highest possible feature controversiality, then, would be the bimodal case with equal numbers of evaluations on the extreme positive and negative bins (Figure 2). Note, however, that controversiality is not simply bimodality. A unimodal normal-like distribution of evaluations centred on zero, for example, should intuitively be somewhat controversial, because there are equal numbers of positive and negative evaluations. Our entropy-based feature controversiality measure is able to take this into account.

To calculate the controversiality of the corpus, a weighted average is taken over the CF controversiality scores, with the weight being equal to one less than the number of evaluations for that CF. We subtract one to eliminate any CF where only one evaluation is made, as that CF has an entropy score of one by default before scaling by importance. This procedure satisfies properties CF-weighting and CF-independence.

$$w(cf_j) = |ps(cf_j)| - 1$$

$$contro(corpus) = \frac{\sum w(cf_j) \times contro(cf_j)}{\sum w(cf_j)}$$

Although the annotations in this corpus range from -3 to +3, it would be easy to rescale opinion annotations of different corpora to apply this metric. Note that empirically, this measure correlates highly with Kappa and Krippendorff's Alpha.

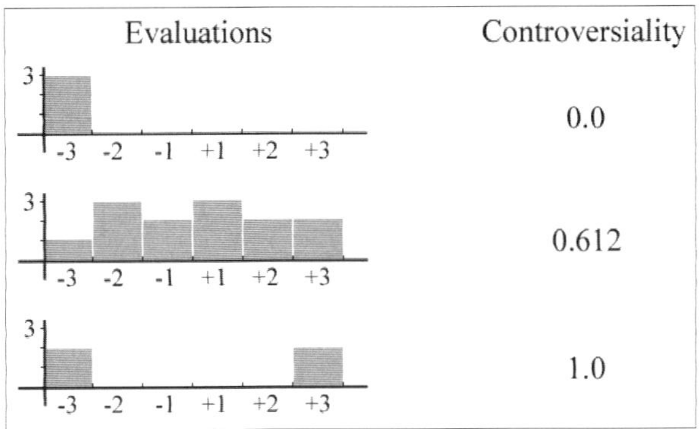

Figure 2: Sample feature controversiality scores for three different distributions of polarity/strength evaluations.

5 User Study

Our main hypothesis that extractive summarization is outperformed even more in the case of controversial corpora was tested by a user study, which compared the results of MEAD* and the modified SEA. First, ten subsets of 30 user reviews were selected from the corpus of 101 reviews of the Apex AD2600 DVD player from amazon.com by stochastic local search. Five of these subsets are controversial, with controversiality scores between 0.83 and 0.88, and five of these are uncontroversial, with controversiality scores of 0. A set of thir-

SEA	MEAD*
Customers had mixed opinions about the Apex AD2600 1,2 possibly because users were divided on the range of compatible disc formats 3,4 and there was disagreement among the users about the video output 5,6. However, users did agree on some things. Some purchasers found the extra features 7 to be very good and some customers really liked the surround sound support 8 and thought the user interface 9 was poor.	When we tried to hook up the first one , it was broken - the motor would not eject discs or close the door . 1 The build quality feels solid , it does n't shake or whine while playing discs , and the picture and sound is top notch (both dts and dd5.1 sound good) . 2 The progressive scan option can be turned off easily by a button on the remote control which is one of the simplest and easiest remote controls i have ever seen or used . 3 It plays original dvds and cds and plays mp3s and jpegs . 4

Figure 3: Sample SEA and MEAD* summaries for a controversial corpus. The numbers within the summaries are footnotes linking the summary to an original user review from the corpus.

ty user reviews per subcorpus was needed to create a summary of sufficient length, which in our case was about 80 words in length.

Twenty university students were recruited and presented with two summaries of the same subcorpus, one generated from SEA and one from MEAD*. We generated ten subcorpora in total, so each subcorpus was assigned to two participants. One of these participants was shown the SEA summary first, and the other was shown the MEAD* summary first, to eliminate the order of presentation as a source of variation.

The participants were asked to take on the role of an employee of Apex, and told that they would have to write a summary for the quality assurance department of the company about the product in question. The purpose of this was to prime them to look for information that should be included in a summary of this corpus. They were given thirty minutes to read the reviews, and take notes.

They were then presented with a questionnaire on the summaries, consisting of ten Likert rating questions. Five of these questions targeted the linguistic quality of the summary, based on linguistic well-formedness questions used at DUC 2005, one targeted the "clickable footnotes" linking to sample sentences in the summary (see section 3.3), and three evaluated the contents of the summary. The three questions targeted *Recall*, *Precision*, and the general *Accuracy* of the summary contents respectively. The tenth question asked for a general overall quality judgement of the summary.

After familiarizing themselves with the questionnaire, the participants were presented with the two summaries in sequence, and asked to fill out the questionnaire while reading the summary. They were allowed to return to the original set of reviews during this time. Lastly, they were given an additional questionnaire which asked them to compare the two summaries that they were shown. Questions in the questionnaire not found in (Carenini et al., 2006) are attached in Appendix A.

6 Results

6.1 Quantitative Results

We convert the Likert responses from a scale from Strongly Disagree to Strong Agree to a scale from 1 to 5, with 1 corresponding to Strongly Disagree, and 5 to Strongly Agree. We group the ten questions into four categories: linguistic (questions 1 to 5), content (questions 6 to 8), footnote (question 9), and overall (question 10). See Table 1 for a breakdown of the responses for each question at each controversiality level.

For our analysis, we adopt a two-step approach that has been applied in Computational Linguistics (Di Eugenio et al., 2002) as well as in HCI (Hinckley et al., 1997).

First, we perform a two-way Analysis of Variance (ANOVA) test using the average response of the questions in each category. The two factors are controversiality of the corpus (high or low) as independent samples, and the summarizer (SEA or MEAD*) as repeated measures. We repeat this procedure for the average of the ten questions, termed *Macro* below. The p-values of these tests are summarized in Table 2.

The results of the ANOVA tests indicate that SEA significantly outperforms MEAD* in terms of linguistic and overall quality, as well as for all the questions combined. It does not significantly outperform MEAD* by content, or in the amount that the included sample sentences linked to by the footnotes aid the summary. No significant differences are found in the performance of the summa-

	Controversial						Uncontroversial					
	SEA		MEAD*		(SEA – MEAD*)		SEA		MEAD*		(SEA – MEAD*)	
Question	Mean	St. Dev.	Mean	St. Dev.	Mean	St. Dev.	Mean	St. Dev.	Mean	St. Dev.	Mean	St. Dev.
Grammaticality	4.5	0.53	3.4	1.26	1.1	0.99	4.2	0.92	2.78	1.3	1.56	1.51
Non-redundancy	4.2	0.92	4	1.07	0.25	1.58	3.7	0.95	3.8	1.14	-0.1	1.45
Referential clarity	4.5	0.53	3.44	1.33	1	1.22	4.2	1.03	3.5	1.18	0.7	1.34
Focus	4.11	1.27	2.1	0.88	2.22	0.83	3.9	1.1	2.6	1.35	1.3	1.57
Structure and Coherence	4.1	0.99	1.9	0.99	2.2	1.14	3.8	1.4	2.3	1.06	1.5	1.9
Linguistic	*4.29*	*0.87*	*2.91*	*1.35*	*1.39*	*1.34*	*3.96*	*1.07*	*3*	*1.29*	*0.98*	*1.63*
Recall	2.8	1.32	1.8	1.23	1	1.33	2.5	1.27	2.5	1.43	0	1.89
Precision	3.9	1.1	2.7	1.64	1.2	1.23	3.5	1.27	3.3	0.95	0.2	1.93
Accuracy	3.4	0.97	3.3	1.57	0.1	1.2	3.1	1.52	3.2	1.03	-0.1	2.28
Content	*3.37*	*1.19*	*2.6*	*1.57*	*0.77*	*1.3*	*3.03*	*1.38*	*3*	*1.17*	*0.03*	*1.97*
Footnote	4	1.05	3.9	0.88	0.1	1.66	3.6	1.07	3.5	1.35	0.1	1.6
Overall	3.8	0.79	2.4	1.17	1.4	1.07	3.2	1.23	2.7	0.82	0.5	1.84
Macro – Footnote	*3.92*	*1.06*	*2.75*	*1.41*	*1.17*	*1.32*	*3.57*	*1.26*	*2.97*	*1.2*	*0.61*	*1.81*
Macro	*3.93*	*1.05*	*2.87*	*1.4*	*1.06*	*1.39*	*3.57*	*1.24*	*3.02*	*1.22*	*0.56*	*1.79*

Table 1: Breakdown of average Likert question responses for each summary at the two levels of controversiality as well as the difference between SEA and MEAD*.

Question Set	Controversiality	Summarizer	Controversiality x Summarizer
Linguistic	0.7226	<0.0001	0.2639
Content	0.9215	0.1906	0.2277
Footnote	0.2457	0.7805	1
Overall	0.6301	0.0115	0.2000
Macro	*0.7127*	*0.0003*	*0.1655*

Table 2: Two-way ANOVA p-values.

rizers over the two levels of controversiality for any of the question sets .

While the average differences in scores between the SEA and MEAD* summarizers are greater in the controversial case for the linguistic, content, and macro averages as well as the question on the overall quality, the p-values for interaction between the two factors in the two-way ANOVA test are not significant.

For the second step of the analysis, we use a one-tailed sign test (Siegel and Castellan, 1988) over the difference in performance of the summarizers at the two levels of controversiality for the questions in the questionnaire. We encode + in the case where the difference between SEA and MEAD* is greater for a question in the controversial setting, – if the difference is smaller, and we discard a question if the difference is the same (e.g. the *Footnote* question). Since the *Overall* question is likely correlated with the responses of the other questions, we did not include it in the test. After discarding the *Footnote* question, the p-value over the remaining eight questions is 0.0352, which lends support to our hypothesis that the abstraction is better by more when the corpus is controversial.

We also analyze the users' summary preferences at the two levels of controversiality. A strong preference for SEA is encoded as a 5, while a strong preference for MEAD* is encoded as a 1, with 3 being neutral. Using a two-tailed unpaired two-sample t-test, we do not find a significant difference in the participants' summary preferences (p=0.6237). However, participants sometimes preferred summaries for reasons other than linguistic or content quality, or may base their judgement only on one aspect of the summary. For instance, one participant rated SEA at least as well as MEAD* in all questions except *Footnote*, yet preferred MEAD* to SEA overall precisely because MEAD* was felt to have made better use of the footnotes than SEA.

6.2 Qualitative Results

The qualitative comments that participants were asked to provide along with the Likert scores confirmed the observations that led us to formulate the initial hypothesis.

In the controversial subcorpora, participants generally agreed that the abstractive nature of SEA's generated text was an advantage. For example, one participant lauded SEA for attempting to "synthesize the reviews" and said that it "did reflect the mixed nature of the reviews, and covered some common complaints." The participant, however, said that SEA "was somewhat misleading in that it understated the extent to which reviews were negative. In particular, agreement was reported on some features where none existed, and problems with reliability were not mentioned."

Participants disagreed on the information coverage of the MEAD* summary. One participant said that MEAD* includes "almost all the information about the Apex 2600 DVD player", while another said that it "does not reflect all information from the customer reviews."

In the uncontroversial subcorpora, more users criticized SEA for its inaccuracy in content selection. One participant felt that SEA "made generalizations that were not precise or accurate." Participants had specific comments about the features that SEA mentioned that they did not consider important. For example, one comment was that "Compatibility with CDs was not a general problem, nor were issues with the remote control, or video output (when it worked)." MEAD* was criticized for being "overly specific", but users praised MEAD* for being "not at all redundant", and said that it "included information I felt was important."

7 Conclusion and Future Work

We have explored the controversiality of opinions in a corpus of evaluative text as an aspect which may determine how well abstractive and extractive summarization strategies perform. We have presented a novel measure of controversiality, and reported on the results of a user study which suggest that abstraction by NLG outperforms extraction by a larger amount in more controversial corpora. We have also presented a document structuring strategy for summarization of controversial corpora.

Our work has implications in practical decisions on summarization strategy choice; an extractive approach, which may be easier to implement because of its lack of requirement for natural language generation, may suffice if the controversiality of opinions in a corpus is sufficiently low.

A future approach to summarization of evaluative text might combine extraction and abstraction in order to combine the different strengths that each bring to the summary. The controversiality of the corpus might be one factor determining the mix of abstraction and extraction in the summary. The footnotes linking to sample sentences in the corpus in SEA are already one form of this combined approach. Further work is needed to integrate this text into the summary itself, possibly in a modified form.

As a final note to our user study, further studies should be done with different corpora and summarization systems to increase the external validity of our results.

Acknowledgements

We would like to thank Raymond T. Ng, Gabriel Murray and Lucas Rizoli for their helpful comments. This work was partially funded by the Natural Sciences and Engineering Research Council of Canada.

References

Regina Barzilay, Kathleen R. McKeown, and Michael Elhadad. 1999. Information fusion in the context of multi-document summarization. In *Proc. 37th ACL*, pages 550–557.

Giuseppe Carenini and Johanna D. Moore. 2006. Generating and evaluating evaluative arguments. *Artificial Intelligence*, 170(11):925-952.

Giuseppe Carenini, Raymond Ng and Adam Pauls. 2006. Multi-document summarization of evaluative text. In *Proc. 11th EACL 2006*, pages 305-312.

Giuseppe Carenini, Raymond T. Ng and Ed Zwart. 2005. Extracting Knowledge from Evaluative Text. In *Proc. 3rd International Conference on Knowledge Capture*, pages 11-18.

Giuseppe Carenini and Johanna D. Moore. 2000. A strategy for generating evaluative arguments. In *First INLG*, pages 47-54, Mitzpe Ramon, Israel.

Barbara Di Eugenio, Michael Glass, and Michael J. Trolio. 2002. The DIAG experiments: Natural language generation for intelligent tutoring systems. In *INLG02, The 2nd INLG*, pages 120-127.

Joseph L. Fleiss. 1971. Measuring nominal scale agreement among many raters. *Psychological Bulletin*. 76:378-382.

U. Hahn and I. Mani. 2000. The challenges of automatic summarization. *IEEE Computer*, 33(11):29-36.

Ken Hinckley, Randy Pausch, Dennis Proffitt, James Patten, and Neal Kassell. 1997. Cooperative bimanual action. In *Proc. CHI Conference*.

Minqing Hu and Bing Liu. 2004. Mining and summarizing customer reviews. In *Proc. 10th ACM SIGKDD conference*, pages 168-177.

Klaus Krippendorff. 1980. *Content Analysis: An Introduction to Its Methodology*. Sage Publications, Beverly Hills, CA.

Chin-Yew Lin. 2004. ROUGE: A Package for Automatic Evaluation of Summaries. In *Proc. of Workshop on Text Summarization Branches Out, Post-Conference Workshop of ACL 2004*, Barcelona, Spain.

2005. Linguistic quality questions from the 2005 document understanding conference. http://duc.nist.gov/duc2005/quality-questions.txt

Kathleen McKeown, Rebecca Passonneau, David Elson, Ani Nenkova, and Julia Hirschberg. 2005. Do summaries help? A task-based evaluation of multi-document summarization. In *Proc. SIGIR 2005.*

Ani Nenkova, Rebecca J. Passonneau, and K. McKeown. 2007. The pyramid method: incorporating human content selection variation in summarization evaluation. *ACM Transactions on Speech and Language Processing*, 4(2).

Ani Nenkova and Rebecca J. Passonneau. 2004. Evaluating content selection in summarization: The pyramid method. In *Proc. NAACL/HLT.*

Rebecca J. Passonneau, Kathleen McKeown, Sergey Sigleman, and Adam Goodkind. 2006. Applying the pyramid method in the 2006 Document Understanding Conference. In *Proc. DUC'06.*

Rebecca J. Passonneau, Ani Nenkova, Kathleen McKeown, and Sergey Sigleman. 2005. Applying the pyramid method in DUC 2005. In *Proc. DUC'05.*

Rebecca J. Passonneau. 1997. Applying Reliability Metrics to Co-Reference Annotation. Department of Computer Science, Columbia University, TR CUCS-017-97.

Dragomir Radev, Hongyan Jing, and Malgorzata Budzikowska. 2000. Centroid-based summarization of multiple documents: sentence extraction, utility-based evaluation, and user studies. In *Proc. ANLP/NAACL Workshop on Automatic Summarization.*

S. Siegel and N. J. Castellan, Jr. 1988. Nonparametric statistics for the behaviorial sciences. McGraw Hill.

Appendix A. Additional Questions

Footnotes: a) Did you use the footnotes when reviewing the summary?

b) Answer this question only if you answered "Yes" to the previous question. The clickable footnotes were a helpful addition to the summary.

Summary Comparison Questions:

1) List any Pros and Cons you can think of for each of the summaries. Point form is okay.

2) Overall, which summary did you prefer?

3) Why did you prefer this summary? (If the reason overlaps with some points from question 1, put a star next to those points in the chart.)

4) Do you have any other comments about the reviews or summaries, the tasks, or the experiment in general? If so, please write them below.

Referring Expressions as Formulas of Description Logic

Carlos Areces
INRIA Nancy Grand Est
Nancy, France
areces@loria.fr

Alexander Koller
University of Edinburgh
Edinburgh, UK
a.koller@ed.ac.uk

Kristina Striegnitz
Union College
Schenectady, NY, US
striegnk@union.edu

Abstract

In this paper, we propose to reinterpret the problem of generating referring expressions (GRE) as the problem of computing a formula in a description logic that is only satisfied by the referent. This view offers a new unifying perspective under which existing GRE algorithms can be compared. We also show that by applying existing algorithms for computing simulation classes in description logic, we can obtain extremely efficient algorithms for relational referring expressions without any danger of running into infinite regress.

1 Introduction

The generation of referring expressions (GRE) is one of the most active and successful research areas in natural language generation. Building upon Dale and Reiter's work (Dale, 1989; Dale and Reiter, 1995), various researchers have added extensions such as reference to sets (Stone, 2000), more expressive logical connectives (van Deemter, 2002), and relational expressions (Dale and Haddock, 1991).

Referring expressions (REs) involving relations, in particular, have received increasing attention recently; especially in the context of spatial referring expressions in situated generation (e.g. (Kelleher and Kruijff, 2006)), where it seems particularly natural to use expressions such as "the book on the table". However, the classical algorithm by Dale and Haddock (1991) was recently shown to be unable to generate satisfying REs in practice (Viethen and Dale, 2006). Furthermore, the Dale and Haddock algorithm and most of its successors (such as (Kelleher and Kruijff, 2006)) are vulnerable to the problem of "infinite regress", where the algorithm jumps back and forth between generating descriptions for two related individuals infinitely, as in "the book on the table which supports a book on the table . . . ".

In this paper, we propose to view GRE as the problem of computing a formula of description logic (DL) that denotes exactly the set of individuals that we want to refer to. This very natural idea has been mentioned in passing before (Krahmer et al., 2003; Gardent and Striegnitz, 2007); however, we take it one step further by proposing DL as an interlingua for comparing the REs produced by different approaches to GRE. In this way, we can organize existing GRE approaches in an expressiveness hierarchy. For instance, the classical Dale and Reiter algorithms compute purely conjunctive formulas; van Deemter (2002) extends this language by adding the other propositional connectives, whereas Dale and Haddock (1991) extends it by allowing existential quantification.

Furthermore, the view of GRE as a problem of computing DL formulas with a given extension allows us to apply existing algorithms for the latter problem to obtain efficient algorithms for GRE. We present algorithms that compute such formulas for the description logics $\mathcal{EL}$ (which allows only conjunction and existential quantification) and $\mathcal{ALC}$ (which also allows negation). These algorithms effectively compute REs for all individuals in the domain at the same time, which allows them to systematically avoid the infinite regress problem. The $\mathcal{EL}$ algorithm is capable of generating 67% of the relational REs in the Viethen and Dale (2006) dataset, in about 15 milliseconds. The $\mathcal{ALC}$ algorithm is even faster; it computes relational REs for all 100 individuals in a random model in 140 milliseconds.

The paper is structured as follows. In Section 2,

we will first define description logics. We will then show how to generate REs by computing DL similarity sets for $\mathcal{ALC}$ and $\mathcal{EL}$ in Section 3. In Section 4, we evaluate our algorithms and discuss our results. Section 5 compares our approach to related research; in particular, it shows how various prominent GRE algorithms fit into the DL framework. Section 6 concludes and points to future work.

2 Description logics and similarity

In this paper, we will represent referring expressions as formulas of description logic (Baader et al., 2003). In order to make this point, we will now define the two description logics we will be working with: $\mathcal{ALC}$ and $\mathcal{EL}$.

Formulas (or *concepts*) φ of $\mathcal{ALC}$ are generated by the following grammar:

$$\varphi, \varphi' ::= \top \mid p \mid \neg\varphi \mid \varphi \sqcap \varphi' \mid \exists R.\varphi$$

where p is in the set of propositional symbols prop, and R is in the set of relational symbols rel. $\mathcal{EL}$ is the negation-free fragment of $\mathcal{ALC}$.

Formulas of both $\mathcal{ALC}$ and $\mathcal{EL}$ are interpreted in ordinary relational first-order models $\mathcal{M} = (\Delta, \|\cdot\|)$ where Δ is a non-empty set and $\|\cdot\|$ is an interpretation function such that:

$$\begin{array}{rcl} \|p\| & \subseteq & \Delta \text{ for } p \in \mathsf{prop} \\ \|R\| & \subseteq & \Delta \times \Delta \text{ for } R \in \mathsf{rel} \\ \|\neg\varphi\| & = & \Delta - \|\varphi\| \\ \|\varphi \sqcap \varphi'\| & = & \|\varphi\| \cap \|\varphi'\| \\ \|\exists R.\varphi\| & = & \{i \mid \text{for some } i', (i,i') \in \|R\| \\ & & \text{and } i' \in \|\varphi\|\}. \end{array}$$

Every formula of a description logic denotes a set of individuals in the domain; thus we can use such formulas to describe sets. For instance, in the model in Fig. 1b, the formula flower denotes the set $\{f_1, f_2\}$; the formula $\mathsf{flower} \sqcap \exists \mathsf{in.hat}$ denotes $\{f_2\}$; and the formula $\mathsf{flower} \sqcap \neg\exists \mathsf{in.hat}$ denotes $\{f_1\}$.

Different description logics differ in the inventory of logical connectives they allow: While $\mathcal{ALC}$ permits negation, $\mathcal{EL}$ doesn't. There are many other description logics in the literature; some that we will get back to in Section 5 are $\mathcal{CL}$ ($\mathcal{EL}$ without existential quantification, i.e., only conjunctions of atoms); $\mathcal{PL}$ ($\mathcal{ALC}$ without existential quantification, i.e., propositional logic); and $\mathcal{ELU}_{(\neg)}$ ($\mathcal{EL}$ plus disjunction and atomic negation).

Below, we will use a key notion of formula preservation that we call *similarity*. For any DL $\mathcal{L}$, we will say that an individual i is *$\mathcal{L}$-similar* to i' in a given model $\mathcal{M}$ if for any formula $\varphi \in \mathcal{L}$ such that $i \in \|\varphi\|$, we also have $i' \in \|\varphi\|$. Equivalently, there is no $\mathcal{L}$-formula that holds of i but not of i'. We say that the *$\mathcal{L}$-similarity set* of some individual i is the set of all individuals to which i is $\mathcal{L}$-similar.

Notice that similarity is not necessarily a symmetrical relation: For instance, f_1 is $\mathcal{EL}$-similar to f_2 in Fig. 1b, but f_2 is not $\mathcal{EL}$-similar to f_1 (it satisfies the formula $\exists \mathsf{in.hat}$ and f_1 doesn't). However, $\mathcal{ALC}$-similarity is a symmetrical relation because the language contains negation; and indeed, f_1 is not $\mathcal{ALC}$-similar to f_2 either because it satisfies $\neg\exists \mathsf{in.hat}$. Because $\mathcal{ALC}$ is more expressive than $\mathcal{EL}$, it is possible for some individual a to be $\mathcal{EL}$-similar but not $\mathcal{ALC}$-similar to some individual b, but not vice versa.

3 Generating referring expressions

Now we apply description logic to GRE. The core claim of this paper is that it is natural and useful to view the GRE problem as the problem of computing a formula of some description logic $\mathcal{L}$ whose extension is a given target set A of individuals.

$\mathcal{L}$-GRE PROBLEM	
Input:	A model $\mathcal{M}$ and a target set $A \subseteq \Delta$.
Output:	A formula $\varphi \in \mathcal{L}$ such that $\|\varphi\| = A$ (if such a formula exists).

In the examples above, it is because $\mathsf{flower} \sqcap \exists \mathsf{in.hat}$ denotes exactly $\{f_2\}$ that we can say "the flower in the hat" to refer to f_2. This perspective provides a general framework into which many existing GRE approaches fit: Traditional attribute selection (Dale and Reiter, 1995) corresponds to building DL formulas that are conjunctions of atoms; relational REs as in Dale and Haddock (1991) are formulas of $\mathcal{EL}$; and so on. We will further pursue the idea of organizing GRE approaches with respect to the variant of DL they use in Section 5.

For the rest of this paper, we assume that we are generating a singular RE, i.e., the target set A will be a singleton. In this case, we will only be able to generate a formula that denotes exactly $A = \{a\}$ (i.e., a RE that uniquely refers to a) if there is no

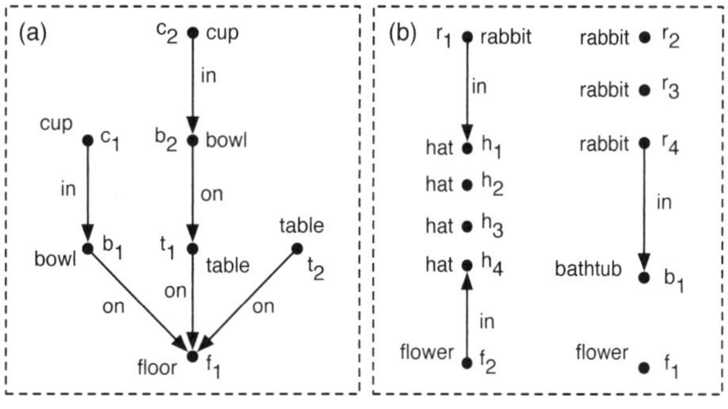

Figure 1: (a) The Dale and Haddock (1991) scenario; (b) the Stone and Webber (1998) scenario.

other individual b to which a is similar; otherwise, any formula that is satisfied by a is also satisfied by b. Conversely, if we know that a is not similar to any other individual, then there is a formula that is satisfied by a and not by anything else; this formula can serve as a unique singular RE. In other words, we can reduce the $\mathcal{L}$-GRE problem for a given model to the problem of computing the $\mathcal{L}$-similarity sets of this model. Notice that this use of similarity sets can be seen as a generalization of van Deemter's (2002) "satellite sets" to relational descriptions.

In the rest of this section, we will present algorithms that compute the similarity sets of a given model for $\mathcal{ALC}$ and $\mathcal{EL}$, together with characteristic formulas that denote them. In the $\mathcal{ALC}$ case, we adapt a standard algorithm from the literature for computing *simulation classes*; we will then further adapt this algorithm for $\mathcal{EL}$. In effect, both algorithms compute REs for all individuals in some model at the same time – very efficiently and without any danger of infinite regress.

3.1 Computing similarity sets

It can be shown that for $\mathcal{ALC}$, the similarity sets of a finite model coincide exactly with the *simulation classes* of this model. Simulation classes have been studied extensively in the literature (see e.g., Blackburn et al. (2001); Kurtonina and de Rijke (1998)), and there are several efficient algorithms for computing $\mathcal{ALC}$-simulation classes (Hopcroft, 1971; Paige and Tarjan, 1987; Dovier et al., 2004). However, these algorithms will only compute the simulation classes themselves. Here we extend the Hopcroft (1971) algorithm such that it computes, along with each set, also a formula that denotes exactly this set. We can then use these formulas as representations of the referring expressions.

The pseudocode for our $\mathcal{ALC}$ algorithm is shown as Algorithm 1 (with $\mathcal{L} = \mathcal{ALC}$) and Algorithm 2. Given a model $\mathcal{M} = (\Delta, \|\cdot\|)$, the algorithm computes a set RE of $\mathcal{ALC}$ formulas such that $\{\|\varphi\| \mid \varphi \in RE\}$ is the set of $\mathcal{ALC}$-similarity sets of $\mathcal{M}$. The algorithm starts with $RE = \{\top\}$ (where $\|\top\| = \Delta$), and successively refines RE by making its elements denote smaller and smaller sets. It maintains the invariant that at the start and end of every iteration, $\{\|\varphi\| \mid \varphi \in RE\}$ is always a partition of Δ. The algorithm iterates over all propositional and relational symbols in prop and rel to construct new formulas until either all formulas in RE denote singletons (i.e., there is only one individual that satisfies them), or no progress has been made in the previous iteration. In each iteration, it calls the procedure $\text{add}_{\mathcal{ALC}}(\varphi, RE)$, which intersects φ with any formula $\psi \in RE$ which does not denote a singleton and which is not equivalent to φ and to $\neg\varphi$. In this case, it replaces ψ in RE by $\psi \sqcap \varphi$ and $\psi \sqcap \neg\varphi$.

The $\mathcal{ALC}$ algorithm computes the $\mathcal{ALC}$-similarity sets of the model in time $O(n^3)$, where n is the number of individuals in the domain. However, it will freely introduce negations in the case distinctions, which can make the resulting formula hard to realize (see also Section 4.3). This is why we also present an algorithm for the $\mathcal{EL}$-similarity sets; $\mathcal{EL}$ corresponds to positive relational REs, which are generally much easier to realize.

We obtain the $\mathcal{EL}$ algorithm by replacing the call to $\text{add}_{\mathcal{ALC}}$ in Algorithm 1 by a call to $\text{add}_{\mathcal{EL}}$, which is defined in Algorithm 3. As before, the algorithm maintains a set $RE = \{\varphi_1, \ldots, \varphi_n\}$ of formulas (this time of $\mathcal{EL}$) such that $\|\varphi_1\| \cup \ldots \cup \|\varphi_n\| = \Delta$, and which it refines iteratively. However, where the $\mathcal{ALC}$ algorithm maintains the invariant that $\|\varphi_1\|, \ldots, \|\varphi_n\|$ is a partition of Δ, we weaken this invariant to the requirement that there are no $m \geq 2$ pairwise different indices $1 \leq i_1, \ldots, i_m \leq n$ such that $\|\varphi_{i_1}\| = \|\varphi_{i_2}\| \cup \ldots \cup \|\varphi_{i_m}\|$. We call φ_{i_1} *subsumed* if such a decomposition exists.

Because it maintains a weaker invariant, the set RE may contain more formulas at the same time in the $\mathcal{EL}$ algorithm than in the $\mathcal{ALC}$ algorithm. Given that Δ has an exponential number of subsets, there is a risk that the $\mathcal{EL}$ algorithm might have worst-case

Algorithm 1: Computing the $\mathcal{L}$-similarity sets

Input: A model $\mathcal{M} = (\Delta, \|\cdot\|)$
Output: A set RE of formulas such that $\{\|\varphi\| \mid \varphi \in RE\}$ is the set of $\mathcal{L}$-similarity sets of $\mathcal{M}$.

$RE \leftarrow \{\top\}$
for $p \in \mathsf{prop}$ **do**
    add$_{\mathcal{L}}(p, RE)$
while *exists some* $\varphi \in RE, |\|\varphi\||^{\mathcal{M}} > 1$ **do**
    for $\varphi \in RE, R \in \mathsf{rel}$ **do**
        add$_{\mathcal{L}}(\exists R.\varphi, RE)$
    if *made no changes to* RE **then**
        exit

Algorithm 2: add$_{\mathcal{ALC}}(\varphi, RE)$

for $\psi \in RE$ *with* $|\|\psi\|| > 1$ **do**
    if $\|\psi \sqcap \varphi\| \neq \emptyset$ *and* $\|\psi \sqcap \neg\varphi\| \neq \emptyset$ **then**
        add $\psi \sqcap \varphi$ and $\psi \sqcap \neg\varphi$ to RE;
        remove ψ from RE;

Algorithm 3: add$_{\mathcal{EL}}(\varphi, RE)$

for $\psi \in RE$ *with* $|\|\psi\|| > 1$ **do**
    if $\psi \sqcap \varphi$ *is not subsumed in* RE **and** $\|\psi \sqcap \varphi\| \neq \emptyset$ **and** $\|\psi \sqcap \varphi\| \neq \|\psi\|$ **then**
        add $\psi \sqcap \varphi$ to RE
        remove subsumed formulas from RE

exponential runtime (although we are not aware of such worst-case examples). We leave a more careful complexity analysis for future work.

We presented both algorithms as first refining RE according to propositional symbols, and then by relational expressions of increasing depth. But actually, propositional symbols can be encoded using new relational symbols (e.g., we could represent that f_1 is a flower in Fig. 1 as a relation labeled flower from f_1 to an additional dummy element d). In this way, we don't need to distinguish between propositions and relations, and any arbitrary preference ordering of properties can be used.

3.2 Some examples

Let's try our algorithms on some examples. We first run the $\mathcal{EL}$ algorithm on the model shown in Fig. 1a, which is taken from Dale and Haddock (1991). The algorithm starts with $RE = \{\top\}$. In the first loop, it adds the formulas floor, bowl, cup, and table, and then removes $\top$ because it is now subsumed. Not all of these formulas denote singletons; for instance, $\|\mathsf{cup}\|$ contains two individuals. So we iterate over the relations to refine our formulas. After the first iteration over the relations, we have $RE = \{\mathsf{floor}, \mathsf{bowl} \sqcap \exists\mathsf{on.floor}, \mathsf{bowl} \sqcap \exists\mathsf{on.table}, \mathsf{cup}, \mathsf{table}\}$. Notice that bowl has become subsumed, but we haven't distinguished the cups and tables further.

Now we can use the split between the bowls to distinguish the cups in the second iteration. The result of this is $RE = \{\mathsf{floor}, \mathsf{bowl} \sqcap \exists\mathsf{on.floor}, \mathsf{bowl} \sqcap \exists\mathsf{on.table}, \mathsf{cup} \sqcap \exists\mathsf{in.}(\mathsf{bowl} \sqcap \exists\mathsf{on.floor}), \mathsf{cup} \sqcap \exists\mathsf{in.}(\mathsf{bowl} \sqcap \exists\mathsf{on.table}), \mathsf{table}\}$. At this point, all formulas except table denote singletons, and further iterations don't allow us to refine table; so the algorithm terminates. Each formula with a singleton extension $\{a\}$ is a unique description of a; for instance, $\mathsf{cup} \sqcap \exists\mathsf{in.}(\mathsf{bowl} \sqcap \exists\mathsf{on.table})$ is only satisfied by c_2, so we may refer to c_2 as "the cup in the bowl on the table". Notice that the algorithm didn't focus on any particular individual; it simultaneously generated REs for all individuals except for the two tables (which are similar to each other).

The $\mathcal{EL}$ algorithm has a harder time with the example in Fig. 1b (Stone and Webber, 1998). While it will correctly identify r_1 as "the rabbit in the hat" and f_2 as "the flower in the hat", it will not be able to compute a RE for f_1 because f_1 is $\mathcal{EL}$-similar to f_2. Indeed, the algorithm terminates with RE containing both flower and $\mathsf{flower} \sqcap \exists\mathsf{in.hat}$. This is a typical pattern for asymmetrical cases of similarity in $\mathcal{EL}$: If there are two formulas φ_1 and φ_2 in the output set with $\|\varphi_1\| \subseteq \|\varphi_2\|$, then there is generally some individual $b \in \|\varphi_2\| - \|\varphi_1\|$ such that all individuals in $\|\varphi_1\|$ are similar to b, but not vice versa. By contrast, the $\mathcal{ALC}$ algorithm can exploit the greater expressivity of $\mathcal{ALC}$ to split flower into the two new formulas $\mathsf{flower} \sqcap \exists\mathsf{in.hat}$ and $\mathsf{flower} \sqcap \neg\exists\mathsf{in.hat}$, generating a unique RE for f_1 as well.

4 Discussion

We will now describe two experiments evaluating the quality of the $\mathcal{EL}$ algorithm's output and the effi-

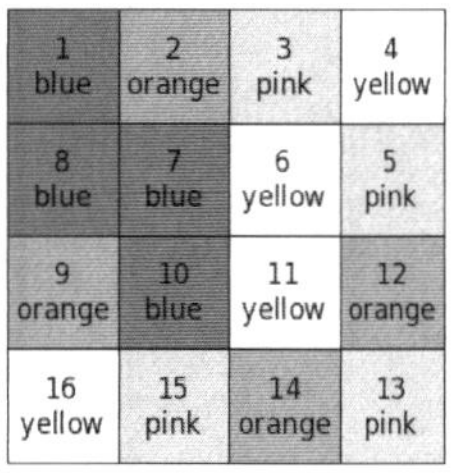

Figure 2: A schematic view of the filing cabinets.

ciency of both of our algorithms, and we discuss the interface between our algorithms and realization.

4.1 Evaluation: Output quality

To compare the descriptions generated by our algorithm to those humans produce, we use a corpus of human-generated referring expressions collected and made available by Jette Viethen and Robert Dale.[1] They asked human subjects to describe one of 16 filing cabinet drawers. The drawers had different colors and were arranged in a four-by-four grid (see Fig. 2). The human subjects used four non-relational properties (the drawer's color, its column and row number, and whether it is in a corner) and five relational properties (above, below, next to, left of, right of). Of the 118 referring expressions obtained in the experiment, only 15 use relations.

Viethen and Dale (2006) describe the data in more detail and present results of evaluating the Full Brevity algorithm, the Incremental Algorithm (both by Dale and Reiter (1995)), and the Relational Algorithm (Dale and Haddock, 1991) on this corpus. The Incremental Algorithm is dependent on a predefined ordering in which properties are added to the description. Viethen and Dale, therefore, try all possible orderings and evaluate what percentage of descriptions an algorithm can generate with any of them. The Full Brevity and the Relational Algorithms choose properties based on their discriminatory power and only use the orderings as tie breakers. Viethen and Dale found that the Incremental Algorithm is capable of generating 98 of the 103 non-relational descriptions. However, the Relational Algorithm was unable to generate even a single one of the human-generated relational descriptions.

We replicated Viethen and Dale's experiment for the $\mathcal{EL}$ algorithm presented above. In the non-relational case, our results are the same as theirs for the Incremental Algorithm: the $\mathcal{EL}$ algorithm generates 98 of the 103 non-relational descriptions, using four (of the possible) orderings. This is because the two algorithms perform essentially the same computations if there are no relations.

When we add relations, our algorithm is able to generate 10 of the 15 human-produced relational descriptions correctly (in addition to the 98 non-relational descriptions). Fig. 3 gives example outputs of the $\mathcal{EL}$ algorithm for three different orderings, which together achieve this coverage. Of the five human-produced descriptions that the $\mathcal{EL}$ algorithm cannot generate, three involve references to sets (*the two blues ones in horizontal sequence/the two yellow drawers*), and two contain so much redundant information that our algorithm cannot reproduce them: Similarly to the Incremental Algorithm, our algorithm allows for some redundancy, but stops once it has found a distinguishing description. It does, however, generate other, simpler descriptions for these referents.

4.2 Evaluation: Efficiency

Both the $\mathcal{EL}$ and the $\mathcal{ALC}$ algorithms took about 15 milliseconds to compute distinguishing formulas for all 16 individuals in the Viethen and Dale dataset.[2]

In order to get a more comprehensive picture of the algorithms' efficiency, we ran them on random models with increasing numbers of individuals. Each model had random interpretations for ten different propositional and four relational symbols; each individual had a 10% chance to be in the extension of each propositional symbol, and each pair of individuals had a 10% chance to be related by a relational symbol. The results (averaged over 10 runs for each model size) are shown in Fig. 4. The $\mathcal{EL}$ algorithm takes about 350 ms on average to generate relational REs for all individuals in the model of size 100, i.e., less than 4 ms on average for each individual. The $\mathcal{ALC}$ algorithm is even faster, at about 140 ms for the model of size 100. As far as we know, these are by far the fastest published runtimes for

[1] http://www.ics.mq.edu.au/~jviethen/drawers

[2] Runtimes were measured on a MacBook Pro (Intel Core 2 Duo, 2.16 GHz) running Java 1.6 beta. We allowed the Java VM to warm up, i.e., just-in-time compile all bytecode, before taking the measurements.

id	*human-produced description* output of the $\mathcal{EL}$ algorithm
2	*the orange drawer above the blue drawer* **orange $\sqcap$ $\exists$above.blue** / orange $\sqcap$ $\exists$above.($\exists$below.(orange) $\sqcap$ blue) / orange $\sqcap$ $\exists$next.(blue) $\sqcap$ $\exists$next.(pink)
4	*the yellow drawer on the top of the pink one* **yellow $\sqcap$ $\exists$above.pink** / yellow $\sqcap$ corner $\sqcap$ $\exists$above.pink / yellow $\sqcap$ corner $\sqcap$ $\exists$above.($\exists$next.(yellow) $\sqcap$ pink)
5	*$*$ the pink drawer in the fourth column below the yellow one* pink $\sqcap$ $\exists$above.orange / pink $\sqcap$ $\exists$below.yellow / pink $\sqcap$ $\exists$next.(yellow) $\sqcap$ $\exists$above.($\exists$next.(yellow) $\sqcap$ orange)
6	*the yellow drawer on top of the yellow drawer (2×) / $*$ the drawer after the two blue ones in horizontal sequence* **yellow $\sqcap$ $\exists$above.yellow** / yellow $\sqcap$ $\exists$below.pink / yellow $\sqcap$ $\exists$next.(blue) $\sqcap$ $\exists$next.(pink)
7	*the blue drawer below the orange one / $*$ the blue drawer below the orange drawer in the second column* blue $\sqcap$ $\exists$above.(blue) $\sqcap$ $\exists$next.($\exists$above.(orange) $\sqcap$ blue) / **blue $\sqcap$ $\exists$below.(orange)** / blue $\sqcap$ $\exists$next.(blue) $\sqcap$ $\exists$next.(yellow)
10	*the blue drawer above the pink drawer (2×)* **blue $\sqcap$ $\exists$above.(pink)** / blue $\sqcap$ $\exists$above.(pink) $\sqcap$ $\exists$below.(blue) / blue $\sqcap$ $\exists$next.(orange) $\sqcap$ $\exists$next.(yellow)
11	*the yellow drawer next to the orange drawer (2×)* yellow $\sqcap$ $\exists$above.orange / yellow $\sqcap$ $\exists$below.yellow / **yellow $\sqcap$ $\exists$next.orange**
12	*the orange drawer below the pink drawer* orange $\sqcap$ $\exists$above.(pink $\sqcap$ corner) / **orange $\sqcap$ $\exists$below.pink** / orange $\sqcap$ $\exists$next.yellow
14	*$*$ the orange drawer below the two yellow drawers (2×)* orange $\sqcap$ $\exists$next.(pink $\sqcap$ corner) $\sqcap$ $\exists$next.(pink) / orange $\sqcap$ $\exists$below.yellow / orange $\sqcap$ $\exists$next.(pink $\sqcap$ corner)

Figure 3: The relational descriptions from Viethen and Dale (2006), annotated with the drawer id and the outputs of the $\mathcal{EL}$ algorithm using three different orderings. Notice that four descriptions occurred twice in the corpus. Descriptions that the $\mathcal{EL}$ algorithm cannot generate with any ordering are marked by $*$. Generated descriptions that match one produced by humans are in boldface.

any relational GRE algorithm in the literature.

4.3 Interface to realization

Our GRE algorithms do not guarantee that the formula they compute can actually be realized in language. For example, none of the formulas our algorithms computed in the Viethen and Dale domain contained an atom that would commonly be realized as a noun; the property drawer is never used because it applies to all individuals in the domain. This particular problem could easily be worked around in a post-processing step. However, another problem arises from the massive use of negation in the $\mathcal{ALC}$ algorithm; it will be hard for any realizer to find a reasonable way of expressing a formula like $\neg\exists R.(\neg P \sqcap \neg Q)$ as a smooth noun phrase. Although we agree with van Deemter (2002) and others that the careful use of negation and disjunction can improve REs, these connectives must not be overused. Thus we consider the formulas computed by the $\mathcal{EL}$ algorithm "safer" with respect to realization.

Of course, we share the problem of interfacing GRE and realization with every other approach that separates these two modules, i.e., almost the entire GRE literature (notable exceptions are, e.g., Horacek (1997) and SPUD (Stone and Webber, 1998)).

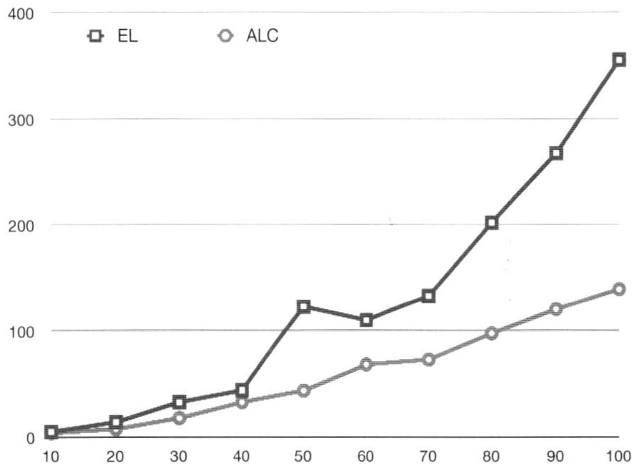

Figure 4: Average runtimes (in ms) of the two algorithms on random models with different numbers of individuals.

In principle, we believe that it is a good idea to handle sentence planning and realization in a single module; for instance, SPUD can use its awareness of the syntactic context to generate succinct REs as in "take the rabbit from the hat". We hope that the ideas we have explored here for efficient and expressive RE generation can eventually be combined with recent efficient algorithms for integrated sentence planning and realization, such as in Koller and Stone (2007).

One problem that arises in our approach is that

both algorithms derive some measure of efficiency from their freedom to build formulas without having to respect any linguistic constraints. It seems straightforward, for instance, to extend Krahmer et al.'s (2003) approach such that it only considers subgraphs that can actually be realized, because their algorithm proceeds by a genuine search for uniquely identifying subgraphs, and will simply take a different branch of the search if some subgraph is useless. This would be harder in our case. Our algorithms don't search in the same way; if we disallow certain refinements of a partition, we have to allow the algorithms to backtrack and thus jeopardize the worst-case polynomial runtime. Investigating this interplay between efficiency and linguistic constraints is an interesting avenue for future research.

5 A unified perspective on GRE

GRE algorithm	DL variant
Dale and Reiter (1995)	$\mathcal{CL}$
van Deemter (2002)	$\mathcal{PL}$
Dale and Haddock (1991)	$\mathcal{EL}$
Kelleher and Kruijff (2006)	$\mathcal{EL}$
Gardent (2002)	$\mathcal{ELU}_{(\neg)}$

Figure 5: DL variants used by different GRE algorithms.

Viewing GRE as a problem of generating DL formulas offers a unified perspective: It is the problem of computing a DL formula with a given extension. Many existing approaches can be subsumed under this view; we have summarized this for some of them in Fig. 5, along with the DL fragment they use. We already discussed some of these approaches in Section 3. Furthermore, the non-relational but negative and disjunctive descriptions generated by van Deemter (2002) are simply formulas of $\mathcal{PL}$; and Gardent (2002) generalizes this into generating formulas of $\mathcal{ELU}_{(\neg)}$, i.e., $\mathcal{EL}$ plus disjunction and atomic negation. The approach presented here fits well into this landscape, and it completes the picture by showing how to generate REs in $\mathcal{ALC}$, which combines all connectives used in any of these previous approaches.

Where our approach breaks new ground is in the way these formulas are computed: It successively refines a decomposition of the domain into subsets. In this way, it is reminiscent of the Incremental Algorithm, which in fact can be seen as a special case of the $\mathcal{EL}$ algorithm. However, unlike Dale and Haddock (1991) and its successors, such as Kelleher and Kruijff (2006), we do not have to take special precautions to avoid infinite regress. While Dale and Haddock's algorithm attempts to generate a RE for a single individual, for successive individuals in the model, our algorithms consider all individuals in parallel. It monotonically refines a partition of the model and never needs to backtrack, and therefore is always guaranteed to terminate.

Perhaps closest in spirit to our approach is Krahmer et al.'s graph algorithm (2003), which also computes REs by extending them successively. However, their subgraphs go beyond the expressive power of $\mathcal{ALC}$ in that they can distinguish between "the dog that bites a dog" and "the dog that bites itself". The price they pay for this increase in expressive power is an NP-complete worst-case complexity. Interestingly, Krahmer et al. themselves discuss the possibility of seeing their subgraphs as formulas of hybrid logic which are satisfied at the points where the subgraph can be embedded; and hybrid logics can be seen as very expressive description logics (Areces and ten Cate, 2006).

6 Conclusion

In this paper, we have explored the idea of viewing the generation of singular REs as the problem of computing a DL formula with a given extension. We have shown how such formulas can be computed efficiently (for $\mathcal{ALC}$ and $\mathcal{EL}$) by adapting existing algorithms from the literature. The $\mathcal{EL}$ algorithm is able to generate 95% of the non-relational and 67% of the relational REs from Viethen and Dale (2006). Both algorithms are extremely efficient (350 ms and 140 ms respectively to generate relational REs for all individuals in a random model with 100 individuals); to our knowledge, these are by far the fastest runtimes for relational GRE reported in the literature. We have made our implementation available online at `http://code.google.com/p/crisp-nlg/wiki/DlGre`.

Because they compute referring expressions for all individuals in the domain at once, our algorithms will perform especially strongly in static settings, such as the generation of descriptions for museum exhibits, in which the individuals and their properties don't change much. However, even in more dynamic settings, our algorithms have a chance to outperform search algorithms like Dale and Haddock's in the average case because they can't get stuck in unproductive branches of the search space. Nevertheless, one interesting question for future research is how to incrementally update simulation classes when the model changes. Similarly, it would be interesting to explore how different linguistic constraints and attribute orderings can be taken into account efficiently, how our algorithms could be integrated with more standard DL T-Box inferences, and how they can be adapted to use inverse relations or to compute REs for sets. In exploring these extensions we will be able to draw on a rich body of literature that has already considered many variants of simulation algorithms addressing similar issues.

In experimenting with the Viethen and Dale data, we found that there is no single ordering that covers all human-produced descriptions, which seems to be in contrast to Dale and Reiter's (1995) assumption that there is only one ordering for each given domain. In fact, it is not even the case that each speaker consistently uses just one ordering. An interesting open research question is thus what factors determine which ordering is used. Unfortunately, both in the Viethen and Dale dataset and in the TUNA corpus (van Deemter et al., 2006), only a minority of referring expressions is relational, maybe because these domains lend themselves very well to row/column style propositional REs. We are currently collecting REs in a domain in which propositional REs are less preferred.

Acknowledgments. We are grateful to Hector Geffner (who independently suggested to view GRE as computation of DL formulas), Kees van Deemter, and Emiel Krahmer for interesting discussions. We also thank Jette Viethen and Robert Dale for making their corpus available, and the reviewers for their comments.

References

C. Areces and B. ten Cate. 2006. Hybrid logics. In P. Blackburn, F. Wolter, and J. van Benthem, editors, *Handbook of Modal Logics*. Elsevier.

F. Baader, D. McGuiness, D. Nardi, and P. Patel-Schneider, editors. 2003. *The Description Logic Handbook: Theory, implementation and applications*. Cambridge University Press.

P. Blackburn, M. de Rijke, and Y. Venema. 2001. *Modal Logic*. Cambridge University Press.

R. Dale and N. Haddock. 1991. Generating referring expressions involving relations. In *Proc. of the 5th EACL*.

R. Dale and E. Reiter. 1995. Computational interpretations of the Gricean maxims in the generation of referring expressions. *Cognitive Science*, 19.

R. Dale. 1989. Cooking up referring expressions. In *Proc. of the 27th ACL*.

A. Dovier, C. Piazza, and A. Policriti. 2004. An efficient algorithm for computing bisimulation equivalence. *Theoretical Computer Science*, 311(1–3).

C. Gardent and K. Striegnitz. 2007. Generating bridging definite descriptions. In H. Bunt and R. Muskens, editors, *Computing Meaning, Vol. 3*. Springer.

C. Gardent. 2002. Generating minimal definite descriptions. In *Proc. of the 40th ACL*.

J. Hopcroft. 1971. An $n \log(n)$ algorithm for minimizing states in a finite automaton. In Z. Kohave, editor, *Theory of Machines and computations*. Academic Press.

H. Horacek. 1997. An algorithm for generating referential descriptions with flexible interfaces. In *Proc. of the 35th ACL*.

J. Kelleher and G.-J. Kruijff. 2006. Incremental generation of spatial referring expressions in situated dialog. In *Proc. of COLING/ACL*.

A. Koller and M. Stone. 2007. Sentence generation as planning. In *Proc. of the 45th ACL*.

E. Krahmer, S. van Erk, and A. Verleg. 2003. Graph-based generation of referring expressions. *Computational Linguistics*, 29(1).

N. Kurtonina and M. de Rijke. 1998. Expressiveness of concept expressions in first-order description logics. *Artificial Intelligence*, 107.

R. Paige and R. Tarjan. 1987. Three partition refinement algorithms. *SIAM Journal on Computing*, 16(6).

M. Stone and B. Webber. 1998. Textual economy through close coupling of syntax and semantics. In *Proc. of the 9th INLG workshop*.

M. Stone. 2000. On identifying sets. In *Proc. of the 1st INLG*.

K. van Deemter, I. van der Sluis, and A. Gatt. 2006. Building a semantically transparent corpus for the generation of referring expressions. In *Proc. of the 4th INLG*.

K. van Deemter. 2002. Generating referring expressions: Boolean extensions of the incremental algorithm. *Computational Linguistics*, 28(1):37–52.

J. Viethen and R. Dale. 2006. Algorithms for generating referring expressions: Do they do what people do? In *Proc. of the 4th INLG*.

Attribute Selection for Referring Expression Generation: New Algorithms and Evaluation Methods

Albert Gatt
Department of Computing Science
University of Aberdeen
Aberdeen AB24 3UE, UK
a.gatt@abdn.ac.uk

Anja Belz
Natural Language Technology Group
University of Brighton
Brighton BN2 4GJ, UK
a.s.belz@brighton.ac.uk

Abstract

Referring expression generation has recently been the subject of the first Shared Task Challenge in NLG. In this paper, we analyse the systems that participated in the Challenge in terms of their algorithmic properties, comparing new techniques to classic ones, based on results from a new human task-performance experiment and from the intrinsic measures that were used in the Challenge. We also consider the relationship between different evaluation methods, showing that extrinsic task-performance experiments and intrinsic evaluation methods yield results that are not significantly correlated. We argue that this highlights the importance of including extrinsic evaluation methods in comparative NLG evaluations.

1 Introduction and Background

The Generation of Referring Expressions (GRE) is one of the most intensively studied sub-tasks of Natural Language Generation (NLG). Much research has focused on content determination in GRE, which is typically framed as an *attribute selection* task in which properties are selected in order to describe an intended referent. Since such properties are typically defined as attribute-value pairs, in what follows, we will refer to this as the ASGRE (*A*ttribute *S*election for *G*enerating *R*eferring *E*xpressions) task.

1.1 Approaches to ASGRE

Since early work on ASGRE, which focused on pragmatic motivations behind different types of reference (Appelt, 1985; Appelt and Kronfeld, 1987), the focus has increasingly been on definite descriptions and identification, where the set of attributes selected should uniquely distinguish the intended referent from other entities (its 'distractors'). *Unique Reference* in this sense is a dominant criterion for selecting attribute sets in classic ASGRE algorithms. Following Dale (1989), and especially Dale and Reiter (1995), several contributions have extended the remit of ASGRE algorithms to handle relations (Dale and Haddock, 1991; Kelleher and Kruijff, 2006) and gradable attributes (van Deemter, 2006); and also to guarantee logical completeness of algorithms (van Deemter, 2002; Gardent, 2002; Horacek, 2004; Gatt and van Deemter, 2007).

Much of this work has incorporated the principle of brevity. Based on the Gricean Quantity maxim (Grice, 1975), and originally discussed by Appelt (1985), and further by Dale (1989), Reiter (1990) and Gardent (2002), this principle holds that descriptions should contain no more information than is necessary to distinguish an intended referent. In ASGRE, this has been translated into a criterion which determines the adequacy of an attribute set, implemented in its most straightforward form in *Full Brevity* algorithms which select the smallest attribute set that uniquely refers to the intended referent (Dale, 1989).

Another frequent property of ASGRE algorithms is *Incrementality* which involves selection of attributes one at a time (rather than exhaustive search for a distinguishing set), and was initially motivated by algorithmic complexity considerations. The Incremental Algorithm of Dale and Reiter (1995) was also justified with reference to psycholinguistic findings that (a) humans overspecify their references (i.e. they are not brief when they produce a reference); and (b) this tends to occur with properties which seem to be very salient or in some sense preferred (Pechmann, 1989; Belke and Meyer, 2002; Arts, 2004). In the Incremental Algorithm (Dale and Reiter, 1995), incrementality took the form of hillclimbing along an attribute order which reflects the preference that humans manifest for certain attributes (such as COLOUR). This *Modelling of Human Preferences* in the Incremental Algorithm has proven influential. Another feature proposed by Dale and Reiter is to hardwire the inclusion of the type of an entity in a description, reflecting the human tendency to always include the category of an object (e.g. *chair* or *man*), even if it has no discriminatory value. A compromise may be reached between incrementality and brevity; for example, Dale's (1989) Greedy Algorithm selects attributes one at a time, and computes the *Discriminatory Power* of attributes, that is, it bases selection on the extent to which an attribute helps distinguish an entity from its distractors.

In the remainder of this paper, we uniformly use the term 'algorithmic property' for the selection criteria and other properties of ASGRE algorithms described above, and refer to them by the following short forms: Full Brevity, Uniqueness, Discriminatory Power, Hardwired Type Selection, Human Preference Modelling and Incrementality.[1]

1.2 ASGRE and Evaluation

Though ASGRE evaluations have been carried out (Gupta and Stent, 2005; Viethen and Dale, 2006; Gatt et al., 2007), these have focused on 'classic' algorithms, and have been corpus-based. The absence of task-performance evaluations is surprising, considering the well-defined nature of the ASGRE task, and the predominance of task-performance studies elsewhere in the NLG evaluation literature (Reiter et al., 2003; Karasimos and Isard, 2004).

Given the widespread agreement on task definition and input/output specifications, ASGRE was an ideal candidate for the first NLG shared task evaluation challenge. The challenge was first discussed during a workshop held at Arlington, Va. (Dale and White, 2007), and eventually organised as part of the UCNLG+MT Workshop in September 2007 (Belz and Gatt, 2007).

The ASGRE Shared Task provided an opportunity to (a) assess the extent to which the field has diversified since its inception; (b) carry out a comparative evaluation involving both automatic methods and human task-performance methods.

1.3 Overview

In the ASGRE Challenge report (Belz and Gatt, 2007) we presented the results of the ASGRE Challenge evaluations objectively and with little interpretation. In this paper, we present the results of a new task-performance evaluation and a new intrinsic measure involving the same 15 systems and compare the new results with the earlier ones. We also examine all results in the light of the algorithmic properties of the participating systems. We thus focus on two issues in ASGRE and its evaluation. We examine the similarities and differences among the systems submitted to the ASGRE Challenge and compare them to classic approaches (Section 2.1). We look at the results of intrinsic and extrinsic evaluations (Section 4) and examine how these relate to algorithmic properties (Section 4.1 and 4.2). Finally we look at how intrinsic and extrinsic evaluations correlate with each other (Section 4.3).

2 The ASGRE Challenge

The ASGRE Challenge used the TUNA Corpus (Gatt et al., 2007), a set of human-produced referring expressions (REs) for entities in visual domains of pictures of furniture or people. The corpus was collected during an online elicitation experiment in which subjects typed descriptions of a target referent in a DOMAIN in which there were also 6 other entities ('distractors'). Each RE in the corpus is paired with a domain representation consisting of the target referent and the set of distractors, each with their possible attributes and values; Figure 1(a) shows an example of an entity representation.

In each human-produced RE, substrings are annotated with the attribute(s) they express ('realise'). For the Challenge, the attributes in each RE were extracted to produce a DESCRIPTION, i.e. a set of

[1]While terms like 'Unique Reference' and 'Brevity' are characteristics of outputs of ASGRE algorithms, we use them as shorthand here for those properties of algorithms which guarantee that they will achieve these characteristics in the attribute sets generated.

```
<ENTITY ID="121" TYPE="target">
<ATTRIBUTE NAME="colour" VALUE="blue" />
<ATTRIBUTE NAME="orientation" VALUE="left" />
<ATTRIBUTE NAME="type" VALUE="fan" />
<ATTRIBUTE NAME="size" VALUE="small" />
<ATTRIBUTE NAME="x-dimension" VALUE="1" />
<ATTRIBUTE NAME="y-dimension" VALUE="3" />
</ENTITY>
```

(a) Entity representation

```
<DESCRIPTION>
<ATTRIBUTE NAME="colour" VALUE="blue" />
<ATTRIBUTE NAME="orientation" VALUE="left" />
<ATTRIBUTE NAME="type" VALUE="fan" />
</DESCRIPTION>
```

(b) Description: *the blue fan facing left*

Figure 1: Example of the input and output data in the ASGRE Challenge

attribute-value pairs to describe the target referent. An example, corresponding to a human-produced RE for Figure 1(a), is shown in Figure 1(b).

For the ASGRE Challenge, the 780 singular descriptions in the corpus were used, and divided into 60% training data, 20% development data and 20% test data. Participants were given both input (DOMAIN) and output (DESCRIPTION) parts in the training and development data, but just inputs in the test data. They were asked to submit the corresponding outputs for test data inputs.

2.1 Systems

The evaluations reported below included 15 of the 22 submitted ASGRE systems. Table 1 is an overview of these systems in terms of five of the classic algorithmic properties described in Section 1, and one property that has emerged in more recent ASGRE algorithms: *Trainability*, or automatic adaptability of systems from data. This classification of systems is based on the reports submitted by their developers to the ASGRE Challenge. Properties are indicated in the first column (abbreviations are explained in the table caption).

The version of the IS-FBS system that was originally submitted to ASGRE contained a bug and did not actually output minimal attribute sets (but added an arbitrary attribute to each set). Unlike the ASGRE Challenge task-performance evaluation, the analysis presented in this paper uses the corrected version of this system.

3 Evaluation methods

Evaluation methods can be characterised as either *intrinsic* or *extrinsic*. While intrinsic methods evaluate the outputs of algorithms in their own right, either relative to a corpus or based on absolute evaluation metrics, extrinsic methods assess the effect of an algorithm on something external to it, such as its effect on human performance on some external task.

3.1 Intrinsic measures

In the evaluation results reported below, we use two of the intrinsic methods used in the ASGRE Challenge. The first of these is *Minimality*, defined as the proportion of descriptions produced by a system that are maximally brief, as per the original definition in Dale (1989). The second is the Dice coefficient, used to compare the description produced by a system (D_S) to the human-produced description (D_H) on the same input domain. Dice is estimated as follows:

$$\frac{2 \times |D_S \cap D_H|}{|D_S| + |D_H|} \tag{1}$$

For this paper, we also computed MASI, a version of the Jaccard similarity coefficient proposed by Passonneau (2006) which multiplies the similarity value by a monotonicity coefficient, biasing the measure towards those cases where D_S and D_H have an empty set difference. Intuitively, this means that those system-produced descriptions are preferred which do not include attributes that are omitted by a human. Thus, two of our intrinsic measures assess *Humanlikeness* (Dice and MASI), while *Minimality* reflects the extent to which an algorithm conforms to brevity, one of the principles that has emerged from the ASGRE literature.

3.2 Extrinsic measures

In the ASGRE Challenge, the extrinsic evaluation was performed via an experiment in which partici-

	CAM					GRAPH		IS				TITCH			
	T	TU	B	BU	DIT-DS	FP	SC	FBS	FBN	IAC	NIL	RS	RS+	AS	AS+
Incr	Y	Y	Y	Y	Y	n	n	n	n	Y	Y	Y	Y	Y	Y
DP	Y	Y	Y	Y	n	n	n	n	n	n	n	Y	Y	Y	Y
Train	Y	Y	n	n	Y	Y	Y	n	Y	Y	Y/n	Y	Y	Y	Y
Type	Y	Y	Y	Y	Y	Y	Y	n	n	n	n	Y	Y	Y	Y
Hum	Y	Y	Y	Y	n	Y	n	n	n	n	n	n	n	n	n
FB	n	n	n	n	n	n	n	Y	n	n	n	n	n	n	n

Table 1: Overview of properties of systems submitted to the ASGRE Challenge. All systems produce outputs with unique reference. The meaning of the abbreviations is as follows (for definitions see Section 1): *Incr = Incrementality*; *DP = Discriminatory Power*; *Train = Trainability*; *Type = Hardwired Type Selection*; *Hum = Human Preference Modelling*; *FB = Full Brevity*

pants were shown visual representations of the domains that were used as inputs in the test data, coupled with a system-generated description on the same screen. Their task was to identify the intended referent in the domain by means of a mouse click. The rationale behind the experiment was to assess the degree to which an algorithm achieved its stated purpose of generating a description that facilitates identification of the intended referent.

Since system outputs were sets of attributes (see Figure 1(b)), they were first mapped to NL strings using a deterministic, template-based method which always maps each attribute to word(s) in the same way and in the same position regardless of context[2].

The present analysis is based on results from a new evaluation experiment which replicated the original methodology with a slight difference. While participants in the ASGRE experiment were shown visual domains and descriptions at the same time, this experiment sought to distinguish reading and identification time. Thus, for each system output, participants first saw the description, using the mouse to call up the visual domain once they had read it. This yields three dependent measures: (a) reading time (RT); (b) identification time (IT); (c) error rate (ER), defined as the proportion of trials per system for which participants identified the wrong referent.

One of the possible complications with the RT measure is that, while it depends on the semantics of a description (the attributes that an algorithm selects), the syntactic complexity of the description will also impact the time it takes to read it. In our setup, the adoption of a deterministic, one-to-one mapping between an attribute and its linguistic representation controls for this to some extent. Since every attribute in any semantic representation will invariably map to the same surface form, there is no variation between systems in terms of how a particular attribute is realised.

Design: As in the original experiment, we used a Repeated Latin Squares design in which each combination of peer system and test set item is allocated one trial. Because there were 148 items in the test set, but 15 peer systems, 2 test set items were randomly selected and duplicated to give a test set size of 150, and 10 Latin Squares. The 150 test set items were divided into two sets of 75; 15 of the 30 participants did the first 75 items (the first 5 Latin Squares), while the other 15 did the rest. This resulted in 2250 trials (each corresponding to a combination of test set item and system) in all. For the purposes of this paper, the duplicate items were treated as fillers, that is, every item was included only once in the analysis.

Participants and procedure: The experiment was carried out by 30 participants recruited from among the faculty and administrative staff of the University of Brighton. Participants carried out the experiment under supervision in a quiet room on a laptop. Stimulus presentation was carried out using DMDX, a Win-32 software package for psycholinguistic experiments involving time measurements (Forster and Forster, 2003). Participants initiated each trial, which consisted of an initial warning bell and a fixation point flashed on the screen for 1000ms. They then read the description and called up the visual domain to identify the referent. Identi-

[2]The template-based string-mapping algorithm was created by Irene Langkilde-Geary at the University of Brighton.

fication was carried out by clicking on the image that a participant thought was the target referent of the description they had read. RT was measured from the point at which the description was presented, to the point at which a participant called up the next screen via mouse click. IT was measured from the point at which pictures (the visual domain) were presented on the screen to the point where a participant identified a referent by clicking on it. In addition to the time taken to identify a referent, the program recorded the location of a participant's mouse click, in order to assess whether the object identified was in fact the correct one. Trials timed out after 15 seconds; this only occurred in 2 trials overall (out of 2250).

4 Results and discussion

Table 2 displays aggregate (mean or percentage) scores for each of the intrinsic and extrinsic measures. As an initial test for differences between the 15 systems separate univariate ANOVAs were conducted using SYSTEM as the independent variable (15 levels), testing its effect on the extrinsic task-performance measures (RT and IT). For error rate (ER), we used a Kruskall-Wallis ranks test to compare identification accuracy rates across systems[3]. The main effect of SYSTEM was significant on RT ($F(14, 2219) = 2.58$, $p < .01$), and IT ($F(14, 2219) = 1.90$, $p < .05$). No significant main effect was found on ER ($\chi^2 = 13.88$, $p > .4$).[4]

Systems also differed significantly on Dice ($F(14, 2219) = 18.66$, $p < .001$) and MASI scores ($F(14, 2219) = 15.94$, $p < .001$).

In the remainder of this section, we first consider the differences between systems based on the algorithmic properties listed in Table 1 (and described in Section 1). For this part of the analysis, we consider intrinsic and extrinsic evaluation measures separately (Section 4.1 and 4.2). Subsequently, we explicitly compare the intrinsic and extrinsic methods (Section 4.3).

[3]The large number of zero values in ER proportions, and a high dependency of variance on the mean, meant that a non-parametric test was more appropriate.

[4]We left out the duplicated items in this analysis.

4.1 Differences between system types

As Table 1 indicates, there are some similarities between the new systems submitted for the ASGRE tasks, and the classic approaches discussed in Section 1. Eleven of the systems are incremental, although only a minority (5 systems) explicitly hardwire human preferences. Furthermore, 8 systems (all variations on two basic systems, CAM and TITCH) compute the discriminatory value of the properties selected. Just one system adopts the Full Brevity approach of Dale (1989), while the majority (11 systems) adopt the Dale and Reiter convention of always adding TYPE. Perhaps the greatest point of divergence between the ASGRE Challenge systems and the classic algorithms discussed in Section 1 is the predominance of data-driven approaches (12 systems are trainable), a characteristic that mirrors trends elsewhere in HLT.

It is worth asking how the particular algorithmic properties impact on performance, as measured with the evaluation methods used. Table 3 displays means computed with all the extrinsic and intrinsic measures, for all system properties except full brevity and discriminatory power. Since the latter are related to Minimality, which was a separate evaluation measure in this study, they are treated separately below (Section 4.2). Note that the aggregate scores in Table 3 are based on unequal-sized samples, since this is a post-hoc analysis which the evaluation studies described above did not directly target.

Table 3 indicates that systems that were directly trained on data display higher agreement (Dice and MASI) scores with the human data. This is relatively unsurprising; what is less straightforwardly predictable is that trainable systems have better task-performance scores (IT and RT). Systems which always include TYPE and those which are incremental apparently score better overall. Somewhat surprisingly, incorporating human attribute preferences results in smaller improvements than incrementality and TYPE inclusion. This is likely due to the fact that the attributes preferred by humans are not straightforwardly determinable in the people subdomain (van der Sluis et al., 2007). In contrast, those in the furniture domain, which include COLOUR, SIZE and ORIENTATION, are fairly predictable as far as human preference goes, based on previous psy-

	Minimality	Dice	MASI	RT	IT	ER
IS-FBN	1.35	0.770	0.601	1837.546	2188.923	6
DIT-DS	0	0.750	0.595	1304.119	1859.246	2
IS-IAC	0	0.746	0.597	1356.146	1973.193	6
CAM-T	0	0.725	0.560	1475.313	1978.237	5.33
CAM-TU	0	0.721	0.557	1297.372	1809.044	4
GRAPH-FP	4.73	0.689	0.479	1382.039	2053.326	3.33
GRAPH-SC	4.73	0.671	0.466	1349.047	1899.585	2
TITCH-RS+	0	0.669	0.459	1278.008	1814.933	1.33
TITCH-AS+	0	0.660	0.452	1321.204	1817.303	4.67
TITCH-RS	0	0.655	0.432	1255.278	1866.935	4.67
TITCH-AS	0	0.645	0.422	1229.417	1766.350	4.67
CAM-BU	10.14	0.630	0.420	1251.316	1877.948	4
NIL	20.27	0.625	0.477	1482.665	1960.314	5.33
CAM-B	8.11	0.620	0.403	1309.070	1952.394	5.33
IS-FBS	100	0.368	0.182	1461.453	2181.883	7.33

Table 2: Results for systems and evaluation measures (in order of Dice).

	trainable		includes type		incremental		human preferences	
	no	yes	no	yes	no	yes	no	yes
Dice	0.561	0.700	0.627	0.676	0.625	0.677	0.656	0.677
MASI	0.370	0.511	0.464	0.477	0.432	0.488	0.468	0.484
RT	1376.13	1371.41	1534.45	1313.83	1507.52	1323.63	1387.49	1343.02
IT	1993.13	1911.55	2076.08	1881.39	2080.93	1879.63	1932.87	1934.19
ER	5.2%	4.2%	6.3%	3.8%	4.7%	4.4%	4.5%	4.5%

Table 3: Means on intrinsic and extrinsic measures, by system type.

	Dice	MASI	IT	RT
Trainable	171.67*	145.63*	.002	4.36
Incremental	47.90*	45.61*	7.43	1.64
Includes type	18.42*	29.38*	6.89	11.27
Human pref.	3.27	5.12	2.11	.83
Incr. × Train.	40.82*	30.99*	.001	7.08

Table 4: Multivariate tests examining impact of system type on evaluation measures. Cells indicate $F-$values with 4 numerator and 2201 error degrees of freedom. $*$: $p \leq .05$ after Bonferroni correction.

cholinguistic results (Pechmann, 1989; Arts, 2004).

As a further test of these differences, a multivariate ANOVA was conducted, comparing scores on the intrinsic and extrinsic measures, as a function of the presence or absence of the 4 algorithmic properties being considered here. The results are shown in Table 4 which displays figures for all main effects and for the one interaction that was significant (incrementality × trainability, bottom row). Since this is a multiple-test post-hoc analysis on unequal-sized samples, all significance values are based on a Bonferroni correction[5] The table does not include ER, as no main effect of SYSTEM was found on this measure.

The results show that trainability, followed by incrementality and inclusion of TYPE had the strongest impact on system quality, as far as this is measured by Dice and MASI.

The incrementality × trainability interaction is mostly due to the huge effect that trainability has on how non-incremental systems perform. In the case of incremental systems, trainability gives rise to marginally better performance: the mean Dice score for non-trainable incremental systems was .625, as compared to .696 for trainable incremental systems. Similar patterns are observable with MASI (.433 vs .439). However, the most significant feature of the interaction is the large benefit that training on data confers on non-incremental systems. Untrained non-incremental systems obtained a mean Dice score of .368 (MASI = .182), while the mean Dice score on trained non-incremental systems was .710, with a mean MASI score of .515. Another,

[5]The Bonferroni correction adjusts for the increased likelihood of finding results statistically significant when multiple tests are applied by lowering the alpha value (the significance threshold) by dividing it by the number of tests involved.

Intrinsic measures		Extrinsic measures		
Dice	MASI	ER	RT	IT
-.904**	-.789**	.505	.183	.560*

Table 5: Correlations between Minimality and other evaluation measures. Legend: **: $p \leq .01$, *: $p \leq .05$

more tentative, conclusion that could be made by looking at these figures is that trainable systems perform better if they are non-incremental; however, the difference (Dice of .710 vs .696) seems rather marginal and would require further testing. What is also striking in this table is the absence of any significant impact of these properties on the task-performance measures of reading and identification time, despite initial impressions based on means (Table 3).

In summary, at least one of the principles that has been widely adopted in ASGRE – incrementality – seems to be validated by the evaluation results for these new algorithms. However, results show that improvement on an automatically computed humanlikeness metric such as MASI or Dice does not necessarily imply an improvement on a task-performance measure. This is a theme to which we return in Section 4.3.

4.2 The role of minimality

Apart from incrementality, the other dominant principle that has emerged from nearly three decades of ASGRE research is brevity. While psycholinguistic research has shown (Pechmann, 1989; Belke and Meyer, 2002; Arts, 2004) that the strict interpretation of the Gricean Quantity Maxim, adopted for example by Dale (1989), is not observed by speakers, brevity has remained a central concern in recent approaches (Gardent, 2002). Only one algorithm adopted a full-brevity approach in the ASGRE Challenge; however, several algorithms emphasised discriminatory power, and some of these, as a comparison between Tables 1 and 2 shows, tended to have higher Minimality scores overall.

Since Minimality was part of the overall design of the evaluation, it is possible to see the extent to which it covaries significantly with other performance measures. The relevant correlations are displayed in Table 5. There are highly significant *negative* correlations between Minimality and the two intrinsic humanlikeness measures (Dice and MASI). The significant positive correlation with IT implies that participants in our evaluation experiment tended to take longer to identify referents in the case of systems which produce more minimal descriptions.

The negative correlation with the humanlikeness measures corroborates previous findings that people do not observe a strict interpretation of the Gricean Quantity Maxim (Pechmann, 1989; Belke and Meyer, 2002; Arts, 2004). On the other hand, the direction of the correlation with IT is somewhat more surprising. One possible explanation is that minimal descriptions often do not include a TYPE attribute, since this seldom has any discriminatory power in the TUNA Corpus domains.

The role of Minimality remains a topic of some debate in the psycholinguistic literature. A recent study (Engelhardt et al., 2006) showed that identification of objects in a visual domain could be delayed if a description of the target referent was overspecified, suggesting a beneficial effect from Minimality. However, Engelhardt et al. also found, in a separate study, that overspecified descriptions tended to be rated as no worse than brief, or minimal ones. Indeed, one of the points that emerges from this study is that intrinsic and extrinsic assessments can yield contrasting results. It is to this issue that we now turn.

4.3 Intrinsic vs. extrinsic methods

Since humanlikeness (intrinsic) and task performance (extrinsic) are different perspectives on the outputs of an ASGRE algorithm, it is worth asking to what extent they agree. This is an important question for comparative HLT evaluation more generally, which has become dominated by corpus-based humanlikeness metrics. To obtain an indication of agreement, we computed correlations between the two humanlikeness measures and the task-performance measures; these are displayed in Table 6.

The two time measures (RT and IT) are strongly correlated, implying that when subjects took longer to read descriptions, they also took longer to identify a referent. This may seem surprising in view of the positive correlation between Minimality and IT (shorter descriptions imply *longer* IT) which was reported in Section 4.2, where Minimality was also

	RT	IT	ER	Dice	MASI
RT	1	.8**	0.46	0.12	.23
IT	.8**	1	.59*	-0.28	-.17
ER	0.46	.59*	1	-0.39	-.29
Dice	0.12	-0.28	-0.39	1	.97**
MASI	0.23	-0.17	-0.29	.97**	1

Table 6: Pairwise correlations between humanlikeness and task-performance measures (*: $p \leq .05$; **: $p \leq .01$)

shown not to correlate with RT (shorter descriptions do not imply longer or shorter RT). What this result indicates is that rather than the number of attributes in a description, as measured by Minimality, it is the content that influences identification latency. Part of the effect may be due to the lack of TYPE in minimal descriptions noted earlier.

Table 6 also shows that error rate is significantly correlated with IT (but not with RT), i.e. where subjects took longer to identify referents, the identification was more likely to be wrong. This points to a common underlying cause for slower reading and identification, possibly arising from the use of attributes (such as SIZE) which impose a greater cognitive load on the reader.

The very strong correlation (0.97) between Dice and MASI is to be expected, given the similarity in the way they are defined.

Another unambiguous result emerges: none of the similarity-based metrics covary significantly with any of the task-performance measures. An extended analysis involving a larger range of intrinsic metrics confirmed this lack of significant covariation for string-based similarity metrics as well as set-similarity metrics across two task-performance experiments (Belz and Gatt, 2008). This indicates that at least for some areas of HLT, task-performance evaluation is vital: without the external reality check provided by extrinsic evaluations, intrinsic evaluations may end up being too self-contained and disconnected from notions of usefulness to provide a meaningful assessment of systems' quality.

5 Conclusion

Comparative evaluation can be of great benefit, especially in an area as mature and diverse as GRE. A shared-task evaluation like the ASGRE Challenge can help identify the strengths and weaknesses of alternative approaches and techniques, as measured by different evaluation criteria. Perhaps even more importantly, such a challenge helps evaluate the evaluation methods themselves and reveals which (combinations of) evaluation methods are appropriate for a given evaluation purpose.

As far as the first issue is concerned, this paper has shown that trainability, incrementality and not aiming for minimality are the algorithmic properties most helpful in achieving high humanlikeness scores. This result is in line with psycholinguistic research on attribute selection in reference by humans. Less clear-cut is the relationship between these properties and task-performance measures that assess how efficiently a referent can be identified based on a description.

The second part of the analysis presented here showed that intrinsic and extrinsic perspectives on the quality of system outputs quality can yield uncorrelated sets of results, making it difficult to predict quality as measured by one based on quality as measured by the other. Furthermore, while intuitively it might be expected that higher humanlikeness entailed better task performance, our results suggest that this is not necessarily the case.

Our main conclusions for ASGRE evaluation are that (a) while humanlikeness evaluation may provide a measure of one aspect of systems but we need to be cautious in relying on humanlikeness as a criterion of overall quality (standard in evaluation of MT and summarisation); and (b) that we must not leave the NLG tradition of task-performance evaluations behind as we move towards more comparative forms of evaluation.

Acknowledgements

We gratefully acknowledge the contribution made to the evaluations by the faculty and staff at Brighton University who participated in the identification experiments. The biggest contribution was, of course, made by the participants in the ASGRE Challenge who created the systems involved in the evaluations: Bernd Bohnet, Ann Copestake, Pablo Gervás, Raquel Hervás, John Kelleher, Emiel Krahmer, Takahiro Kurosawa, Advaith Siddharthan, Philipp Spanger, Takenobu Tokunaga, Mariet Theune, Pascal Touset and Jette Viethen.

References

D. Appelt and A. Kronfeld. 1987. A computational model of referring. In *Proc. 10th International Joint Conference on Artificial Intelligence (IJCAI-87)*, pages 640–647.

D. Appelt. 1985. Planning English referring expressions. *Artificial Intelligence*, 26(1):1–33.

A. Arts. 2004. *Overspecification in Instructive Texts*. Ph.D. thesis, University of Tilburg.

E. Belke and A. Meyer. 2002. Tracking the time course of multidimensional stimulus discrimination: Analysis of viewing patterns and processing times during same-different decisions. *European Journal of Cognitive Psychology*, 14(2):237–266.

A. Belz and A. Gatt. 2007. The Attribute Selection for GRE Challenge: Overview and evaluation results. In *Proc. 2nd UCNLG Workshop: Language Generation and Machine Translation (UCNLG+MT)*, pages 75–83.

A. Belz and A. Gatt. 2008. Intrinsic vs. extrinsic evaluation measures for referring expression generation. In *Proc. 46th Annual Meeting of the Association for Computational Linguistics (ACL-08)*. To appear.

R. Dale and N. Haddock. 1991. Generating referring expressions containing relations. In *Proc. 5th Conference of the European Chapter of the Association for Computational Linguistics (EACL-91).*, pages 161–166.

R. Dale and E. Reiter. 1995. Computational interpretation of the Gricean maxims in the generation of referring expressions. *Cognitive Science*, 19(8):233–263.

R. Dale and M. White, editors. 2007. *Shared tasks and comparative evaluation in Natural Language Generation: Workshop Report.*

Robert Dale. 1989. Cooking up referring expressions. In *Proc. 27th Annual Meeting of the Association for Computational Linguistics (ACL-89).*, pages 68–75.

P. E. Engelhardt, K.G.D Bailey, and F. Ferreira. 2006. Do speakers and listeners observe the Gricean Maxim of Quantity? *Journal of Memory and Language*, 54:554–573.

K. I. Forster and J. C. Forster. 2003. DMDX: A windows display program with millisecond accuracy. *Behavior Research Methods, Instruments, & Computers*, 35(1):116–124.

C. Gardent. 2002. Generating minimal definite descriptions. In *Proc. 40th Annual Meeting of the Association for Computational Linguistics (ACL-02).*, pages 96–103.

A. Gatt and K. van Deemter. 2007. Incremental generation of plural descriptions: Similarity and partitioning. In *Proc. 2007 Joint Conference on Empirical Methods in Natural Language Processing and Computational Natural Language Learning (EMNLP/CONLL-07)*, pages 102–111.

A. Gatt, I. van der Sluis, and K. van Deemter. 2007. Evaluating algorithms for the generation of referring expressions using a balanced corpus. In *Proc. 11th European Workshop on Natural Language Generation (ENLG-07).*, pages 49–56.

H. P. Grice. 1975. Logic and conversation. In P. Cole and J. L. Morgan, editors, *Syntax and Semantics: Speech Acts.*, volume III. Academic Press.

S. Gupta and A. J. Stent. 2005. Automatic evaluation of referring expression generation using corpora. In *Proc. 1st Workshop on Using Corpora in NLG (UCNLG-05).*, pages 1–6.

H. Horacek. 2004. On referring to sets of objects naturally. In *Proc. 3rd International Conference on Natural Language Generation (INLG-04).*, pages 70–79.

A. Karasimos and A. Isard. 2004. Multilingual evaluation of a natural language generation system. In *Proc. 4th International Conference on Language Resources and Evaluation (LREC-04).*

J. D. Kelleher and G-J Kruijff. 2006. Incremental generation of spatial referring expressions in situated dialog. In *Proc. joint 21st International Conference on Computational Linguistics and 44th Annual Meeting of the Association for Computational Linguistics (ACL/COLING-06).*, pages 1041–1048.

R. Passonneau. 2006. Measuring agreement on set-valued items (MASI) for semantic and pragmatic annotation. In *Proc. 5th International Conference on Language Resources and Evaluation (LREC-06).*, pages 831–836.

Thomas Pechmann. 1989. Incremental speech production and referential overspecification. *Linguistics*, 27:89–110.

E. Reiter, R. Robertson, and L. Osman. 2003. Lessons from a failure: Generating tailored smoking cessation letters. *Artificial Intelligence*, 144:41–58.

E. Reiter. 1990. The computational complexity of avoiding conversational implicatures. In *Proc. 28th Annual Meeting of the Association for Computational Linguistics (ACL-90).*, pages 97–104.

K. van Deemter. 2002. Generating referring expressions: Boolean extensions of the incremental algorithm. *Computational Linguistics*, 28(1):37–52.

K. van Deemter. 2006. Generating referring expressions that involve gradable properties. *Computational Linguistics*, 32(2):195–222.

I. van der Sluis, A. Gatt, and K. van Deemter. 2007. Evaluating algorithms for the generation of referring expressions: Going beyond toy domains. In *Proc. International Conference on Recent Advances in Natural Language Processing (RANLP-07).*

J. Viethen and R. Dale. 2006. Algorithms for generating referring expressions: Do they do what people do? In *Proc. 4th International Conference on Natural Language Generation (INLG-06).*, pages 63–72.

The Use of Spatial Relations in Referring Expression Generation

Jette Viethen
Centre for Language Technology
Macquarie University
Sydney, Australia
jviethen@ics.mq.edu.au

Robert Dale
Centre for Language Technology
Macquarie University
Sydney, Australia
rdale@ics.mq.edu.au

Abstract

There is a prevailing assumption in the literature on referring expression generation that relations are used in descriptions only 'as a last resort', typically on the basis that including the second entity in the relation introduces an additional cognitive load for either speaker or hearer. In this paper, we describe an experiemt that attempts to test this assumption; we determine that, even in simple scenes where the use of relations is not strictly required in order to identify an entity, relations are in fact often used. We draw some conclusions as to what this means for the development of algorithms for the generation of referring expressions.

1 Introduction

In recent years, researchers working on referring expression generation have increasingly moved towards collecting their own data on the human production of referring expressions (REs) (Krahmer and Theune, 2002; van der Sluis and Krahmer, 2004; Gatt and van Deemter, 2006; Belz and Varges, 2007); and the recent Attribute Selection in the Generation of Referring Expressions (ASGRE) Challenge used the TUNA corpus (Gatt et al., 2007), which is the most extensive collection of referring expressions to date. While there is a substantial body of experimental work in psycholinguistics that looks at the human production of referring expressions (see, amongst more recent work, (Clark and Wilkes-Gibbs, 1986; Stevenson, 2002; Haywood et al., 2003; Jordan and Walker, 2005)) the large range of factors that play a role in language production mean that it is often the case that the specific question that one is interested in has not been studied before. So, NLG researchers have tended towards data gathering exercises that explore some specific aspect of referring expression generation, focussing on hypotheses relevant to algorithm development.

This paper is in the same mold. We are particuarly interested in how people use spatial relations in referring expressions, and so in this paper we describe an experiment that explores the generation of relational referring expressions in a simple scene. Section 2 elaborates on our reasons for exploring this aspect of reference. Section 3 describes the experiment and provides some discussion of the results: our primary conclusion is that the assumption in the literature that relations are used 'as a last resort' does not appear to hold; relations are often used, even in simple scenes, when they are not strictly required, and it is likely that they would be more heavily used in more complex real-world scenes. We conclude in Section 4 with some observations as to how the results presented here might impact on the development of algorithms for referring expression generation, and outline some future work.

2 Spatial Relations in Referring Expression Generation

The bulk of the existing literature on referring expression generation (see, for example, Dale (1989), Dale and Reiter (1995), van Deemter (2006), Horacek (2004), Gatt and van Deemter (2006)) generally focuses on the use of non-relational properties, which can either be absolute (for example, colour) or relative (for example, size). We are interested in the use of relational expressions, and in particular the use of spatial relations; the contexts of use we are interested in are task-specific, where, for example, we might want an omniscient domestic agent to tell us where we have placed a lost object (*You left your keys under the folder on the desk …*), or to identify a hearer-new object in a cluttered scene (*the magazine at the bottom of the pile of papers next to the lampshade in the corner*). To develop agents with these kinds of referential capabilities, we want to acquire data that will inform the development of algorithms, either by automatically checking their ability to replicate the corpus, or as a baseline for assessing the performance of humans in an identification task based on the output of these algorithms.

In this paper, we describe an experiment that looks at how and when people use spatial relations in a simple scene. More specifically, we aim to explore the hypothesis that relations are always dispreferred over non-relational properties. This hypothesis appears to underly most approaches to referring expression generation that handle relations:

Gardent (2002) adopts a constraint based approach to deal with relations specifically geared at generating referring expressions that are as short as possible. As including a relation in a referring expression always entails the additional mention of at least a head noun for the related object, this approach inherently prefers properties over relations.

Krahmer and Theune (2002) extend the Incremental Algorithm (IA; Dale and Reiter (1995)) to handle relations. This requires a preference list over all properties and relations to be specified in advance. They explicitly choose to put spatial relations right at the end of that preference list, on the basis that 'It seems an acceptable assumption that people prefer to describe an object in terms of simple properties, and only shift to relations when properties do not suffice […] it takes less effort to consider and describe only one object'.

As the referents in Varges' 2005 domain are all points on a map distinguishable only by their spatial relations to other objects, he has no choice but to use relations. However, he also adopts brevity as a main criterion for choosing which spatial relations to use.

Kelleher and Kruijff (2005, 2006) cite Clark and Wilkes-Gibbs' (1986) Principle of Minimal Cooperative Effort and Dale and Reiter's (1995) Principle of Sensitivity, as well as van der Sluis and Krahmer's (2004) production study, to motivate the ordering over the types of properties that can be used by their system; accordingly, their system only includes spatial (and hence relational) information in a referring expression if it is not possible to construct a description from non-relational properties.

These approaches would appear to favour the production of referring expressions containing long sequences of non-relational properties when a single relational property might do the job. We are interested, then, in whether it really is the case that relational expressions are dispreferred, and in determining when they might in fact be preferred.

To date, we are not aware of any substantial data sets that would allow this question to be explored. Both the TUNA corpus (Gatt et al., 2007) and the Macquarie Drawer data (Viethen and Dale, 2006) contain too few relational descriptions to allow us to draw conclusions about any kind of patterns; the GREC corpus (Belz and Varges, 2007) is not concerned with content selection at all, but rather studies the form of referring expressions used over a whole text; i.e. the choice between fully descriptive NPs, reduced NPs, *one*-anaphora and pronouns.

There are a number of corpora resulting from experiments involving human participants which contain referring expressions, such as Brennan and Clark's (1996) collection of tangram descriptions, the HCRC Map Task Corpus (Thompson et al., 1993), the COCONUT corpus (Jordan and Walker, 2005), and Byron and Fosler-Lussier's (2006) OSU Quake corpus. However, these contain whole conversations between communicative partners cooperating on a task, making it difficult to factor out the impact of prior discourse context on the referring expressions used.

3 The Data Gathering Experiment

3.1 General overview

We conducted a web-based production experiment to elicit referring expressions describing singular objects in very simple scenes. The study was aimed at shedding light on the question of whether spatial relations are indeed as dispreferred as suggested by the literature in those situations where non-relational descriptions are possible.

The Desiderata section of the report from the Workshop on Shared Tasks and Comparative Evaluation in NLG (Paris et al., 2007) emphasises the difficulties inherent in evaluating NLG systems due to the context dependency of language production: the output appropriate for any given referring expression generation system entirely depends on the particular task being performed. The data gathered in this experiment is intended to inform the development and evaluation of algorithms for the production of one-shot, fully distinguishing descriptions of simple objects in 3-dimensional scenes. The experiment is focussed on the adequate use of spatial relations in referring expressions.

In designing the materials for the experiment, we were conscious of a number of factors which we might expect to have an influence on the use of spatial relations: the prominence of other properties such as colour and size (i.e. whether most objects are of the same or similar size and colour, so that none are very distinct from the point of view of their direct properties); how easy it is to distinguish the target from the other objects around it; how easy it is to identify the target in the scene without using any locational information; and the visual salience of other objects which could serve as relatees in relational descriptions.

3.2 Method

3.2.1 Participants

In total, 74 participants completed the experiment. They were recruited by emailing 120 native English speakers and asking them to pass on the call for participation to other native or fluent English speakers. This resulted in a range of participants from a wide variety of backgrounds and age groups; most participants were in their early or mid twenties.

One participant indicated they were colour-blind, and another requested that their data be discarded. The data for a further nine participants was excluded from the analysis for reasons outlined in Section 3.2.4 below. Of the remaining 63 participants, 34 were male and 29 were female.

3.2.2 Materials

The stimuli for this study consisted of 20 jpeg images of simple scenes generated using Google SketchUp. Each scene contained three objects; each object was either a sphere or a cube. The objects could also be either large or small and were one of two colours; scenes either contained blue and green objects, or red and yellow objects. The *target object*, to be described by the participant, was marked by a grey arrow pointing to it; the target was always located either directly in front of or on top of one of the other two objects. We will refer to this other related object as the *landmark*, although there is of course no guarantee that participants actually included it into the description as the ground object in a spatial relation. The third object, which we refer to as the *distractor*, was located either to the left or the right of the target and landmark objects.

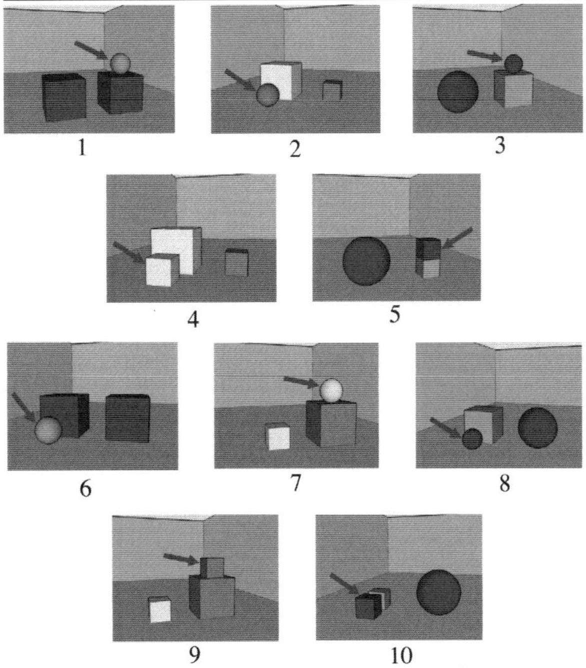

Figure 1: Trial Set 1: The five base configurations 1–5 and their counterparts 6–10 using the other type of target–landmark relation and orientation.

The 20 scenes are generated from five *base configurations*, differing in the type and size of the objects pictured. Figure 1 shows the five base configurations. They can be categorised by the length of the shortest possible description for the target object:

- in two of the base configurations it is possible to identify the target object using its type only;
- in one base configuration size alone would suf-

fice, although in line with past observations in the literature we would expect that type is always included as well;

- in one base configuration, colour and type are both necessary; and
- in the final base configuration, both size and colour are necessary, and again we would expect type to be included.

Importantly, there is no configuration in which the spatial relations between the objects are *required* in order to identify the target.

For each base configuration, we generated two scenes: in one scene, the target is located on top of the landmark object, and in the other, the target lies in front of the landmark. This allows us to investigate whether people prefer to use one type of spatial relation more than the other.

Five of the resulting 10 scenes were in the blue–green colour scheme, while the other five used red and yellow. The different colour schemes were an attempt to decrease the monotony of the task, so that we could show each participant more scenes. These 10 scenes, numbered 1 through 10, constituted our first trial set. A second trial set, with scenes numbered 11 through 20, was generated by producing the mirror image of each scene and using the opposite colour scheme. Mirroring the scenes had the same purpose as using the two different colour schemes. However, to be able to control any unwanted effect of these two variables we always used both variants.[1]

3.2.3 Procedure

On the experiment website, each participant was shown the scenes from one of the two trial sets in the order of the scene numbers. Under each scene, they had to complete the sentence *Please, pick up the ...* as if they were describing the object marked by the arrow to an onlooker.

To encourage the use of fully distinguishing referring expressions, participants were told that they had only one chance at describing the object. They were shown a sample scene for which they could provide an unrecorded (and unchecked) description. After being presented with all ten scenes in the trial, participants were asked to complete an exit questionnaire, which also gave them the option of having their data discarded, and asked for their opinion on whether the task became easier over time, and any other comments they might wish to make.

3.2.4 Data Processing

740 descriptions were elicited in the experiment. 10 of these were discarded in line with the participant's request, and 10 because the participant reported that they were colour-blind. After the data was cleaned and parsed, another 90 descriptions from 9 participants were discarded:

- One participant had consistently produced extremely long and complex descriptions using the ternary relation *between* and direct reference to the onlooker, the ground and parts of the objects: a typical example is *the red cube which rests on the ground and is between you and the yellow cube of equal size*. While these descriptions are interesting, in relation to the rest of the data they are such outliers that no real conclusions can be drawn from them.
- A further eight participants consistently used highly under-specified descriptions. We decided to discard the data from these participants since it seemed that they had not understood the need to provide a distinguishing description, rather than, for example, just indicating the type of the object.[2]

This resulted in a total of 630 referring expressions, with 30 for each scene in Trial Set 1 and 33 for each scene in Trial Set 2. We then applied some normalisation steps: the data was stripped of punctuation marks and other extraneous material (such as repetition of the *Please, pick up the*); in four cases, the dynamic spatial preposition *from* was deleted from descriptions such as *the green ball from on top of the blue cube*;[3] and spelling was normalised. The

[1] For brevity, where relevant we will use the form 'Scenes n+m' to refer to paired scenes across the two trial sets.

[2] Of course, underspecified descriptions are justified in many circumstances, and in real-life situations may even be necessary. However, the simple scenes used in this study do not fall into these classes.

[3] We are only interested in the static locative in these expressions; the use of the dynamic preposition is most likely due to the movement implied by the indicated picking-up action.

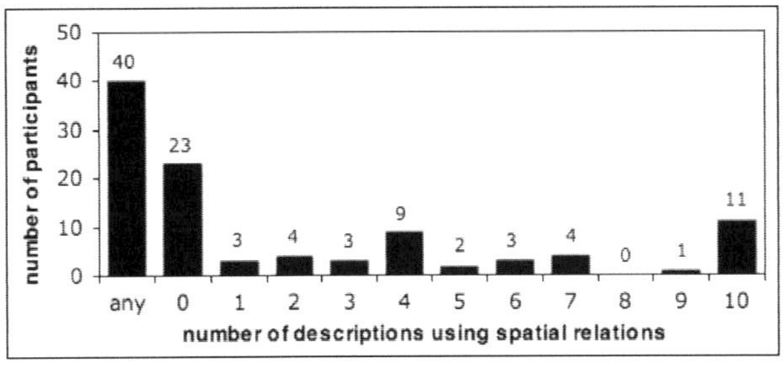

Figure 2: Number of participants who delivered n (0...10) relational descriptions.

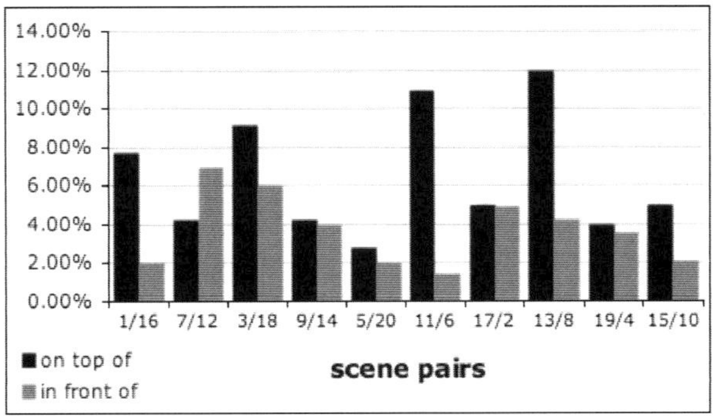

Figure 3: % of relational descriptions for each scene out of all relational descriptions produced by participants not using an exclusive strategy. Scenes are paired with their counterpart using the other target–landmark relation.

second object was stripped from comparatives such as *the smaller of the two green cubes* and converted to the form *the smaller green cube*, which in the context of our simple scenes is semantically equivalent.

3.3 Results

Over a third (231 or 36.6%) of the 630 descriptions in the resulting corpus use spatial relations despite the fact that relations were never necessary for the identification of the target. These 231 relational descriptions were produced by 40 (63.5%) of the 63 participants, while 23 (36.5%) of the participants never used spatial relations. This suggests that the use of relations is very much dependent on personal preference, a hypothesis that is further supported by the fact that 11 (i.e. over 25%) of the relation-using participants did so in *all* 10 referring expressions they delivered. Figure 2 shows the number of participants who produced exactly n descriptions containing at least one spatial relation, for n in the range $\{0 \ldots 10\}$.

From the above, we might hypothesise that some participants adopt a strategy of always using relational properties, and that others adopt a strategy of avoiding relational properties as much as possible. We further analysed the descriptions produced by participants who did *not* follow either of these two exclusive strategies to see how their choices varied across the different scenes; the spread is shown in Figure 3. Looking only at the descriptions produced by participants who sometimes, but not always, used spatial relations allows us to get a clearer view on which objects received most and least relational descriptions. This in turn affords an analysis of the impact the different features in the respective scenes have on the use of spatial relations.

41.7% of the remaining descriptions used relations. Interestingly, 63.6% of these relational descriptions were used for scenes where the target was located on top of the landmark object, while only 36.4% were from scenes where the target was in front of the landmark, suggesting that the use of the in-front-of relation may be relatively dispreferred.

Because the first scene always had the target on top of the landmark, this preference for using relational descriptions in on-top-of scenes might be due to a training effect that discourages people from using relations over time. However, if we do not take into account descriptions for the first 4 scenes of each trial set, this ratio is still large: 58.8% of the the remaining relational descriptions stemmed from scenes where the target was on top of the landmark, 41.2% of them from scenes with an on-top-of relation.

As expected, the orientation of the scenes and the colour scheme used did not have a significant impact on the use of spatial relations. For both these variables, the difference between values in use of relations was under 6 percentage points.

3.4 Discussion

We noted earlier that existing relation-handling referring expression generation algorithms generally disprefer relations and only add them to a description if absolutely necessary. This in essence mimics the behaviour of our participants who adopted the exclusive Never-Use-Relations strategy.[4] These algorithms therefore only represent slightly more than one third of the participants in our study.

The analysis of the descriptions given by people who did not follow one of the two exclusive strategies indicates that the distribution of relational descriptions over the scenes is not random. In addition to modelling exclusive strategies, then, we may also want to capture in an algorithm the reasons why referring expressions for some scenes are more likely to include spatial relations than others.

In the remainder of this section we consider the conclusions that can be drawn from our data regarding the factors that impact on the choice of whether to use spatial relations in a referring expression.

Spatial Relations Are Used Even When Unnecessary: The main observation that can be made is that even in very simple scenes, where locatives are not necessary to distinguish the target from the other objects present, people show a tendency to use spatial relations to describe a target object to an onlooker. This contradicts the prevailing approach to the use of relations in referring expression generation. It is important to bear in mind that the scenes used in this study were extremely simple and could easily be taken in at one glance; it seems likely that when faced with a more crowded scene containing more complex objects, the tendency to incorporate possibly unnecessary spatial relations into descriptions would increase.

Training Effect: Note in Figure 4 that the targets in Scenes 1+11 received a disproportionally high number of descriptions containing spatial relations. While this fact could be attributed to the similar features of the two scenes (they only differed in orientation and colour scheme), it is much more likely that this is due to Scenes 1 and 11 being the first scenes of the respective trial sets. The drop-off in relational descriptions from beginning to end of the trial sets almost certainly results from a training effect, where people realised over time that relations were not necessary in any of the scenes. If we only consider the first two scenes in each trial set, where no training effect has taken hold, we find that 36 of

[4]On the assumption that these participants would also resort to relations if they had to.

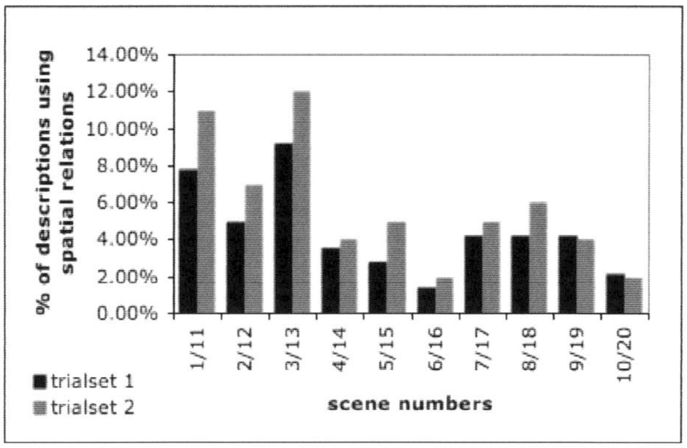

Figure 4: % of relational descriptions for each scene out of all relational descriptions produced by participants not using an exclusive strategy. Scenes are paired with their counterpart from the other trial set.

the 58 (62.1%) descriptions for these scenes use spatial relations. The presence of some kind of training effect was also reported in the exit questionnaire by half of the participants.

This training effect in itself is an interesting phenomenon. It suggests that people are much more likely to use spatial relations when they come anew to the task of identifying an object rather than when they are describing an object in a similar domain on a subsequent occasion.

Landmark Salience Encourages Use of Relations: Figure 4 shows that the highest spike in usage of spatial relations was recorded for Scenes 3+13; interestingly another, although much less pronounced, peak occurs for their counterpart scenes only differing in the type of target–landmark relation, 8+18.

These peaks cannot be explained by the training effect; in fact, they seem to be running contrary to it, indicating that some other reasonably strong factors are prompting the use of relations in these scenes.

Scenes 3, 8, 13, and 18 are the only scenes in which the landmark object is distinguishable from both other objects only by its type (cube) or its colour (see Figure 1). In addition, in each case the landmark is large resulting in high visual salience for the landmark. This in turn makes the relation to the landmark a salient feature of the target. The salience of the relation then causes people to add it to an already distinguishing description or even to prefer it over the use of absolute properties.

***on top of* Is Preferred over *in front of*:** Although these four scenes all share the same base set of objects, the usage of spatial relations is considerably higher for Scenes 3+13 than for 8+18. This could either be entirely due to the training effect, but may also be influenced by the only difference between these two scenes: in Scenes 3+13, the target sits on top of the landmark, while in Scenes 8+18 it is lying in front of the landmark. The overall comparison of the data for scenes featuring an on-top-of relation with that for scenes with an in-front-of relation suggests that this also is a factor. Even if we only take into account Scenes 5–10 and 15–20, where we might expect the effect of training to have stabilised, people were almost one and a half times more likely to use a relation in a scene where the target was on top of rather than in front of the landmark (30 vs. 21 of the 111 relational descriptions for those scenes from people not using an exclusive strategy).

This finding is in accordance with Kelleher and Kruijff's (2006) approach of preferring topological spatial relations over projective ones. The semantics of projective spatial relations, such as *in front of*, depend on a frame of reference defining directions from some origin (in this case the landmark object), while topological relations, such as *on top of*, are semantically defined by relations such as intersection, containedness, and contiguity, and pose a lighter cognitive load on both discourse partners (see Tenbrink (2005) for an overview).

The impact of landmark salience and the preference for the on-top-of relation can also explain the low use of spatial relations for Scenes 4+14, 6+16 and 10+20 (see Figure 1). In these scenes it is very hard or even impossible to distinguish the landmark from the other objects using only non-relational properties, and the target is located in front of rather than on top of it. The possibility of describing the target in Scenes 6+16 only by its type or colour may be the reason for the extremely low usage of spatial relations in these scenes.

4 Conclusions

4.1 Consequences for Algorithm Development

We noted above that some participants adopted a Never-Use-Relations strategy, and some adopted an Always-Use-Relations stratgy. This might be modelled by the use of a parameter akin to the the Risky/Cautious distinction proposed by Carletta (1992) in her work on references in the Map Task corpus. The effect of this parameter in the context of the Incremental Algorithm would be to put spatial relations either at the front or at the end of the preference list of properties; this would ensure that they are either considered first for inclusion into a referring expression, or only when the other properties of the target do not suffice.

A more interesting problem is how to model the apparent preference of our participants to use relations in some scenes more than in others. Following our discussion above, the factors that lead to this preference seem to include the folllowing:

- the ease with which a potential landmark can be distinguished from the other objects in the scene;
- the visual salience of a potential landmark (in our case its size);
- the type of spatial relation between the target and a potential landmark; and
- the ease with which the target can be described without the use of spatial relations.

The visual salience of the target object is likely to also play a role; however, this was not tested in the current study, since all target objects were small.

Factors like these can be incorporated into a referring expression generation algorithm by taking them into account in the step that calculates which property of the target object should next be considered for inclusion in the referring expression. Instead of using a static preference list over all possible domain properties, a preference score for each property needs to be determined 'at run time'. Such a dynamic approach would also allow the consideration of the discourse salience of a property (perhaps due to its recent use in another referring expression), as well as the consideration that some properties are more likely to be used in combination with other specific properties. An example of this phenomenon is the combination of the property *hair-colour* with either *has-hair* or *has-beard* in the TUNA data. If *hair-colour* is included in a referring expression, at least one of the other two properties is present as well.

The preference scores of the properties in a referring expression under construction would then combine into an adequacy score for the overall description, similar to Edmonds' (1994) concept of the speaker's confidence that a referring expression suffices for the communicative task at hand.

4.2 Future Work

As a next step, we aim to run experiments to separately confirm the impact that each of the different factors listed in Section 3.4 has on the use of spatial relations in referring expressions. In parallel, we will evaluate the human-produced descriptions in task-based evaluation schemes to assess whether the use of relations in certain categories of scenes is advantageous for an onlooker trying to identify the object that is being referred to.

Ultimately, the aim of this research is to develop an algorithm that incorporates the findings from both types of studies into the generation of referring expressions. Such an algorithm should not simply mimic the behaviour that our participants have displayed during the production experiment, but also take into account the findings of the task-based study, to ensure both naturalness and usefulness for the listener.

References

Anja Belz and Sebastian Varges. 2007. Generation of repeated references to discourse entities. In *Proceedings of the 11th European Workshop on Natural Language Generation*, pages 9–16.

Susan E. Brennan and Herbert H. Clark. 1996. Conceptual pacts and lexical choice in conversation. *Journal of Experimental Psychology: Learning, Memory, and Cognition*, 22:1482–1493.

Donna K. Byron and Eric Fosler-Lussier. 2006. The OSU Quake 2004 corpus of two-party situated problem-solving dialogs. In *Proceedings of the 15th Language Resources and Evaluation Conference*.

Jean C. Carletta. 1992. *Risk-taking and Recovery in Task-Oriented Dialogue*. Ph.D. thesis, University of Edinburgh.

Herbert H. Clark and Deanna Wilkes-Gibbs. 1986. Referring as a collaborative process. *Cognition*, 22(1):1–39.

Robert Dale and Ehud Reiter. 1995. Computational interpretations of the Gricean maxims in the generation of referring expressions. *Cognitive Science*, 19(2):233–263.

Robert Dale. 1989. Cooking up referring expressions. In *Proceedings of the 27th Annual Meeting of the Association for Computational Linguistics*, Vancouver, BC.

Philip G. Edmonds. 1994. Collaboration on reference to objects that are not mutually known. In *Proceedings of the 15th International Conference on Computational Linguistics*, Kyoto, Japan.

Claire Gardent. 2002. Generating minimal definite descriptions. In *Proceedings of the 40th Annual Meeting of the Association for Computational Linguistics*, Philadelphia, USA.

Albert Gatt and Kees van Deemter. 2006. Conceptual coherence in the generation of referring expressions. In *Proceedings of the 21st COLING and the 44th ACL Conference*, Sydney, Australia.

Albert Gatt, Ielka van der Sluis, and Kees van Deemter. 2007. Evaluating algorithms for the generation of referring expressions using a balanced corpus. In *Proceedings of the 11th European Workshop on Natural Language Generation*, pages 49–56.

Sarah Haywood, Martin J. Pickering, and Holly P. Branigan. 2003. Co-operation and co-ordination in the production of noun phrases. In *Proceedings of the 25th Annual Meeting of the Cognitive Science Society*, pages 533–538, Boston, MA.

Helmut Horacek. 2004. On referring to sets of objects naturally. In *Proceedings of the 3rd International Conference on Natural Language Generation*, pages 70–79, Brockenhurst, UK.

Pamela W. Jordan and Marilyn A. Walker. 2005. Learning content selection rules for generating object descriptions in dialogue. *Journal of Artificial Intelligence Research*, 24:157–194.

John Kelleher and Geert-Jan M. Kruijff. 2005. A context-dependent model of proximity in physically situated environments. In *Proceedings of the 2nd ACL-SIGSEM Workshop on The Linguistic Dimensions of Prepositions and their Use in Computational Linguistics Formalisms and Applications*, Colchester, U.K.

John Kelleher and Geert-Jan M. Kruijff. 2006. Incremental generation of spatial referring expressions in situated dialog. In *Proceedings of the 21st COLING and the 44th ACL Conference*, Sydney, Australia.

Emiel Krahmer and Mariët Theune. 2002. Efficient context-sensitive generation of referring expressions. In Kees van Deemter and Rodger Kibble, editors, *Information Sharing: Reference and Presupposition in Language Generation and Interpretation*, pages 223–264. CSLI Publications, Stanford, CA.

Cécile Paris, Donia Scott, Nancy Green, Kathy McCoy, and David McDonald. 2007. Desiderata for evaluation of natural language generation. In Robert Dale and Michael White, editors, *Proceedings of the Workshop on Shared Tasks and Comparative Evaluation in Natural Language Generation*, pages 9–15, Arlington, VA.

Rosemary Stevenson. 2002. The role of salience in the production of referring expressions: A psycholinguistic perspective. In Kees van Deemter and Rodger Kibble, editors, *Information Sharing: Reference and Presupposition in Language Generation and Interpretation*. CSLI, Stanford.

Thora Tenbrink. 2005. Semantics and application of spatial dimensional terms in English and German. Technical Report Series of the Transregional Collaborative Research Center SFB/TR 8 Spatial Cognition, No. 004-03/2005, Universities of Bremen and Freiburg, Germany.

Henry S. Thompson, Anne Anderson, Ellen Gurman Bard, Gwyneth Doherty-Sneddon, Alison Newlands, and Cathy Sotillo. 1993. The HCRC map task corpus: natural dialogue for speech recognition. In *Proceedings of the 1993 Workshop on Human Language Technology*, pages 25–30, Princeton, New Jersey.

Kees van Deemter. 2006. Generating referring expressions that involve gradable properties. *Computational Linguistics*, 32(2):195–222.

Ielka van der Sluis and Emiel Krahmer. 2004. The influence of target size and distance on the production of speech and gesture in multimodal referring expressions. In *Proceedings of the 8th International Conference on Spoken Language Processing (INTERSPEECH 2004)*, Jeju, Korea.

Sebastian Varges. 2005. Spatial descriptions as referring expressions in the maptask domain. In *Proceedings of the 10th European Workshop On Natural Language Generation*, Aberdeen, UK.

Jette Viethen and Robert Dale. 2006. Algorithms for generating referring expressions: Do they do what people do? In *Proceedings of the 4th International Conference on Natural Language Generation*, pages 63–70, Sydney, Australia, July.

Using Tactical NLG to Induce Affective States: Empirical Investigations

Ielka van der Sluis
Computing Science,
University of Aberdeen
i.v.d.sluis@abdn.ac.uk

Chris Mellish
Computing Science
University of Aberdeen
c.mellish@abdn.ac.uk

Abstract

This paper reports on attempts at Aberdeen[1] to measure the effects on readers' emotions of positively and negatively "slanted" texts with the same basic message. The "slanting" methods could be implemented in an (NLG) system. We discuss a number of possible reasons why the studies were unable to show clear, statistically significant differences between the effects of the different texts.

1 Introduction: Affective NLG

"Affective NLG" has been defined as "NLG that relates to, arises from or deliberately influences emotions or other non-strictly rational aspects of the Hearer" (De Rosis and Grasso, 2000). Although this term could cover a range of types of NLG, in practice, a lot of work on affective NLG emphasises the *depiction* of emotional states/personalities (Oberlander and Gill, 2004), rather than the *induction* of emotional effects on readers. However, there are many applications where the intention is, for instance, to motivate or discourage, as well as to inform.

How can NLG influence the emotions of its readers? It is apparent that strategical decisions ("what to say") can make a difference on how a reader responds emotionally to a text. If you tell someone good news, they will be happier than if you tell them bad news. On the other hand, much of NLG is concerned with tactical decisions ("how to say it"), and the affective relevance of these is less clear. Can tactical NLG choices be used to achieve goals in terms of the reader's emotions? In the area of affective computing, there has been some work on assessing the effects of interfaces on the emotions of their users, e.g. on their frustration levels (Prendinger et al., 2006) or their feelings of support/trust (Lee et al., 2007). In NLG there has been some work on task-based evaluation cf. STOP (Reiter et al., 2003) and SKILLSUM (Williams and Reiter, forthcoming). However, to our knowledge, there has not yet been any demonstration of tactical decisions making a difference on a reader's emotions.

The paper is organised as follows: Section 2 introduces the tactical choices we are studying, our test texts and a text validation study. Section 3 discusses a pilot study that was conducted to try out potential psychological measurement methods. Section 4 presents a full study to measure the affect of text invoked in readers. The paper closes with a discussion of the findings and their possible implications.

2 Tactical Choices

We decided that a safe way to start would be to choose primitive positive versus negative emotions (such as sadness, joy, disappointment, surprise, anger), as opposed to more complex emotions related to trust, persuasion, advice, reassurance. Therefore we focus here on alternatives that give a text a positive or negative "slant". These could be applied by an NLG system whose message has "positive" and "negative" aspects, where "positive" information conjures up scenarios that are pleasant and acceptable to the reader, makes them feel happy and cooperative etc. and "negative" information conjures up unpleasant or threatening situations and

[1] Ielka van der Sluis is now at the Department of Computer Science, Trinity College, Dublin

so makes them feel more unhappy, confused etc. For instance, (DeRosis et al., 1999) discuss generating instructions on how to take medication which have to both address positive aspects ('this will make you feel better if you do the following') and also negative ones ('this may produce side-effects, which I have to tell you about by law'). An NLG system in such a domain could make itself popular by only mentioning the positive information, but then it could leave itself open to later criticism (or litigation) if by doing so it clearly misrepresented the true situation. Although it may be inappropriate grossly to misrepresent the provided message, there are more subtle (tactical) ways to "colour" or "slant" the presentation of the message in order to emphasise either the positive or the negative aspects.

We assume that the message to be conveyed is a simple set of propositions, each classified in an application-dependent way as having positive or negative *polarity* according to whether the reader is likely to welcome it or be unhappy about it in the context of the current message.[2] In general, this classification could, for instance, be derived from the information that a planning system has about which propositions support which goals (e.g. to stay healthy one needs to eat healthy food). We also assume that a possible phrasing for a proposition has a *magnitude*, which indicates the degree of impact it has. This is independent of the polarity. We will not need to actually measure magnitudes, but when we make claims that one wording of a proposition has a smaller magnitude than another we indicate this with <. For instance, we would claim that usually:

"a few rats died" < *"many rats died"*

Thus we claim that "a few rats died" has less impact than "many rats died", whether or not rats dying is considered a good thing (i.e. whether the polarity is positive or negative). In general, an NLG system can manipulate the magnitude of wordings of the propositions it expresses, to indicate its own (subjective) view of their importance. In order to slant a text positively, it can express positive polarity propositions in ways that have high magnitudes and negative polarity propositions in ways that have low magnitudes. The opposite applies for negative slanting. Thus, for instance, in an application where it is bad for rats to die, expressing a given proposition by "a few rats died" would be giving more of a positive slant, whereas saying "many rats died" would be slanting it more negatively.

Whenever one words a proposition in different ways, it can be claimed that a (perhaps subtle) change of meaning is involved. In an example like this, therefore, perhaps the content of the message changes between the two wordings and so this is in fact a strategic alternation. In this work, we take the view that it is legal to make changes that relate to the writer's attitude to the material of the text. The difference between "a few rats" and "many rats" is (in our view) that the number of rats is either less than or more than *the writer would have expected.* We can therefore choose between these alternatives by varying the writer, not the underlying message. Another reason for considering this choice as tactical is that in an NLG system, it would likely be implemented somewhere late in the "pipeline". Our claim that pairs such as this can appropriately describe the same event is also supported by our text validation experiments described below.

2.1 Test Texts

We started by composing by hand two messages containing mainly negative and positive polarity propositions respectively. The negative message tells the reader that a cancer-causing colouring substance is found in some foods available in the supermarkets. The positive message tells the reader that foods that contain Scottish water contain a mineral which helps to fight cancer. The first paragraph of both texts states that there is a substance found in consumer products that has an effect on people's health and it addresses the way in which this fact is handled by the relevant authorities. The second paragraph of the text elaborates on the products that contain the substance and the third paragraph explains in what way the substance can affect people's health.

To study the effects of different wordings, for each text a positive and a negative version was produced by slanting propositions in either a positive or a negative way. This resulted in four texts in total, two texts with a negative message one positively

[2] Note that this sense of "polarity" is not the same as the one used to describe "negative polarity items" in Linguistics

and one negatively phrased (NP and NN), and two texts with a positive message one positively and one negatively verbalised (PP and PN). To maximise the impact aimed for, various slanting techniques were used by hand as often as possible without loss of believability (this was assessed by the intuition of the researchers). The positive and negative texts were slanted in parallel as far as possible, that is in both texts similar sentences were adapted so that they emphasised the positive or the negative aspects of the message. The linguistic variation used in the texts was algorithmically reproducible and the techniques are illustrated below. A number of these were suggested by work on "framing" in Psychology (Moxey and Sanford, 2000; Teigen and Brun, 2003). Indeed, that work also suggests further variations that could be manipulated, for instance, the choice between using numerical and non-numerical values for expressing quantities.

SLANTING EXAMPLES FOR THE NEGATIVE MESSAGE

Here it is assumed that recalls of products, risks of danger etc. involve negative polarity propositions. Therefore negative slanting will amongst other things choose high magnitude realisations for these.

Techniques involving adjectives and adverbs:

- "*A recall*" < "*A large-scale recall*" of infected merchandise was triggered

Techniques involving quantification:

- Sausages, tomato sauce and lentil soup are "*some*" < "*only some*" of the affected items

Techniques involving a change in polarity

Proposition expressed with positive polarity:

- Tests on monkeys revealed that as many as "*40 percent*" of the animals infected with this substance "*did not develop any tumors*"

Proposition expressed with negative polarity:

- Tests on monkeys revealed that as many as "*60 percent*" of the animals infected with this substance "*developed tumors*".

Techniques manipulating rhetorical prominence

Positive slant:

- "So your health is at risk, but every possible thing is being done to tackle this problem"

Negative slant:

- "So although every possible thing is being done to tackle this problem, your health is at risk"

SLANTING EXAMPLES FOR THE POSITIVE MESSAGE

Here it is assumed that killing cancer, promoting Scottish water etc. involve positive polarity propositions. Therefore positive slanting will amongst other things choose high magnitude realisations for these.

Techniques involving adjectives and adverbs:

- Neolite is a "*detoxifier*" < "*powerful detoxifier*" preventing cancer cells

Techniques involving quantification:

- "*Cancer-killing Neolite*" < "*Substantial amounts of cancer-killing Neolite*" was found in Scottish drinking water

Techniques involving a change in polarity

Proposition expressed with negative polarity:

- A study on people with mostly stage 4 cancer revealed that as many as "*40 percent*" of the patients that were given Neolite "*still had cancer*" at the end of the study.

Proposition expressed with positive polarity:

- A study on people with mostly stage 4 cancer revealed that as many as "*60 percent*" of the patients that were given Neolite "*were cancer free*" at the end of the study.

Techniques manipulating rhetorical prominence

Negative slant:

- "Neolite is certainly advantageous for your health, but it is not a guaranteed cure for, or defence against cancer"

Positive slant:

- "So Although Neolite is not a guaranteed cure for, or defence against cancer, it is certainly advantageous for your health"

2.2 Text validation

To check our intuitions on the effects of the textual variation between the four texts described above, a text validation experiment was conducted in which 24 colleagues participated. The participants were randomly assigned to one of two groups (i.e. P and N), group P was asked to validate 23 sentence pairs from the positive message (PN versus PP) and group N was asked to validate 17 sentence pairs from the negative message (NN versus NP). Each pair consisted of two sentences intended to differ in their magnitude but to be possible realisations of the same underlying content (as in the examples in the last section). Both the N and the P group sentence pairs included four filler pairs. The participants in group

P were asked which of the two sentences in each pair they thought most positive in the context of the message about the positive effects of Scottish water. The participants in group N were asked which of the two sentences in each pair they found most alarming in the context of the message about the contamination of food available for consumption. All participants were asked to indicate if they thought the sentences in each pair could be used to report on the same event (i.e. represented purely tactical variations).

Results in the N group indicated that in 89.75% of the cases participants agreed with our intuitions about which one of the two sentences was most alarming. On average, per sentence pair 1.08 of the 12 participants judged the sentences differently than what we expected. In 7 of the 13 sentence pairs (17 - 4 fillers) participants unanimously agreed with our intuitions. In the other sentence pairs 1 to, maximally, 4 participants did not share our point of view. In the two cases in which four participants did not agree with or were unsure about the difference we expected, we adapted our texts. One of these cases was the pair:

> "*just 359*" infected products have been withdrawn < "*as many as 359*" infected products have been withdrawn "*already*"

We thought that the latter of the two would be more alarming (and correspond to negative slanting) because it is a bad thing if products have to be withdrawn (negative polarity). However, some participants felt that products being withdrawn was a good thing (positive polarity), because it meant that something was being done to tackle the problem, in which case the latter would be imposing a positive slant. As a consequence of the validation results, it was decided to 'neutralise' this sentence in both the NP and NN versions of the text to "359 infected products have been withdrawn". Overall, in 78.85% of the cases the participants thought that both sentences in a pair could report on the same event.

Results in the P group were similar. In 82.46% of the cases participants agreed with our intuitions about which one of the two sentences was most positive. In two cases, minor changes were made to make the texts clearer. Overall, in 86.84 % of the cases the participants thought that both sentences in a pair could report on the same event.

3 Pilot Study: Testing Psychological Methods to Measure Emotions

3.1 Psychological Methods

The next step was to determine plausible methods to measure the emotional effect of a text. There are two broad ways of measuring the emotions of human subjects – physiological methods and self-reporting. Because of the technical complications and the conflicting results to be found in the literature, we opted to ignore physiological measurement methods and to investigate self-reporting. To measure these emotions we decided do a pilot study to try out three well-established methods that are used frequently in the field of psychology, the Russel Affect Grid (Russell et al., 1989), the Positive and Negative Affect Scale (PANAS) (Watson et al., 1988), and the Self Assessment Manikin (SAM) (Lang, 1980). The PANAS test is a scale consisting of 20 words and phrases (10 for positive affect and 10 for negative affect) that describe feelings and emotions. Participants read the terms and indicate to what extent they experience(d) the emotions indicated by each of them using a five point scale ranging from (1) very slightly/not at all, (2) a little, (3) moderately, (4) quite a bit to (5) extremely. A total score for positive affect is calculated by simply adding the scores for the positive terms, and similarly for negative affect. The Russel Affect Grid and the SAM test both assess valence and arousal on a nine-point scale.

3.2 Method: Subjects, Stimuli and Setting

Our pilot study aimed to test a general experiment set up, and to help us find the most promising of the above methods to measure emotions evoked by text. 24 colleagues and students (other than the ones involved in the text validation experiments) participated as subjects in this pilot study in which they were asked to fill in a few forms about how they felt after reading a particular text. All, except three, were native or fluent speakers of English and none was familiar with the purposes of the study. The subjects were divided in two groups of 12 subjects each, and were asked to fill in some questionnaires and to read a text about a general topic with a particular consequence for the addressee. For this experiment, just the negative message texts illustrated in the previous section were used (i.e. "some of your food contains a substance that causes cancer"). One group of subjects, the NP-group, was given this negative message verbalised in a neutral way giving the impression that although there was a problem every possible thing was being done to tackle it. The other group, the NN-group, was given the same negative message presented in a negative way implying that although many things were being done to tackle the problem, there still was a problem. We expected that after the subjects had read the text, the emotions of the subjects in the NN-group would be more negative than the emotions of the subjects in the NP-group. We also expected the subjects in the NN-group to be more strongly affected than the subjects in the NP-group.

For ethical reasons, both in this experiment and the following one, the main experimental procedure was followed by a debriefing session in which the subjects were informed that they had been deceived by the texts presented and during which it was possible to provide support for subjects if their emotional reactions had been especially strong.

3.3 Results and Discussion

Overall, t-test results failed to find significant differences between the the NN-group and the NP-group for any of the emotion measurement methods used. The Russel test, which was taken before the participants read the test text[3], indicated that the participants in the NP group might be feeling slightly more positive and less aroused than the participants in the NN group. The results for the PANAS test, taken after the participants read the test text, show that the NP group might be feeling a little bit more positive that the NN group about the content of the text they just read. The Sam test, which the participants were also asked to fill out with respect to their feelings after reading the test text, indicates that the NP group might be feeling less positive and more aroused than the NN group.

How to interpret the outcomes of the pilot study? There are several factors that could have caused the lack of significant results. One reason could be that the differences between the NP and NN texts were not large enough. Yet another reason could be that the people that took part in the study were not really involved in the topic of the text or the consequences of the message. When looking at the three emotion measurement methods used, some participants did indicate that the SAM and Russel tests were difficult to interpret. Also some participants showed signs of boredom or disinterest while rating the PANAS terms, which were all printed on one A4 page; some just marked all the terms as 'slightly/not at all' by circling them all in one go instead of looking at the terms separately. Also, some participants indicated that they found it difficult to distinguish particular terms. For example the PANAS test includes both 'scared' and 'afraid'. As a consequence, there were several things that could be improved and adjusted before going ahead with a full scale experiment in which all four texts were tested.

[3]Ideally we would have presented all tests both before and after the text was read, but we believed that this would overload the subjects and lead to distorted results.

4 Full Study: Measuring Emotional Effects of Text

This section presents a full scale experiment conducted to assess the emotional effect invoked in readers of a text. The experimental set up attempts to take into account the results found in the pilot study presented in the previous section. However, there were obviously a number of things that could be improved after this study, and so many things were changed without any direct evidence that they would improve the experiment. Below the method, data processing and results are presented and discussed.

4.1 Method: subjects, stimuli and experimental setting

Based on the pilot results, the setup of this study was adapted in a number of ways. For instance, we decided to increase the likelihood of finding measurable emotional effects of text by targeting a group of subjects other than our sceptical colleagues. Because it has been shown that young women are highly interested in health issues and especially health risks (Finucane et al., 2000), we decided on young female students as our participants.

In total 60 female students took part in the experiment and were paid a small fee for their efforts. The average age of the participants was about 20.57 (std. 2.41) years old. The participants were evenly and randomly distributed over the four texts (i.e. NN, NP, PN, PP) tested in this study, that is 15 participants per group. The texts were tailored to the subject group, by for example mentioning food products that are typically consumed by students as examples in the texts and by specifically mentioning young females as targets of the consequences of the message. On a more general level, the texts were adapted to a Scottish audience by, for instance, mentioning Scottish products and a Scottish newspaper as the source of the article. Although the results of the pilot study did not indicate that the texts were not believable, we thought that the presentation of the texts could be improved by making them look more like newspaper articles, with a date and a source indication.

To enhance the experimental setting, the emotion measurement methods were better tailored to the task. The SAM test as well as the Russel Grid were removed from the experiment set up, because they caused confusion for the participants in the pilot study. Another reason for removing these tests was to reduce the number of questions to be answered by the participants and to avoid bored answering. For the latter reason, also a previously used reduced version of the PANAS test (Mackinnon et al., 1999) was used, in which the number of emotion terms that participants had to rate for themselves was decreased from 20 to 10. This PANAS set, consisting of five positive (i.e. alert, determined, enthusiastic, excited, inspired) and five negative terms (i.e. afraid, scared, nervous, upset, distressed), was used both before and after participants read the test text. Before the participants read the test text, they were asked to indicate how they felt at that point in time using the PANAS terms. After the participants read the test text, they were asked to rate the affect terms with respect to their feelings about the text. Note that this is different from asking them about their current feelings, because we wanted to emphasise that we wanted to know about their emotions related to the content of the text they just read and not about their feelings in general. We expected that the reduced PANAS test would produce reliable results because of its previous successful use. Whereas in the pilot study each test was handled individually, the PANAS terms were now interleaved with other questions about recall and opinions to further avoid boredom.

4.2 Hypotheses

In this full study four texts were tested on four different groups of subjects. Two groups read the positive message (PP-group and PN-group) two groups read the negative message (NN-group and NP-group). Of the two groups that read the positive message, we expected the positive emotions of the participants that read the positive version of this message (PP-group) to be stronger than the positive emotions of the participants that read the neutral/negative version of this message (PN-group). Of the two groups that read the negative message, we expected the participants that read the negative version of this message (NN-group) to be more negative than the participants that read the positive version of the message (NP-group).

4.3 Results

Overall, participants in this study were highly interested in the experiment and in the text they were asked to read. Participants that read the positive message, about the benefits of Scottish water, appeared very enthusiastic and expressed disappointment when they read the debriefing from which they learned that the story contained no truth. Similarly, participants that read the negative message expressed anger and fear in their comments on the experiment and showed relief when the debriefing told them that the story on food poisoning was completely made up for the purposes of the experiment. Only a few participants that read a version of the negative message commented that they had got used to the fact that there was often something wrong with food and were therefore less scared. Table 1 shows some descriptives that underline these impressions. For instance, on a 5-point scale the participants rated the texts they read more than moderately interesting (average of *po-i* = 3.74). They also found the text informative (average of *inform* = 3.82) and noted that it contained new information (average of *new* = 4.05). These are surprisingly positive figures when we consider that the participants indicated only an average interest in food (average of

	PN	PP	NN	NP
pr-i	2.47(1.13)	3.07(1.03)	3.00(.85)	3.00(1.25)
inf	3.87(.83)	3.80(.94)	3.67(1.05)	3.93(.70)
pos	3.93(.96)	4.27(1.03)	1.67(.98)	1.67(.97)
neg	1.53(.64)	1.27(5.94)	4.07(1.22)	3.53(1.19)
new	4.13(1.18)	4.53(.64)	3.87(1.30)	3.67(1.59)
po-i	3.67(.82)	3.80(.78)	3.67(.72)	3.80(1.01)

Table 1: Means and Standard deviations (between brackets) for the PN, PP, NP and NN texts for various variables: *pr-i* interest in food before reading the text, the *inf*ormativeness of the message, the *pos*itive or *neg*ative polarity of the message, *new* information and the *po-i* post interest in the message. All measured on a 5-point Scale: 1 = not at all, . . ., 5 = extremely.

pr-i = 2.89) before they read the test text. The participants that read the negative messages (NN and NP) recognised that the message was negative (cf. *pos* and *neg* in Table 1). Moreover, the NN-group rated the text more negatively than the NP-group (4.07 vs 3.53). The participants that read the positive message found that they had read a positive message. The PP-group rated their text slightly more positive than the PN-group rated theirs.

The bar chart presented in Figure 1 illustrates the results of the PANAS questionnaire after reading the texts. In terms of the differences in message content (P* vs N*), there is a difference between the ratings of the negative terms, which is as expected. However, there is no significant difference for the positive terms, which were rated fairly similarly for all groups. Also, contrary to what was expected, the rating of the negative PANAS terms by both N* groups is lower than their rating of the positive terms. The hoped-for results for the positive/negative slanting are also not forthcoming - t-tests show no significant differences between the PN-group and the PP-group and no significant differences between the NN-group and the NP-group. All mean ratings stay far below 3, the 'moderate' average of the scale. When looking at these results in more detail, it appears that, of the positive PANAS terms, only 'excited' and 'inspired' had a higher mean for the positively worded message when comparing the positive and the negative version of the positive message (PP and PN). When comparing the positive and the negative version of the negative message (NP vs NN), as expected, the NN-group has lower means for all 5 positive terms than the NP group.

From this study various conclusions can be

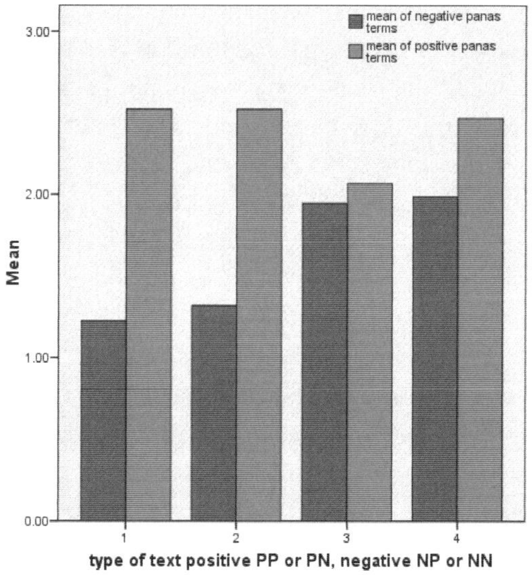

Figure 1: Positive and negative PANAS means after the Participants read the test text.

drawn. First of all, from the fact that only the lower half of the 5-point PANAS scale was used it can be concluded that the participants in this study seem to have difficulties with reporting on their emotions. This was the case both before and after the test text was read. Furthermore, participants seem to have a preference for reporting their positive emotions and focus less on their negative emotions. This can be inferred from the fact that the negative PANAS terms of the PP-group and the PN-group were lower than the means of the negative PANAS terms of the NN-group and the NP-group, but all groups had about the same means for the positive PANAS terms. The inference that self-reporting of emotions is troublesome is also indicated by the fact that the participants of this full study seemed highly interested and involved in the experiment and in what they read in the experiment texts. The participants generally believed the story they read and they expressed disappointment or relief when they were told the truth after the experiment. In addition, the descriptives in Table 1 show that participants generally correctly identified the text they read as either positive or negative. Note that in this respect the more fine-grained differences between the PP-group and the PN-group as well as the differences between the NN-group and the NP-group also confirm our expectations.

5 Conclusion and Discussion

This paper presented our efforts to measure differences in emotional effects invoked in readers. These efforts were based on our assumption that the wording used to present a particular proposition matters in how the message is received. Participants' judgements of the negative or positive nature of a text (in both the text validation and in the full study) are in accord with our predictions. In terms of *reflective analysis* of the text, therefore, participants behave as we expected. Although we strongly emphasised that we were interested in emotions with respect to the test text, our attempts to measure the *emotional effects* invoked in readers caused by tactical text differences did, however, not produce any significant results.

There are several reasons that may have played a role in this. It may be that the emotion measuring methods we tried are not fine-grained enough to measure the emotions that were invoked by the texts. As mentioned above, participants only used part of the PANAS scale and seemed to be reluctant to record their emotions (especially negative ones). Other ways of recording levels of emotional response that are more fine-grained than a 5-point scale, such as magnitude estimation (Bard et al., 1996), might be called for here. Carrying out experiments with even more participants might reveal patterns that are obscured by noise in the current study, but this would be expensive.

Alternatively, it could be that the differences between the versions of the messages are just too subtle and/or that there is not enough text for these subtle differences to produce measurable effects. Indeed, we are not aware of PANAS being used to assess purely textual effects before. Perhaps it is necessary to immerse participants more fully in slanted text in order to really affect them differently. Or perhaps more extreme versions of slanting could be found. Perhaps indeed the main way in which NLG can achieve effects on emotions is through appropriate content determination (strategy), rather than through lexical or presentation differences (tactics).

Another reason could still be a lack of involvement of the participants of the study. Although the participants of the full study indicated their enthusiasm for the study as well as their interest in the topic and the message, they may have felt that the news did not affect them too much, because they considered themselves as responsible people when it comes to health and food issues. We are designing a follow up experiment in which, to increase the reader's involvement, a feedback task is used, where participants play a game or answer some questions after which they receive feedback on their performance. The study will aim to measure the emotional effects of slanting this feedback text in a positive or a negative way. As in such a feedback situation the test text is directly related to the participants' own performance, we expect an increased involvement and stronger emotions.

As argued above, the results of our study seem to indicate that self-reporting of emotions is difficult. This could be because participants do not like to show their emotions, because the emotions invoked by what they read were just not very strong or because they do not have good conscious access to their emotions. Although self-reporting is widely used in Psychology, it could be that participants are not (entirely) reporting their true emotions, and that maybe this matters more when effects are likely to be subtle. In all of these situations, the solution could be to use additional measuring methods (e.g. physiological methods), and to check if the results of such methods can strengthen the results of the questionnaires. Another option is to use an objective observer during the experiment (e.g. videotaping the participants and observing the duration of smiles or frowns) to judge whether the subject is affected.

Yet another possibility would be only to measure emotional effects via performance on a task that is known to be facilitated by particular emotions. For instance, one could use the methods of (Carenini and Moore, 2000) to measure persuasiveness of different textual realisations that may induce emotions.

Acknowledgments

This work was supported by the EPSRC grant 'Affecting people with natural language' (EP/E011764/1) and also in part by Science Foundation Ireland under a CSET grant (NGL/CSET). We would like to thank the people who contributed to this study, most notably Louise Phillips, Emiel Krahmer, Linda Moxey, Graeme Ritchie, Judith Masthoff, Albert Gatt and Kees van Deemter.

References

E. G. Bard, D. Robertson, and A. Sorace. 1996. Magnitude estimation of linguistic acceptability. *Language*, 72(1):32–68.

G. Carenini and J. D. Moore. 2000. An empirical study of the influence of argument conciseness on argument effectiveness. In *Proceedings of the 38th annual meeting of the Association for Computational Linguistics*.

F. DeRosis, F. Grasso, and D. Berry. 1999. Refining instructional text generation after evaluation. *Artificial Intelligence in Medicine*, 17(1):1–36.

M. Finucane, P. Slovic, C. Mertz, J. Flynn, and T. Satterfield. 2000. Gender, race, and perceived risk: the 'white male' effect. *Health, Risk & Society*, 2(2):159 – 172.

P. Lang, 1980. *Technology in Mental Health Care Delivery Systems*, chapter Behavioral Treatment and Biobehavioral Assessment: Computer Applications, page 119 137. Norwood, NJ: Ablex.

J.-E. Lee, C. Nass, S. Brave, Y. Morishima, H. Nakajima, and R. Yamada. 2007. The case for caring co-learners: The effects of a computer-mediated co-learner agent on trust and learning. *Journal of Communication*.

A. Mackinnon, A. Jorm, H. Christensen, A. Korten, P. Jacomb, and B. Rodgers. 1999. A short form of the positive and negative affect schedule: evaluation of factorial validity and invariance across demographic variables in a community sample. *Personality and Individual Differences*, 27(3):405–416.

L. Moxey and A. Sanford. 2000. Communicating quantities: A review of psycholinguistic evidence of how expressions determine perspectives. *Applied Cognitive Psychology*, 14(3):237–255.

J. Oberlander and A. Gill. 2004. Individual differences and implicit language: Personality, parts-of-speech and pervasiveness. In *Proceedings of the 26th Annual Conference of the Cognitive Science Society*.

Helmut Prendinger, Christian Becker, and Mitsuru Ishizuka. 2006. A study in users' physiological response to an empathic interface agent. *International Journal of Humanoid Robotics*, 3(3):371–391.

E. Reiter, R. Robertson, and L. Osman. 2003. Lessons from a failure: Generating tailored smoking cessation letters. *Artificial Intelligence*, 144:41–58.

F. De Rosis and F Grasso. 2000. Affective natural language generation. In A. Paiva, editor, *Affective Interactions*. Springer LNAI 1814.

J. Russell, A. Weiss, and G. Mendelsohn. 1989. Affect grid: A single-item scale of pleasure and arousal. *Journal of Personality and Social Psychology*, 57:493–502.

K. Teigen and W. Brun. 2003. Verbal probabilities: A question of frame. *Journal of Behavioral Decision Making*, 16:53–72.

D. Watson, L. Clark, and A. Tellegen. 1988. Development and validation of brief measures of positive and negative affect: The PANAS scales. *Journal of Personality and Social Psychology*, 54(1063-1070).

S. Williams and E. Reiter. forthcoming. Generating basic skills reports for lowskilled readers. *Journal of Natural Language Engineering*.

Practical Grammar-Based NLG from Examples

David DeVault and **David Traum** and **Ron Artstein**
USC Institute for Creative Technologies
13274 Fiji Way
Marina del Rey, CA 90292
{devault,traum,artstein}@ict.usc.edu

Abstract

We present a technique that opens up grammar-based generation to a wider range of practical applications by dramatically reducing the development costs and linguistic expertise that are required. Our method infers the grammatical resources needed for generation from a set of declarative examples that link surface expressions directly to the application's available semantic representations. The same examples further serve to optimize a run-time search strategy that generates the best output that can be found within an application-specific time frame. Our method offers substantially lower development costs than hand-crafted grammars for application-specific NLG, while maintaining high output quality and diversity.

1 Introduction

This paper presents a new example-based generation technique designed to reduce the development costs and linguistic expertise needed to integrate a grammar-based generation component into an existing application. We believe this approach will broaden the class of applications in which grammar-based generation may feasibly be deployed.

In principle, grammar-based generation offers significant advantages for many applications, when compared with simpler template-based or canned text output solutions, by providing productive coverage and greater output variety. However, realizing these advantages can require significant development costs (Busemann and Horacek, 1998).

One possible strategy is to exploit a wide-coverage realizer that aims for applicability in multiple application domains (White et al., 2007; Cahill and van Genabith, 2006; Zhong and Stent, 2005; Langkilde-Geary, 2002; Langkilde and Knight, 1998; Elhadad, 1991). These realizers provide a sound wide-coverage grammar (or robust wide-coverage language model) for free, but demand a specific input format that is otherwise foreign to an existing application. Unfortunately, the development burden of implementing the translation between the system's available semantic representations and the required input format can be quite substantial (Busemann and Horacek, 1998). Indeed, implementing the translation might require as much effort as would be required to build a simple custom generator; cf. (Callaway, 2003). Thus, there currently are many applications where using a wide-coverage generator remains impractical.

Another strategy is for system builders to hand craft an application-specific grammar for generation. This approach can be initially attractive to system builders because it allows syntactic coverage and semantic modeling to be tailored directly to application needs. However, writing grammatical rules by hand ultimately requires a painstaking, time-consuming effort by a developer who has detailed linguistic knowledge as well as detailed application knowledge. Further, the resulting coverage is inevitably limited to the set of linguistic constructions that have been selected for careful modeling.

A third strategy is to use an example-based approach (Wong and Mooney, 2007; Stone, 2003; Varges and Mellish, 2001) in which the connection between available application semantic representations and desired output utterances is specified by example. Example-based approaches aim to allow system builders to specify a productive generation capacity while leaving the representations and reasoning that underlie that productive capacity mostly implicit in a set of training examples. This methodology insulates system builders from the detailed expertise and technical infrastructure needed to implement the productive capacity directly, and has made example-based approaches attractive not only in text generation but also in related areas such as concatenative speech synthesis and motion capture based animation; see, e.g., (Stone et al., 2004).

The technique we present in this paper is a new example-based approach to specifying application-specific text generation. As in other hand-crafted and example-based approaches, our technique allows syntactic coverage and semantic modeling to follow the needs and available semantic representations in an application. One contribution of our technique is to relieve the generation content author of the burden of manual syntactic modeling by leveraging an off-the-shelf parser; defects in the syntax provided by the parser are effectively overcome using a machine learning technique. Additionally, our technique organizes the authoring task in a way that relieves the generation author of carefully modeling the connections between particular syntactic constructions and available semantic representations.

Together, we argue, these features dramatically reduce the linguistic expertise and other development costs that are required to integrate a grammar-based generation component into an existing system. In a case study application, we show that our approach allows an application developer who lacks detailed linguistic knowledge to extend grammatical coverage at an expense of less than one minute per additional lexical entry.

2 Case Study: Doctor Perez

Our approach has been tested as a replacement for the generation component of interactive virtual humans used for social training purposes (Swartout et al., 2006). Virtual humans are embodied conversational agents that play the role of people in simulations or games. The case study we present in this paper is the generation of output utterances for a particular virtual human, Doctor Perez, who is designed to teach negotiation skills in a multi-modal, multi-party, non-team dialogue setting (Traum et al., 2008). The human trainee who talks to the doctor plays the role of a U.S. Army captain named Captain Kirk. The design goals for Doctor Perez create a number of requirements for a practical NLG component. We briefly summarize these requirements here; see (DeVault et al., 2008) for more details.

Doctor Perez has a relatively rich internal mental state including beliefs, goals, plans, and emotions. He uses an attribute-value matrix (AVM) semantic representation to describe an utterance as a set of core speech acts and other dialogue acts. Speech acts generally have semantic contents that describe propositions and questions about states and actions in the domain. To facilitate interprocess communication, and statistical processing, this AVM structure is linearized into a "frame" of key values in which each non-recursive terminal value is paired with a path from the root to the final attribute. Figure 1 shows a typical frame. See (Traum, 2003) for additional details and examples of this representation.

While only hundreds of frames currently arise in actual dialogues, the number of potential frames is orders of magnitude larger, and it is difficult to predict in advance which frames might occur. The utterances that realize these frames need to take a variety of syntactic forms, including simple declarative sentences, various modal constructions relating to hypothetical actions or plans, yes/no and wh-questions, and abbreviated dialogue forms such as elliptical clarification and repair requests, grounding, and turn-taking utterances. Highly fluent output is not a necessity for this character, since Doctor Perez is designed to simulate a non-native English speaker. However, in order to support compelling real-time conversational interaction and effective training, the generation module must be able to identify an utterance for Doctor Perez to use within approximately 200ms on modern hardware.

Finally, the development team for Doctor Perez's language capabilities includes approximately 10 programmers, testers, linguists, and computational linguists. Wherever possible, it is better if any developer can improve any aspect of Doctor Perez's language processing; e.g., if a programmer discovers a bug or disfluency in the NLG output, it is better if she can fix it directly rather than requiring a (computational) linguist to do so.

3 Technical Approach

Our approach builds on recently developed techniques in statistical parsing, lexicalized syntax modeling, generation with lexicalized grammars, and search optimization to automatically construct all the resources needed for a high-quality run-time generation component. In particular, we leverage the increasing availability of off-the-shelf parsers such as (Charniak, 2001; Charniak, 2005) to automatically (or semi-automatically) assign syntactic analyses to a set of suggested output sentences. We then draw on lexicalization techniques for statistical language models (Magerman, 1995; Collins, 1999; Chiang, 2000; Chiang, 2003) to induce a probabilistic, lexicalized tree-adjoining grammar that supports the derivation of all the suggested output sentences, and many others besides.

The final step is to use the training examples to learn an effective search policy so that our run-time generation component can find good output sentences in a reasonable time frame. In particular, we use variants of existing search optimization (Daumé and Marcu, 2005) and ranking algorithms (Collins and Koo, 2005) to train our run-time component to find good outputs within a specified time window; see also (Stent et al., 2004; Walker et al., 2001). The result is a run-time component that treats generation as an anytime search problem, and is thus suitable for applications in which a time/performance tradeoff is necessary (such as real-time dialogue).

3.1 Specification of Training Examples

Each training example in our approach specifies a target output utterance (string), its syntax, and a set of links between substrings within the utterance and system semantic representations. Formally, a training example takes the form $(u, \mathrm{syntax}(u), \mathrm{semantics}(u))$. We will illustrate this format using the training example in Figure 1. In this example, the generation content author suggests the output utterance u = *we don't have medical supplies here captain*. Each utterance u is accompanied by $\mathrm{syntax}(u)$, a syntactic analysis in Penn Treebank format (Marcus et al., 1994). In the figure, we show two alternative syntactic analyses that might be specified: one is the uncorrected output of the Charniak parser on this sentence, and the other a hand-corrected version of that parse; we evaluate the utility of this hand correction in Section 4.

To represent the meaning of utterances, our approach assumes that the system provides some set $M = \{m_1, ..., m_j\}$ of semantic representations. The meaning of any individual utterance is then identified with some subset of M. For Doctor Perez, M comprises the 232 distinct key-value pairs that appear in the system's various generation frames. In this example, the utterance's meaning is captured by the 8 key-value pairs indicated in the figure.

Our approach requires the generation content author to link these 8 key-value pairs to contiguous surface expressions within the utterance. The technique is flexible about which surface expressions are chosen (e.g. they need not correspond to constituent boundaries); however, they do need to be compatible with the way the syntactic analysis tokenizes the utterance, as follows. Let $t(u) = \langle t_1, ..., t_n \rangle$ be the terminals in the syntactic analysis, in left-to-right order. Formally, $\mathrm{semantics}(u) = \{(s_1, M_1), ..., (s_k, M_k)\}$, where $t(u) = s_1 @ \cdots @ s_k$ (with @ denoting concatenation), and where $M_i \subseteq M$ for all $i \in 1..k$. In this example, the surface expression *we don't*, which tokenizes as $\langle \mathrm{we, do, n't} \rangle$, is connected to key-values that indicate a negative polarity assertion.

This training example format has two features that are crucial to our approach. First, the semantics of an utterance is specified *independently* of its syntax. This greatly reduces the amount of linguistic expertise a generation content author needs to have. It also allows making changes to the underlying syntax without having to re-author the semantic links.

Second, the assignment of semantic representations to surface expressions must span the *entire utterance*. No words or expressions can be viewed as "meaningless". This is essential because, otherwise, the semantically motivated search algorithm used in generation has no basis on which to include those particular expressions when it constructs its output utterance. Many systems, including Doctor Perez, lack some of the internal representations that would be necessary to specify semantics down to the lex-

Utterance we don't have medical supplies here captain

Syntax

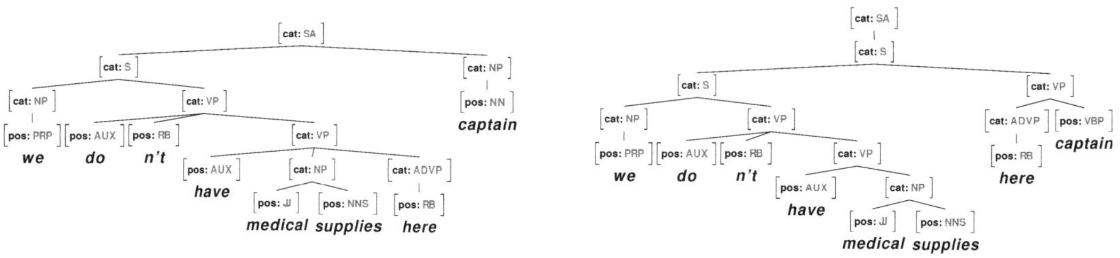

(corrected Charniak parse) *or* (uncorrected Charniak parse)

Semantics

	semantic frame
we do n't .... {	speech-act.action = assert
	speech-act.content.polarity = negative
have	speech-act.content.attribute = resourceAttribute
medical supplies ..	speech-act.content.value = medical-supplies
here	speech-act.content.object-id = market
captain .... {	addressee = captain-kirk
	dialogue-act.addressee = captain-kirk
	speech-act.addressee = captain-kirk

Figure 1: A generation training example for Doctor Perez. If uncorrected syntax is used, the generation content author only writes the utterance and the links to the semantic frame.

ical level. An important feature of our approach is that it allows an arbitrary semantic granularity to be employed, by mapping the representations available in the system to appropriate multi-word chunks.

3.2 Automatic Grammar Induction

We adopt essentially the probabilistic tree-adjoining grammar (PTAG) formalism and grammar induction technique of (Chiang, 2003). Our approach makes three modifications, however. First, while Chiang's model includes both full adjunction and sister adjunction operations, our grammar has only sister adjunction (left and right), exactly as in the TAGLET grammar formalism of (Stone, 2002). Second, to support lexicalization at an arbitrary granularity, we allow Chiang's tree templates to be associated with more than one lexical anchor. Third, to unify syntactic and semantic reasoning in search, we augment lexical anchors with semantic information. Formally, wherever Chiang's model has a lexical anchor w, ours has a pair $(\langle w_1, ..., w_n\rangle, M')$, where $M' \subseteq M$ is connected to lexical anchors $\langle w_1, ..., w_n\rangle$ by the generation content author, as in Figure 1. The result is that the derivation probabilities the grammar assigns depend not only on the implicated syntactic structures and lexical anchors but also on the *senses* of those lexical anchors in application terms.

We induce our grammar from training examples such as Figure 1 using heuristics to assign derivations to the examples, exactly as in (Chiang, 2003). The process proceeds in two stages. In the first stage, a collection of rules is used to automatically "decorate" the training syntax with a number of features. These include deciding the lexical anchor(s) for each non-terminal constituent and assigning complement/adjunct status for nonterminals which are not on their parent's lexicalization path; see (Magerman, 1995; Chiang, 2003; Collins, 1999). In addition, we deterministically add features to improve several grammatical aspects, including (1) enforcing verb inflectional agreement in derived trees, (2) enforcing consistency in the finiteness of VP and S complements, and (3) restricting subject/direct object/indirect object complements to play the same grammatical role in derived trees.

In the second stage, the complements and adjuncts in the decorated trees are incrementally re-

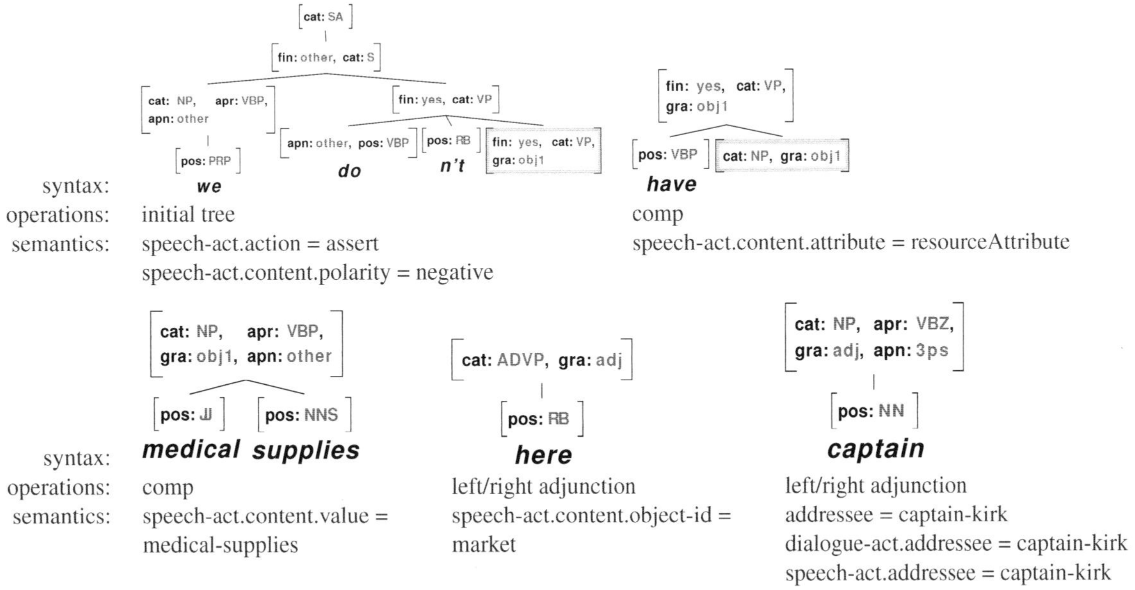

Figure 2: The linguistic resources inferred from the training example in Figure 1.

moved, yielding the reusable linguistic resources in the grammar, as illustrated in Figure 2, as well as the maximum likelihood estimates needed to compute operation probabilities.

Our approach uses this induced grammar to treat generation as a search problem: given a desired semantic representation $M' \subseteq M$, use the grammar to incrementally construct an output utterance u that expresses M'. We treat generation as anytime search by accruing multiple goal states up until a specified timeout (for Doctor Perez: 200ms) and returning a list of alternative outputs ranked by their derivation probabilities.

3.3 Optimizing the Search Strategy

The search space created by a grammar induced in this way is too large to be searched exhaustively in most applications. The solution we have developed is a beam search strategy that uses weighted features to rank alternative grammatical expansions at each step. In particular, the beam size and structure is optimized so that, with high probability, the beam can be searched exhaustively before the timeout.[1] The second step of automated processing, then, is a training problem of finding weighted features such that for every training problem, nodes that lead to good generation output are ranked highly enough by those features to make it into the beam.

We use domain-independent rules to automatically define a set of features that could be heuristically useful for a given induced grammar. These include features for various syntactic structures and operations, numbers of undesired and desired meanings of different types added by an expansion, derivation probabilities, etc. (For Doctor Perez, this yields about 600 features.) Our training algorithm is based on the search optimization algorithm of (Daumé and Marcu, 2005), which updates feature weights when mistakes are made during search on training examples. For the weight update step, we use the boosting approach of (Collins and Koo, 2005), which performs feature selection and identifies weight values that improve the ranking of alternative derivation steps when mistakes are made during search. We discuss the resulting success rate and quality in the next section.

4 Cost/Benefit Analysis

The motivation that underlies our technical approach is to reduce the development costs and linguistic expertise needed to develop a grammar-based generation component for an existing system. In this section, we assess the progress we have made by ana-

[1]For Doctor Perez, we use a wider beam for initial trees, since the Doctor's semantic representation is particularly impoverished at the level of main verbs. At search depths > 1, we use beam size 1 (i.e. greedy search).

lyzing the use of our approach for Doctor Perez.

Method. We began with a sample of 220 instances of frames that Doctor Perez's dialogue manager had requested of the generation component in previous dialogues with users. Each frame was associated with a hand-authored target output utterance. We then constructed two alternative training examples, in the format specified in Section 3.1, for each frame. One example had uncorrected output of the Charniak parser for the syntax, and another had hand-corrected parser output (see Figure 1). The connections between surface expressions and frame key-value pairs were identical in both uncorrected and corrected training sets.

We then built two generators using the two sets of training examples. We used 90% of the data for training and held out 10% for testing. The generators sometimes failed to find a successful utterance within the 200ms timeout. For example, the success rate of the version of our generator trained on uncorrected syntax was 96.0% for training examples and 81.8% for test examples.

Quality of generated output. To assess output quality, 5 system developers rated each of 494 utterances, in relation to the specific frame for which it was produced, on a single 1 ("very bad") to 5 ("very good") scale. The 494 utterances included all of the hand-authored (suggested) utterances in the training examples. They also included all the top-ranked utterances that were successfully generated by the two generators. We asked our judges to make an overall assessment of output quality, incorporating both accuracy and fluency, for the Doctor Perez character. Judges were blind to the conditions under which utterances were produced. We discuss additional details of this rating task in (DeVault et al., 2008).

The judges achieved a reliability of $\alpha = 0.708$ (Krippendorff, 1980); this value shows that agreement is well above chance, and allows for tentative conclusions. We ran a small number of planned comparisons on these ratings. Surprisingly, we found no significant difference between generated output trained on corrected and uncorrected syntax ($t(29) = 0.056, p > 0.9$ on test items, $t(498) = -1.1, p > 0.2$ on all items).[2] However, we did

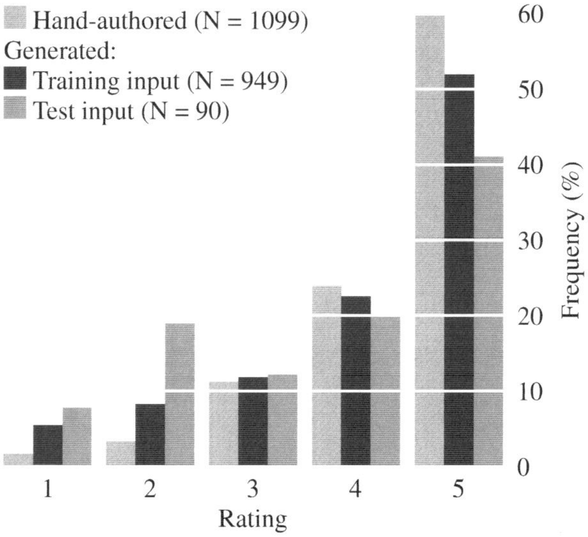

Figure 3: Observed rating frequencies for hand-authored vs. generated utterances (uncorrected syntax).

find that hand-authored utterances (mean rating 4.4) are significantly better ($t(388) = 5.9, p < 0.001$) than generated utterances (mean rating 3.8 for uncorrected syntax). These ratings are depicted in Figure 3. While the figure suggests a slight reduction in quality for generated output for test frames vs. training frames, we did not find a significant difference between the two ($t(19) = 1.4228, p > 0.15$).

Variety of generated output. In general our anytime algorithm delivers a ranked list of alternative outputs. While in this initial study our judges rated only the highest ranked output generated for each frame, we observed that many of the lower ranked outputs are of relatively high quality. For example, Figure 4 shows a variety of alternative outputs that were generated for two of Doctor Perez's training examples. Many of these outputs are not present as hand-authored utterances (for any frame); this illustrates the potential of our approach to provide a variety of alternative outputs or paraphrases, which in some applications may be useful even for meanings for which an example utterance is hand-authored. Figure 5 shows the overall distribution in the number of outputs returned for Doctor Perez.

Development costs. The development costs included implementation of the approach and specification of Doctor Perez's training set. Implementa-

[2]The distribution of ratings across utterances is not normal; to validate our results we accompanied each t-test by a non-parametric Wilcoxon rank sum test, and significance always fell in the same general range.

Rank	Time (ms)	Novel?	
1	16	no	*the clinic is up to standard captain*
2	94	no	*the clinic is acceptable captain* (hand-authored for this input)
3	78	yes	*the clinic should be in acceptable condition captain*
4	16	yes	*the clinic downtown is currently acceptable captain*
5	78	yes	*the clinic should agree in an acceptable condition captain*
1	94	no	*there are no medical supplies downtown captain*
2	172	no	*we don't have medical supplies downtown captain*
3	125	yes	*well captain i do not think downtown there are medical supplies*
4	16	yes	*i do not think there are medical supplies downtown captain*

Figure 4: All the utterances generated (uncorrected syntax) for two examples. Rank is determined by derivation probability. Outputs marked as novel are different from any suggested output for any training example.

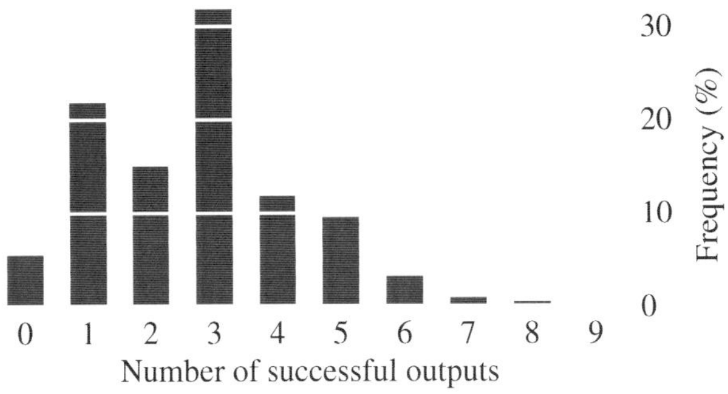

Figure 5: Variety of outputs for each input.

tion required an effort of approximately six person months. The developer who carried out the implementation initially had no familiarity with the Doctor Perez domain, so part of this time was spent understanding Doctor Perez and his available semantic representations. The bulk of the development time was spent implementing the grammar induction and training processes. Grammar induction included implementing the probabilistic grammar model and writing about 40 rules that are used to extract grammatical entries from the training examples. Of these 40 rules, only 3 are specific to Doctor Perez.[3] The remainder are broadly applicable to syntactic analyses in Penn Treebank format, and thus we expect they would transfer to applications of our approach in other domains. Similarly, the training algorithms are entirely domain neutral and could be expected to transfer well to additional domains.

Specification of Doctor Perez's training data took about 6 hours, or about 1.6 minutes per training example. This time included hand correction of syntactic analyses generated by the Charniak parser and definition of semantic links between surface expressions and frame key-value pairs. Since we found that hand-correcting syntax does not improve output quality, this 1.6 minutes/example figure overestimates the authoring time required by our approach. The remaining work lies in defining the semantic links. For Doctor Perez, approximately half of the semantic links were automatically assigned with simple ad hoc scripts.[4] The semantic linking process might be further sped up through a streamlined authoring interface offering additional automation, or even using a machine learning approach to suggest appropriate links.

Linguistic expertise required. Since we found that hand-correcting syntax does not improve output quality, a developer who wishes to exploit our approach may use the Charniak parser to supply the syntactic model for the domain. Thus, while one developer with linguistic expertise is required to implement the approach, anybody on the application team can contribute by hand authoring additional utterances and defining semantic links. The benefit of this authoring effort is the ability to generate high quality output for many novel semantic inputs.

Cost/benefit. The grammar induced from the 198 training examples (with uncorrected syntax) contains 426 lexical entries of the type depicted in Figure 2. These 426 lexical entries were produced automatically from about 6 hours worth of authoring ef-

[3]These 3 rules compensate for frequent errors in Charniak parser output for the words *captain*, *elder*, and *imam*, which are often used to signal the addressee of Doctor Perez's utterances.

[4]Time to compose these scripts is included in the 1.6 minutes/example.

fort together with domain-neutral algorithms. This translates to a rate of grammar expansion of less than 1 minute per lexical entry, on average, for this small application-specific grammar. This constitutes a dramatic improvement over our previous experience hand-crafting grammars. It would be challenging for an expert to specify a lexical entry such as those in Figure 2 in under one minute (and probably impossible for someone lacking detailed linguistic knowledge). In our experience, however, the bulk of development lies in additional time spent considering and investigating possible interactions between lexical entries in generation. Our technique helps with both problems: the grammar induction streamlines the specification of lexical entries, and the training removes the need for a developer to manually trace through the various complex interactions between lexical entries during generation.

5 Limitations

Currently, we do not support semantic links from non-contiguous expressions, which means a desired output like "we rely heavily on medical supplies" would be difficult to annotate if *rely...on* corresponds to a single semantic representation. This is not an intrinsic limitation to our general approach, but rather a simplification in our initial implementation.

As discussed in Section 3.2, our grammar induction process adds syntactic features related to verb inflection, finiteness, and grammatical role to the inferred lexical entries. Such features improve the fluency and accuracy of output derived with the grammar. While we believe such features can always be assigned using domain-independent rules, developing these rules requires linguistic expertise, and it is likely that additional rules and features (not yet implemented) would improve coverage of linguistic phenomena such as control verbs, various kinds of coordination, and relative clauses, inter alia.

A more entrenched limitation of our approach is its assumption that the generator does not need context as a separate input. This means, for example, that our approach cannot generate referring expressions (by selecting disambiguating semantic properties); rather, all semantic properties must be pre-selected and included in the generation request. Generation of anaphoric expressions is also limited, since contextual ambiguities are not considered.

6 Related Work

To our knowledge, this is the first implemented generation technique that does all three of the following: directly interfaces to existing application semantic representations, infers a phrase structure grammar from examples, and does not require hand-authored syntax as input. (Varges and Mellish, 2001) also aims to reduce the authoring burden of domain-specific generation; however, they seem to use a special purpose semantic annotation rather than pre-existing application semantics, and their task is defined in terms of the Penn Treebank, so hand-authored syntax is used as input. (Wong and Mooney, 2007) also interfaces to existing application semantics, and does not require hand-authored syntax as input. Their technique infers a synchronous grammar in which the hierarchical linguistic analysis is isomorphic to the hierarchy in the application semantics, and differs from phrase structure. It would be interesting to compare their output quality with ours; their automated alignment of words to semantics might also provide a way to further reduce the authoring burden of our approach.

7 Conclusion and Future Work

We have presented a new example-based approach to specifying text generation for an existing application. We have used a cost/benefit analysis to argue that our approach offers productive coverage and high-quality output with less linguistic expertise and lower development costs than building a hand-crafted grammar. In future work, we will evaluate our approach in additional application settings, and study the performance of our approach as the size and scope of the training set grows.

Acknowledgments

Thanks to our anonymous reviewers, Arno Hartholt, Susan Robinson, Thomas Russ, Chung-chieh Shan, and Matthew Stone. This work was sponsored by the U.S. Army Research, Development, and Engineering Command (RDECOM), and the content does not necessarily reflect the position or the policy of the Government, and no official endorsement should be inferred.

References

S. Busemann and H. Horacek. 1998. A flexible shallow approach to text generation. In *Proceedings of INLG*, pages 238–247.

Aoife Cahill and Josef van Genabith. 2006. Robust PCFG-based generation using automatically acquired LFG approximations. In *ACL*, pages 1033–1040.

C. B. Callaway. 2003. Evaluating coverage for large symbolic NLG grammars. *Proceedings of IJCAI*.

E. Charniak. 2001. Immediate-head parsing for language models. In *ACL*, pages 124–131, Morristown, NJ, USA. Association for Computational Linguistics.

E. Charniak. 2005. ftp://ftp.cs.brown.edu/pub/nlparser/parser05Aug16.tar.gz.

D. Chiang. 2000. Statistical parsing with an automatically-extracted tree adjoining grammar. In *ACL '00: Proceedings of the 38th Annual Meeting on Association for Computational Linguistics*, pages 456–463, Morristown, NJ, USA. Association for Computational Linguistics.

D. Chiang. 2003. Statistical parsing with an automatically extracted tree adjoining grammar. In R. Bod, R. Scha, and K. Sima'an, editors, *Data Oriented Parsing*, pages 299–316. CSLI Publications, Stanford.

M. Collins and T. Koo. 2005. Discriminative reranking for natural language parsing. *Computational Linguistics*, 31(1):25–70.

M. Collins. 1999. *Head-Driven Statistical Models for Natural Language Parsing*. Ph.D. dissertation, University of Pennsylvania.

H. Daumé and D. Marcu. 2005. Learning as search optimization: approximate large margin methods for structured prediction. In *ICML '05: Proceedings of the 22nd international conference on Machine learning*, pages 169–176, New York, NY, USA. ACM.

David DeVault, David Traum, and Ron Artstein. 2008. Making grammar-based generation easier to deploy in dialogue systems. In *Ninth SIGdial Workshop on Discourse and Dialogue (SIGdial)*.

M. Elhadad. 1991. FUF: the universal unifier user manual version 5.0. Technical Report CUCS-038-91.

K. Krippendorff, 1980. *Content Analysis: An Introduction to Its Methodology*, chapter 12, pages 129–154. Sage, Beverly Hills, CA.

I. Langkilde and K. Knight. 1998. Generation that exploits corpus-based statistical knowledge. In *COLING-ACL*, pages 704–710.

I. Langkilde-Geary. 2002. An empirical verification of coverage and correctness for a general-purpose sentence generator.

D. M. Magerman. 1995. Statistical decision-tree models for parsing. In *Proceedings of the 33rd annual meeting on Association for Computational Linguistics*, pages 276–283, Morristown, NJ, USA. Association for Computational Linguistics.

M. P. Marcus, B. Santorini, and M. A. Marcinkiewicz. 1994. Building a large annotated corpus of english: The penn treebank. *Computational Linguistics*, 19(2):313–330.

A. Stent, R. Prasad, and M. Walker. 2004. Trainable sentence planning for complex information presentation in spoken dialog systems. In *ACL*.

Matthew Stone, Doug DeCarlo, Insuk Oh, Christian Rodriguez, Adrian Stere, Alyssa Lees, and Chris Bregler. 2004. Speaking with hands: creating animated conversational characters from recordings of human performance. *ACM Trans. Graph.*, 23(3):506–513.

M. Stone. 2002. Lexicalized grammar 101. In *ACL Workshop on Tools and Methodologies for Teaching Natural Language Processing*.

Matthew Stone. 2003. Specifying generation of referring expressions by example. In *AAAI Spring Symposium on Natural Language Generation in Spoken and Written Dialogue*, pages 133–140.

W. Swartout, J. Gratch, R. W. Hill, E. Hovy, S. Marsella, J. Rickel, and D. Traum. 2006. Toward virtual humans. *AI Mag.*, 27(2):96–108.

D. R. Traum, W. Swartout, J. Gratch, and S. Marsella. 2008. A virtual human dialogue model for non-team interaction. In L. Dybkjaer and W. Minker, editors, *Recent Trends in Discourse and Dialogue*. Springer.

D. Traum. 2003. Semantics and pragmatics of questions and answers for dialogue agents. In *proceedings of the International Workshop on Computational Semantics*, pages 380–394, January.

Sebastian Varges and Chris Mellish. 2001. Instance-based natural language generation. In *NAACL*, pages 1–8.

M. Walker, O. Rambow, and M. Rogati. 2001. Spot: A trainable sentence planner. In *Proceedings of the North American Meeting of the Association for Computational Linguistics*.

M. White, R. Rajkumar, and S. Martin. 2007. Towards broad coverage surface realization with CCG. In *Proc. of the Workshop on Using Corpora for NLG: Language Generation and Machine Translation (UCNLG+MT)*.

Yuk Wah Wong and Raymond Mooney. 2007. Generation by inverting a semantic parser that uses statistical machine translation. In *Proceedings of NAACL-HLT*, pages 172–179.

H. Zhong and A. Stent. 2005. Building surface realizers automatically from corpora using general-purpose tools. In *Proc. Corpus Linguistics '05 Workshop on Using Corpora for Natural Language Generation*.

Accurate and Robust LFG-Based Generation for Chinese

Yuqing Guo
NCLT, School of Computing
Dublin City University
Dublin 9, Ireland
yguo@computing.dcu.ie

Haifeng Wang
Toshiba (China)
Research and Development Center
Beijing, 100738, China
wanghaifeng@rdc.toshiba.com.cn

Josef van Genabith
NCLT, School of Computing
Dublin City University
IBM CAS, Dublin, Ireland
josef@computing.dcu.ie

Abstract

We describe three PCFG-based models for Chinese sentence realisation from Lexical-Functional Grammar (LFG) f-structures. Both the lexicalised model and the history-based model improve on the accuracy of a simple wide-coverage PCFG model by adding lexical and contextual information to weaken inappropriate independence assumptions implicit in the PCFG models. In addition, we provide techniques for lexical smoothing and rule smoothing to increase the generation coverage. Trained on 15,663 automatically LFG f-structure annotated sentences of the Penn Chinese treebank and tested on 500 sentences randomly selected from the treebank test set, the lexicalised model achieves a BLEU score of 0.7265 at 100% coverage, while the history-based model achieves a BLEU score of 0.7245 also at 100% coverage.

1 Introduction

Sentence generation, or surface realisation can be described as the problem of producing syntactically, morphologically, and orthographically correct sentences from a given abstract semantic / logical representation according to some linguistic theory, e.g. Lexical Functional Grammar (LFG), Head-Driven Phrase Structure Grammar (HPSG), Combinatory Categorial Grammar (CCG), Tree Adjoining Grammar (TAG) etc. Grammars, such as these, are declarative formulations of the correspondences between semantic and syntactic representations. Traditionally, grammar rules have been carefully handcrafted, such as those used in LinGo (Carroll et al., 1999), OpenCCG (White, 2004) and XLE (Crouch et al., 2007). As handcrafting grammar rules is time-consuming, language-dependent and domain-specific, recent years have witnessed research on extracting wide-coverage grammars automatically from annotated corpora, for both parsing and generation. FERGUS (Bangalore and Rambow, 2000) took dependency structures as inputs, and produced XTAG derivations by a stochastic tree model automatically acquired from an annotated corpus. Nakanishi et al. (2005) presented log-linear models for a chart generator using a HPSG grammar acquired from the Penn-II Treebank. From the same treebank, Cahill and van Genabith (2006) automatically extracted wide-coverage LFG approximations for a PCFG-based generation model.

In addition to applying statistical techniques to automatically acquire generation grammars, over the last decade, there has been a lot of interest in a generate-and-select paradigm for surface realisation. The paradigm is characterised by a separation between generation and selection, in which symbolic or rule-based methods are used to generate a space of possible paraphrases, and statistical methods are used to select one or more outputs from the space. Starting from Langkilde (2002) who used a n-gram language model to rank generated output strings, a substantial number of traditional handcrafted surface realisers have been augmented with sophisticated stochastic rankers (Velldal and Oepen, 2005; White et al., 2007; Cahill et al., 2007).

It is interesting to note that, while the study of how the granularity of context-free grammars (CFG) affects the performance of a parser (e.g. in the form

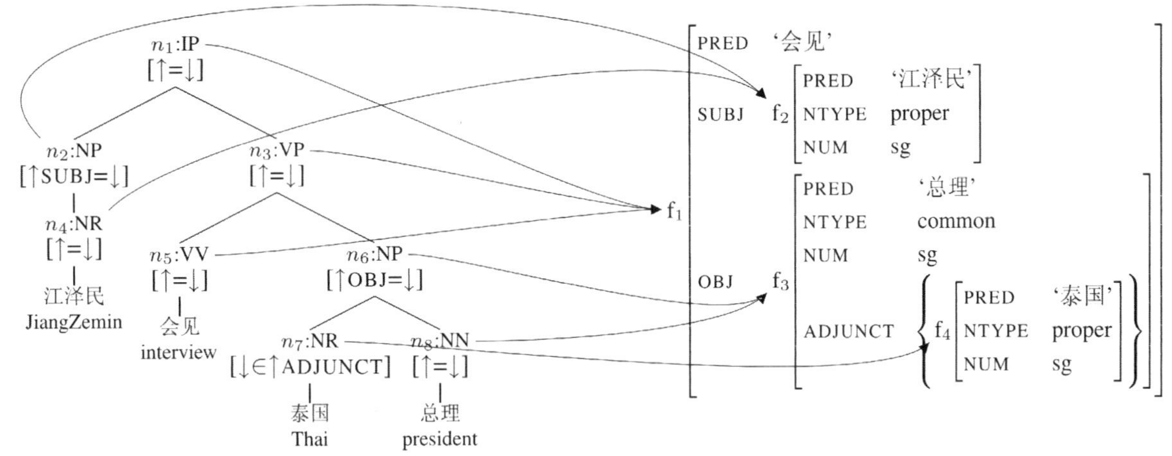

$$\phi : N \rightarrow F$$

$$\phi(n_1)=\phi(n_3)=\phi(n_5)=f_1 \quad \phi(n_2)=\phi(n_4)=f_2 \quad \phi(n_6)=\phi(n_8)=f_3 \quad \phi(n_7)=f_4$$

Figure 1: C- and f-structures with ϕ links for the sentence "江泽民会见泰国总理"

of grammar transforms (Johnson, 1998) and lexicalisation (Collins, 1997)) has attracted substantial attention, to our knowledge, there has been a lot less research on this subject for surface realisation, a process that is generally regarded as the reverse process of parsing. Moreover, while most of the research so far has concentrated on English or European languages, we are also interested in generation for other languages with diverse properties, such as Chinese which is currently a focus language in parsing (Bikel, 2004; Cao et al., 2007).

In this paper, we investigate three generative PCFG models for Chinese generation based on wide-coverage LFG grammars automatically extracted from the Penn Chinese Treebank (CTB). Our work is couched in the framework of Lexical Functional Grammar and is implemented in a chart-style generator. We briefly describe LFG and the basic generation model in Section 2. We improve the baseline PCFG model by weakening the independence assumptions in two disambiguation models in Section 3. Section 4 describes the smoothing algorithms adopted for the chart generator and Section 5 gives the experimental details and results.

2 LFG-Based Generation

2.1 Lexical Functional Grammar

Lexical Functional Grammar (Kaplan and Bresnan, 1982) is a constraint-based grammar formalism which postulates (minimally) two levels of representation: c(onstituent)-structure and f(unctional)-structure. C-structure takes the form of phrase structure trees and captures surface grammatical configurations. F-structure encodes more abstract grammatical functions (GFs) such as SUBJ(ect), OBJ(ect), ADJUNCT and TOPIC etc., in the form of hierarchical attribute-value matrices. C-structures and f-structures are related by a piecewise correspondence function ϕ that goes from the nodes of a c-structure tree into units of f-structure spaces (Kaplan, 1995). As illustrated in Figure 1, given a c-structure node n_i, the corresponding f-structure component f_j is $\phi(n_i)$. Admissible c-structures are specified by a context-free grammar. The corresponding f-structures are derived from functional annotations attached to the CFG rewriting rules.

(1)	a.	IP	⟶	NP [↑SUBJ=↓]	VP [↑=↓]
	b.	VP	⟶	VV [↑=↓]	NP [↑OBJ=↓]
	c.	NP	⟶	NR [↑ADJ=↓]	NN [↑=↓]
	d.	NP	⟶	NR [↑=↓]	

(1) shows a miniature set of annotated CFG rules (lexical entries omitted) which generates the c- and f-structure in Figure 1. In the functional annotations, (↓) refers to the f-structure associated with the local c-structure node n_i, i.e. $\phi(n_i)$, and (↑) refers to the

Model	Grammar Rule	Conditions
PCFG	VP[↑=↓] → VV[↑=↓] NP[↑OBJ=↓]	VP[↑=↓], {PRED, SUBJ, OBJ}
HB-PCFG	VP[↑=↓] → VV[↑=↓] NP[↑OBJ=↓]	VP[↑=↓], {PRED, SUBJ, OBJ}, TOP
LEX-PCFG	VP(会见)[↑=↓] → VV(会见)[↑=↓] NP(总理)[↑OBJ=↓]	VP(会见)[↑=↓], {PRED, SUBJ, OBJ}

Table 1: Examples of f-structure annotated CFG rules (from Figure 1) in different models

f-structure associated with the mother (M) node of n_i, i.e. $\phi(M(n_i))$.

2.2 Generation from f-Structures

The generation task in LFG is to determine which sentences correspond to a specified f-structure, given a particular grammar, such as (1). Kaplan and Wedekind (2000) proved that the set of strings generated by an LFG grammar from fully specified f-structures is a context-free language. Based on this theoretical cornerstone, Cahill and van Genabith (2006) presented a PCFG-based chart generator using wide-coverage LFG approximations automatically extracted from the Penn-II treebank. The LFG-based statistical generation model defines the conditional probability $P(T|F)$, for each candidate functionally annotated c-structure tree T (which fully specifies a surface realisation) given an f-structure F. The generation model searches for the T_{best} that maximises $P(T|F)$ (Eq. 1). $P(T|F)$ is then decomposed as the product of the probabilities of all the functionally annotated CFG rewriting rules $X \rightarrow Y$ (conditioned on the left hand side (LHS) X and local features of the corresponding f-structure $\phi(X)$) contributing to the tree T (Eq. 2). The first line (PCFG) of Table 1 shows the f-structure annotated CFG rule to expand node n_3 in Figure 1.

$$T_{best} = \underset{T}{\text{argmax}}\, P(T|F) \quad (1)$$

$$P(T|F) = \prod_{\substack{X \rightarrow Y in\, T \\ Feats = \{a_i | a_i \in \phi(X)\}}} P(X \rightarrow Y | X, Feats) \quad (2)$$

3 Disambiguation Models

The basic generation model presented in (Cahill and van Genabith, 2006) used simple probabilistic context-free grammars. However, the independence assumptions implicit in PCFG models may not be appropriate to best capture natural language phenomena. Methodologies such as lexicalisation (Collins, 1997; Charniak, 2000) and tree transformations (Johnson, 1998), weaken the independence assumptions and have been applied successfully to parsing and shown significant improvements over simple PCFGs. In this section we study the effect of such methods in LFG-based generation for Chinese.

3.1 A History-Based Model

The history-based (HB) approach which incorporates more context information has worked well in parsing (Collins, 1997; Charniak, 2000). Resembling history-based models for parsing, Hogan et al. (2007) presented a history-based generation model to overcome some of the inappropriate independence assumptions in the basic generation model of (Cahill and van Genabith, 2006). The history-based model increases the context by simply including the parent grammatical function GF of the f-structure in addition to the local ϕ-linked feature set in the conditioning context (Eq. 3). The f-structure annotated CFG rule expanding n_3 in the history-based model is shown in the second line (HB-PCFG) of Table 1.[1]

$$P(T|F) = \prod_{\substack{X \rightarrow Y in\, T \\ Feats = \{a_i | a_i \in \phi(X)\} \\ \exists f\, (f\, \mathbf{GF}) = \phi(X)}} P(X \rightarrow Y | X, Feats, \mathbf{GF}) \quad (3)$$

The history-based model is motivated by English data, for example, to generate the appropriate case for pronouns in subject position and object position, respectively. Though Chinese does not distinguish cases, we expect the f-structure parent GF to help predict grammar rule expansions more accurately in the tree derivation than the simple PCFG model. We will investigate how the HB model performs while migrating it from English to Chinese data.

[1]The parent grammatical function of the outermost f-structure is assumed to be a dummy GF TOP.

3.2 A Lexicalised Model

Compared to the HB model which includes the parent grammatical function in the conditioning context, lexicalised grammar rules contain more fine-grained categorial information. To the best of our knowledge, lexicalised parsers (Bikel, 2004) outperform unlexicalised parsers for Chinese. The expectation is that a lexicalised PCFG model also works better than a simple PCFG model in Chinese generation, considering e.g. prepositional phrase (PP) modification in Chinese. Some prepositions indicating directions can occur either before or after the main verbs, for instance both (2a) and (2b) are acceptable in Chinese. However, most PP modifiers only act as adverbial adjuncts between the subjects and verbal predicates. For instance "对/to" never follows a verb as exemplified in the ungrammatical sentence (3b).

(2) a. 这 趟 列车 开 **往北京**
this CLS train run **to Beijing**
'The train is bound for Beijing.'

b. 这 趟 列车 **往北京** 开
this CLS train **to Beijing** run

(3) a. 泰国 总理 **对中国** 进行 访问
Thai president to China make visit
'The Thai president paid a visit to China.'

b. * 泰国 总理 进行 访问 **对中国**
Thai president make visit to China

In order to model phenomena such as these, we head-lexicalise our grammar by associating each non-terminal node with the head word[2] in the c-structure tree along the head-projection line. A non-terminal node is written as $X(x)$, where x is the lexical head of X. The example generation grammar rule in the lexicalised model is shown in the last line (LEX-PCFG) of Table 1.

As in CKY chart parsing, generation grammars are binarised in our chart generator. Thus all grammar rules are either unary of the form $X \rightarrow H$ or binary $X \rightarrow YH$ (or $X \rightarrow HY$), where H is the head constituent and Y is the modifier. To handle the problem of sparse data while estimating rule probabilities, a back-off to baseline model is employed. As, from a linguistic perspective, it is the modifier rather than the head word which plays the main role in determining word order, a back-off to partial lexicalisation on the modifier only is also used for binary rules. As a result, the probabilities of lexicalised unary and binary CFG rules are calculated as in Eq. (4) and Eq. (5), respectively.

$$P_{bk}(H(h)|X(h)) = \lambda_1 P(H(h)|X(h)) + \lambda_2 P(H|X) \quad (4)$$

$$P_{bk}(Y(y)H(h)|X(h)) = \lambda_1 P(Y(y)H(h)|X(h)) + \lambda_2 P(Y(y)H|X) + \lambda_3 P(YH|X) \quad (5)$$

$$where \quad \sum_{i=1} \lambda_i = 1$$

In principle, grammars binarisation from left-to-right (left-) or from right-to-left (right-) are equivalent to represent the original grammar and the probability distributions. However the head word is the final constituent for most phrasal categories in Chinese.[3] In lexicalised model, the head word immediately projects to the top level in a left-binary tree, and as a result, the intermediate $\overline{\text{NP}}$ nodes cannot be lexicalised with the head word as illustrated in Figure (2b). By contrast, right-binary rules are lexicalised and the head word is percolated from the bottom of the tree (Figure (2c)). Therefore we adopt the right binarisation method in our generation algorithm.

4 Chart Generation and Smoothing Algorithms

4.1 Chart Generation Algorithm

The PCFG-based generation algorithms are implemented in terms of a chart generator (Kay, 1996). In the generation algorithm, each (sub-)f-structure indexes a (sub-)chart. Each local chart generates the most probable trees for the local f-structure in a bottom-up manner:

- generating lexical edges from the the local GF PRED and some atomic features representing function words, mood or aspect etc.

[2]We use a mechanism similar to (Collins, 1997) but adapted to Chinese data to find lexical heads in the treebank data.

[3]Except for prepositional phrases, localiser and some verbal phrases.

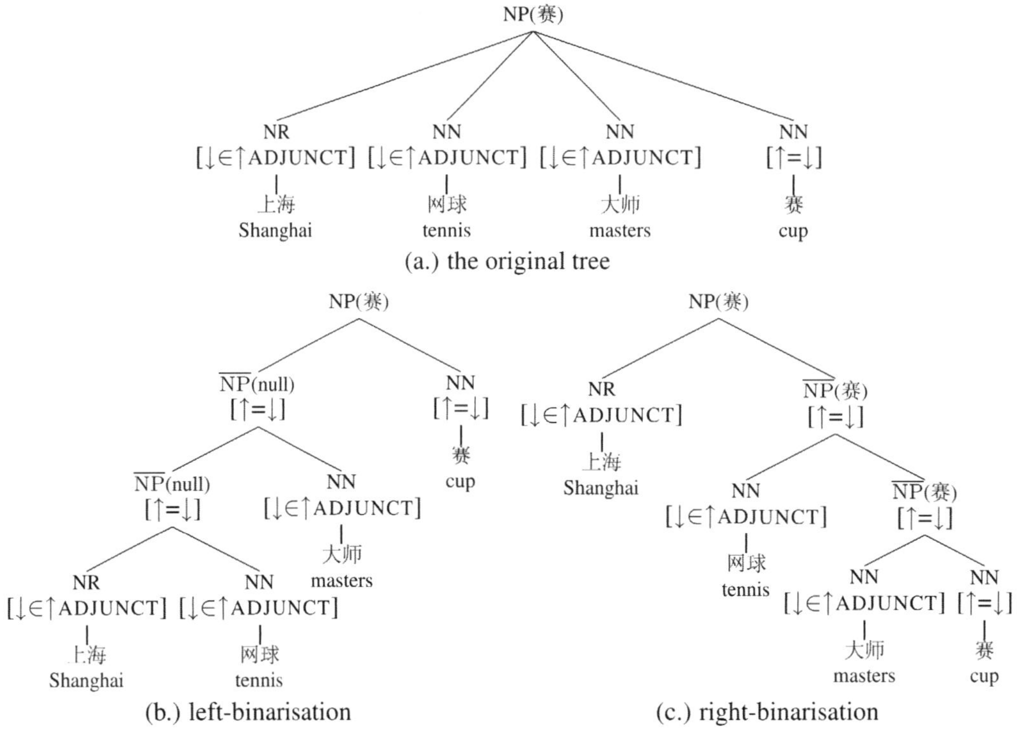

Figure 2: Lexicalised binary trees

- applying unary rules and binary rules to generate new edges until no any new edges can be generated in the current local chart.
- propagating compatible edges to the upper-level chart.

For efficiency, the generation algorithm does Viterbi-pruning for each local chart, viz. if two edges have equivalent categories and lexical coverage, only the most probable one is kept.

The generation coverage is impacted on by unknown words[4] and unmatched grammar rules in chart generation. We present a lexical smoothing and a rule smoothing strategy in the following subsections.

4.2 Lexical Smoothing

In LFG f-structure, the surface form of the lemma is represented via lexical rules involving a particular set of features, e.g. the lemma "总理/president" is represented as {↑PRED='总理', ↑NTYPE=common, ↑NUM=sg}. Particular lexical rules can be captured in general lexical macros abstracting away from particular surface forms to lemmas, e.g. the lexical macro encapsuling the above lexical rule is {↑PRED=$LEMMA, ↑NTYPE=common, ↑NUM=sg}, which generally associates to common nouns NN in the CTB. According to the assumption that unknown words have a probability distribution similar to hapax legomenon (Baayen and Sproat, 1996), we predict the part-of-speech of unknown words from infrequent words in the training set by automatically extracting lexical macros corresponding to the particular set of f-structure features. The probability of the potential POS tag t associated to a feature set f is estimated according to Eq. (6).

$$P(t|f) = \frac{count(t, f)}{\sum_{i=1}^{n} count(t_i, f)} \quad (6)$$

[4]We use unknown words as a cover term to refer to all words occurring in the test set but not in the training set.

4.3 Rule Smoothing

The coverage of grammar rules increases with the size of training data and in theory all the rules can be fully covered by a training set, if it is big enough. With limited training resources we have to resort to fuzzy matching of grammar rules. Two smoothing strategies are carried out at the level of grammar rules.

	Mathched Grammar Rule
Nonsmooth	VP[↑=↓] → VV[↑=↓] NP[↑OBJ=↓], {SUBJ, OBJ, PRED}
Feature smooth	VP[↑=↓] → VV[↑=↓] NP[↑OBJ=↓]
Partial match	VP → VV [↑OBJ=↓], {SUBJ, OBJ, PRED}

Table 2: Smoothing of CFG rules

- Reducing the conditioning f-structure features during rule matching;
- Applying partial match during rule application.

A node in each unlexicalised grammar rule $X \rightarrow Y H$ includes two parts: constituent category c, such as IP, NP, VP etc.; functional f-structure annotation a, such as [↑SUBJ=↓], [↑=↓] etc. As a heuristic based on linguistic experience, we define the order of importance of these elements as follows:

$$X(c) > H(c) > Y(a) > Y(c) > X(a) > H(a)$$

(4) IP[↑COMP=↓] → NP[↑SUBJ=↓] VP[↑=↓]

For the above example rule (4), the importance of the elements is:

IP > VP > [↑SUBJ=↓] > NP > [↑COMP=↓] > [↑=↓]

The elements can be deleted from the rules in an importance order from low to high.[5] The partial rules adopted in our system ignore the least important 3 elements, viz. the functional annotation of the head node $H(a)$, the functional annotation on LHS $X(a)$ and constituent category of the modifier node $Y(c)$. Examples of the two types of smoothed rules are shown in Table 2.

5 Experimental Results

Our experiments are carried out on the newly released Penn Chinese treebank version 6.0 (CTB6) (Xue et al., 2005), excluding the portion of ACE broadcast news. We follow the recommended splits (in the list-of-file of CTB6) to divide the data into test set, development set and training set. The training set includes 756 files with a total of 15,663 sentences. The CTB trees of the training set were automatically annotated with LFG f-structure equations following (Guo et al., 2007). Table 3 shows the number of different grammar rule types extracted from the training set. From the test files, we randomly select 500 sentences as test data with minimal sentence length 5 words, maximal length 80 words, and average length 28.84 words. The development set also includes 500 sentences randomly selected from the development files with sentence length between 5 and 80 words. The c-structure trees of the test and development data were also automatically converted to f-structures as input to the generator.

Type	with features	without features
PCFG	22,372	8,548
HB-PCFG	28,487	11,969
LEX-PCFG	325,094	286,468

Table 3: Number of rules in the training set

The generation system is evaluated against the raw text of the test data in terms of accuracy and coverage. Following (Langkilde, 2002) and other work on general-purpose generators, we adopt BLEU score (Papineni et al., 2002), average simple string accuracy (SSA) and percentage of exactly matched sentences for accuracy evaluation.[6] For coverage evaluation, we measure the percentage of input f-structures that generate a sentence.

Table 4 reports the initial experiments on the simple PCFG, HB-based PCFG and lexicalised PCFG models. The results in the left column evaluate all input f-structures, the right column evaluate only those f-structures which yield a complete sentence. The results show that the lexicalised model outperforms the baseline PCFG model. The HB model is the most accurate for complete sentences, but with reduced coverage compared to the other two models. However the low coverage of sentences completely generated due to unknown words and unmatched rules makes the results unusable in prac-

[5] However c and a on the same node can't be deleted at the same time.

[6] We are aware of the limitations in fully automatic evaluation metrics, and in an ideal scenario, we would complement the BLEU and SSA scores by a human evaluation. Unfortunately, this is beyond the scope of the current paper.

	All Output Strings				Complete Output Sentences			
	Coverage	ExMatch	BLEU	SSA	Coverage	ExMatch	BLEU	SSA
PCFG	100%	7.2%	0.5401	0.6261	36.40%	19.78%	0.7101	0.7687
HB-PCFG	100%	8.60%	0.5474	0.6281	34.80%	24.71%	**0.7513**	**0.8092**
LEX-PCFG	100%	**9.40%**	**0.5687**	**0.6537**	37.00%	**25.41%**	0.7431	0.8024

Table 4: Results without smoothing

	All Output Strings				Complete Output Sentences			
	Coverage	ExMatch	BLEU	SSA	Coverage	ExMatch	BLEU	SSA
PCFG	100%	11.00%	0.6894	0.7240	94.20%	11.68%	0.7047	0.7388
HB-PCFG	100%	11.80%	0.7108	0.7348	94.00%	12.55%	0.7284	0.7506
LEX-PCFG	100%	**14.00%**	**0.7152**	**0.7595**	94.40%	**14.83%**	**0.7302**	**0.7754**

Table 5: Results with lexical smoothing

	Partial match				Feature smooth			
Complete Sentences	Coverage	ExMatch	BLEU	SSA	Coverage	ExMatch	BLEU	SSA
PCFG	97.20%	11.32%	0.7022	0.7356	100%	11.20%	0.7021	0.7330
HB-PCFG	96.20%	12.27%	0.7263	0.7458	100%	12.00%	0.7245	0.7413
LEX-PCFG	97.80%	**14.31%**	**0.7265**	**0.7696**	100%	**14.20%**	**0.7265**	**0.7675**

Table 6: Results with lexical and rule smoothing

tice.

Table 5 gives the results with lexical smoothing. The coverage for complete sentences increases by nearly 60% absolute for all models. The increased coverage also improves the overall results evaluated against all sentences. The HB model performs better than the simple PCFG model in nearly all respects and in turn the lexicalised model comprehensively outperforms the HB model.

The final results with both lexical smoothing and rule smoothing by two different strategies are tabulated in Table 6. The left column provides the results of smoothing by partial match and the right column the results by reducing conditioning f-structure features. All results are evaluated for completely generated sentences only. The feature smoothing results in a full coverage of 100%, while slightly degrading the quality of sentences generated compared with partial match smoothing. We feel the tradeoff at the cost of a small decrease in quality is still worth the full coverage. Throughout the experiments, the lexicalised model exhibits consistently better performance than the unlexicalised models, which proves our intuition that successful techniques in parsing also work well in generation.

6 Conclusion and Further Work

We have presented an accurate, robust chart generator for Chinese based on treebank-based, automatically acquired LFG resources. Our model improves the baseline provided by (Cahill and van Genabith, 2006): (i) accuracy is increased by creating a lexicalised PCFG grammar and enriching conditioning context with parent f-structure features; and (ii) coverage is increased by providing lexical smoothing and fuzzy matching techniques for rule smoothing.

The combinational explosion of grammar rules encountered in the chart generator is similar to that in parsing. In the current system, we only keep the most probable realisation for each input f-structure. An alternative model in line with the generate-and-select paradigm, would pack all the locally equivalent edges in a forest and re-rank all the realisations by a separate language model. This might help us to reduce some errors caused in our current model, for instance, the generation of function words in fixed phrases. As shown in ex. (5), the function word "之" is incorrectly generated as "的". This is because they share the same part-of-speech DEG in CTB, however "的" has a much higher frequency than "之" in Chinese text and thus has a higher probability to be generated.

(5) a. 万物 之 中
all things DE in
'among all things'

b. * 万物 的 中
all things DE in

Acknowledgments

The research reported in this paper is supported by Science Foundation Ireland grant 04/IN/I527. Also, we would like to thank Aoife Cahill for many helpful and insightful discussions on the work. And we gratefully acknowledge the anonymous reviewers.

References

Harald Baayen and Richard Sproat. 1996. Estimating Lexical Priors for Low-Frequency Morphologically Ambiguous Forms. *Computational Linguistics*, 22(2): 155–166.

Srinivas Bangalore and Owen Rambow. 2000. Exploiting a Probabilistic Hierarchical Model for Generation. *Proceedings of the 18th International Conference on Computational Linguistics*, pages 42–48. Saarbrücken, Germany.

Daniel M. Bikel. 2004. On the Parameter Space of Generative Lexicalized Statistical Parsing Models. Ph.D. Thesis of Department of Computer & Information Science, University of Pennsylvania.

Aoife Cahill and Josef van Genabith. 2006. Robust PCFG-Based Generation Using Automatically Acquired LFG Approximations. *Proceedings of the 21st International Conference on Computational Linguistics and 44th Annual Meeting of the Association for Computational Linguistics*, pages 1033–1040. Sydney, Australia.

Aoife Cahill and Martin Forst and Christian Rohrer. 2007. Stochastic Realisation Ranking for a Free Word Order Language. *Proceedings of the 11th European Workshop on Natural Language Generation*, pages 17–24. Schloss Dagstuhl, Germany.

John Carroll and Ann Copestake and Dan Flickinger and Victor Poznanski. 1999. An efficient chart generator for (semi-)lexicalist grammars. *Proceedings of the 7th European Workshop on Natural Language Generation*, pages 86–95. Toulouse, France.

Hailong Cao and Yujie Zhang and Hitoshi Isahara. 2007. Empirical study on Parsing Chinese Based on Collins' Model. *Proceedings of the 10th Conference of the Pacific Association for Computational Linguistics*, pages 113–119. Melbourne, Australia.

Eugene Charniak. 2000. A Maximum-Entropy-Inspired Parser. *Proceedings of the 1st Annual Meeting of the North American Chapter of the Association for Computational Linguistics*, pages 132–139. Seattle, WA.

Michael Collins. 1997. Three Generative, Lexicalized Models for Statistical Parsing. *Proceedings of the 35th Annual Meeting of the Association for Computational Linguistics*, pages 16–23. Madrid, Spain.

Dick Crouch and Mary Dalrymple and Ron Kaplan and Tracy King and John Maxwell and Paula Newman. 2007. XLE Documentation. Palo Alto Research Center, CA.

Yuqing Guo and Josef van Genabith and Haifeng Wang. 2007. Treebank-based Acquisition of LFG Resources for Chinese. *Proceedings of LFG07 Conference*, pages 214–232. Stanford, CA, USA.

Deirdre Hogan and Conor Cafferkey and Aoife Cahill and Josef van Genabith. 2007. Exploiting Multi-Word Units in History-Based Probabilistic Generation. *Proceedings of the 2007 Joint Conference on Empirical Methods in Natural Language Processing and Computational Natural Language Learning*, pages 267–276. Prague, Czech Republic.

Mark Johnson. 1998. PCFG Models of Linguistic Tree Representations. *Computational Linguistics*, 24(4): 613–632. MIT Press, Cambridge, MA,

Ronald M. Kaplan. 1995. The formal architecture of lexical-functional grammar. *Formal Issues in Lexical-Functional Grammar*, pages 7–27. CSLI Publications, Standford, USA.

Ronald M. Kaplan and Joan Bresnan. 1982. Lexical Functional Grammar: a Formal System for Grammatical Representation. *The Mental Representation of Grammatical Relations*, pages 173-282. MIT Press, Cambridge, MA.

Ronald M. Kaplan and Jurgen Wedekind. 2000. LFG Generation Produces Context-free Languages. *Proceedings of the 18th International Conference on Computational Linguistics*, pages 425–431. Saarbrücken, Germany.

Martin Kay. 1996. Chart Generation. *Proceedings of the 34th Annual Meeting of the Association for Computational Linguistics*, pages 200–204. Santa Cruz, USA.

Irene Langkilde. 2000. Forest-Based Statistical Sentence Generation. *Proceedings of 1st Meeting of the North American Chapter of the Association for Computational Linguistics*, pages 170–177. Seattle, WA.

Langkilde, Irene. 2002. An Empirical Verification of Coverage and Correctness for a General-Purpose Sentence Generator. *Proceedings of the Second International Conference on Natural Language Generation*, 17–24. New York, USA.

Hiroko Nakanishi and Yusuke Nakanishi and Jun'ichi Tsujii. 2005. Probabilistic Models for Disambiguation of an HPSG-Based Chart Generator. *Proceedings of the 9th International Workshop on Parsing Technology*, pages 93–102. Vancouver, British Columbia.

Kishore Papineni and Salim Roukos and Todd Ward and Wei-Jing Zhu. 2002. Bleu: a Method for Automatic Evaluation of Machine Translation. *Proceedings of the 40th Annual Meeting of the Association for Computational Linguistics*, pages 311-318. Philadelphia, USA.

Erik Velldal and Stephan Oepen. 2005. Maximum entropy models for realization ranking. *Proceedings of the MTSummit '05*.

Michael White. 2004. Reining in CCG Chart Realization. *Proceedings of the third International Natural Language Generation Conference*. Hampshire, UK.

Michael White and Rajakrishnan Rajkumar and Scott Martin. 2007. Towards Broad Coverage Surface Realization with CCG. *Proceedings of the MT Summit XI Workshop on Language Generation and Machine Translation*, pages 22–30. Copenhagen, Danmark.

Nianwen Xue and Fei Xia and Fu dong Chiou and Martha Palmer. 2005. The Penn Chinese TreeBank: Phrase Structure Annotation of a Large Corpus. *Natural Language Engineering*, 11(2): 207–238.

Automated Metrics That Agree With Human Judgements On Generated Output for an Embodied Conversational Agent

Mary Ellen Foster
Informatik VI: Robotics and Embedded Systems
Technische Universität München
Boltzmannstraße 3, D-85748 Garching bei München, Germany
foster@in.tum.de

Abstract

When evaluating a generation system, if a corpus of target outputs is available, a common and simple strategy is to compare the system output against the corpus contents. However, cross-validation metrics that test whether the system makes exactly the same choices as the corpus on each item have recently been shown not to correlate well with human judgements of quality. An alternative evaluation strategy is to compute intrinsic, task-specific properties of the generated output; this requires more domain-specific metrics, but can often produce a better assessment of the output. In this paper, a range of metrics using both of these techniques are used to evaluate three methods for selecting the facial displays of an embodied conversational agent, and the predictions of the metrics are compared with human judgements of the same generated output. The corpus-reproduction metrics show no relationship with the human judgements, while the intrinsic metrics that capture the number and variety of facial displays show a significant correlation with the preferences of the human users.

1 Introduction

Evaluating the output of a generation system is known to be difficult: since generation is an open-ended task, the criteria for success can be difficult to define (cf. Mellish and Dale, 1998). In the current state of the art, there are two main strategies for evaluating the output of a generation system: the behaviour or preferences of humans in response to the output may be measured, or automated measures may be computed on the output itself. A study involving human judges is the most complete and convincing evaluation of generated output. However, such a study is not always practical, as recruiting sufficient subjects can be time-consuming and expensive. So automated metrics are also used in addition to—or instead of—human studies.

When automatically evaluating generated output, the goal is to find metrics that can easily be computed and that can also be shown to correlate with human judgements of quality. Such metrics have been introduced in other fields, including PARADISE (Walker et al., 1997) for spoken dialogue systems, BLEU (Papineni et al., 2002) for machine translation,[1] and ROUGE (Lin, 2004) for summarisation. Many automated generation evaluations measure the similarity between the generated output and a corpus of "gold-standard" target outputs, often using measures such as precision and recall. Such measures of corpus similarity are straightforward to compute and easy to interpret; however, they are not always appropriate for generation systems. One of the main advantages of choosing dynamic generation over canned output is its flexibility and its ability to produce a range of different outputs; as pointed out by Paris et al. (2007), "[e]valuation studies that ignore the potential of the system to generate a range of appropriate outputs will be necessarily limited." Indeed, several recent studies (Stent et al., 2005; Belz and Reiter, 2006; Foster and White, 2007) have shown that strict corpus-similarity measures tend to favour repetitive generation strategies that do not diverge much, on average, from the corpus data, while human judges often prefer output with more variety.

[1] Although Callison-Burch et al. (2006) have recently called into question the utility of BLEU.

Automated metrics that take into account other properties than strict corpus similarity have also been used to evaluate the output of generation systems. Walker (2005) describes several evaluations that used corpus data in a different way: each of the corpus examples was associated with some reward function (e.g., subjective user evaluation or task success), and machine-learning techniques such as reinforcement learning or boosting were then used to train the output planner. Foster and White (2007) found that automated metrics based on factors other than corpus similarity (e.g., the amount of variation in the output) agreed better with user preferences than did the corpus-similarity scores. Belz and Gatt (2008) compare the predictions of a range of measures, both intrinsic and extrinsic, that were used to evaluate the systems in a shared-task referring-expression generation challenge. One main finding from this comparison was that there was no significant correlation between the intrinsic and extrinsic (task success) measures for this task.

All of the above studies considered only systems that generate text, but many of the same factors also apply to the generation of non-verbal behaviours for an embodied conversational agent (ECA) (Cassell et al., 2000). The behaviour of such an agent is normally based on recorded human behaviour, which can provide targets similar to those used in corpus-based evaluations of text-generation systems. However, just as in text generation, a multimodal system that scores well on corpus similarity tends to produce highly repetitive non-verbal behaviours, so it is equally important to gather human judgements to accompany any automated evaluation.

This paper presents three corpus-driven methods of selecting facial displays for an embodied conversational agent and describes two studies comparing the output of the different methods. All methods are based on annotated data drawn from a corpus of human facial displays, and each uses the corpus data in a different way. The first evaluation study uses human judges to compare the output of the selection methods against one another, while the second study uses a range of automated metrics: several corpus-reproduction measures, along with metrics based on intrinsic properties of the outputs. The results of the two studies are compared using multiple regression, and the implications are discussed.

2 Corpus-based generation of facial displays for an ECA

The experiments in this paper make use of the output components of the COMIC multimodal dialogue system (Foster et al., 2005), which adds a multimodal talking-head interface to a CAD-style system for redesigning bathrooms. The studies focus on the task of selecting appropriate ECA head and eyebrow motions to accompany the turns in which the system describes and compares the options for tiling the room, as those are the parts of the output with the most interesting and varied content.

The implementations were based on a corpus of conversational facial displays derived from the behaviour of a single speaker reading approximately 450 scripted sentences generated by the COMIC output-generation system. The OpenCCG syntactic derivation trees (White, 2006) for the sentences form the basis of the corpus. The leaf nodes in these trees correspond to the individual words, while the internal nodes correspond to multi-word constituents. Every node in each tree was initially labelled with all of the applicable contextual features produced by the output planner: the user-preference evaluation of the tile design being described (positive/negative/neutral), the information status (given/new) of each piece of information, and the predicted speech-synthesiser prosody. The annotators then linked each facial display produced by the speaker to the node or span of nodes in the derivation tree covering the words temporally associated with the display. Full details of this corpus are given in Foster (2007a).

The most common display used by the speaker was a downward nod, while the user-preference evaluation had the single largest differential effect on the displays used. When the speaker described features of the design that the user was expected to like, he was relatively more likely to turn to the right and to raise his eyebrows (Figure 1(a)); on features that the user was expected to dislike, on the other hand, there was a higher probability of left leaning, lowered eyebrows, and narrowed eyes (Figure 1(b)). In a previous study, users were generally able to recognise these "positive" and "negative" displays when they were resynthesised on an embodied conversational agent (Foster, 2007b).

(a) Positive

(b) Negative

Figure 1: Characteristic facial displays from the corpus

Based on this corpus, three different strategies were implemented for selecting facial displays to accompany the synthesised speech: one strategy using only the three characteristic displays described above, along with two data-driven strategies drawing on the full corpus data. All of the strategies use the same basic process to select the displays to accompany a sentence. Beginning with the contextually-annotated syntactic tree for the sentence, the system proceeds depth-first, selecting a face-display combination to accompany each node in turn. The main difference among the strategies is the way that each selects the displays for a node as it is encountered.

The **rule-based** strategy includes displays only on derivation-tree nodes corresponding to specific tile-design properties: that is, manufacturer and series names, colours, and decorative motifs. The displays for such a node are entirely determined by the user-preference evaluation of the property being described, and are based on the corpus patterns described above: for every node associated with a positive evaluation, this strategy selects a right turn and brow raise; for a negative node, it selects a left turn, brow lower, and eye squint; while for all other design-property nodes, it chooses a downward nod.

While the rule-based strategy selects displays only on nodes describing tile-design features, the two data-driven strategies consider all nodes in the syntactic tree for a sentence as possible sites for a facial display. To choose the displays for a given node, the system considers the set of displays that occurred on all nodes in the corpus with the same syntactic, semantic, and pragmatic context, and then chooses a display from this set in one of two ways. The **majority** strategy selects the most common option in all cases, while the **weighted** strategy makes a stochastic choice among all of the options based on the relative frequency. As a concrete example, consider a hypothetical context in which the speaker made no motion 80% of the time, a downward nod 15% of the time, and a downward nod with a brow raise the other 5% of the time. For nodes with this context, the majority strategy would always choose no motion, while the weighted strategy would choose no motion with probability 0.8, a downward nod with probability 0.15, and a nod with a brow raise with probability 0.05.

Table 1 shows a sample sentence from the corpus, the original facial displays used by the speaker, and the displays selected by each of the strategies. In the figure, *nd=d* indicates a downward nod, *bw=u* and *bw=d* a brow raise and lower, respectively, *sq* an eye squint, *ln=l* a left lean, and *tn=r* a right turn. Most of the displays in these schedules are associated with leaf nodes in the derivation tree, and therefore with single words in the output. However, both the left lean in the original schedule and the right turn in the weighted schedule are associated with internal nodes in the tree, and therefore cover more than one word in the surface string.

3 User-preference studies

As a first comparison of the evaluation strategies, human judges were asked to compare videos based on the output of each of the generation strategies to one another and to resynthesised versions of the original displays from the corpus. This section gives the details of a study in which the judges chose

	Although	*it's*	*in*	*the*	*family*	*style,*	*the*	*tiles*	*are*	*by*	*Alessi.*
Original	nd=d	nd=d	nd=d		nd=d				nd=d,bw=u		
	....	....	....	....	....	ln=l	....	....	....	....	....
Rule-based					ln=l,bw=d						tn=r,bw=u
Majority					nd=d						nd=d
Weighted	nd=d				nd=d		.. tn=r ..				

Table 1: Face-display schedules for a sample sentence

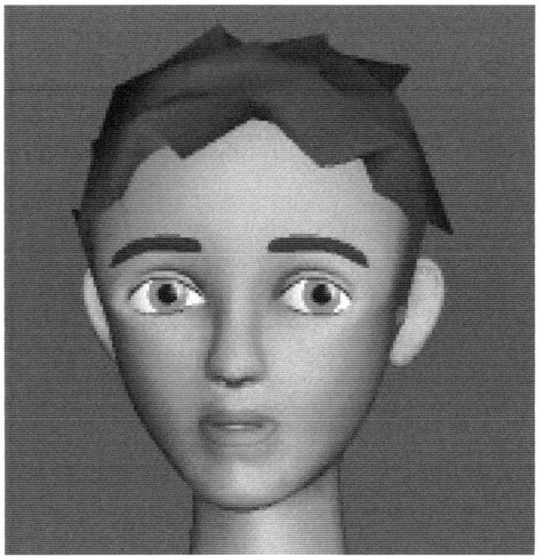

Figure 2: RUTH talking head

among the original displays and the output of the weighted and rule-based strategies. At the end of the section, the results of this study are discussed together with the results of a similar previous study comparing the two data-driven strategies to each other; the full details of the earlier study are given in Foster and Oberlander (2007).

3.1 Subjects

Subjects were recruited for this experiment through the Language Experiments Portal,[2] a website dedicated to online psycholinguistic experiments. There were 36 subjects (20 female), 50% of whom identified themselves as native English speakers; most of the subjects were between 20 and 29 years old.

3.2 Materials

The materials for this experiment were based on 18 randomly-selected sentences from the corpus. For each sentence, face-display schedules were generated using both the rule-based and the weighted strategies. The Festival speech synthesiser (Clark et al., 2004) and the RUTH animated talking head (DeCarlo et al., 2004) (Figure 2) were used to create video clips of the two generated schedules for each sentence, along with a video clip showing the original facial displays annotated in the corpus.

3.3 Method

Each subject saw a series of pairs of videos. Both videos in a pair had identical spoken content, but the face-display schedules differed: each trial included two of rule-based, weighted, and original. For each pair of videos, the subject was asked to select which of the two versions they preferred. Subjects made each pairwise comparison between schedule types six times—three times in each order—for a total of 18 judgements. All subjects saw the same set of sentences, in an individually randomly-selected order: the pairwise choices between schedule types were also allocated to items at random.

3.4 Results and analysis

The overall pairwise preferences of the subjects in this study are shown in Figure 3(a). A χ^2 goodness-of-fit test can be used to evaluate the significance of the choices made on each individual comparison. For the comparison between original and rule-based schedules, the preference is significant: $\chi^2(1, N = 216) = 4.17$, $p < 0.05$. The results are similar for the original vs. weighted comparison: $\chi^2(1, N = 215) = 4.47$, $p < 0.05$. However, the preferences for the weighted vs. rule-based comparison are not significant: $\chi^2(1, N = 217) = 2.44$, $p \approx 0.12$.

Figure 3(b) shows the results from a similar previous study (Foster and Oberlander, 2007) in which the subjects compared the two data-driven strategies to the original displays, using a design identical to that used in the current study with 54 subjects and 24 sentences. The responses given by the subjects in this study also showed a signifi-

[2] `http://www.language-experiments.org/`

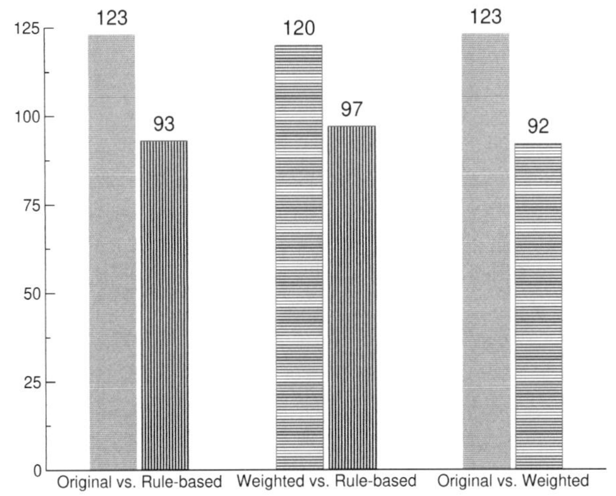

(a) Original, weighted, rule-based

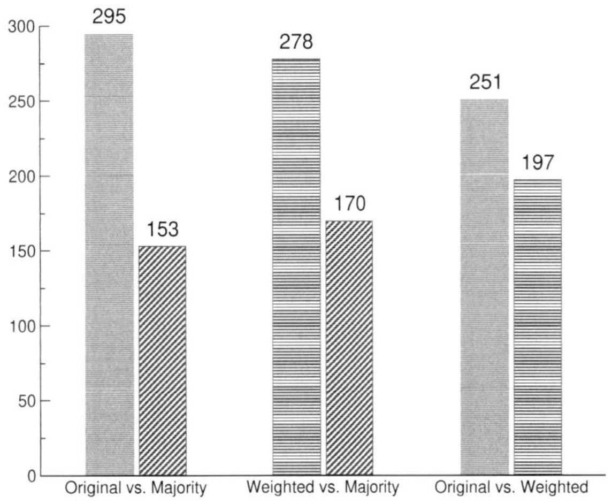

(b) Original, weighted, majority (Foster and Oberlander, 2007)

Figure 3: Pairwise preferences from the user evaluations

cant preference for the original schedules over the weighted ones ($\chi^2(1, N = 448) = 6.51$, $p < 0.05$). Both the weighted and the original schedules were very strongly preferred over the majority schedules ($\chi^2(1, N = 448) = 45$ and 26, respectively; $p \ll 0.0001$). The original vs. weighted comparison was included in both studies (the rightmost pair of bars on the two graphs in Figure 3), and the response patterns across the two studies for this comparison did not differ significantly from each other: $\chi^2(1, N = 664) = 0.02$, $p \approx 0.89$.

3.5 Discussion

Taken together, the results of these two studies suggest a rough preference ordering among the different strategies for generating facial displays. In both studies, the judges significantly preferred the original displays from the corpus over any of the automatically-generated alternatives. This suggests that, for this generation task, the data in the corpus can indeed be treated as a "gold standard"—unlike, for example, the corpus used by Belz and Reiter (2006), where the human judges sometimes preferred generated output to the corpus data. The schedules generated by the majority strategy, on the other hand, were very obviously disliked by the judges in the Foster and Oberlander (2007) study. The ranking between the rule-based and weighted schedules from the current study is less clear, although there was a tendency to prefer the latter.

4 Automated evaluation

Since the subjects in the user-preference studies generally selected the corpus schedules over any of the alternatives, any automated metric for this task should favour output that resembles the examples in the corpus. The most obvious form of corpus similarity is exact reproduction of the displays in the corpus, which suggests using metrics such as precision and recall that favour generation strategies whose output on every item is as close as possible to what was annotated in the corpus for that sentence. In Section 4.1, several such **corpus-reproduction** metrics are described and their results presented.

For this type of open-ended generation task, though, it can be overly restrictive to allow *only* the displays that were annotated in the corpus for a sentence and to penalise any deviation. Indeed, as mentioned in the introduction, a number of previous studies have found that the output of generation systems that score well on this type of metric is often disliked in practice by users. Section 4.2 therefore presents several **intrinsic** metrics that aim to capture corpus similarity of a different type: rather than requiring the system to exactly reproduce the corpus on each sentence, these metrics instead favour strategies resulting in global behaviour that exhibits similar patterns to those found in the corpus, without necessarily agreeing exactly with the corpus on any specific sentence.

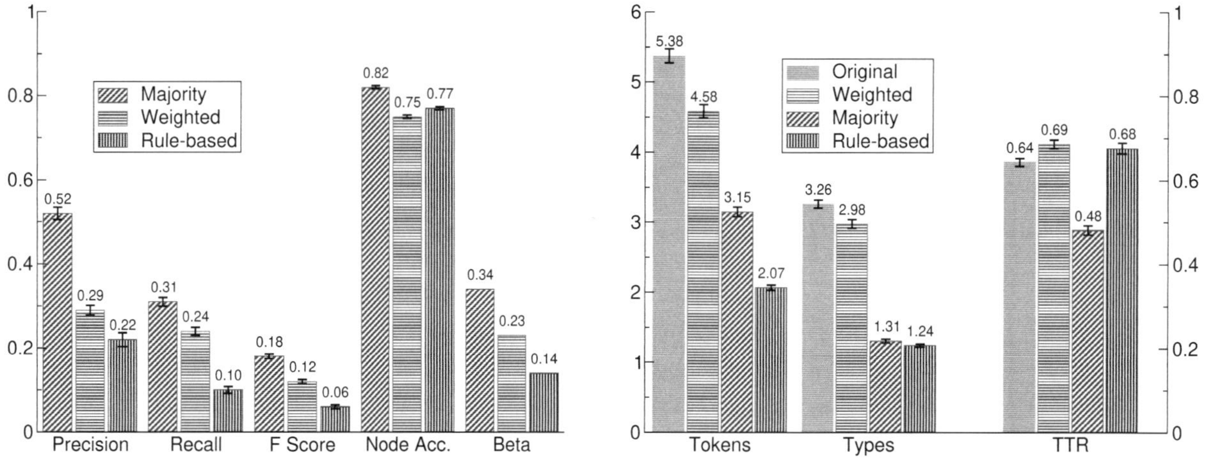

(a) Corpus-reproduction metrics

(b) Intrinsic metrics

Figure 4: Results of the automated evaluations

4.1 Corpus-reproduction metrics

This first set of metrics compared the generated schedules against the original schedules annotated in the corpus, using 10-fold cross-validation. The first three metrics that were tested are standard for this sort of corpus-comparison task: recall, precision, and F score. Recall was computed as the proportion of the corpus displays for a sentence that were reproduced exactly in the generated output, while precision was the proportion of generated displays that had exact matches in the corpus; the F score for a sentence is then the harmonic mean of these two values, as usual. The leftmost three columns in Table 2 show the precision, recall, and F score for the sample schedules in Table 1.

In addition to the above commonly-used metrics, two other corpus-reproduction metrics were also computed. The first, *node accuracy*, represents the proportion of nodes in the derivation tree for a sentence where the proposed displays were correct, including those nodes where the system correctly selected no motion—a baseline system that never proposes any motion scores 0.79 on this measure. The fourth column of Table 2 shows the node-accuracy score for the sample sentences. The final corpus-reproduction metric compared the proposed displays to the annotated corpus displays using the β agreement measure (Artstein and Poesio, 2005). β is a weighted measure that permits different levels of agreement when annotations overlap, and that can therefore capture a more fine-grained form of agreement than other measures such as κ.

	P	R	F	NAcc	Tok	Typ	TTR
Original	–	–	–	–	6	3	0.5
Rule-based	0	0	0	0.65	2	2	1
Majority	0.50	0.14	0.11	0.70	2	1	0.5
Weighted	0.67	0.29	0.20	0.74	3	2	0.67

Table 2: Automated evaluation of the sample schedules

Figure 4(a) shows the results for all of these corpus-reproduction measures, averaged across the sentences in the corpus; the results for the weighted and majority strategies are from Foster and Oberlander (2007). The majority strategy scored uniformly higher than the weighted strategy on all of these measures—particularly on precision—while the weighted strategy in turn scored higher than the rule-based strategy on all measures except for node accuracy. Using a Wilcoxon rank sum test with a Bonferroni correction for multiple comparisons, all of the differences among the strategies on precision, recall, F score, and node accuracy are significant at $p < 0.001$. Significance cannot be assessed for the differences in β scores, as noted by Artstein and Poesio (2005), but the results are similar. Also, the node accuracy score for the majority strategy is significantly better than the no-motion baseline of 0.79, while those for the weighted and rule-based strategies are worse (also all $p < 0.001$).

As expected—and as noted by Foster and Oberlander (2007)—all of the corpus-reproduction metrics strongly favoured the weighted strategy over the weighted strategy and generally penalised the rule-based strategy. Since the majority strategy always chooses the most probable option, it is not surprising that it agrees more often with the corpus than do the other strategies, which deliberately select less frequent options; this led to its relatively high scores on the corpus-reproduction metrics. It is also not surprising that the weighted strategy beat the rule-based strategy on most of these metrics, as the former selects from the most frequent options, while the latter uses the most *marked* options, which are not generally the most frequent.

4.2 Intrinsic metrics

The metrics in the preceding section compared the displays selected for a sentence against the displays found in the corpus for that sentence. This section describes other measures that are computed directly on the generated schedules, without any reference to the corpus data. For each sentence, the following values were counted: the total number of face-display combinations (i.e., the number of display *tokens*), and the number of different combinations (*types*). In addition to being used as metrics themselves, these two counts were also used to compute a third value: the *type/token ratio* (TTR) (i.e., $\frac{\#\,types}{\#\,tokens}$), which captures the diversity of the displays selected for each sentence.

These intrinsic metrics were computed on each sentence produced in the cross-validation study from the preceding section and then averaged to produce the final results. Since these metrics do not require the original corpus data for comparison, they were also computed on the original corpus schedules. The rightmost columns in Table 2 show the intrinsic results for the sample schedules in Table 1.

The overall results for these metrics across the entire corpus are shown in Figure 4(b). The original corpus had both the most displays types and the most tokens; the values for weighted choice were a fairly close second, those for majority choice third, while the rule-based strategy scored lowest on both of these metrics. Except for the difference between majority and rule-based on the facial-display types—which is not significant—all of the differences between schedule types on these two measures are significant at $p < 0.001$ on a Wilcoxon rank sum test with Bonferroni correction. When it comes to the type/token ratio, the value for the majority-choice schedule is significantly lower than that for the other three schedule types (all $p < 0.0001$), while the value for weighted choice is somewhat higher than that for the original schedules ($p < 0.01$); no other differences are significant.

Since the original corpus schedules scored the highest on the user study, these metrics should be considered in the context of of how close the results are to those of the corpus. Figure 4(b) shows that the weighted strategy is most similar to the corpus in both the number and the diversity of displays it selects, while the other two strategies have much lower diversity. However, even though the rule-based strategy selects fewer displays all of the other strategies, its TTR is more similar to that of the corpus and the weighted strategy, while the majority strategy has a much lower TTR. In fact, in the schedules generated by the majority-choice strategy, nearly 90% of the displays that were selected were downward nods.

5 Comparing the automated metrics with human preferences

Qualitatively, the results of the corpus-reproduction metrics differ greatly from the preferences of the human judges. The users generally liked the majority schedules the least, while all of these metrics scored this strategy the highest. Among the intrinsic metrics, the type and token counts placed the weighted schedules closest to the corpus, while the majority and rule-based strategies were further away; this agrees with the human results for the two data-driven strategies, but not for the rule-based strategy. On the other hand, the TTR indicated that the output of the rule-based and weighted schedules was similar to the schedules found in the corpus, while the majority-choice strategy produced sentences with TTRs more different from the corpus, generally agreeing with the human results.

To permit a more quantitative comparison between the predictions of the automated metrics and the judges' preferences, the pairwise preferences from the user study were converted into a numeric value called the *selection ratio*. The selection ratio for an item (i.e., a sentence with a particular set of facial displays) was computed as the number of trials on which that item was selected, divided by the total number of trials on which that item was an option. For example, an item that was always preferred over any of the alternatives on all trials would score 1.0 on this measure, while an item that was selected a quarter of the time would score 0.25. The selection ratios of the items used in the human-preference studies ranged from 0.13 to 0.85. As a concrete example, when the sentence in Table 1 was used in the Foster and Oberlander (2007) study, the selection ratios were 0.43 for the original version, 0.33 for the majority version, and 0.24 for the weighted version.

The relationship between the selection ratio and the full set of automated metrics from the preceding section was assessed through multiple linear regression. An initial model including all of the automated metrics as predictor variables had an adjusted R^2 value of 0.413. Performing stepwise selection on this initial model resulted in a final model with two significant predictor variables—display tokens and TTR—and an adjusted R^2 of 0.422. The regression coefficients for both of these predictor variables are positive, with high significance ($p < 0.001$). While the R^2 values indicate that neither the initial nor the final model fully explains the selection ratios from the user study, the details of the models themselves are relevant to the overall goal of finding automated metrics that agree with human preferences.

The results of the stepwise selection have backed up the qualitative intuition that none of the corpus-reproduction metrics had any relationship to the users' preferences, while the number and diversity of displays per sentence appear to have contributed much more strongly to the choices made by the human judges. This adds to the growing body of evidence that intrinsic measures are the preferred option for evaluating the output of generation systems, particularly those that are designed to incorporate variation into their output, while measures based on strict corpus similarity are less likely to be useful.

6 Conclusions

This paper has presented three methods for using corpus data to select facial displays for an embodied agent and shown the results from two studies comparing the output generated by these methods. When human judges rated the output, they preferred the original displays from the corpus and strongly disliked the displays selected by a majority-choice strategy, with the weighted and rule-based strategies in between. In the automated evaluation, the metrics that directly compared the generated output against the corpus data favoured the majority strategy and did not show any relationship with the user preferences. On the other hand, the number of displays accompanying a sentence and the diversity of those displays both had a positive relationship with the rate at which users selected that display schedule.

These results confirm those of previous text-generation evaluations and extend these results to the multimodal-generation case. This adds to the body of evidence that, even though direct corpus reproduction is often the easiest factor to analyse automatically, it is rarely an accurate reflection of user reactions to generated output. If a system performs well on this type of metric, its output tends to be constrained to a small space; for example, the majority-choice strategy used in these studies nearly always selected a nodding expression. For most generation tasks, output options beyond those in the corpus are often equally valid, and users seem to prefer a system that makes use of this wider space of variations.

This suggests that corpus-based generation systems should use strategies that retain the full range of variation, and—perhaps most importantly—that metrics based on factors other than strict similarity are more likely to capture human preferences when evaluating generated output.

The user study described here was based only on the preferences of human judges. In future, it would be informative to include more task-based measures such as task success and time taken, as user preferences do not always correlate with performance (Nielsen and Levy, 1994), to see if a different style of automated measure agrees better with the results of this sort of user study.

Acknowledgements

This work was partly supported by the EU projects COMIC (IST-2001-32311) and JAST (FP6-003747-IP). Thanks to Jon Oberlander, Jean Carletta, and the INLG reviewers for helpful feedback.

References

R. Artstein and M. Poesio. 2005. Kappa^3 = alpha (or beta). Technical Report CSM-437, University of Essex Department of Computer Science. http://cswww.essex.ac.uk/technical-reports/2005/csm-437.pdf.

A. Belz and A. Gatt. 2008. Intrinsic vs. extrinsic evaluation measures for referring expression generation. In *Proceedings of ACL/HLT 2008*.

A. Belz and E. Reiter. 2006. Comparing automatic and human evaluation of NLG systems. In *Proceedings of EACL 2006*. acl:E06-1040.

C. Callison-Burch, M. Osborne, and P. Koehn. 2006. Re-evaluating the role of BLEU in machine translation research. In *Proceedings of EACL 2006*. acl:E06-1032.

J. Cassell, J. Sullivan, S. Prevost, and E. Churchill, editors. 2000. *Embodied Conversational Agents*. MIT Press.

R. A. J. Clark, K. Richmond, and S. King. 2004. Festival 2 – build your own general purpose unit selection speech synthesiser. In *Proceedings of the 5th ISCA Workshop on Speech Synthesis*. http://www.ssw5.org/papers/1047.pdf.

R. Dale and M. White, editors. 2007. *Report from the Workshop on Shared Tasks and Comparative Evaluation in Natural Language Generation*. http://ling.ohio-state.edu/nlgeval07/NLGEval07-Report.pdf.

D. DeCarlo, M. Stone, C. Revilla, and J. Venditti. 2004. Specifying and animating facial signals for discourse in embodied conversational agents. *Computer Animation and Virtual Worlds*, 15(1):27–38. doi:10.1002/cav.5.

M. E. Foster. 2007a. Associating facial displays with syntactic constituents for generation. In *Proceedings of the ACL 2007 Linguistic Annotation Workshop*. acl:W07-1504.

M. E. Foster. 2007b. Generating embodied descriptions tailored to user preferences. In *Proceedings of Intelligent Virtual Agents 2007*. doi:10.1007/978-3-540-74997-4_24.

M. E. Foster and J. Oberlander. 2007. Corpus-based generation of head and eyebrow motion for an embodied conversational agent. *Language Resources and Evaluation*, 41(3–4):305–323. doi:10.1007/s10579-007-9055-3.

M. E. Foster and M. White. 2007. Avoiding repetition in generated text. In *Proceedings of ENLG 2007*. acl:W07-2305.

M. E. Foster, M. White, A. Setzer, and R. Catizone. 2005. Multimodal generation in the COMIC dialogue system. In *Proceedings of the ACL 2005 Demo Session*. acl:P05-3012.

C. Y. Lin. 2004. ROUGE: A package for automatic evaluation of summaries. In *Proceedings of the ACL 2004 Workshop on Text Summarization*. acl:W04-1013.

C. Mellish and R. Dale. 1998. Evaluation in the context of natural language generation. *Computer Speech and Language*, 12(4):349–373. doi:10.1006/csla.1998.0106.

J. Nielsen and J. Levy. 1994. Measuring usability: preference vs. performance. *Communications of the ACM*, 37(4):66–75. doi:10.1145/175276.175282.

K. Papineni, S. Roukos, T. Ward, and W.-J. Zhu. 2002. BLEU: A method for automatic evaluation of machine translation. In *Proceedings of ACL 2002*. acl:P02-1040.

C. Paris, D. Scott, N. Green, K. McCoy, , and D. McDonald. 2007. Desiderata for evaluation of natural language generation. In Dale and White (2007), chapter 2.

A. Stent, M. Marge, and M. Singhai. 2005. Evaluating evaluation methods for generation in the presence of variation. In *Computational Linguistics and Intelligent Text Processing*, pages 341–351. Springer. doi:10.1007/b105772.

M. A. Walker. 2005. Can we talk? Methods for evaluation and training of spoken dialogue systems. *Language Resources and Evaluation*, 39(1):65–75. doi:10.1007/s10579-005-2696-1.

M. A. Walker, D. J. Litman, C. A. Kamm, and A. Abella. 1997. PARADISE: A general framework for evaluating spoken dialogue agents. In *Proceedings of ACL/EACL 1997*. acl:P97-1035.

M. White. 2006. Efficient realization of coordinate structures in Combinatory Categorial Grammar. *Research on Language and Computation*, 4(1):39–75. doi:10.1007/s11168-006-9010-2.

Simple but effective feedback generation to tutor abstract problem solving

Xin Lu, Barbara Di Eugenio, Stellan Ohlsson and Davide Fossati
University of Illinois at Chicago
Chicago, IL 60607, USA
xinlu@northsideinc.com
bdieugen,stellan,dfossa1@uic.edu

Abstract

To generate natural language feedback for an intelligent tutoring system, we developed a simple planning model with a distinguishing feature: its plan operators are derived automatically, on the basis of the association rules mined from our tutorial dialog corpus. Automatically mined rules are also used for realization. We evaluated 5 different versions of a system that tutors on an abstract sequence learning task. The version that uses our planning framework is significantly more effective than the other four versions. We compared this version to the human tutors we employed in our tutorial dialogs, with intriguing results.

1 Introduction

Intelligent Tutoring Systems (ITSs) are software systems that provide individualized instruction, like human tutors do in one-on-one tutoring sessions. Whereas ITSs have been shown to be effective in engendering learning gains, they still are not equivalent to human tutors. Hence, many researchers are exploring Natural Language (NL) as the key to bridging the gap between human tutors and current ITSs. A few results are now available, that show that ITS with relatively sophisticated language interfaces are more effective than some other competitive condition (Graesser et al., 2004; Litman et al., 2006; Evens and Michael, 2006; Kumar et al., 2006; VanLehn et al., 2007; Di Eugenio et al., 2008). Ascertaining which specific features of the NL interaction are responsible for learning still remains an open research question.

In our experiments, we contrasted the richness with which human tutors respond to student actions with poorer forms of providing feedback, e.g. only graphical. Our study starts exploring the role that *positive* feedback plays in tutoring and in ITSs. While it has long been observed that most tutors tend to avoid direct negative feedback, e.g. (Fox, 1993; Moore et al., 2004), ITSs mostly provide negative feedback, as they react to student errors.

In this paper, we will first briefly describe our tutorial dialog collection. We will then present the planning architecture that underlies our feedback generator. Even if our ITS does not currently allow for student input, our generation architecture is inspired by state-of-the art tutorial dialog management (Freedman, 2000; Jordan et al., 2001; Zinn et al., 2002). One limitation of these approaches is that plan operators are difficult to maintain and extend, partly because they are manually defined and tuned. Crucially, our plan operators are automatically derived via the association rules mined from our corpus. Finally, we will devote a substantial amount of space to evaluation. Our work is among the first to show not only that a more sophisticated language interface results in more learning, but that it favorably compares with human tutors. Full details on our work can be found in (Lu, 2007).

2 Task and curriculum

Our domain concerns extrapolating letter patterns, such as inferring EFMGHM, given the pattern ABMCDM and the new initial letter E. This task is used in cognitive science to investigate human information processing (Kotovsky and Simon, 1973; Reed and Johnson, 1994; Nokes and Ohlsson, 2005). The curriculum we designed consists of 13 patterns of increasing length and difficulty; it was used unchanged in both our human data collection and ITS experiments. The curriculum is followed by two

Tutor Moves
Answer student's questions
Evaluate student's actions
Summarize what done so far
Prompt student into activity
Diagnose what student is doing
Instruct
Demonstrate how to solve (portions of) problem
Support – Encourage student
Conversation – Acknowledgments, small talk
Student Moves
Question
Explain what student said or did
Reflect – Evaluate own understanding
Answer tutor's question
Action Response – Perform non-linguistic action (e.g. write letter down)
Complete tutor's utterance
Conversation – Acknowledgments, small talk

Table 1: Tutor and student moves

post-test problems, each 15 letter long: subjects (all from the psychology subject pool) have n trials to extrapolate each pattern, always starting from a different letter ($n = 6$ in the human conditions, and $n = 10$ in the ITS conditions). While the earlier example was kept simple for illustrative purposes, our patterns become very complex. Starting e.g. from the letter L, we invite the reader to extrapolate problem 9 in our curriculum: *BDDFFFCCEEGGGC*, or the second test problem: *ACZDBYYDFXGEWWGI*.[1]

3 Human dialogs

Three tutors – one expert, one novice, and one (the *lecturer*) experienced in teaching, but not in one-on-one tutoring – were videotaped as they interacted with 11 subjects each.[2] A repeated measures ANOVA, followed by post-hoc tests, revealed that students with the expert tutor performed significantly better than the students with the other two tutors on both test problems ($p < 0.05$ in both cases).

36 dialog excerpts were transcribed, taken from 18 different subjects (6 per tutor), for a total of about 2600 tutor utterances and 660 student utterances (transcription guidelines were taken from (MacWhinney, 2000)). For each subject, these two dialog excerpts cover the whole interaction with the tutor on one easy and one difficult problem (# 2 and 9 respectively). 2 groups of 2 coders each, annotated half of the transcripts each, with dialogue moves. Our move inventory comprises 9 tutor moves and 7 student moves, as listed in Table 1.[3] Table 2 presents an annotated fragment from one of the dialogues with the expert tutor. Kappa measures for intercoder agreement had values in the following ranges, according to the scale in (Rietveld and van Hout, 1993): for tutor moves, from moderate (0.4 for *Support*) to excellent (0.82 for *Prompt*); for student moves, from substantial (0.64 for *Explanation*) to excellent (0.82 for *Question*, 0.97 for *ActionResponse*). Whereas some of these Kappa measures are lower than what we had strived for, we decided to nonetheless use the move inventory in its entirety, after the coders reconciled their codings. In fact, our ultimate evaluation measure concerns learning, and indeed the ITS version that uses that entire move inventory engenders the most learning. Please see (Lu et al., 2007) for a detailed analysis of these dialogs and for a discussion of differences among the tutors in terms of tutor and student moves.

The transcripts were further annotated by one coder for tutor attitude (whether the tutor agrees with the student's response – *positive*, *negative*, *neutral*), for correctness of student move and for student confidence (*positive*, *negative*, *neutral*). Student hesitation time (*long*, *medium*, *short*) was estimated by the transcribers. Additionally, we annotated for the problem features under discussion. Of the 8 possible relationships between letters, most relevant to the examples discussed in this paper are *forward, backward, progression* and *marker*. E.g. in ABMCDM, M functions as chunk *marker*, and the sequence moves *forward* by one step, both *within* one chunk and *across* chunks. *Within* and *across* are two out of 4 *relationship scopes*, which encode the coverage of a particular relationship within the sequence.

[1]The solutions are, respectively: *LNNPPPMMOOQQQM*, and *LNZOMYYOQXRPWWRT*.

[2]One goal of ours was to ascertain whether expert tutors are indeed more effective than non-expert tutors, not at all a foregone conclusion since very few studies have contrasted expert and non expert tutors, e.g. (Glass et al., 1999).

[3]There is no explicit tutor *question* move because we focus on the goal of a tutor's question, either *prompt* or *diagnose*.

Line	Utterances	Annotation
38	**Tutor:** how'd you actually get the *n* in the first place?	Diagnose
39	**Student:** from here I count from *c* to *g* and then just from *n* to *r*.	Answer
40	**Tutor:** okay so do the *c* to *g*.	Prompt
41	**Tutor:** do it out loud so I can hear you do it.	Prompt
42	**Student:** *c d e f.*	Explain
43	**Student:** so it's three spaces.	Answer
44	**Tutor:** okay so it's three spaces in between.	Summarize

Table 2: An annotated fragment from a dialogue with the expert tutor

4 Learning rules to provide feedback

Once the corpus was annotated, we mined the expert tutor portion via Classification based on Associations (CBA) (Liu et al., 1998). CBA generates understandable rules and has been effectively applied to various domains. CBA finds all rules that exist in the data, which is especially important for small training sets such as ours.

To modularize what the rules should learn, we decomposed *what the tutor should do* into two components pertaining to content: letter relationship and relationship scope; and two components pertaining to how to deliver that content: tutor move and tutor attitude. Hence, we derived 4 sets of tutorial rules. Features used in the rules are those annotated on the tutoring dialogs, plus the student's Knowledge State (KS) on each type of letter relationship *rel*, computed as follows:

$$KS(rel) = \lfloor \frac{p \times 0.5 + w}{t} \times 5 \rfloor \qquad (1)$$

p is the number of partially correct student inputs, w is the number of wrong student inputs and t is the total number of student inputs ("inputs" here are only those relevant to the relationship rel, as logged by the ITS from the beginning of the session). $KS(rel)$ ranges from 0 to 5. The higher the value, the worse the performance on rel. The scale of 5 was chosen to result in just enough values for KS(rel) to be useful for classification.

We ran experiments with different lengths of dialog history, but using only the last utterance gave us the best results. Three of the four rule sets have accuracies between 88 and 90% (results are based on 6-way cross-validation, and the cardinality of each set of rules is in the low hundreds.). Whereas the tutor move rule set only has 57% accuracy, as for some of the low Kappa values mentioned earlier, our ultimate evaluation measure is that the NL feedback based on these rules does improve learning.

relation-marker = No, relation-forward = Yes, student-move = ActionResponse
→ **relation-forward = Yes**
(Confidence = 100%, Support = 4.396%)

correctness = wrong, scope-within = No, KS(backward) = 0, relation-forward = Yes
→ **tutor-move = Summarize**
(Confidence = 100%, Support = 6.983%)

correctness = wrong, relation-forward = Yes, KS(forward) = 1, hesitation = no
→ **tutor-attitude = negative**
(Confidence = 100%, Support = 1.130%)

Figure 1: Example Tutorial Rules

Figure 1 shows three example rules, for choosing relationship, move and attitude respectively – we'll discuss two of them. The first rule predicts that the ITS will continue focusing on the *forward* relation, if it was focusing on *forward* and not on *marker*, and the student just input something. The second rule chooses the *summarize* move if the student made a mistake, the ITS was focusing on *forward* but not on relationships within chunks, and the student showed perfect knowledge of *backward*.

Two strength measurements are associated with each rule $X \rightarrow y$. A rule holds with confidence *conf* if *conf*% of cases that contain X also contain y; and with support *sup* if *sup*% of cases contain X or y. Rules are ordered, with confidence having precedence over support. Ties over confidence are solved via support; any remaining ties are solved according to the order rules were generated.

For each Tut-Move-Rule $TMR_{i,k}$ whose Left-Hand Side LHS matches IS_i do:

1. **Create and Populate New Plan** $p_{i,k}$:
   (a) *preconditions* = IS_i; *actions* = tutor move from $TMR_{i,k}$; *strength* = confidence and support from $TMR_{i,k}$
   (b) Fill remaining slots in $p_{i,k}$:
      i. *contents* = relationship $\cup$ scope (from highest ranked rules that match IS_i from relationship and scope rule sets);
      ii. *modifiers* = attitude (from highest ranked rule that matches IS_i from tutor attitude rule set)
2. **Augment Plan:** do the following *n* times :
   (a) make copy of IS_i and name it IS_{i+1};
   (b) change *agent* to "tutor";
   (c) change corresponding elements in IS_{i+1} to move, attitude, letter relationship and scope from $p_{i,k}$;
   (d) from the two rule sets for tutor move and tutor attitude, retrieve highest ranked rules that match IS_{i+1}, $TMR_{i+1,j}$ and $TAR_{i+1,j}$
   (e) add to *actions* tutor move from $TMR_{i+1,j}$; add to *modifiers* tutor attitude from $TAR_{i+1,j}$

Figure 2: Plan generation

5 From rules to plans

For our task of extrapolating abstract sequences, we built a model-tracing ITS by means of the Tutoring Development Kit (TDK) (Koedinger et al., 2003). Model-tracing ITSs codify cognitive skills via production rules. The student's solution is monitored by rules that fire according to the underlying model. When the student steps differ from that model, an error is recognized. A portion of the student interface of the ITS is shown in Figure 4a. It mainly includes two rows, one showing the *Example Pattern*, the other for the student to input the *New Pattern* extrapolated starting with the letter in the first cell.

In model-tracing ITSs, production rules provide the capability to generate simple template-based messages. We developed a more sophisticated NL feedback generator consisting of three major modules: update, planning and feedback realization.

The update module maintains the context, represented by the Information State (IS) (Larsson and Traum, 2000), which captures the overall dialog context and interfaces with external knowledge sources (e.g., curriculum, tutorial rules) and the production rule system. As the student performs a new action, the IS is updated. The planning module generates or revises the system plan and selects the next tutoring move based on the newly updated IS. At last the feedback realization module transforms this move into NL feedback.

The planning module consists of three components, plan generation, plan selection and plan monitoring. A plan includes an ordered collection of tutoring moves meant to help the student correctly fill a single cell. The structure of our plans is shown in Figure 3.

Plan generation generates a plan set which contains one plan for each tutor move rule that matches the current IS_i. Each of these plans is augmented at plan generation time by 'simulating' the next IS_{i+1} that would result if the move is executed but its effects are not achieved. The algorithm is sketched in Figure 2. The planner iterates through the *tutor move* rule set.[4] Recall that our four rule sets are totally ordered. Also, note that each rule set contains a default rule that fires when no rule matches the current IS_i. In Step 1b, at every iteration *only* the rules that have not been checked yet from those three rule sets are considered. In Step 2, n is set to 3, i.e., each plan contains 3 additional moves and corresponding attitudes, which will provide hints when no response from the student occurs. Three hints plus one original move makes 4, which is the average number of moves in one turn of the expert tutor.

An example plan is shown in Figure 3. It is generated in reaction to the mistake in Figure 4a, and by

[4] Since there is no language input, rules which include student moves other than *ActionResponse* in their LHS will never be activated. Additionally, we recast tutor *answers* as *confirm* moves, since students cannot ask questions.

Preconditions	(same as the IS in Figure 4b)
Effects	student's input = *W*
Contents	relationship = *forward* scope = *across*
Actions	*summarize, evaluate, prompt, summarize*
Modifiers	*negative, negative, neutral, neutral*
Strength	conf = *100%*, sup = *6.983%*

Figure 3: An Example Plan

firing, among others, the rules in Figure 1. The IS in Figure 4b reflects some of the history of this interaction (in the slots *Relationships, Scopes* and *KS*), and as such corresponds to the situation depicted in Figure 4a in a specific context (this plan was generated in one of our user experiments).

The plan selection component retrieves the highest ranked plan in the newly generated plan set, selects a template for each tutoring move in its "Actions" slot and puts each tutoring move onto the dialog move (DM) stack. Earlier we mentioned that rules are totally ordered according to confidence, then support and finally rule generation order. When a plan set contains more than one plan, plans are also totally ordered, since they inherit strength measurements from the rule that engenders the first tutor move in the *Actions* slot.

After the student receives the message which realizes the top tutoring move in the DM stack, plan monitoring checks whether its intended effects have been obtained. If the effects have not been obtained, and the student's input is unchanged, the next move from the DM stack will be executed to provide the student with hint messages until either the student's input changes or the DM stack becomes empty. If the DM stack becomes empty, the next plan is selected from the original plan set and the tutoring moves within that plan are pushed onto the DM stack. Whenever the student's input changes, or after every plan in the plan set has been selected, control returns to plan generation.

The realization module. A tutor move is pushed onto the DM stack by plan selection together with a template to realize it. 50 templates were written manually upon inspection of the expert tutor dialogs. Since several templates can realize each tutor move, we used CBA to learn rules to choose among templates. Features used to learn when to use each

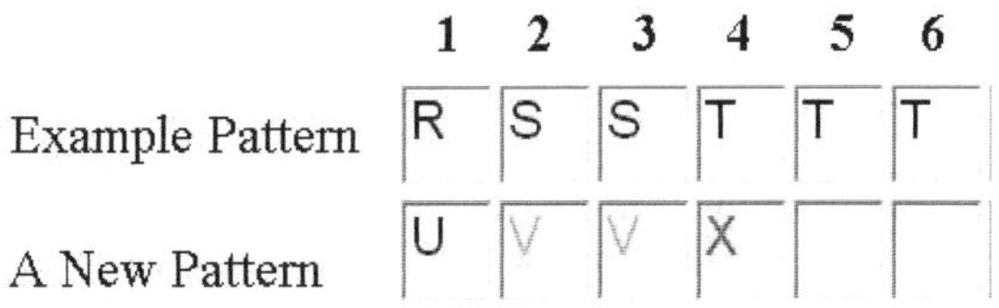

(a) A Student Action in Problem 4

1. **Agent**: *student* (producer of current move);
2. **Relationships**: *forward, progress in length*
3. **Scopes**: *across* (for 'forward'), *within* (for 'progress in length');
4. **Agent's move**: *action response*;
5. **Agent's attitude**: *positive* (since student shows no hesitation before inputting letter);
6. **Correctness**: *wrong* (correct letter is *W*);
7. **Student's input**: *X*;
8. **Student's selection**: 4th cell in *New Pattern* row;
9. **Hesitation time**: *no*;
10. **Student's knowledge state (KS)**: *1* (on "forward"), *3* (on "progress in length").

(b) The corresponding IS

Figure 4: A snapshot of an ITS interaction

template also include the tutor attitude. For the first *Summarize* move in the plan in Figure 3, given the IS in Figure 4b, the rule in Fig. 5 will fire (tutor attitude does not affect this specific rule). As a result, the following feedback message is generated: "From *V* to *X*, you are going forward 2 in the alphabet."

6 Evaluation

To demonstrate the utility of our feedback generator, we developed five different versions of our ITS, named according to how feedback is generated:

1. **No feedback**: The ITS only provides the basic interface, so that subjects can practice solving the 13 problems in the curriculum, but does not provide any kind of feedback.
2. **Color only**: The ITS provides graphic feedback by turning the input green if it is correct or red if it is wrong.
3. **Negative**: In addition to the color feedback, the

scope-within = No, relation-marker = No, relation-forward = Yes, move= Summarize → **template = TPL11**
[where TPL11: From "<reference-pattern>" to "<input>", you are going <input-relation> <input-number> in the alphabet.]

Figure 5: Example Realization Rule

ITS provides feedback messages when the input is wrong.

4. **Positive**: In addition to the color feedback, the ITS provides feedback messages when the input is correct.

5. **Model**: In addition to the color feedback, the ITS provides feedback messages generated by the feedback generator just described.

Feedback is given for each input letter. Positive and negative verbal feedback messages are given out whenever the student's input is correct or incorrect, respectively. Positive feedback messages confirm the correct input and explain the relationships which this input is involved in. Negative feedback messages flag the incorrect input and deliver hints. The feedback messages for the "negative" and "positive" versions were developed earlier in the project, to avoid repetitions and inspired by the expert tutor's language but before we performed any annotation and mining. They are directly generated by TDK production rules.

Although in reality positive and negative feedback are both present in tutoring sessions, one study for the letter pattern task shows that positive/negative feedback, given independently, perform different functions (Corrigan-Halpern and Ohlsson, 2002). In addition, our *negative* condition is meant to embody the "classical" model-tracing ITS, that only reacts to student errors. Hence, in our experiments, we elected to keep these two types of feedback separate, other than in the "model" version of the ITS.

To evaluate the five versions of the ITS, we ran a between-subjects study in which each group of subjects interacted with one version of the system. A group of control subjects took the post-test with no training at all but only read a short description of the domain.[5] Subjects were trained to solve the same 13 problems in the curriculum that were used in the human tutoring condition. They also did the same post-test (2 problems, each pattern 15 letters long). For each post-test problem, each subject had 10 trials, where each trial started with a new letter.

	Condition	Score		
		Prob 1	Prob 2	Total
0	Control	36.50	32.84	69.34
1	No feedback	58.21	75.27	133.48
2	Color only	68.32	66.30	134.62
3	Negative	70.33	66.06	141.83
4	Positive	75.06	79.00	154.06
5	Model	91.95	101.76	193.71

Table 3: Average Post-test Scores of the ITS

6.1 Results

Table 3 reports the average post-test scores of the six groups of subjects, corresponding to the five versions of the ITS and the control condition. Performance on each problem is measured by the number of correct letters out of a total of 150 letters (15 letters by 10 trials); hence, cumulative post-test score, is the number of correct letters out of 300 possible.

A note before we proceed. In ITS research it is common to administer the same test before (pre-test) and after treatment (post-test), but we only have the post-test. The pre/post-test paradigm is used for two reasons. First, for evaluation proper, to gauge learning gains. Second, to verify that the groups have the same level of pre-tutoring ability, as shown when the pre-tests of the different groups are statistically indistinguishable, and hence, that they can be rightly compared. Even without a pre-test we can assess this. An ANOVA on "time spent on the first 3 problems" revealed no significant differences across the different groups. Since time spent on the first 3 problems is highly correlated with post-test score (multiple regression, $p < 0.03$), this provides indirect evidence that all subjects before treatment have equivalent ability for this task. Hence, we can trust that our evaluation, in terms of absolute scores, does reveal differences between conditions.

Our main findings are based on one-way ANOVAs, followed by Tukey post-hoc tests:

[5] The number of subjects in each condition varies from 32 to 38. Groups differ in size because of technical problems.

- A **main effect** of ITS ($p \leq 0.05$). Subjects who interacted with any version of the ITS had significantly higher total post-test scores than subjects in the control condition.
- A **main effect** of modeled feedback ($p < 0.05$). Subjects who interacted with the "model" version of the ITS had significantly higher total post-test scores than control subjects, and subjects with any other version of the ITS.
- No other effects. Subjects trained by the three versions "color only", "negative", "positive", did not have significantly higher total post-test scores than subjects with the "no feedback" version; neither did subjects trained by the two versions "negative", "positive", wrt subjects with the "color-only" version.

If we examine individual problems, the same pattern of results hold, other than, interestingly, the *model* and *positive* versions are not significantly different any more. As customary, we also analyze *effect sizes* , i.e., how much *more* subjects learn with the 'model' ITS in comparison to the other conditions. On the Y axis, Figure 6 shows *Cohen's d*, a common measure of effect size. Each point represents the difference between the means of the scores in the 'model' ITS and in one of the other condition, divided by the standard deviation of either condition. According to (Cohen, 1988), the effect sizes shown in Figure 6 are large as concerns the comparison with the "no feedback", "color only" and "negative" conditions, and moderate as concerns the "positive" condition.[6]

ITSs and Human Tutors. After we established that, at least cumulatively, the "model" ITS is more effective than the other ITSs, we wanted to assess how well the "model" ITS fares in comparison to the expert tutor it is modeled on. Since in the human data each post-test problem consists of only 6 trials, the first 6 trials per problem from the ITSs are used to run this comparison, for a maximum total score of 180 (15 letters by 6 trials, by 2 problems). Figure 7 shows the overall post-test performance of all 9 conditions. The error bars in the figure represent the standard deviations.

[6]A very large effect size with respect to control is not shown in Figure 6.

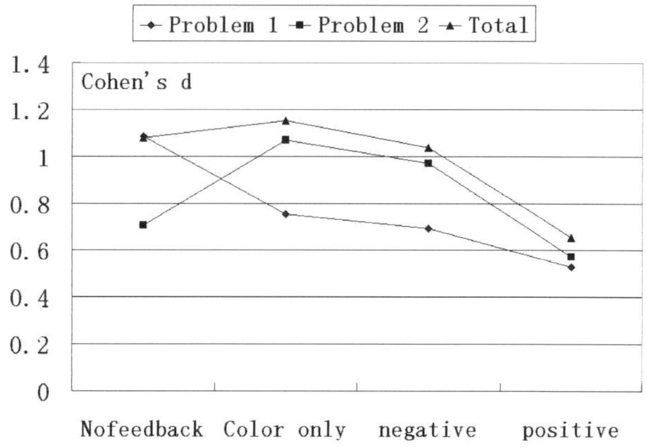

Figure 6: Effect sizes: how much more subjects learn with the "model" ITS

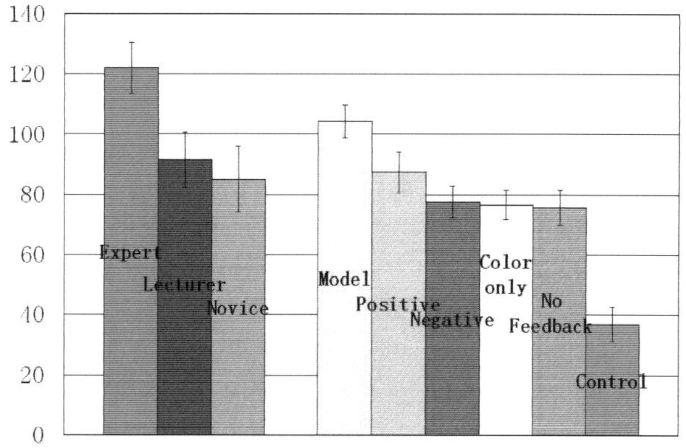

Figure 7: Post-test performance – all conditions

Paired t-tests between the model ITS and each of the human tutors show that:[7]

- on problem 1, the 'model' ITS is indistinguishable from the expert tutor, and is significantly better than the novice and the lecturer ($p = 0.05$ and $p = 0.039$ respectively);
- on problem 2, the model ITS is significantly worse than the expert tutor ($p = 0.020$), and is not different from the other two tutors;
- cumulatively, there are no significant differences between the 'model' ITS and any of the three human tutors.

[7]A 9-way ANOVA among all conditions is not appropriate, since in a sense we have two "super conditions", human and ITS. It is better to compare the 'model' ITS to each of the human tutors via t-tests, as a follow-up to the differences highlighted by the separate analyses on the two "super conditions".

7 Discussion and Conclusions

Our results add to the growing body of evidence that language feedback engenders more learning not only than simple practice, but also, than less sophisticated language feedback. Importantly, our 'model' ITS appears intriguingly close to our expert tutor in effectiveness: on post-test problem 1, it is as effective as the expert tutor himself, and significantly better than the other two tutors, as the expert tutor is. It appears our 'model' ITS does capture at least some features of successful tutoring.

As concerns the specific language the ITS generates, we compared different ways of providing verbal feedback. A subject receives both positive and negative verbal feedback when interacting with the "model" version, while a subject receives only one type of verbal feedback when interacting with the "positive" and "negative" versions (recall that in all these versions including the "model" ITS the red/green graphical feedback is provided on every input). While we cannot draw definite conclusions regarding the functions of positive and negative feedback, since the 'model' version provides other tutorial moves beyond positive / negative feedback, we have suggestive evidence that negative feedback by itself is not as effective. Additionally, positive feedback appears to play an important role. First, the 'model' and the 'positive' versions are statistically equivalent when we analyze performance on individual problems. Further, in the "model" version, the ratio of positive to negative messages turns out to be 9 to 1. In our tutoring dialogs, positive feedback still outnumbers negative feedback, but by a lower margin, 4 to 1. We hypothesize that conveying a positive attitude in an ITS is perhaps even more important than in human tutoring since a human has many more ways of conveying subtle shades of approval and disapproval.

From the NLG point of view, we have presented a simple generation architecture that turns out to be rather effective. Among its clear limitations are the lack of hierarchical planning, and the fact that different components of a plan are generated independently one from the other. Among its strengths are that the plan operators are derived automatically via the rules we mined, both for content planning and, partly, for realization.

It clearly remains to be seen whether our NLG framework can easily be ported to other domains – the issue is not domain dependence, but whether a more complex domain will require some form of hierarchical planning. We are now working in the domain of Computer Science data structures and algorithms, where we continue exploring the role of positive feedback. We collected data with two tutors in that domain, and there again, we found that in the human data positive feedback occurs about 8 times more often than negative feedback. We are now annotating the data to mine it as we did here, and developing the core ITS.

Acknowledgments

This work was supported by awards N00014-00-1-0640 and N00014-07-1-0040 from the Office of Naval Research, by Campus Research Board S02 and S03 awards from the University of Illinois at Chicago, and in part, by awards IIS 0133123 and ALT 0536968 from the National Science Foundation.

References

J. Cohen. 1988. *Statistical power analysis for the behavioral sciences (2nd ed.)*. Hillsdale, NJ: Lawrence Earlbaum Associates.

Andrew Corrigan-Halpern and Stellan Ohlsson. 2002. Feedback effects in the acquisition of a hierarchical skill. In *Proceedings of the 24th Annual Conference of the Cognitive Science Society*.

Barbara Di Eugenio, Davide Fossati, Susan Haller, Dan Yu, and Michael Glass. 2008. Be brief, and they shall learn: Generating concise language feedback for a computer tutor. *International Journal of AI in Education*, 18(4). To appear.

Martha W. Evens and Joel A. Michael. 2006. *One-on-one Tutoring by Humans and Machines*. Mahwah, NJ: Lawrence Erlbaum Associates.

Barbara A. Fox. 1993. *The Human Tutorial Dialogue Project: Issues in the design of instructional systems*. Lawrence Erlbaum Associates, Hillsdale, NJ.

Reva K. Freedman. 2000. Plan-based dialogue management in a physics tutor. In *Proceedings of the Sixth Applied Natural Language Conference*, Seattle, WA, May.

Michael Glass, Jung Hee Kim, Martha W. Evens, Joel A. Michael, and Allen A. Rovick. 1999. Novice vs. expert tutors: A comparison of style. In *MAICS-99, Proceedings of the Tenth Midwest AI and Cognitive Science Conference*, pages 43–49, Bloomington, IN.

Arthur C. Graesser, S. Lu, G.T. Jackson, H. Mitchell, M. Ventura, A. Olney, and M.M. Louwerse. 2004. AutoTutor: A tutor with dialogue in natural language. *Behavioral Research Methods, Instruments, and Computers*, 36:180–193.

Pamela Jordan, Carolyn Penstein Rosé, and Kurt VanLehn. 2001. Tools for authoring tutorial dialogue knowledge. In *Proceedings of AI in Education 2001 Conference*.

Kenneth R. Koedinger, Vincent Aleven, and Neil T. Heffernan. 2003. Toward a rapid development environment for cognitive tutors. In *12th Annual Conference on Behavior Representation in Modeling and Simulation*.

K. Kotovsky and H. Simon. 1973. Empirical tests of a theory of human acquisition of information-processing analysis. *British Journal of Psychology*, 61:243–257.

Rohit Kumar, Carolyn P. Rosé, Vincent Aleven, Ana Iglesias, and Allen Robinson. 2006. Evaluating the Effectiveness of Tutorial Dialogue Instruction in an Exploratory Learning Context. In *Proceedings of the Seventh International Conference on Intelligent Tutoring Systems*, Jhongli, Taiwan, June.

Staffan Larsson and David R. Traum. 2000. Information state and dialogue management in the trindi dialogue move engine toolkit. *Natural Language Engineering*, 6(3-4):323–340.

Diane J. Litman, Carolyn P. Rosé, Kate Forbes-Riley, Kurt VanLehn, Dumisizwe Bhembe, and Scott Silliman. 2006. Spoken versus typed human and computer dialogue tutoring. *International Journal of Artificial Intelligence in Education*, 16:145–170.

Bing Liu, Wynne Hsu, and Yiming Ma. 1998. Integrating classification and association rule mining. In *Knowledge Discovery and Data Mining*, pages 80–86, New York, August.

Xin Lu, Barbara Di Eugenio, Trina Kershaw, Stellan Ohlsson, and Andrew Corrigan-Halpern. 2007. Expert vs. non-expert tutoring: Dialogue moves, interaction patterns and multi-utterance turns. In *CICLING07, Proceedings of the 8th International Conference on Intelligent Text Processing and Computational Linguistics*, pages 456–467. Best Student Paper Award.

Xin Lu. 2007. *Expert tutoring and natural language feedback in intelligent tutoring systems*. Ph.D. thesis, University of Illinois - Chicago.

Brian MacWhinney. 2000. *The CHILDES project. Tools for analyzing talk: Transcription Format and Programs*, volume 1. Lawrence Erlbaum, Mahwah, NJ, third edition.

Johanna D. Moore, Kaska Porayska-Pomsta, Sebastian Varges, and Claus Zinn. 2004. Generating Tutorial Feedback with Affect. In *FLAIRS04, Proceedings of the Seventeenth International Florida Artificial Intelligence Research Society Conference*.

Timothy J. Nokes and Stellan Ohlsson. 2005. Comparing multiple paths to mastery: What is learned? *Cognitive Science*, 29:769–796.

Jonathan Reed and Peder Johnson. 1994. Assessing implicit learning with indirect tests: Determining what is learned about sequence structure. *Journal of Experimental Psychology: Learning, Memory, and Cognition*, 20(3):585–594.

Toni Rietveld and Roeland van Hout. 1993. *Statistical Techniques for the Study of Language and Language Behaviour*. Mouton de Gruyter, Berlin - New York.

Kurt VanLehn, Arthur C. Graesser, G. Tanner Jackson, Pamela W. Jordan, Andrew Olney, and Carolyn P. Rosé. 2007. When are tutorial dialogues more effective than reading? *Cognitive Science*, 31(1):3–62.

Claus Zinn, Johanna D. Moore, and Mark G. Core. 2002. A 3-tier planning architecture for managing tutorial dialogue. In *ITS 2002, 6th. Intl. Conference on Intelligent Tutoring Systems*, pages 574–584, Biarritz, France.

What's In a Message? Interpreting Geo-referenced Data for the Visually-impaired

Kavita E. Thomas
Department of Computing Science
University of Aberdeen
Aberdeen, Scotland
tkavita@abdn.ac.uk

Somayajulu Sripada
Department of Computing Science
University of Aberdeen
Aberdeen, Scotland
yaji.sripada@abdn.ac.uk

Abstract

In this paper we describe content determination issues involved in the Atlas.txt project, which aims to automatically describe geo-referenced information such as census data as text for the visually-impaired (VI). Texts communicating geo-referenced census information contain census data abstractions and their corresponding geographic references. Because visually impaired users find interpreting geographic references hard, we hypothesized that an introduction message about the underlying geography should help the users to interpret the geographic references easily. We performed user studies to design and evaluate the introduction message. An initial evaluation study with several sighted users and one partially sighted user showed that an introduction message is certainly preferred by most participants. Many of them used an introduction message themselves when they described maps textually. But the study also showed that the introduction message made no difference when the participants were asked to draw maps using the information in the textual descriptions.

1 Introduction

Atlas.txt is a data-to-text natural language generation (NLG) system which aims to communicate geo-referenced information to VI people. Geo-referenced data are data which has a geographic component, and is distributed over a region on Earth. Such data is often visualised as thematic maps, as shown in Figure 1, where colour shading indicates density of distribution, so that dark or intense regions on such maps indicate where the variable, for example unemployment, is most frequently located. Geo-referenced data is frequently stored in long data tables which hinder VI users, who must rely on screenreaders to read out the values in the data table, from quickly and easily forming an overview of how the data is distributed. For example, although the table corresponding to Figure 1 only has 31 rows (corresponding to the 31 council areas of Scotland), VI users still need to listen to each of these values and remember them in order to form a mental picture of the overall trends in population distribution which sighted users can infer from the map in under a minute. Furthermore, tables do not communicate where regions are located. This means that although they might be able to pick out maxima and minima, inferring trends is a much harder task, and mentally visualising how the data is distributed is impossible for unfamiliar areas given named locations in tables. Atlas.txt aims to automatically interpret this tabular geo-referenced data and communicate its central information as texts which can then be read out to VI users via a screenreading application. We start by describing some of the issues involved in communicating geo-referenced information in the census domain. Then we address content determination issues in the system and present some user needs requirements for communicating geo-referenced information to VI users, principle among which is the need for texts to enable mentally visualising the region and how the data is distributed. This motivates our decision to include introduction messages which describe the region before communicating how the

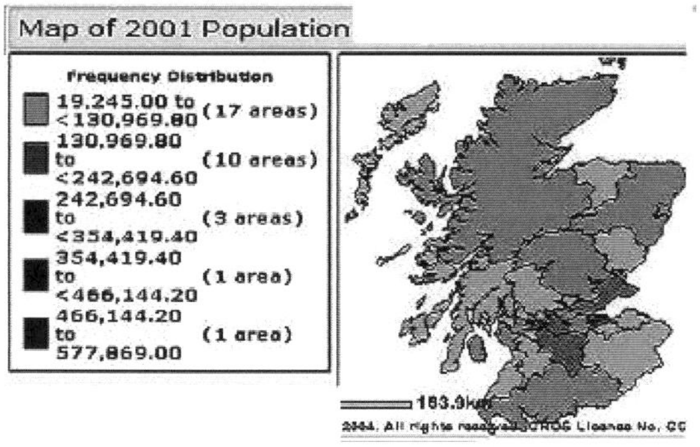

Figure 1: A typical map showing geo-referenced data

data is distributed, and present an experiment into this choice, focusing on evaluating whether introduction messages are beneficial.

2 Related Work

Systems which generate descriptions of numerical data are not uncommon, e.g., the FOG system (Goldberg et al, 1994), TREND (Boyd, 1997) and MULTI-METEO (Coch, 1998) all generate textual summaries of numerical weather data. (Ferres et al, 2006) generates textual descriptions of information in graphs and enables user querying. SumTime[1] summarises time-series data and RoadSafe[2] generates travel advisories and looks at spatial time-series data. While there is no prior work on generating textual descriptions of geo-referenced data, there have been studies on describing spatial data in the context of route directions ((Geldof, 2003), (Marciniak and Strube, 2004)), scene descriptions (Novak, 1986), geometric descriptions (Mitkov, 1990) and spatial descriptions (Ebert et al, 1996).

Data-to-text generation projects like Atlas.txt differ from the traditional three-stage pipeline generation architecture of most NLG systems (Reiter and Dale, 2000) because they need to analyse the data in order to determine data abstractions before then going on to the traditional three stages of document planning, micro-planning and realisation, as was put forward by (Sripada, Reiter et al, 2001). Content determination has been described as involving a collective classification problem (Barzilay and Lapata, 2005) and in the context of data-to-text systems. Since our system involves data-to-text NLG, content determination has more in common with the two-stage process of (Sripada, Reiter et al, 2001) than the classification process of (Barzilay and Lapata, 2005). However a notable difference between our domain and the meteorology domain described in (Sripada, Reiter et al, 2001), is that for us, arriving at an overview before communicating the data to the end-user involves not just data analysis but also scene description to aid in our visualisation goal.

3 Content Determination in Atlas.txt System

The Atlas.txt system aims to be able to take georeferenced data in tabular form, perform data analysis to determine significant features in the data, and then communicate these significant features via text. Data analysis for Atlas.txt involves clustering to find regions in the geography with similar values of census variable. Data analysis also involves trending to find spatial trends in the data. Information obtained from data analysis forms the input to the content determination module.

In order to select which information to communicate (i.e., content selection), we ran a corpus study on online census texts to try and determine what messages they communicate (Thomas and Sripada, 2008). Of course, these documents are not written for the VI user group. On the other hand, without evidence to the contrary, we cannot assume that VI users require census information (i.e., census statistics) that is different from what sighted users require. But VI users do need additional content that helps them to interpret any geographic references associated with census information. An experiment conducted in Ottawa on a group of 5 blind and 5 sighted participants indicated that both blind and sighted participants (without access to a map) need additional information to ground proper name reference to unfamiliar places. Because we did not find examples of these kind in our corpus texts, we hypothesised that all texts produced by Atlas.txt system should start with what we called an 'introduction' messages which help VI users to interpret geographic information better.

This means, we need knowledge of two kinds of

[1] More information can be found at http://www.csd.abdn.ac.uk/research/sumtime.

[2] See http://www.csd.abdn.ac.uk/research/roadsafe.

messages for building Atlas.txt, ones that communicate census information and the others that help VI users understand the geography better. Designing the first type of census messages requires a good understanding of user goals. We have noticed a broad range of goals census users have, and we consider a number of use cases illustrating particular user goals below:

1. You want to buy a house somewhere safe, i.e., with a low crime rate, and within commuting distance of City X.

2. You want to start a business selling expensive furniture and you want to pick a location near potential clientele who are profiled as wealthy based on income level data.

This illustrates the huge range of purposes people might have when accessing census data, and many of these examples were found via online documents on census uses.[3] We determined which content to communicate from the data in this domain by considering both evidence from use cases like the ones above and also online census documents. In many online census documents there is no corresponding data available in tabular form. This could be because the information in different modalities is intended to be complimentary rather than equivalent. The lack of corresponding data in most cases makes it hard to learn what sorts of results constitute interesting data which should be reported. From a qualitative study of corpus documents, we notice that most such texts at the least describe where the variable they focus on (e.g., unemployment) has its high values, low values, and spatial trends of the variable's distribution if there are any. Some scenarios require additional information, e.g., the vicinity of a major road, the coast, a city, etc. We aim for a scenario-generic solution for now as a first step given that the system is not interactive. However we hope that communicating the basic statistics in a meaningful way (i.e., via useful spatial expressions) and also introducing the region and its salient features will improve accessibility to this information. The goal of such a system is of course to eventually become interactive so that it can eventually address users' specific goals and answer more specific questions about how the data is distributed. As explained above Atlas.txt includes the following census messages:

- Maxima message: location/s of high values from Data Analysis

- Minima message: location/s of low values from Data Analysis

- Trend message: location/s of trends from Data Analysis

All these census messages make explicit references to geographic locations which are hard to interpret for VI users. We assume that the introduction messages introduced earlier enable hearers to visualise the underlying geography which helps them to make sense of spatial descriptions in census messages. The introduction message also gives a general summary by communicating the overall average value-range of the data (e.g., "Overall, unemployment frequencies are low"), inspired by Gestalt principles of grouping in perception (Metzger, 2006) and the visual information seeking mantra (Schneiderman, 1996) which argues that one should start with an overview, zoom and filter, and only provide details upon demand (the latter of which is only applicable to interactive systems). The following components of introduction messages are currently considered:

- Boundary geographic information, which indicates geographic features which bound the region as a whole on any side

- Gestalt-driven overview of data (average value-range)

- Location of where population is densest

In order to communicate the boundary geographic information, we ran a survey eliciting spatial descriptions of Aberdeenshire which indicated that people's spatial descriptions when presented with a census map seem to fall into the following three categories of geographic information:

- Human geography: cities, roads, towns, urban/rural distinctions, census ward boundaries, etc.

[3] Business Uses of Census Data: www.incontext.indiana.edu/2001/july01/spotlight.html, Uses of Census Data: www.laria.gov.uk/content/articles/2003_conference_pdf/boag.pdf

- Physical geography: lakes, mountains, sea, desert, etc.
- Orientation geography: cardinal directions

In other words, we saw many descriptions which used terms like "urban", "rural", which pointed out major roads as indicators of where population might be denser, and also many of the descriptions which referred to areas as "coastal", "inland", "[in the] hills", etc. Cardinal directions (e.g., "North", "Southwest", etc.) were also frequently used to locate phenomena and are absolute coordinates in the survey frame of reference involved in Atlas.txt, which describes maps from a bird's eye view, (Taylor and Tversky, 1996).

Determining salient geographic information which describes where maxima, minima and trends are involves overlaying the clusters (and ends of trends) with geographic layers in the human and physical geographies discussed above. Then if we find that any of the geographic elements contained in any of the geographic overlays aligns spatially with the cluster, we add this to a list of multiple possible spatial expressions which can be used to describe the location of the cluster. Appropriately describing clusters via selecting informative spatial expressions is a central aspect of communicating the maximum, minimum and trend messages. Overlaying different layers like this is a standard "intersect overlay" operation in Geographic Information Systems (GIS) and data containing altitude information, urban/road information and physical geography exist online which can be used as the alignment layers in a GIS. We want to select features which intersect our clusters even minimally, as they help to describe where features are located. If no intersecting regions exist, we choose the nearest. Note that the layers considered all fall within the different geographic types, i.e., human and physical geographies. Orientation information does not require overlaying maps to identify which parts are North, etc. Orientation information can be calculated for the region in question by overlaying it with a square 8 by 8 grid for the various cardinal directions. The location of the maxima and minima clusters can then be described as lying in a particular cardinal direction by simply checking which square/s of the grid they fall in. Determining cardinal direction has been implemented in the Roadsafe project.

In future we will consider how to handle situations in which multiple possible features intersect (or are near to) our clusters, which will involve us ranking some of these features higher than others. We will also want to consider the effects of other factors than proximity on selection of spatial descriptions, e.g., discourse context and causality could affect the choice of spatial description. The results from our survey eliciting spatial descriptions of Aberdeen showed more spatial descriptions from the human geography (58%) than from the physical geography (42%). The survey involved a between-subjects design where the 24 participants were blocked into 3 groups, one group getting coarse maps with only 3 or 4 large wards covering all of Aberdeenshire while the other two groups had medium (around 28 wards) and fine grained maps (around 50 wards) covering the shire. Coarse-grained maps had higher percentages of scores for physical geography descriptions than for human geography descriptions (62% vs. 37%) while both medium and fine-grained maps had larger percentages for human geography descriptions (62% and 57% respectively). There were also a higher number of human descriptions used per turn on average, 4.2 vs. 2.6 for physical descriptions.

Most census variables describe information which pertains to human populations, (e.g., unemployment statistics, or employment in hunting, agriculture and forestry in our survey), indicating that human geographic features might be causally linked to most census data. As was indicated in our initial survey, human geographic features like the locations of cities and roads seem to be most related to these population variables and might form the most meaningful description for the hearer, since they may help the hearer to infer useful correlations between the presence of (e.g.) a maxima and a geographic feature. However there might also be correlations between physical geographic features and these variables, for example, logging in forests, fishing industry in coastal areas, etc.

Context will certainly also play a large role, e.g., if the prior message uses a description from the physical geography (e.g., "coastal"), this might result in "inland" being preferred over "urban", particularly if the messages have opposite content (e.g., one reports maxima while the other reports minima).

We also saw that participants tended to mix geographies more often than not, involving both physical and human geography descriptions in their texts, as 60% of the number of turns which had descriptions from both geographies. Describing cluster locations with two geographies leads to sentences like "Unemployment is highest in *rural* and *coastal* areas," which leads to a range of inferences about how coastal and rural areas might be similar where unemployment is concerned. Mixed geography descriptions are more informative, since they convey additional information, so our view is that extra descriptors, particularly if they come from other geographies, will only clarify and help listeners to ground the locations of clusters.

So the content determination module takes the document plan containing the four messages to be communicated and gets the locations of maxima, minima and trends (which come from data analysis). These are then overlaid with data of the area containing physical or human geographies for the region. Proximity is our current selection factor, so aligning features are currently selected if they intersect (though as discussed earlier, if no features intersect, the nearest ones are chosen) and are saved as possible spatial expressions to be used in the message. In future work we will also need to account for causality and context in this selection of appropriate spatial descriptions.

4 Evaluation

Unlike many of the other data-to-text systems described, the Atlas.txt system's goal is much more general. Rather than generating specific texts for specific audiences with particular expertise and tasks in mind, this project aims to communicate census data to a VI audience of varying expertise who, unlike for most other NLG systems, have a range of tasks in mind. As we argued earlier, the messages we choose to communicate enable the vast majority of users to at least get an overview of the salient features in the data and we leave more specific informational requirements for an interactive version of Atlas.txt.

One issue that arises for a broad-focus non-task-specific domain like this is that evaluation methods are not as well-specified as for other NLG systems for content determination. (Dale and Mellish, 1998) present four questions one can ask when evaluating content determination: (1) truth (is the output true), (2) quantity–does the output say enough, (3) quantity–does the output say too much, and (4) appropriateness (is the output inappropriate to the context). But what if we want to ask the more high level question of utility? That is, do we really need the introduction message (assuming it is not misleading)? The two quantity considerations–have we said too much or too little–are probably the best ways to guage whether the introduction message is informative enough (and not too verbose). But again, this is a bit too fine-grained for us, as we want to first ask whether the introduction message is necessary or not in the first place before attempting to refine its contents.

The general-purpose task aspect of this domain also implies that we cannot compare our texts with an expert's texts based on the underlying data, as it is difficult to find simple summarising expert-written census texts online. The vast majority of census texts are far longer than ours and tend to discuss the implications of what the data presents which is beyond our scope. Furthermore, we cannot compare Atlas.txt output against expert-written text because there is no expert-produced parallel data where texts summarise the information contained in tables or maps. Also, experts (statisticians) are not used to summarising tables as simple, general-purpose texts like this and they vary in the sorts of texts they produce. Our experiment in Ottawa indicated that different statisticians employed at Statistics Canada vary both in terms of the analyses they make of both tabular and textual census data (under experimental conditions) and in their post-edits of expert-written census texts (Thomas and Sripada, 2008). This means that we need to rethink how we should evaluate Atlas.txt's texts.

4.1 Study

Given that instructions rich in imagery help subjects to form a spatial mental model (Gyselinck et al, 2006), our end goal is to discover if introduction messages actually aid in visualisation. Given the lack of conclusive evidence to the contrary, we operate under the premise that VI people have spatial comprehension abilities (Kitchin et al, 1997) and can benefit from texts which enable visualisation. We run the study with sighted people because they can draw maps which they visualise from our texts.

We ran a study which presented a group of 20 randomly recruited sighted participants with a pair of texts where one member of the pair included the introduction message and the other member did not include the introduction message. The introduction message contains the two geographic elements we discussed earlier: locations of boundary information, the location of where population is densest and the trend for population density. The messages were identical in content (though names and directions were changed so that participants would not assume that the same country was being described), and both texts have a maxima, minima and trend message (each), as can be seen in Examples 1 and 2 below:

1. The land of Bosk is bounded to the East by the Bale Ocean, and its largest city is Wristwath, on the East coast. Population is densest around Wristwath and gradually decreases as one moves Westward, though there are clusters of medium-high population in cities like Slangin in Central Bosk. Crime rates are highest in Wristwath and Southern suburbs of Wristwath. Additionally, Slangin also has high crime rates. Crime is lowest in Northwestern and East-Central Bosk. Crime tends to decrease as one goes East or West from Central Bosk with the exception of the Wristwath area.

2. Poverty rates are highest in Galen and Western suburbs of Galen. Additionally, Boroos also has high poverty rates. Poverty rates are lowest in Northwestern and East-Central Dagor. Poverty rates tends to decrease as one goes East or West from Central Dagor with the exception of the Galen area.

For each text, participants were asked to draw a map of the area they visualise based on the text, indicating where the maxima and minima are and where all other information mentioned in the text is located. Then they were asked two task-based questions per text which aim to check whether they can use the information appropriately. The first question asks whether they can identify the minima/maxima, e.g., "You want to relocate to Bosk. Considering only crime rates, where might you want to move?" The second question gives them a piece of additional information which sighted people would be able to pick off from the map, e.g., that there is a coastline, harbours, roads, etc., e.g., "You work in Wristwath and need to commute in daily. Given this and the above info, where might you want to live in Bosk?" After each of the two pairs of texts and questions, participants are asked to indicate which text was easier to visualise and to state why. Participants were also presented with two thematic maps and asked to write descriptions of them so that someone who is blind can visualise them.

We hypothesized that Ex.2 above will cause difficulties for map drawing. There is no introduction message helping readers to orient themselves to the region, and one does not know a priori whether Galen is the name of a city or the region itself, or where it is in the region if it is indeed a city. This might seem purposefully difficult, but this is what one typically finds in census texts online. For example, if you want to know where in Canada Saskatoon is, you need to look it up in a map. This makes it hard (even for sighted people) when you read many unfamiliar place names and are trying to get an overall picture of where places are.

4.2 Results and Discussion

The maps drawn for the text stimuli are scored on a number of features, but the primary goal is to ascertain whether readers visualised the locations of the maximum, minimum and trend correctly. Each text is based on an underlying map which is used as the gold standard against which participants' maps are compared. This gold standard map includes a range of variation in location of maximum, minimum and trend based on the ambiguity present in the text. For example, "East-Central" in Ex. 2 is hard to define. Participants were given a point each for correctly identifying the maximum, minimum and trend in each message, or a zero if they failed to do so correctly or if their answer was uninterpretable. These three scores were also totalled giving a total score per text for the maps drawn. Here we did not see a huge difference in scores for the different mes-

Table 1: Average & std. deviation scores for map drawing

Text	Maximum	Minimum	Trend	Total
Text 1	1; 0	0.80; 0.41	0.80; 0.41	0.87; 0.23
Text 2	0.85; 0.37	0.70; 0.47	0.65; 0.49	0.73; 0.32

sages, as can be seen in the table; Text 1 has an introduction message (and is seen in Ex. 1) and Text 2 (Ex. 2) lacks the introduction message. The total column corresponds to the average score for the three messages (maximum, minimum and trend). A t-test on the total scores for Texts 1 and 2 gives a non-significant result with a p-value of 0.110. On the other hand, almost all the participants preferred Text 1 to Text 2; a signed ranks test on the preference judgements (participants ticked which text they preferred, 1 or 2) was significant with a p-value $<$ 0.001. When asked to state their reasons for preferring Text 1, participants identified the geographic information from the introduction message as the only reason. Also when participants wrote texts for map stimuli they tended to include introduction messages in them; a binomial test on whether introduction messages were included in either of their two texts was significant with a p-value < 0.041. Interestingly enough, shape was a feature used in many of these introduction messages when the map had a particularly non-square shape. In the part of the experiment where participants answered task-based questions based on texts with and without introduction messages they performed well on all questions following both types of texts.

It is encouraging that participants preferred texts with introduction messages and also used them in their own texts. But it is disappointing that the absence of introduction messages seems to make no difference to mental visualisation of Text 2. In fact, many of the maps for Text 2 were incomplete; participants simply marked the required information and their nearby geographic entities. The problem with evaluating maps is that they partly measure the geometrical relationships in the map which could bias such evaluations against participants with poor drawing skills. Poor drawing skills could also obscure whether they have visualised the correct information.

Many participants said that drawing the map and accounting for all of the information contained in the introduction message was very difficult, so there might have additionally been some cognitive overload on drawing maps for Text 1 which biased the results in favour of Text 2. Generally all the participants complained that the whole experiment took longer than they had expected. This indicates that the texts were challenging enough and not trivial. (Murray, 1979) claims that there are variations among people's ability to draw mentally visualised geographic information, indicating that evaluating elicited maps might have a large amount of individual variation. Ideally we need to find alternative ways (other than eliciting map drawing) of assessing the effectiveness of introduction messages.

Other factors could also have affected these results. For example, we did not randomise the order of stimuli. Furthermore, our task-based questions proved too easy for participants because they can be answered by simply searching for the named region with the highest value etc. Another issue which we will want to explore in future work is whether using spatial descriptions (e.g., "a medium-sized city" instead of "Slangin" from Text 1, etc.) in both texts would have helped people to make more sense of the texts, particularly Text 2.

We also ran the text stimuli of the experiment with a VI computing undergraduate who clearly indicated that the texts without the introduction message were much harder to visualise, as he did not know where the cities (referred to by proper name alone) were located. He also indicated that some information required to partially visualise the region could be inferred indirectly from information presented in these texts lacking introduction messages. For example, in Ex. 2, he could deduce that poverty rates are high in Central Dagor, since it decreases as one goes East or West from Central Dagor. However there was not enough information for him to place Boroos in Central Dagor.

5 Conclusions and Future Directions

In this paper we describe how content determination in Atlas.txt is achieved and report on evaluation of one message in our content determination schema: the introduction message. Our end goal is to enable VI users to mentally visualise the region being described in order to locate where areas with high and low values of the census variable described are and also to visualise spatial trends for this variable in the region. In order to evaluate whether introduction messages in our texts help users to mentally visualise the region, we elicited drawings of maps visualised by sighted participants based on our texts with and without the introduction message. This was based on the assumption that VI people also have spatial cognition abilities, and because sighted participants can draw the maps they visualise. We did not see a significant difference between texts with and without introduction messages from the elicited drawings of maps which were scored on the correct locations of maximum, minimum and trend information. However we saw that participants overwhelmingly preferred texts with introduction messages to those without, and also tended to include introduction messages in texts describing maps when asked to describe the maps to blind readers.

The question then arises as to how one should ideally evaluate message inclusion when communicating spatial data. Although drawing maps seemed a natural way to evaluate visualisation, we saw that it was fraught with difficulties. We leave the question of finding an appropriate evaluation methodology for message choice in spatial data-to-text systems such as ours for future work.

Evaluating the utility of the individual components of the introduction message has also been left as future work. Furthermore, we also plan on investigating the factors involved in selecting description geographies, e.g., causality and context, in order to produce informative spatial descriptions in our messages.

References

R. Barzilay and M. Lapata. 2005. Collective Content Selection for Concept-to-text Generation. *Human Language Technology Conference*.

S. Boyd. 1997. Detecting and Describing Patterns in Time-varying Data Using Wavelets. *Advances in Intelligent Data Analysis: Reasoning About Data, Lecture Notes in Computer Science*, 1280.

J. Coch. 1998. Multimeteo: Multilingual Production of Weather Forecasts. *ELRA Newsletter*, 3(2).

R. Dale and C. Mellish. 1998. Towards the Evaluation of Natural Language Generation. *Proceedings of the First International Conference on Evaluation of Natural Language Processing Systems*.

C. Ebert, D. Glatz, M. Jansche, R. Meyer-Klabunde and R. Porzel. 1996. From Conceptualization to Formulation in Generating Spatial Descriptions. *Proceedings fo the 5th European Conference on Cognitive Modelling*.

L. Ferres, A. Parush, S. Roberts and G. Lindgaard. 2006. Helping People with Visual Impairments Gain Access to Graphical Information Through Natural Language: The iGraph System. *Proceedings of ICCHP 2006, Lecture Notes in Computer Science*, 4061.

S. Geldof. 2003. Corpus Analysis for NLG. *Proceedings of the 9th EWNLG*.

E. Goldberg, N. Driedger and R.L. Kittredge. 1994. Using Natural-Language Processing to Produce Weather Forecasts. *IEEE Expert*, 9(2).

V. Gyselinck, R. De Beni, F. Pazzaglia, C. Meneghetti and A. Mondoloni. 2006. Spatial Knowledge Acquisition from Maps and from Navigation in Real and Virtual Environments. *Memory and Cognition*, 27.

R. Kitchin, M. Blades and R. Golledge. 1997. Understanding Spatial Concepts at the Geographic Scale Without the Use of Vision. *Human Geography*, 21(2).

T. Marciniak and M. Strube. 2004. Classification-based Generation Using TAG. *Proceedings of Natural Language Generation: 3rd International Conference, Lecture Notes in Artificial Intelligence*, 3123.

W. Metzger. 2006. Laws of Seeing. *MIT Press*.

R. Mitkov. 1990. A Text-Generation System for Explaining Concepts in Geometry. *Proceedings of the 13th Conference on Computational Linguistics*.

D. Murray and C. Spencer. 1979. Individual Differences in the Drawing of Cognitive Maps: the Effects of Geographical Mobility, Strength of Mental Imagery and Basic Graphic Ability. *Transactions of the Institute of British Geographers*, New Series, Vol.4, No.3.

H.J. Novak. 1986. Generating a Coherent Text Describing a Traffic Scene. *Proceedings of the 11th Conference on Computational Linguistics*.

E. Reiter and R. Dale. 2000. Building Natural Language Generation Systems. *Cambridge University Press*.

B. Schneiderman. 1996. The Eyes Have It: A Task by Data Type Taxonomy for Information Visualisations. *Proceedings of Visual Language*.

S. Sripada, E. Reiter, J. Hunter and J. Yu. 2001. A Two-Stage Model for Content Determination. *Proceedings of the 8th ACL-EWNLG*.

S. Sripada, E. Reiter, J. Hunter and J. Yu. 2003. Exploiting a Parallel TEXT-DATA Corpus. *Proceedings of Corpus Linguistics*.

H. Taylor and B. Tversky. 1996. Perspective in Spatial Descriptions. *Journal of Memory and Language, vol. 35*.

K. Thomas and S. Sripada. 2008. Atlas.txt: First Steps Towards Bridging the Gap Between Geo-Referenced Data and Text. *Proceedings of the Cross-Disciplinary Conference on Web Accessibility*.

J. Yu, E. Reiter, J. Hunter and C. Mellish. 2005. Choosing the Content of Textual Summaries of Large Time-series Data Sets. *Natural Language Engineering, vol. 11*.

Evolving Questions in Text Planning

Mick O'Donnell
Escuela Politecnica Superior,
Universidad Autónoma de Madrid,
Cantoblanco, Spain
michael.odonnell@uam.es

Abstract

This paper explores how the main question addressed in Text Planning has evolved over the last twenty years. Earlier approaches to text planning asked the question: *How do we write a good text?*, and whatever answers were found were programmed directly into code. With the introduction of search-based text planning in recent years, the focus shifted to the evaluation function, and thus the question became: *How do we tell if a text is good?* This paper will explore these evolving questions, and subsequent refinements of them as the field matures.

Introduction

Given the growing interest in the application of search-based planning methods in NLG, we can describe how text planning has evolved from its beginning in terms of the kinds of questions that have been addressed.

1 How do we compose a good text?

The object in text planning is to write a program which can compose a text to meet some input specification. Traditionally, the programs themselves embody decision making procedures coded to make textual decisions, such as whether or not to include some content, how to rhetorically link it to the rest of the text, and in what order should the content nodes appear.

How one writes a good text has many answers, and depends partly on the type of text one is writing. For some texts, a schematic approach is possible: a text can be composed by using predefined schemas, which nominate what information should appear, and in what order (McKeown 1985). Sometimes the system makes the inclusion of a schema element conditional on the context of the text, for instance, deciding to include or exclude content based on the type of user that the message is being generated for (DiMarco *et al.* 1997).

For other types of text, the application of schemas is less appropriate. Some text planners take as their goal the delivery of a single fact, or a set of facts, but take into account that other information may need to be given first for each message to be understood, other information may need to be given after to counter misconceptions, and examples may be given to aide assimilation (for instance, the RST text planners, such as Hovy 1988). The system thus composes a text which delivers the facts required of it, and any other facts which will facilitate the uptake of these facts.

In another text genre, the goal is not to deliver specific facts, but rather to describe an entity, for instance, museum artefacts (e.g., ILEX: O'Donnell *et al.* 2001), or animals (*Peba*: Milosavljevic 1999). A basic strategy to generate a reasonable text of this kind is to list the different attributes of the target entity, possibly sorted into relevant topics. Good systems are aware of which information is already known to the intended audience, what should be interesting, etc. In ILEX, the system followed various strategies to generate better texts, such as allowing digressions (describing secondary entities), generalisations, defeating misconceptions, aggregation, etc.

Systems have increasingly tried to address larger sets of the issues needed to produce good quality text. We not only need to ensure that appropriate content is selected, and that adequate grounding is given to ensure the audience can understand the content. Increasingly issues of coherence dominate. Entities should be referred to in a contextually appropriate form, related sentences should be aggregated to avoid repetition, the sequence of sentence themes should be structured to express a logical development of messages, etc.

As systems address more and more of these issues, the planning algorithms become more complex. Systems which need to produce texts meeting content and coherence constraints are reaching the limit of what they can do, because the programming needs to address too many issues.

2 What texts can be produced?

The text-planning problem gets more complex when text planners need to address global as well as local goals. In Ilex, one constraint on the planner was that the generated text needed to fit in a specified space on a web page. During the generation process, the decision of whether or not to include a given fact in the page was difficult to make, since while the inclusion of the fact might help achieve the communicative goals, it also increases the size of the text. However, the system cannot know until the whole text is produced whether including this fact would push the text size over the limit. One can only calculate the real cost of including extra content when the text is finished. In the Ilex case, we selected an incremental text planning approach, adding facts into the text structure in order of their relevance, until the space limit is reached. But this approach is not compatible with all generation goals.

In the 1990s, several approaches started to recharacterise the text planning process as one of searching the space of possible text structures for those structures which were optimal when seen as a completed whole. These approaches split the question: *how do we produce a good text?* into two parts:

- How can we search the space of texts which could be produced for given content?
- How can we select the text in this space which optimally meets our goals?

In this section, we will discuss the first of these questions. Marcu (1997) characterised the text planning process as follows. He assumed that the knowledge base (KB) consists of a set of semantic units to express, and that an additional resource provided a set of rhetorical relations, which can hold between two semantic units in the KB. A pair of semantic units may have no relation between them, one relation, or multiple.

The set of units to express is finite, and the relations that can hold between them is finite, so if we assume that each semantic unit can only appear once in the text tree, then it is clear that the set of text structures that can realise the KB is also finite. We can model the space of possible text structures as a lattice, where each point in the lattice represents a given set of included facts, with a given set of relationships between them, and a given sequencing of these facts in relation to each other.

Seen in this light, one might naively propose the following approach to text planning: generate all possible text plans for the given input, evaluate each tree as a whole, and choose the one with the highest value. However, even for a small number of facts, the number of trees is huge, and this approach is not feasible.

A more feasible approach is to treat this as a search problem. Each text plan represents one point in the space of all possible plans. Adjacent points in this lattice represent similar text plans differing in one detail (the insertion of a fact, the deletion of a subtree, the reordering of nucleus and satellite, etc.). Given a starting text plan, we can move from point to point in the space, searching for a text plan which is optimal for our goals.

The earliest of work to take this approach was that of Zukerman and McConachy (1994). They were concerned with generating texts which conveyed content adequately but concisely. A text adequately conveys the facts it is given to convey if these facts are understood by the addressee. Where a given fact requires other facts to be given for it to be understood, these facts need also to be included. If a given fact or set of facts may cause the reader to make an unintended inference, facts are included to prevent this. Additionally, the inclusion of a fact sometimes made the inclusion of other facts unnecessary (e.g., including an example might clarify a concept better than a longer explanation). The conciseness goal required that as few facts as possible are used to convey the information that needs to be conveyed.

Given these constraints, traditional planning methods which made decisions locally were not appropriate. The conciseness and communicative adequacy of the text is a property of a set of facts as a whole, and thus text plans need to be evaluated as a whole. They thus rephrased the text planning issue as optimisation at a global text level.

They only addressed part of text planning as an optimisation problem: content selection. They take as a starting point the set of facts that are categorically required to be expressed. They then use an incremental graph search algorithm to search for optimal sets of facts to include in a text: on each iteration, facts are added to or deleted from each solution to produce new solutions, until the program finds one solution which adequately conveys the designated facts, with the fewest facts possible. Marcu (1997) experimented with several different search methods. Firstly, he assumed that *all* the units in the KB need to be included in the text plan (the problem of content selection was thus not relevant). His goal was thus to find RST trees which optimally covered all facts.

In his first algorithm, he used a chart mechanism to construct all possible text plans for the given content and the set of possible relations. However, as he notes, for any non-trivial number of facts, with multiple possible relations between them, this approach is computationally expensive. I also note that Marcu assumed all facts in the KB were to be expressed. If content selection is included in the process, meaning all facts are optional, the solution is even less tractable.

His second proposal restricts the chart mechanism to a greedy algorithm, which at each level, selects only the best tree to take to the next level. However, this basically amounts to make decisions locally, not globally, and thus is not relevant to this section.

His third algorithm is more relevant here. He splits the problem into two parts. Firstly, determine an ordering of content units such that as many as possible of the ordering and adjacency constraints in the potential relations are satisfied. Secondly, derive an RST tree for this ordering of content units.

He uses a constraint satisfaction algorithm for the first step. A small corpus study was used to derive, for each relation, the relative probability of nucleus-satellite vs. satellite-nucleus ordering, and also the degree to which the connected text segments are required to be linearly adjacent.

Given a set of facts, for each possible relation between a pair of facts, the process asserts a constraint stating what the nucleus-satellite order should be, and another constraint asserting that the connected facts should be adjacent. The strength of the constraint depends on the values obtained in the corpus study, for instance, if a relation allows relatively free ordering of a satellite, the constraint strength would be low.

The constraint satisfaction algorithm then derives the ordering of facts which maximises the constraints. Marcu elsewhere provides an algorithm to build a text tree on top of a given ordering of facts, again using adjacency and order propensities.

Mellish *et al.* (1998) made the point that even this restricted approach would soon become intractable with more than a small set of facts when one allows weak RST relations such as Joint and Elaboration into the model.

An alternative approach, which I haven't seen implemented (although Mellish mentions the possibility), would be to apply hill climbing techniques to the problem of finding a text which optimally satisfies a set of locally and globally stated text constraints. The idea would be to start with a single text structure, generated in a simple manner. The system then tries each possible single mutation on this text structure, (e.g., adding a fact in each location in the tree this is possible; deleting each subtree in the tree; grafting a subtree from one location to another, etc.). Each of the resulting text structures is then evaluated, and the one which scores higher is taken as the text structure for the next cycle. When no one-step change to the tree results in an improvement, the process stops.

The problem with all hill-climbing applications is that we might reach a local maximum, a point where no simple change can produce an improvement, but radical restructuring could produce better structures. One partial solution is to repeat the process a number of times from different starting structures, and select the best structure produced in all the trials. But the problem remains.

Genetic algorithms offer an alternative to hill-climbing methods, and are less susceptible to stopping at local maxima. In the late 1990s, Chris Mellish implemented the first stochastic text planner (Mellish *et al.* 1998). He replaced the procedural text planner of the ILEX system, with one based on a genetic approach.

Like the above approaches, a genetic algorithm can be seen as a means to search the space of possible texts. The system starts with a small population of randomly produced text structures, and, on each iteration (each generation), randomly mutates some or all of the structures. Each new text structure is then evaluated by an "evaluation function".

In each generation, those text structures with the highest 'fitness' are more likely to produce offspring, while those under a certain threshold are dropped from the population. In this way, mutations which improve the text structure should be preserved in the population, while those which weaken the text should disappear. After a certain number of iterations, the process is stopped, and the highest scoring text-structure is selected as the one to give the user.

The advantage of a genetic algorithm over a hill-climbing approach is that mutations which may by themselves lower the text value can survive in the population, and later combine with other mutations to produce a high-value text structure. The evolutionary approach has its cost, however, in that far more processing time is required. For this reason, the text mutation stage is usually kept fairly simple.

Like Marcu, Mellish also assumes that the search algorithm is given a set of facts, all of which need to be included. He proposes 3 algorithms. The first mutates a selected tree by randomly swapping two subtrees, and then 'repairing' any relation which is no longer valid (where the relation which links a nucleus and satellite no longer holds between these facts, select another relation which does, or if none exist, use the generic relation, Joint).

Mellish noted that, often, different trees in the population develop good structure for different subsets of facts. He thus introduced a cross-over mechanism, allowing the grafting of structure from one tree to another. He simplifies the process somewhat in a manner similar to Marcu, assuming that the genetic algorithm only manipulates the surface ordering of facts, and that an RST tree can be derived from that ordering (he assumes satellites always follow the nucleus). He differs from Marcu in that evaluation is of the final text tree, rather than the fact sequence. Mellish thus allows for two forms of mutation: moving a fact from one place to another within a single fact sequence, and inserting a sequence of facts from one fact-sequence into a random place in another (then deleting any facts which are repeated).

I have two problems with the approach above. Firstly, I do not believe that a given sequencing of facts so deterministically relates to a particular tree structuring of those facts. Two trees with the same surface ordering of facts could be fundamentally different in structure and in terms of the relations used, and thus will be evaluated very differently. By not including the text structure in the search process, the process cannot search for an optimal text structure.

My second problem with this approach is that the mutations used are fairly destructive of the text plans. When as a human writer I cut and paste text from one document to another, I generally find the amount of repair needed out-weighs the time saved by reusing text. And even the simpler mutation, randomly moving a text node within a sequence, will have far more chance of fracturing coherence than of creating it.

For these two reasons, I believe it is better to use a genetic text planner which firstly operates directly on text trees, and secondly, only allows mutations which preserve the legality of the tree. I also assume the genetic algorithm is used to determine selected content as well as structuring and ordering it. In this hypothetical text planner, no cross-over is used, only operations on a target tree. We start with a population of trees of one fact each (all related to the entity being described). The mutations include:

- *Insert Fact*: select a fact not in the tree and attach it as satellite to a fact which permits such a relation.
- *Delete Subtree*: randomly select a subtree and delete it.
- *Move Subtree*: randomly select a subtree and move it to another location where it can legally attach.
- *Change Top Nucleus*: break off a subtree from the main tree, make its nucleus the top of the tree, and graft the original tree into this tree at a legal point.
- *Switch Order*: change the order of a satellite in relation to the nucleus, or in regards to other satellites of the same nucleus.
- *Switch Focus*: the assessment of text trees includes the evaluation of the focus movement throughout the tree, each fact in the tree nominates a focus. This operation changes that focus for another of the entities in the fact, which will affect which entity is realised as subject in the final text.

All of these operations preserve the legality of the tree, but may change the global evaluation of the tree, given that suboptimal focus movements may result, information prerequisite for understanding may occur late, or not at all, etc.

By only allowing legal mutations, the system needs to do less work repairing the illegalities introduced by mutations. Good solutions should be reached quicker, although as said above, this approach is still in an early stage of development,

To a degree, this approach mirrors the way humans write texts. We start off with a rough draft with the core of what we want to say, and revise parts, sometimes adding in an explanation, sometimes adding a digression to provide background material. We may erase material because a change in another part of the document made the material redundant. Or we might cut/paste material from one part of the document to another.

Another approach to the problem of satisfying global constraints in text planning has been the 'generate and revise' approach, where a text is generated with only partial regard to the global constraints, and the resulting text is then revised to fit the global constraints (e.g., Robin and McKeown, 1996). In the STOP system (Reiter 2000), texts are constrained to fit a certain length. The system generates texts of approximately the right length, and then prunes the text until the size requirement is met. Piwek and van Deemter (2007) expand this approach to handle more than a single global constraint, exemplifying using both global length and communicative effectiveness as (sometimes) contradictory goals. Their approach is to generate a single starting text, and then apply revision operations to work towards an optimal text.

If one sees a revision operation as similar to the text mutations applied above, then it seems the revision approach is not so different to the genetic algorithm approach above. One difference is that the revision approach uses procedural means to generate a reasonable starting text, while the stochastic approaches generally start with easy-to-generate texts and mutate these towards higher complexity and optimality. Another important difference, at least in the work of Piwek and van Deemter, is that they apply their revisions exhaustively, looking at all possible combinations of revisions to locate the optimal one. For more complex text planning tasks, this may become less tractable.

3 How do we tell if a text is good?

One of the consequences of using genetic algorithms for text planning is that much of one's effort is spent on developing the evaluation function, defining the formulas used to decide how good a particular text is. The main focus in building a text planner thus moves from deciding *how do we compose the text?* to one of deciding: *how do we tell if a text is good?*

The important point here is that with procedural planners, we need to take a cognitive approach, trying to perceive how a text is constructed from scratch, which decisions are made, and in what order. Using an evolutionary approach, we can ignore the *process* of writing, and focus on the *products* of writing. We can then function as linguists: our concern is to decide what makes a text function well, and what interferes with its success. These are more important, more abstract questions to address.

Of the systems discussed above, the evaluation functions vary. The system of Zukerman and McConachy (1993) introduced the idea of global criteria for evaluating text, such as conciseness (meeting the informational goals of the system in the fewest facts), and ILEX used text length as a global criteria. Marcu (1997) set the goal of maximising 'global coherence' of the text, which basically amounts to maximising the sum of local decisions made throughout the tree. Marcu used a corpus study to determine how flexible the adjacency and ordering constraints of each relation were, and penalised instances of the relation which did not meet the constraint, the size of the penalty depending on the observation in the corpus.

He does however mention that his approach could be set up to "ensure that the resulting plans satisfy multiple high-level communicative goals" (p629).

The evaluation function of Mellish *et al.* (1998) also was calculated over a sum of local features of the tree, although a wider set of features were involved. These included: rewarding 'interesting' relations and penalising the Joint relation; penalising separation between a nucleus and satellite; penalising unsatisfied precondition of a relation; rewarding good focus movements and penalising bad ones.

While it is clear each of these criteria is contributory to good text, the numbers used were made up. Basing these numbers on a corpus study of good texts may be useful for future work.

Following on from Mellish *et al.*, some work took place focusing on improving the evaluation function, for instance Cheng and Mellish (2000) expanded on the criteria for evaluating focus movement (there called 'discourse topic movement'), and also allowed for embedding of facts in others, providing criteria for evaluating how good an embedding is. Karamanis also examined focus movement (or as he calls it, *entity coherence*) in text evaluation (Karamanis and Manurung 2002; Karamanis 2003; Karamanis *et al.* 2004; Karamanis and Mellish 2005). He proposes dropping the use of rhetorical structure, and taking the goal of text planning as sequencing facts so as to achieve smooth focus movement. Mutations thus change the ordering of facts in a given sequence (as in the Mellish work), but evaluation is applied directly to the fact sequence, penalising discontinuous focus movements.

In summary of this section, the movement to search-based text planning allowed the researcher to move away from issues regarding how to program a system to generate texts, focusing instead on the problems of deciding how to evaluate the quality of a text.

4 How good is this text?

A major problem with the search-based systems described above is that the system-maker needs to formulate the evaluation function: to specify the criteria used to determine how good a text is. This is a difficult problem, with no simple answers.

In some cases, corpus studies have been performed to find the patterns used in good texts, and base the evaluation metric on these results. However, this approach requires significant amounts of time spent on corpus analysis.

One way around this problem is the use of machine learning (ML). The basic idea in ML is to provide the computer with lots of example texts, along with the classification of the text. The system then builds a classification model from the training data. This classification model can then be applied to previously unseen examples to assign a class.

Applying ML to text planning, we provide the computer with a corpus of finished texts, each rated from 0 to 10 in terms of quality, and leave the computer to work out an evaluation function on its own. This step would move the work of the investigator from deciding how to evaluate a text to a far simpler one, of just saying *if* each text is good or not, something we all can do with or without linguistic training.

The problem here is that ML techniques can only function on the range of features that they have access to. In the worst case, only the surface text is provided to the system. Some approaches work simply with the n-gram sequences of words, for instance, to select between alternative sentences generated to express some content (e.g., Langkilde and Knight 1998). N-grams have even been used to assess the global quality of texts, not for text planning, but to assess student exam questions (Pérez *et al.* 2004). However, the sequence of words within a sentence cannot tell us anything about the quality of the text structure.

In recent years, there has been substantial work that assumes that the quality of a text can be judged in relation to the degree to which the sequence of sentences in the generated text corresponds to a 'golden standard' (Lapata 2003; Dimitromanolaki and Androutsopoulos 2003; Karamanis *et al.* 2004). This work, referred to as 'Input Ordering', assumes that content selection is done as a separate task, and the role of text planning can be seen as simply ordering the facts output from content planning. A corpus of human-written texts, (in most approaches tagged by propositional content), is provided. These represent a "golden standard". Text plans generated by the computer are evaluated in terms of the degree to which the terminals of the text structures occur in the same order as the golden standard.

For me, this approach is problematic: two texts may have the same surface ordering of facts, yet very different rhetorical structure. One text may be well structured, and the other badly structured. The surface ordering of facts is by itself a poor indicator of the overall quality of the text.

This recent focus on input ordering results partly from the fact that it is an aspect of text that can easily be recognised. Focusing on input order just because it is easy is something like looking for your watch under the street-light, even though you lost it in the dark alley. The looking might be easier, but if the answers are in the dark, then that is where we should be looking.

Rather than explore surface features of language which are easier to recognise, I believe we should be either:

- building discourse-level tree-banks of real texts, to provide real information to inform the automatic derivation of evaluation functions, or,
- building tools to automatically recognise discourse structure of text, (RST, focus movement, etc.)

Daniel Marcu has been a leader in both directions, working both on building an RST-tagged corpus, and also exploring the automatic recognition of rhetorical structure (Marcu 2000). In regards to the latter, unfortunately, the results have not so far been useful for real applications. If one wants to rhetorically annotate a corpus, one needs to do it by hand, which involves a substantial investment of time. The case is similar for annotation of other discourse structures, such as focus movement.

Within the context of NLG, another approach is possible. For each generated text, we have at hand the deeper structure which was produced in constructing the text. In the case of ILEX for instance, a side-product of generating a text is the rhetorical structure of the text, information regarding coidentity of the entities mentioned in the text, etc. The machine-learning program can thus be provided with all of this information as input, as well as derived focus-movement, etc. We can produce a corpus of generated texts, tagged with structural information, and ask a human, to assign a level of goodness to each text. The program can then derive an evaluation function of its own.

The work of the human in the process thus becomes simply to assign a level of goodness assessment to each of the texts in the training set.

5 What features of a text are critical in evaluating worth?

The effectiveness of any machine leaning program is very limited by the value of the text features it receives. While the previous point started out with a focal question *How good is this text?*, we saw that the real question becomes: *What factors do we feed the system to optimise classification?*

In a sense, this is a movement back towards question 3: *How do we tell if a text is good?* However, note the difference: question 3 concerns the investigator assigning values to particular text features, typically making them up as they go.

With this new question however, the investigator is not *assigning values* to text features. Rather, the investigator need only include the feature in the data, and it is up to the learning algorithm to decide to what degree that feature improves or worsens the text quality. The investigator only needs to hypothesise whether the text feature could be influential in this decision.

The main advantage here is the movement away from investigators making up evaluation function in their heads, or performing corpus studies. In the machine learning approach, we need only include the feature in the corpus. For instance, the evaluation function of Mellish *et al.* (1998) assigned +3 for each instance of subject-repetition. In an ML system, the human just decides that subject-repetition should be considered, and the system derives an appropriate parameter for this feature.

It is possible that many of the features we provide to the system are not actually used by the system. If we use an ML approach which allows access to its evaluation model in an understandable form, then the approach has the added value of revealing to the investigator *which* of the features provided to the system are important to text value, and which are not. One product of this approach, apart from an improved text generator, will be an improved understanding of what it is that makes a text good or bad.

Early approaches to applying ML in this way are calculating the relative frequency of particular discourse features (e.g., of types of focus movements, of types of rhetorical relations and their ordering). Each generated text can then be evaluated in terms of the relative frequency of its discourse features in comparison with the tagged corpus.

One problem with this approach is that many aspects of text structure cannot be said to be good or bad *per se*, it is only in relation to the context of use that such can be judged. Almost any RST relation can appear in a text, and the value of the use needs to be judged in the context of its appearance. However, it is difficult for a machine learning system to infer in which contexts the use of a particular relation is good and in which it is bad.

We have assumed a supervised learning approach, where a human evaluated the quality of each text in the corpus. Because there is a cost to producing such a corpus (human evaluation of each text), some prefer an *unsupervised* approach, whereby the input at the training phase is not valued: it is assumed that all of the texts in the training corpus are good representatives of the genre.

6 Summary

We have represented recent developments in text planning in terms of an evolution in the principle question addressed. While earlier work in text planning addressed the question of *how we compose texts*, the movement into search-based planning split the question into two parts: *how we search the space of possible texts*, and *how we evaluate a text.*

The second of these questions has been increasingly in focus, and the need to move away from made-up evaluation functions leads to the corpus-based derivation of text metrics. At first glance, this seems to leave the analyst with the simple task of evaluating the overall quality of a text, and leaving it to the machine to derive the evaluation function (the question thus becomes: *how good is this text?*).

However, on deeper analysis, the learning system needs to be fed structured input to be able to derive intelligent evaluation functions. The focal question thus needs to shift to considering *what features of discourse structure need to be provided to the ML system.*

The field of search-based text planning is still young, and evolving quickly. In the last 10 years, the focal questions have evolved rapidly. The question is, what will we be asking in another 10 years?

References

H. Cheng and C. Mellish. 2000. Capturing the Interaction between Aggregation and Text Planning in Two Generation Systems. *Proceedings of the 1st Int. NLG Conference*, Mitzpe Ramon, Israel, 108-115.

A. Dimitromanolaki and I. Androutsopoulos. 2003. Learning to order facts for discourse planning in natural language generation. *Proceedings of the 9th European Workshop on NLG.*

C. DiMarco, G. Hirst and E. Hovy. 1997. Generation by selection and repair as a method for adapting text for the individual reader. *Proceedings Workshop on Flexible Hypertext*, 8th ACM International Hypertext Conference, Southampton, U.K., April 1997, 20-23.

E. Hovy. 1988. Planning coherent multisentential text. *Proceedings of the 26th Annual Meeting of ACL*, 163-169.

N. Karamanis. 2003. *Entity Coherence for Descriptive Text Structuring.* Ph.D. thesis, Informatics, University of Edinburgh.

N. Karamanis and H. Manurung. 2002. Stochastic Text Structuring using the Principle of Continuity. *Proceedings of the 2nd Int. NLG Conference.*

N. Karamanis, C. Mellish, J. Oberlander and M. Poesio. 2004. A corpus-based methodology for evaluating metrics of coherence for text structuring. *Proceedings of INLG04*, Brockenhurst, 90-99.

I. Langkilde and K. Knight. 1998. The Practical Value of N-Grams in Generation. *Proceedings of the 9th Int. Workshop on NLG*, Ontario, Canada, 1998.

M. Lapata. 2003. Probabilistic text structuring: Experiments with sentence ordering. *Proceedings of ACL 2003*, 545-552.

D. Marcu. 1997. From local to global coherence: A bottom-up approach to text planning. *Proceedings of the National Conference on Artificial Intelligence* (AAAI'97), 629-635.

D. Marcu. 2000. The Rhetorical Parsing of Unrestricted Texts: a Surface-Based Approach. *Computational Linguistics*, 26 (3), 395-448.

K. McKeown. 1985. *Text Generation.* Cambridge University Press, Cambridge.

C. Mellish, A. Knott, J. Oberlander and M. O'Donnell. 1998. Experiments using stochastic search for text planning. *Proceedings of the 9th Int. Workshop on NLG*, Ontario, Canada, 98-107.

M. Milosavljevic. 1999. *The automatic generation of comparisons in descriptions of entities.* PhD Thesis. Department of Computing, Macquarie University, Australia.

M. O'Donnell, C. Mellish, J. Oberlander and A. Knott. 2001. ILEX: An architecture for a dynamic hypertext generation system. *Natural Language Engineering* 7, 225-250.

D. Pérez, E. Alfonseca, and P. Rodríguez. 2004. Application of the BLEU method for evaluating free-text answers in an e-learning environment. *Proceedings of the Language Resources and Evaluation Conference* (LREC-2004), Portugal.

P. Piwek and K. van Deemter. 2007. Generating under Global Constraints: the Case of Scripted Dialogue. *Journal of Research on Language and Computation*, 5(2):237-263.

E. Reiter. (2000). Pipelines and Size Constraints. *Computational Linguistics.* 26:251-259.

J. Robin and K. McKeown. 1996. Empirically designing and evaluating a new revision-based model for summary generation', *Artificial Intelligence.* 85(1-2).

I. Zukerman and R. McConachy. 1994. Discourse Planning as an Optimization Process. *Proceedings of the 7th Int. Workshop on NLG*, Kennebunkport, Maine, 37-44.

Generation of Output Style Variation in the SAMMIE Dialogue System

Ivana Kruijff-Korbayová, Ciprian Gerstenberger
Olga Kukina
Saarland University, Germany
{korbay|gerstenb|olgak}@coli.uni-sb.de

Jan Schehl
DFKI, Germany
jan.schehl@dfki.de

Abstract

A dialogue system can present itself and/or address the user as an active agent by means of linguistic constructions in personal style, or suppress agentivity by using impersonal style. We describe how we generate and control personal and impersonal style variation in the output of SAMMIE, a multimodal in-car dialogue system for an MP3 player. We carried out an experiment to compare subjective evaluation judgments and input style alignment behavior of users interacting with versions of the system generating output in personal vs. impersonal style. Although our results are consistent with earlier findings obtained with simulated systems, the effects are weaker.

1 Introduction

One of the goals in developing dialogue systems that users find appealing and natural is to endow the systems with contextually appropriate output. This encompasses a broad range of research issues. Our present contribution concerns the generation of personal and impersonal style.

We define the personal/impersonal style dichotomy as reflecting primarily a distinction with respect to *agentivity*: personal style involves the explicit realization of an agent, whereas impersonal style avoids it. In the simplest way this is manifested by the presence of explicit reference to the dialogue participants (typically by means of personal pronouns) vs. its absence, respectively. More generally, active voice and finite verb forms are typical for personal style, whereas impersonal style often, though not exclusively, employs passive constructions or infinite verb forms:

(1) Typical personal style constructions:
  a. I found 20 albums.
  b. You have 20 albums.
  c. Please search for albums by The Beatles.

(2) Typical impersonal style constructions:
  a. 20 albums have been found.
  b. There are 20 albums.
  c. The database contains 20 albums.
  d. 20 albums found.

The dialogue system SAMMIE developed in the TALK project uses either personal or impersonal output style, employing constructions such as (1a–1c) and (2a–2d), respectively, to manifest its own and the user's agentivity linguistically. We ran an experiment to assess the effects of the system output style on users' judgments of the system's usability and performance and on their input formulation.

In Section 2 we review related work on system output adaptation and previous experiments concerning the effect of system output style on users' judgments and style. We describe the SAMMIE system and the generation of style variation in Section 3. In Section 4 we describe our experiment and in Section 5 present the results. In Section 6 we provide a discussion and conclusions.

2 Previous Work

Although recently developed dialogue systems adapt their output to the users in various ways, this usually concerns content selection rather than surface realization. There is to our knowledge no system that varies the style of its output in the interpersonal dimension as we have done in SAMMIE. Work on animated conversational agents has addressed various issues concerning agents displaying their *personality*, but this usually concerns emotional states and personality traits, rather than the personal/impersonal alteration. (Isard et al., 2006) model personality and alignment in generated dialogues between pairs of agents using OpenCCG and an over-generation and ranking approach, guided by a set of language models. Their approach probably could produce the personal/impersonal style variation as an effect of personality or a side-effect of syntactic alignment.

The question whether a system should generate output in personal or impersonal style has been addressed by (Nass and Brave, 2005): They observe that agents that use "I" are generally perceived more like a person than those that do not. However, systems tend to be more positively rated when consistent with respect to such parameters as personality, gender, ontology (human vs. machine), etc. On the basis of an investigation of a range of user attitudes to their simulated system with a synthetic vs. a recorded voice, they conclude that a recorded voice system is perceived as more human-like and thus entitled to use "I", whereas a synthetic-voice system is not perceived as human enough to use "I" to refer to itself (Nass et al., 2006).

Another question is whether system output style influences users' input formulation, as would be expected due to the phenomenon of *alignment*, which is generally considered a basic principle in natural language dialogue (Garrod and Pickering, 2004).[1]

Experiments targeting human-human conversation show that speakers in spontaneous dialogues tend to express themselves in similar ways at lexical and syntactic levels (e.g., (Hadelich et al., 2004; Garrod and Pickering, 2004). Lexical and syntactic alignment is present in human-computer interaction, too. (Brennan, 1996) suggested that users adopt system's terms to avoid errors, expecting the system to be inflexible. However, recent experiments show that alignment in human-computer interaction is also automatic and its strength is comparable to that in human-human communication (Branigan et al., 2003; Pearson et al., 2006).

Early results concerning users' alignment to system output style in the interpersonal dimension are reported in (Brennan and Ohaeri, 1994): They distinguish three styles: anthropomorphic (the system refers to itself using first person pronouns, like in (1a) above, fluent (complete sentences, but no self-reference) and telegraphic, like (2d). They found no difference in users' perception of the system's intelligence across the different conditions. However, they observed that the anthropomorphic group was more than twice as likely to refer to the computer using the second person pronoun "you" and it used more indirect requests and conventional politeness than the other groups. They conclude that the anthropomorphic style is undesirable for dialogue systems because it encourages more complex user input which is harder to recognize and interpret.

The described experiments used either the Wizard-of-Oz paradigm (Brennan and Ohaeri, 1994) or preprogrammed system output (Branigan et al., 2003; Nass and Brave, 2005) and involved written communication. Such methods allow one to test assumptions about idealized human-computer interaction. Experimenting with the SAMMIE system allows us to test whether similar effects arise in an interaction with an actual dialogue system, which is plagued, among other factors, by speech recognition problems.

3 The SAMMIE System

SAMMIE is a multimodal dialogue system developed in the TALK project with particular emphasis on multimodal turn-planning and natural language generation to support intuitive mixed-initiative interaction.

The SAMMIE system provides a multimodal interface to an in-car MP3 player through speech and haptic input with a BMW iDrive input device, a button which can be turned, pushed down and sideways in four directions. System output is by speech and a graphical display integrated into the car's dashboard. SAMMIE has a German and an English version with the same functionality.

[1]This dialogue phenomenon goes under a variety of terms in the literature, besides alignment, e.g., accommodation, adaptation, convergence, entrainment or shaping (used, e.g., by (Brennan and Ohaeri, 1994)).

The MP3 player application offers a wide range of tasks: The user can control the currently playing song, search and browse by looking for fields in the MP3 database (song, artist, album, etc.), search and select playlists and construct and edit them. A sample interaction is shown below (Becker et al., 2006).

(3) U: Show me the Beatles albums.

S: I have these four Beatles albums. [shows a list of album names]

U: Which songs are on this one? [selects the Red Album]

S: The Red Album contains these songs [shows a list of the songs]

U: Play the third one.

S: [song "From Me To You" plays]

The system puts the user in control of the interaction. Input can be given through any modality and is not restricted to answers to system queries. On the contrary, the user can provide new tasks as well as any information relevant to the current task at any time. This is achieved through modeling the interaction as a collaborative problem solving (CPS) process, modeling the tasks and their progression as *recipes* and a multimodal interpretation that fits any user input into the context of the current task (Blaylock and Allen, 2005). To support dialogue flexibility, we model discourse context, the CPS state and the driver's attention state by an enriched information state (Kruijff-Korbayová et al., 2006a).

3.1 System Architecture

The SAMMIE system architecture follows the classical approach of a pipelined architecture with multimodal fusion and fission modules encapsulating the dialogue manager (Bunt et al., 2005). Figure 1 shows the modules and their interaction: Modality-specific recognizers and analysers provide semantically interpreted input to the multimodal fusion module (interpretation manager in Figure 1), that interprets them in the context of the other modalities and the current dialog context. The dialogue manager decides on the next system move, based on its CPS encoded task model, on the current context and also on the results from calls to the MP3 database. The multimodal fission component then generates the system reaction on a modality-dependent level

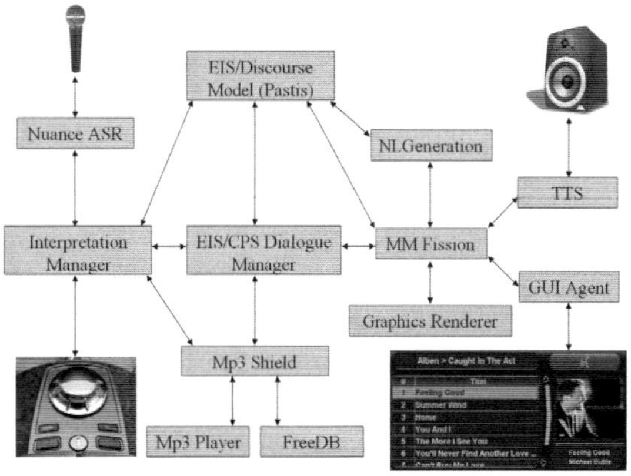

Figure 1: SAMMIE system architecture.

by selecting the content to present, distributing it appropriately over the available output modalities and finally co-ordinating and synchronizing the output. Modality-specific output modules generate spoken output and an update of the graphical display. All modules interact with the extended information state in which all context information is stored.

Many tasks in the SAMMIE system are modeled by a rule-based approach. Discourse modeling, interpretation management, dialogue management, turn planning and linguistic planning are all based on the production rule system PATE (Pfleger, 2004; Kempe, 2004). For speech recognition, we use Nuance. The spoken output is synthesized with the Mary TTS (Schröder and Trouvain, 2003).[2]

3.2 Generation of Natural Language Output with Variation

To generate natural language output in SAMMIE, we developed a template-based generator. It is implemented by a set of sentence planning rules in PATE to build the templates, and a set of XSLT transformations for sentence realization, which yield the output strings. German and English output is produced by accessing different dictionaries in a uniform way. The output is either plain text, if it is to be displayed in the graphical user interface (e.g., captions in tables, written messages to the user) or it is text with mark-up for speech synthesis using the MaryXML format (Schröder and Trouvain, 2003), if it is to be spoken by a speech synthesizer.

[2]http://mary.dfki.de/

The SAMMIE generator can produce alternative realizations for a given content that it receives as input from the turn planner. The implemented range of system output variation involves the following aspects, which have been determined by an analysis of a corpus of dialogues collected in a Wizard-of-Oz experiment using several wizards who were free to formulate their responses to the users (Kruijff-Korbayová et al., 2006b):

1. Personal vs. impersonal style: *Ich habe 3 Lieder gefunden* (*I've found three songs*) vs. *3 Lieder wurden gefunden* (*Three songs have been found*);
2. Telegraphic vs. non-telegraphic style: *23 Alben gefunden (23 albums found)* vs. *Ich habe 23 Alben gefunden (I found 23 albums)*
3. Reduced vs. non-reduced referring expressions: *der Song "Kinder An Die Macht"* (*the song "Kinder An Die Macht"*) vs. *der Song* (*the song*) vs. *"Kinder An Die Macht"* (*"Kinder An Die Macht"*);
4. Lexical choice for (quasi-)synonyms: *Song* vs. *Lied* vs. *Titel* (*song* vs. *track*)
5. Presence vs. absence of adverbs/adverbials: *Ich spiele jetzt den Song* (*I'll now play the song*) vs. *Ich spiele den Song* (*I'll play the song*).

The generation of alternatives is achieved by conditioning the sentence planning and realization decisions. The system can be set either to use one style consistently throughout a dialogue, or to align to the user, i.e., mimic the user's style on a turn-by-turn basis. For the purpose of experimenting with system output variation, the generator supports three sources of control for the available choices: (a) global (default) parameter settings (resulting in no variation); (b) random selection (resulting in random variation); (c) contextual information (resulting in variation based on the dialogue context).

The contextual information used by the generator to control realization includes (i) the grounding status of the content to be communicated (e.g., to decide for vs. against reducing a referring expression); and (ii) linguistic features extracted from the recognized user input (e.g., to make the corresponding syntactic and lexical choices in the output).

3.3 Personal/Impersonal Style Variation

The style variation in SAMMIE amounts to varying between active voice for personal style and passive voice or the "es-gibt" ("there is") construction for impersonal style whenever applicable, as illustrated for several typical dialogue moves below (where (i) always shows the impersonal, and (ii) the personal version).

(4) Search result:[3]
- i. Es gibt 20 Alben.
  There are 20 albums.
- ii. Ich habe 20 Alben gefunden.
  I found 20 albums.
  Sie haben 20 Alben. / Du hast 20 Alben.
  You have 20 albums
  Wir haben 20 Alben.
  We have 20 albums.

(5) Song addition:
- i. Der Titel Bittersweet Symphony wurde zu der Playliste 2 hinzugefügt.
  The track Bittersweet Symphony has been added to Playlist 2.
- ii. Ich habe den Titel Bittersweet Symphony zu der Playliste 2 hinzugefügt.
  I added the track Bittersweer Symphony to Playlist 2.

(6) Song playback:
- i. Der Titel Männer von Herbert Grönemeyer wird gespielt.
  The track Männer by Herbert Grönemeyer is playing.
- ii. Ich spiele den Titel Männer von Herbert Grönemeyer.
  I am playing the track Männer by Herbert Grönemeyer.

(7) Non-understanding:
- i. Das wurde leider nicht verstanden.
  That has unfortunately not been understood.
- ii. Das habe ich leider nicht verstanden.
  I have unfortunately not understood that.

(8) Clarification request:
- i. Welches von diesen acht Liedern?/Welches von diesen acht Liedern wird gewünscht?
  Which of these eight songs? / Which of these eight songs is desired?
- ii. Welches von diesen acht Liedern möchtest du / möchten Sie hören?
  Which of these eight songs would you like to hear?

[3]When referring to the user, personal style has several variants which differ in formality (formal and informal address) and first vs. second person reference.

Figure 2: Experiment setup

The personal/impersonal style variation is not applicable for some dialogue moves, e.g., (9), and for output in telegraphic style.

(9) Song interpreter:
Der Titel Bongo Girl ist von Nena.
The track Bongo Girl is by Nena.

4 Experiment

In order to assess the effects of style manipulation in the SAMMIE system, we ran an experiment in simulated driving conditions, comparing two versions of the system: one consistently using personal and the other impersonal style output.[4] The experiment employed the German version of SAMMIE. The setup (see Figure 2), participants, procedure and collected data are described in detail in (Kruijff-Korbayová and Kukina, 2008), and summarized below.

There were 28 participants, all native speakers of German. We balanced gender and background when assigning them to the style conditions. The experiment followed a fixed script for each participant: welcome, instruction, warm-up driving, 2 trial and 11 experimental tasks, evaluation questionnaire, payment and farewell. The participants were instructed to use mainly spoken input, although they could also use the iDrive button. It took them about 40 minutes to complete all the tasks. The tasks involved exploring the contents of a database of about 25 music albums and were of four types: (1) finding some specified title(s); (2) selecting some title(s) satisfying certain constraints; (3) manipulating the playlists by adding or removing songs and (4) free-use of the system.

[4]For the time being we have not evaluated the version of the system aligning to the user's style.

The experimental tasks were presented to each participant in randomized order apart from the free use of the system, which was always the last task. The experimenter (E) repeated each task assignment twice to the participant, once in personal and once in impersonal style, as shown in the example below.

(10) E: *Bitte frage das System nach den Liedern von "Pur". Du willst also wissen welche Lieder von "Pur" es gibt.*
E: Please ask the the system about the songs by "Pur". You would like to know which songs by "Pur" there are.

The questionnaire was based on (Nass and Brave, 2005) and (Mutschler et al., 2007). It contained questions with a 6-point scale ranging from 1 (low grade) to 6 (high grade), such as *How do you assess the system in general:* technical (1) – human-like (6); *Communication with the system seemed to you:* boring (1) – exciting (6); *In terms of usability, the system is:* inefficient (1) —efficient(6).

The recorded dialogues have been transcribed, the questionnaire responses tabulated. We manually annotated the participants' utterances (on average 95 per session) with the following features for further analysis:

- Construction type:

  Personal (+/-) Is the utterance a complete sentence in active voice or imperative form

  Impersonal (+/-) Is the utterance expressed by passive voice, infinite verb form (e.g., "Lied abspielen" (*lit.* "song play")), or expletive "es-gibt" ("there-is") construction

  Telegraphic (+/-) Is the utterance expressed by a phrase, e.g., "weiter" ("next")

- Personal pronouns: (+/-) Does the utterance contain a first or second person pronoun

- Politeness marking: (+/-) Does the utterance contain a politeness marker, such as "bitte" ("please"), "danke" ("thanks") and verbs in subjunctive mood (eg. "ich hätte gerne")

5 Results

The results concerning users' attitudes and alignment are presented in detail in (Kruijff-Korbayová and Kukina, 2008). Here we summarize the significant findings and provide an additional analysis of the influence of speech recognition problems.

5.1 Style and Users' Attitudes

The first issue addressed in the experiment was whether the users have different judgments of the personal vs. impersonal version of the system. Since the system used a synthetic voice, the judgments were expected to be more positive in the impersonal style condition (Nass and Brave, 2005). Based on factor analysis performed on attitudinal data from the user questionnaires we created the six indices listed below. All indices were meaningful and reliable. (A detailed description of the indices including the contributing factors from the questionnaires can be found in (Kruijff-Korbayová and Kukina, 2008).)

1. General satisfaction with the communication with the system (Cronbach's α=0.86)
2. Easiness of communication with the system (α=0.83)
3. Usability of the system (α=0.76)
4. Clarity of the system's speech (α=0.88)
5. Perceived "humanness" of the system (α=0.69)
6. System's perceived flexibility and creativity (α=0.78)

We did not find any significant influence of system output style on users' attitudes. Only for *perceived humanness of the system* we found a weak tendency in the predicted direction (independent samples test: t(25)=1.64, p=0.06 (one-tailed)), in line with the earlier observation that an interface that refers to itself by a personal pronoun is perceived to be more human-like than one that does not (Nass and Brave, 2005).

5.2 Style and Alignment

The next issue we investigated was whether the users formulated their input differently in the personal vs. impersonal system version. For each dialogue session, we calculated the percentage of utterances containing the feature of interest relative to the total number of user utterances in the session.

In accordance with the expectation based on style alignment in terms of agentivity, we observed a significant difference in the number of personal constructions across style conditions (t(19)=1.8, p=0.05 (one-tailed)). But we did not find a significant difference in the distribution of impersonal constructions. Not surprisingly, there was also no significant difference in the distribution of telegraphic constructions. An unexpected finding was the higher proportion of telegraphic constructions than verb-containing ones within the impersonal style condition (t(13)=3.5, p<0.001 (one-tailed)). However, no such difference was found in the personal style condition. Contrary to expectations, we also did not find any significant effect of style-manipulation on the number of personal pronouns, nor on the number of politeness markers.

Since alignment can also be seen as a process of gradual adjustment among dialogue participants over time we compared the proportion of personal, impersonal and telegraphic constructions in the first and second halves of the conversations for both style conditions. The only significant effect we found was a decrease in the number of personal constructions in the second halves of the impersonal style interactions (t(13)=2.5, p=0.02 (one-tailed)).

5.3 Influence of Speech Recognition Problems

Unlike an interaction in a Wizard-of-Oz simulation or similar, an interaction with a real system is bound to suffer from speech recognition problems. Therefore, we made a post-hoc analysis with respect to how much speech recognition difficulty the participants experienced, in terms of the proportion of participant utterances not recognized by the system relative to the total number of participant utterances in a session.

On average, around 33% of participant utterances were not understood by the system.[5] We classified the participants into three groups according to the performance of speech recognition they experienced: the *good* group with less than 27% of input not understood (7 participants); the *poor* group

[5]This is admittedly rather bad performance, nevertheless it mostly does not prevent the participants from getting their tasks successfully completed within a reasonable time, as was shown in an rigorous usability evaluation of the system in normal driving conditions (Mutschler et al., 2007).

Speech Recognition Group		Satisfaction with Communication	Usability of the System	Perceived Flexibility of the System	Clarity of the System's Speech	Perceived Humanness of the System	Ease of Communication
good SR	Mean	3.8889	3.6444	3.2963	4.2222	3.7407	3.0889
	S. D.	.91287	.81104	1.12354	.97183	.54716	1.16237
poor SR	Mean	3.0000	3.0222	2.5556	3.2778	4.0000	2.8667
	S. D.	1.06719	.73106	.79931	1.03414	.66667	.93808

Figure 3: Judgments of the system by the "good" and "poor" speech recognition group

with more than 37% of input not uderstood (7 participants); the *average* group (the remaining 14 participants).

Speech Recognition and Attitudinal Data We suspected that speech recognition problems might be neutralizing a potential influence of style. Therefore we contrasted the judgments on all six factors between the good and the poor speech recognition group (see Figure 3). The "good" speech recognition group showed higher satisfaction with the communication (t(16)=1.9, p=0.04 (one-tailed)) and evaluated the clarity of the system's speech better (t(16)= 2.0, p=0.03 (one-tailed)). The good speech recognition group also showed a tendency to assess the usability and flexibility of the system higher than the poor speech recognition group (t(16)=1.71, p=0.05 and t(16)=1.61, p=0.06, respectively (marginally significant results)). The two groups did not differ with respect to their judgments of the ease of communication and perceived humanness of the system (t(16)=0.45, p=0.66 and t(16)=0.90, p=0.38). These results are not surprising. They confirm that speech recognition does have an effect on the user's perception of the system.

Speech Recognition and Style Alignment We also checked post-hoc whether differences in the experienced speech recognition performance had an influence on the style employed by the participants, again in terms of the proportion of utterances with personal, impersonal and telegraphic constructions, personal pronouns and politeness marking. However, we found no significant effect on the linguistic structure of the participant input across the groups (politeness marking: F(2)=1.5, p=0.24; all other Fs<1 (ANOVA)).

6 Discussion and Conclusions

We presented the generation of personal/impersonal style variation in the SAMMIE multimodal dialogue system, and the results of an experiment evaluating the influence of the system output style on the users' subjective judgments and their formulation of input. Although our results are not conclusive, they point at a range of issues for further research.

Regarding users' attitudes to the system, we found no significant difference among the styles. This is similar to (Brennan and Ohaeri, 1994) who found no difference in intelligence attributed to the system by the users, but it is at odds with the earlier finding that a synthetic voice interface was judged to be more useful when avoiding self-reference by personal pronouns (Nass and Brave, 2005).

Whereas (Brennan and Ohaeri, 1994) used a flight reservation dialogue system, (Nass and Brave, 2005) used a phone-based auction system which read out an introduction and five object descriptions. There are two points to note: First, the subjects heard system output that was a read out continuous text rather than turns in an interaction. This may have reinforced the activation of particular style features. Second, the auction task may have sensibilized the subjects to the distinction between subjective (the system's) vs. objective information presentation, and thus make them more sensitive to whether the system presents itself as an active agent or not.

Regarding the question whether users align their style to that of the system, where previous experiments showed strong effects of alignment (Brennan and Ohaeri, 1994), our experiment shows some effects, but some of the results are conflicting. On the one hand, subjects interacting with the personal style version of the system used more personal constructions than those interacting with the impersonal style version. However, subjects in either condition did not show any significant difference with respect to the use of impersonal constructions or telegraphic forms. We also found a higher proportion of telegraphic constructions than verb-containing ones within the impersonal style condition, but no such difference in the personal style. Finally, when we considered alignment over time, we found no change in construction use in the personal style, whereas we found a decrease in the use of personal constructions in the impersonal style. It is possible that dividing the interactions into three parts and comparing alignment in the first and the last part might lead to stronger results.

That there is no difference in the use of telegraphic constructions across conditions is not surprising. Being just phrasal sentence fragments, these constructions are neutral with respect to style. But why does there seem to be an alignment effect for personal constructions and not for others? One way of explaining this is that (some of) the constructions that we counted as impersonal are common in both styles. Besides their deliberate use as means to avoid explicit reference to oneself, they also have their normal, neutral usage, and therefore, some of the utterances that we classified as impersonal style may just be neutral formulations, rather than cases of distancing or "de-agentivization". However, we could not test this hypothesis, because we have not found a way to reliably distinguish between neutral and marked, truly impersonal utterances. This is an issue for future work.

The difference between our results concerning alignment and those of (Brennan and Ohaeri, 1994) is not likely to be due to a difference in the degree of interactivity (as with (Nass and Brave, 2005)). We now comment on other differences between our systems, which might have contributed to the differences in results.

One aspect where we differ concerns our distinction between personal and impersonal style, both in the implementation of the SAMMIE system and in the experiment: We include the presence/absence of agentivity not only in the system's reference to itself (akin to (Nass and Brave, 2005) and (Brennan and Ohaeri, 1994)), but also in addressing the user. This concept of the personal/impersonal distinction was inspired by such differences observed in a study of instructional texts in several languages (Kruijff et al., 1999), where the latter dimension is predominant. The present experiment results make it pertinent that more research into the motives behind expressing or suppressing agentivity in both dimensions is needed.

Apart from the linguistic design of the system's output, other factors influence users' behavior and perception of the system, and thus might confound experiment results, e.g., functionality, design, ergonomics, speech synthesis and speech recognition.

A system with synthesized speech should be more positively rated when it does not refer to itself as an active agent by personal pronouns (Nass and Brave, 2005). (Brennan and Ohaeri, 1994) used a system with written interaction, the SAMMIE system employs the MARY text-to-speech synthesis system (Schröder and Trouvain, 2003) with an MBROLA diphone synthesiser, which produces an acceptable though not outstanding output quality. Our post-hoc analysis showed a tendency towards better judgements of the system by the participants experiencing less speech recognition problems. This is as expected. We did not find any statistically significant effect regarding the style-related features we analyzed. A future experiment should address the possibility of an interaction between system style and speech recognition performance as both factors might be influencing the user simultaneously.

One radical difference between our experiment and the earlier ones is that the users of the SAMMIE system are occupied by the driving task, and thus only have a limited cognitive capacity left for the interaction with the system. This may make them less susceptible to the subtleties of style manipulation than would be the case if they were free of other tasks. A possible future experiment could address this issue by including a non-driving condition.

Finally, the SAMMIE system has also the style-alignment mode, where it mimics the user's style on turn-to-turn basis. We plan to present experimental results comparing the alignment-mode with the fixed personal/impersonal style in a future publication.

Acknowledgments

This work was carried out in the TALK project (www.talk-project.org) funded by the EU as project No. IST-507802 within the 6th Framework Program.

References

T. Becker, N. Blaylock, C. Gerstenberger, I. Kruijff-Korbayová, A. Korthauer, M. Pinkal, M. Pitz, P. Poller, and J. Schehl. 2006. Natural and intuitive multimodal dialogue for in-car applications: The SAMMIE system. In *Proceedings of ECAI, PAIS Special section*.

N. Blaylock and J. Allen. 2005. A collaborative problem-solving model of dialogue. In L. Dybkjær and W. Minker, editors, *Proceedings of the 6th SIGdial Workshop on Discourse and Dialogue*, pages 200–211, Lisbon, September 2–3.

H. Branigan, M. Pickering, J. Pearson, J. F. McLean, and C. Nass. 2003. Syntactic alignment between computer and people: the role of belief about mental states. In *Proceedings of the Annual Conference of the Cognitive Science Society*.

S. Brennan and J.O. Ohaeri. 1994. Effects of message style on user's attribution toward agents. In *Proceedings of CHI'94 Conference Companion Human Factors in Computing Systems*, pages 281–282. ACM Press.

S. Brennan. 1996. Lexical entrainment in spontaneous dialogue. In *Proceedings of the International Symposium on Spoken Dialogue (ISSD-96)*, pages 41–44.

H. Bunt, M. Kipp, M. Maybury, and W. Wahlster. 2005. Fusion and coordination for multimodal interactive information presentation: Roadmap, architecture, tools, semantics. In O. Stock and M. Zancanaro, editors, *Multimodal Intelligent Information Presentation*, volume 27 of *Text, Speech and Language Technology*, pages 325–340. Kluwer Academic.

S. Garrod and M. Pickering. 2004. Why is conversation so easy? *TRENDS in Cognitive Sciences*, 8.

K. Hadelich, H. Branigan, M. Pickering, and M. Crocker. 2004. Alignment in dialogue: Effects of feedback on lexical overlap within and between participants. In *Proceedings of the AMLaP Conference*. Aix en Provence, France.

Amy Isard, Carsten Brockmann, and Jon Oberlander. 2006. Individuality and alignment in generated dialogues. In *Proceedings of the 4th International Natural Language Generation Conference (INLG-06)*, pages 22–29, Sydney, Australia.

Benjamin Kempe. 2004. PATE a production rule system based on activation and typed feature structure elements. Bachelor Thesis, Saarland University, August.

G.J.M. Kruijff, I. Kruijff-Korbayová, J. Bateman, D. Dochev, N. Gromova, T. Hartley, E. Teich, S. Sharoff, L. Sokolova, and K. Staykova. 1999. Deliverable TEXS2: Specification of elaborated text structures. Technical report, AGILE Project, EU INCO COPERNICUS PL961104.

I. Kruijff-Korbayová and O. Kukina. 2008. The effect of dialogue system output style variation on users' evaluation judgements and input style. In *Proceedings of SigDial'08*, Columbus, Ohio.

I. Kruijff-Korbayová, G. Amores, N. Blaylock, S. Ericsson, G. Pérez, K. Georgila, M. Kaisser, S. Larsson, O. Lemon, P. Manchón, and J. Schehl. 2006a. Deliverable D3.1: Extended information state modeling. Technical report, TALK Project, EU FP6, IST-507802.

Ivana Kruijff-Korbayová, Tilman Becker, Nate Blaylock, Ciprian Gerstenberger, Michael Kaisser, Peter Poller, Verena Rieser, and Jan Schehl. 2006b. The SAMMIE corpus of multimodal dialogues with an MP3 player. In *Proceedings of LREC*, Genova, Italy.

H. Mutschler, F. Steffens, and A. Korthauer. 2007. Deliverable D6.4: Final report on multimodal experiments Part I: Evaluation of the SAMMIE system. Technical report, TALK Project, EU FP6, IST-507802.

C. Nass and S. Brave, 2005. *Should voice interfaces say "I"? Recorded and synthetic voice interfaces' claims to humanity*, chapter 10, pages 113–124. The MIT Press, Cambridge.

C. Nass, S. Brave, and L. Takayama. 2006. Socializing consistency: from technical homogeneity to human epitome. In *P. Zhang & D. Galletta (Eds.), Human-computer interaction in management information systems: Foundations*, pages 373–390. Armonk, NY: M. E. Sharpe.

J. Pearson, J. Hu, H. Branigan, M. J. Pickering, and C. I. Nass. 2006. Adaptive language behavior in HCI: how expectations and beliefs about a system affect users' word choice. In *CHI '06: Proceedings of the SIGCHI conference on Human Factors in computing systems*, pages 1177–1180, New York, NY, USA. ACM.

N. Pfleger. 2004. Context based multimodal fusion. In *ICMI '04: Proceedings of the 6th international conference on Multimodal interfaces*, pages 265–272, New York, NY, USA. ACM Press.

M. Schröder and J. Trouvain. 2003. The German text-to-speech synthesis system MARY: A tool for research, development and teaching. *International Journal of Speech Technology*, 6:365–377.

Evaluating an Ontology-Driven WYSIWYM Interface

Feikje Hielkema **Chris Mellish** **Peter Edwards**
Computing Science
School of Natural & Computing Sciences
University of Aberdeen
Aberdeen, AB24 3FX, UK
{f.hielkema, c.mellish, p.edwards}@abdn.ac.uk

Abstract

This paper describes an evaluation study of an ontology-driven WYSIWYM interface for metadata creation. Although the results are encouraging, they are not as positive as those of a similar tool developed for the medical domain. We believe this may be due, not to the WYSIWYM interface, but to the complexity of the underlying ontologies and the fact that subjects were unfamiliar with them. We discuss the ways in which ontology development might be influenced by issues stemming from using an NLG approach for user access to data, and the effect these factors have on general usability.

1 Introduction

In the PolicyGrid[1] project we are investigating how best to support social science researchers through the use of Semantic Grid (De Roure et al., 2005) technologies. The Semantic Grid is often described as an 'extension of the current Grid in which information and services are given well-defined meaning, better enabling computers and people to work in cooperation'. Semantic Grids thus not only share data and compute resources, but also share and process metadata and knowledge, e.g. through the use of RDF[2] (Resource Description Framework, a metadata model for making statements about resources) or OWL[3] (knowledge representation language for authoring ontologies).

Numerous e-science applications rely on metadata descriptions of resources. But how does metadata come into existence? Ideally the user should create it. However, metadata creation is a complex task, and few users know how to create them in RDF. To enable our users to describe their resources, we need to provide a tool that facilitates creation, querying and browsing of metadata by users with no prior experience of such technologies.

Existing tools that provide access to RDF metadata are often graphical, e.g. (Handschuh et al., 2001; Catarci et al., 2004). However, we believe that, for social scientists, natural language is the best medium to use, as the way they conduct their research and the structure of their documents and data indicate that they are more oriented towards text than graphics. Natural language approaches include GINO (Bernstein and Kaufmann, 2006), an ontology editor with an approach reminiscent of Natural Language Menus (Tennant et al., 1983), and using Controlled languages such as PENG-D (Schwitter and Tilbrook, 2004). Such natural language approaches tend to restrict expressivity to ensure that every entry can be parsed, limiting the language and often making it stilted, so that there is a small learning curve before the user knows which structures are allowed. In order to maintain full expressivity and to shorten the learning curve, we have elected to use WYSIWYM (What You See Is What You Meant) (Power et al., 1998). This is a natural language generation approach where the system generates a feed-

[1]Funded under the UK Economic and Social Research Council *e-Social Science* programme; grant reference RES-149-25-1027 (http://www.policygrid.org)

[2]http://www.w3.org/RDF/

[3]http://www.w3.org/TR/owl-features/

back text for the user that is based on a semantic representation. This representation is edited directly by the user by manipulating the feedback text. WYSIWYM has been used by a number of other projects, such as MILE (Piwek et al., 2000) and CLEF (Hallett, 2006). As evaluation results in both of these projects were very positive (Piwek, 2002; Hallett et al., 2007), we felt that WYSIWYM would be a suitable approach to use in our work.

We have developed a metadata elicitation tool that enables users to create metadata in the shape of *ontology instance data*; the tool is driven by the ontologies that define those instances. We are currently implementing a WYSIWYM tool for querying, that uses the same interface as the metadata creation tool. We also aim to develop a tool for presenting the results of the query, and for browsing the descriptions in the database. These three tools will be integrated into one consistent interface, so that users can switch effortlessly between querying, browsing and editing ontology instance data. This aim is similar to the support that the graphical tool SHAKEN provides for ontology editing and browsing (Thoméré et al., 2002). We want to ensure that these tools are generic, so that if the ontologies change over time or are replaced, the tools will still function. That means that all domain specific information (as much as is possible) should be contained in the ontologies. In this paper we explore the ways in which Natural Language Generation issues influence ontology building and vice versa.

This paper is structured as follows: section 2 describes the tool for metadata creation that we have implemented; section 3 discusses issues in ontology development and Natural Language Generation; and section 4 presents an evaluation study of the metadata creation tool. In section 5 the results of this study are discussed and compared to those of the CLEF project; we argue that different domains and ontologies affect the usability and complexity of metadata access interfaces.

2 The Metadata Creation Tool

We have developed a WYSIWYM tool that enables users to upload resources (e.g. acadamic papers, statistical datasets, interview transcripts) and create metadata descriptions for them, even if these users

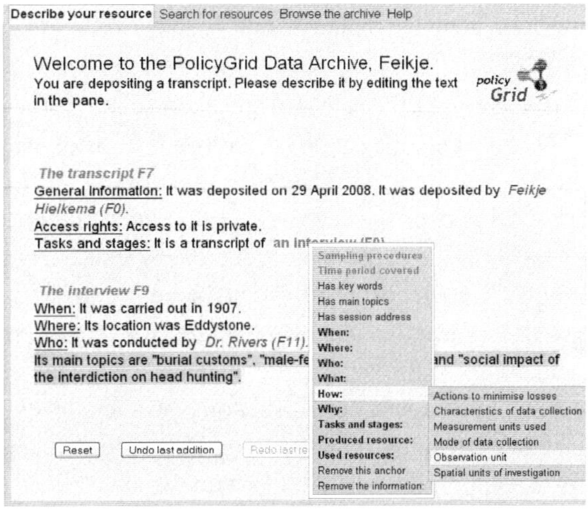

Figure 1: The Metadata Creation Tool.

are unfamiliar with ontologies. First, the user selects the type of resource he is depositing (e.g. a *Transcript*). The tool then generates a brief *feedback text* that presents the information specified by the user. The feedback text contains *anchors*, phrases in red boldface and blue italics that signal where new information can be added. When the user clicks on an anchor, a menu pops up listing the kinds of information that can be added here (see Figure 1). After selecting a menu item, the user is prompted to enter an appropriate value; this may be a date, a free-text string, or another object that may or may not be in the text already. The feedback text is regenerated whenever the user has added some information.

The tool is driven by one or more ontologies. Their class hierarchies are presented when users are selecting a resource type, or creating a new object as range for a property. The anchors correspond to individuals in the ontology; the menu items to the properties of those individuals. The feedback text is divided into paragraphs which correspond to the individuals; each property of an individual is realised as (part of) a sentence in its paragraph. Each property in the ontology is associated with a linguistic specification, a Dependency Tree (Mel'cuk, 1988) that corresponds to a sentence. The specification has slots where the source and target of the property should be inserted, and is sufficiently detailed to support processes such as aggregation, through which the feedback text is made more fluent. For a more extensive description of the metadata creation tool and its implementation, see Hielkema et al. (2007b).

In August 2007 we ran a pilot evaluation study (Hielkema et al., 2007a) on this tool. This study was heuristic in nature, with subjects discussing the interface with the experimenter while performing set tasks. It highlighted a number of aspects which we felt it was necessary to improve before embarking on the formal evaluation. Apart from there being standard usability considerations such as a need for better undo and help functions, it became evident that the underlying ontology was neither extensive enough nor sufficiently well-structured: subjects struggled to find the options they needed, and were often not satisfied with the options' names or their location in the sub-menus. We therefore decided that, as well as improving the basic usability of the interface, we needed to redevelop the ontology that was driving the interface. Users, we felt, would find it easier to navigate the menus when this ontology matched their mental model of the domain. Throughout the development of this new ontology, user requirements and feedback were gathered through a number of focus group sessions. The next section describes the ways in which this ontology development was affected by the demands of the metadata interface.

3 Ontologies in NLG

Portability has always been a major issue in NLG. Language generation involves the use of much information that is domain-specific, and cannot be generalised without a cost in the expressivity of the resulting text. If we want to create an application that is domain-independent, we have to find a way to store all domain-specific information in a structure that is easily extended or replaced.

We have decided to use an ontology, a common structure whose use has become widespread in knowledge representation. Ideally, we would like to create a generator that can be applied to any domain, provided there is an appropriate domain-specific ontology. But what information should such an ontology contain? How should it be structured? In this section we explore issues that occur when developing or adapting ontologies for use in the WYSIWYM tool; we believe that this can at least in part be generalised to NLG. The ontologies we have used so far were developed at the same time as the WYSIWYM tool, so that both tool and ontology influenced each other's development. We are currently adapting an ontology from another e-science project for use in our WYSIWYM interface, to further investigate such issues (see section 5).

There are a number of existing tools that generate language from ontologies, using various approaches. Wilcock (2003) describes an ontology verbaliser using XML-based generation. As Wilcock states, his approach is domain-specific, and therefore probably incompatible with more general ontologies (and presumably with ontologies from a different domain).

MIAKT (Bontcheva and Wills, 2004) is a system that generates textual medical reports from an RDF description. It uses a medical domain ontology and an NLG lexicon that contains lexicalisations for the concepts and instances in the ontology. In order to verbalise properties, MIAKT's surface realiser needs lexical specifications for them. Four basic property types are distinguished whose sub-properties can mostly be realised automatically through the grammar rules in the realiser. This technique increases the portability of the system, but does affect the variability and expressivity of the generator.

We do not aim to generate from any ontology in a domain, but to generate texts with high expressivity and clarity from ontologies that are designed in an 'NLG-aware' way. We are investigating what requirements an ontology has to meet in order to be usable for our application, so that for any domain an ontology can be built or adapted which we can use to produce a usable NL-interface. As many ontology developers are not linguists, ideally we want to support the adaptation to 'NLG-aware' ontologies without requiring linguistic expertise, for instance through a supporting software tool. Ontologies are primarily built to model domain-specific knowledge, making domain assumptions explicit, and to facilitate reasoning with this knowledge. These aims may sometimes conflict with the requirements of NLG applications, but they do frequently coincide (e.g. the need for clear, unambiguous resource names.

3.1 Domain Ontologies for WYSIWYM

What information does our WYSIWYM application need its ontologies to provide? First of all, the parts of it that will be shown to the user need to be easily mapped to natural language. The purpose of the tool is to support creation of ontology instance data by users unfamiliar with ontologies, so the parts they see should be comprehensible to novices. The names of properties are used to populate the pop-up menus, while the class names are shown in the class hierarchy. These names are mapped to natural language by replacing capitals and underscores with whitespace, and if necessary adding a determiner. Therefore, they need to correspond to phrases in natural language in order to be understood by the user, with individual words separated by capitals or underscores. If there is no intuitive NL-phrase to represent a class, it probably does not correspond to a concept in the domain either and might confuse the user, so it should be removed from the hierarchy. Classes whose instances are best presented by some distinctive name (e.g. *Person* or *Paper*) should have a *name* or *title* property whose value can be used (e.g. 'John'). For other classes (e.g. *Interview*), the class name can be used (e.g. 'some interview').

We need a linguistic specification for each property, sufficiently detailed to support aggregation and pronominalisation, but also to produce more than one surface form: a query is presented differently than a description, even if it contains the same information (compare the texts in Figure 1 and 2). The linguistic specification should be sufficiently rich to support the generation of these different surface forms. For this purpose we are using Dependency Trees, whose richness in both syntactic and semantic information provides ample support for such transformations. These trees can be associated with the domain ontology[4]. This specification also contains the header of the submenu in which the property should appear.

Some peculiarities in natural language are domain-independent. For instance, an address is presented in a very specific way and cannot be realised in the standard manner without sacrificing clarity (e.g. 'The address' street is Union Street. Its place is Aberdeen'). Such 'utility' classes are used across domains. In PolicyGrid we have created a utility ontology that contains classes such as 'Person', 'Address' and 'Date' [5]. Instances of these classes are generated to a special surface form. In order to get the best realisation from the WYSIWYM tool, domain ontologies should use the classes from this utility ontology. As the properties of the utility classes are already furnished with linguistic specifications, they are already NLG-aware. Another way to hasten the process is to use, where possible, properties from this ontology instead of those from the domain ontology.

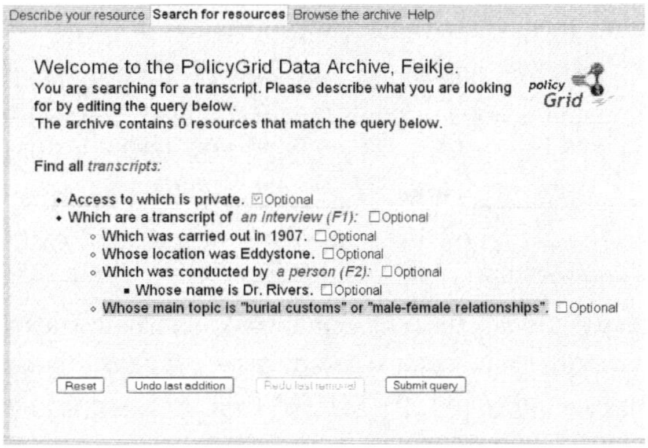

Figure 2: The Query Tool.

3.2 WYSIWYM for Ontologies

What should the WYSIWYM application do in order to provide access to ontologies? For metadata creation it is essential that users can only produce 'correct' metadata, which does not violate the constraints in the ontology. The feedback text should be presented coherently, while the Text Planner only uses information that is either domain independent or present in the ontology. Perhaps most importantly, the application should support easy creation of the linguistic information that the ontology must contain, as we cannot expect ontology developers to have the linguistic expertise to create Dependency Trees. We are devising a way for users to create a specification by manipulating the surface form of a 'template' specification. We currently have 12 templates which represent commonly used sen-

[4]For an example of how this is done, see http://www.csd.abdn.ac.uk/research/policygrid/ontologies/Lexicon/Lexicon.owl

[5]http://www.policygrid.org/utility.owl

tences to present ontology properties in text. The user can fine-tune the surface form by adding adjectives, changing morphological information and the root of individual words; actions for which only a basic linguistic knowledge is needed. This approach is outlined in more detail in (Hielkema et al., 2007b). The main challenge with this approach is that the specification is used to generate two surface forms; it remains to be seen whether a specification that is fine-tuned through one surface form will accommodate the accurate generation of another.

The Penman Upper Model (Bateman, 1990) supports the specification of linguistic information through a different approach. The Upper Model is a domain-independent ontology that supports sophisticated NLP. To make a domain ontology available for NLP, its resources have to be placed in the hierarchy of the Upper Model; their place there determines their surface realisation. This task appears to require considerable linguistic expertise, but like the creation of our Dependency Trees could probably be made easier for non-linguists through some special-purpose interface.

4 Usability Evaluation

The best evaluation of our tool would be to let users deposit their resources in real-life contexts, but our tool is not ready for a full deployment. Another way would be to compare its usability to another metadata creation tool in an experiment where users completed the same tasks with both tools. Unfortunately, most metadata tools focus on providing support for ontology editing (e.g. Protégé[6] or GINO (Bernstein and Kaufmann, 2006)), or query formulation (e.g. SEWASIE (Catarci et al., 2004)). A number of tools for metadata creation use formal (RDF) or controlled languages, which are difficult to use for those wholly unfamiliar with formal logic. Other tools were developed for one specific purpose, e.g. CREAM (Handschuh et al., 2001) which was developed for the annotation of web pages, and could not easily be adapted to our purposes. We were not aware of any tool that we could adapt to the e-social science ontologies and thus use in an experiment.

Alternatively, we could have compared our interface to direct authoring of RDF; but in an environment where most users have no experience of ontologies or metadata this seemed spurious. Instead, we adopted an approach similar to that used in the CLEF project (Hallett et al., 2007). They evaluated their WYSIWYM system (which enabled users to create SQL queries for a database in a medical domain) by measuring the performance of fifteen subjects on four consecutive tasks, after a brief introduction. These subjects were all knowledgeable in the domain, and all but two knew the representation language of the repository and how the data contained in it was structured. These subjects achieved perfect results from the second task onwards, and became faster with each task, especially after the first. We also expected users to become faster and more accurate with each completed task, and indeed hoped for perfect scores on their last task.

Subjects Sixteen researchers and PhD students from various social science-related disciplines participated in the experiment. None of them had prior experience of the metadata elicitation interface, and only two of the subjects had any previous experience of using ontologies. The ontology driving the system models the description of social science resources and was based on requirements gathering sessions, in which a few subjects had participated. None of the subjects knew its precise structure.

Methodology After providing some information about their background, subjects viewed a video introduction[7] of six minutes. This video showed the construction of a simple resource description, highlighting the main functionalities of the interface, while a voice-over explained what was happening on the screen.

Subjects were then handed four short resource descriptions expressed as paragraphs of English (see 'Materials') and asked to reproduce these descriptions as closely as possible using the tool. To avoid making the choice of the correct options too obvious, we tried to avoid phrases that corresponded literally to those in the menus. Each subject received the descriptions in a different order, in case there were differences in the complexity of the tasks. Subjects were allowed as much time as they needed to

[6]http://protege.stanford.edu/

[7]This video can be viewed at http://www.csd.abdn.ac.uk/research/policygrid/demos/WysiwymIntroduction1.mov

Task order	Completion time		Operations		Total errors		Avoidable errors	
	μ	σ	μ	σ	μ	σ	μ	σ
First	512.81	366.132	48.38	24.527	3.31	1.922	1.56	.727
Second	329.50	95.716	37.75	12.228	2.69	2.442	1.38	.957
Third	260.06	90.542	35.13	9.749	2.75	2.720	1.63	1.310
Fourth	309.81	106.049	39.38	10.844	2.00	1.966	1.44	1.504

Table 1: Mean completion times, operations and errors per completed task.

complete each task.

For each task, the tool recorded the completion time, the produced description, the number of operations used to produce it, and the frequency with which various operation types were used, such as 'undo' or the 'help' functions. After the subjects had completed all four tasks, they were asked to rate the usability (very difficult - difficult - OK - easy - very easy) and usefulness (useless - not much use - adequate - useful - very useful) of the tool on a five-point Likert scale, and to note any feedback they might have. The entire experiment took on average 50 min. per subject.

Materials We used four resource descriptions, one of which was:

> You are depositing the transcript of an interview that was held by Dr. Rivers in 1907, at Eddystone. The interview mainly discussed 'male-female relationships', 'burial practices' and 'the social impact of the interdiction on head hunting'. Access to this transcript should remain private.

Figure 1 shows the corresponding description that could be produced with the tool. The separation of the transcript from the interview is an example of the clear distinctions necessary for knowledge representation. In natural language, this distinction would not necessarily be made, and indeed this step was missed by a number of users.

To ensure that tasks did not repeat identical subtasks, we tried to use different parts of the ontology in each task. Every task described a different resource type (conference paper, transcript, academic paper, report), which corresponded to a different class in the ontology. We were also careful to choose varying menu items (corresponding to properties in the ontology), although some repetition was unavoidable (e.g. specifying names). In fact, a real-life use of the tool would involve rather more task repetition (specifying titles, authors and dates would be necessary for practically any resource) than the artificial descriptions in this study.

Results To analyse the accuracy of the produced descriptions, we divided each description task into 8 to 10 subtasks. For the task shown in the previous paragraph, these subtasks were:

- Specify that you are depositing a 'Transcript'
- Specify that access is private
- Specify that it is a transcript of an 'Interview' (creating an 'interview' object)
  - Specify the three main topics
  - Add an interviewer (creating a 'Person' object)
    - Call this person 'Dr. Rivers'
  - Specify the location of the interview
  - Specify the date of the interview

As some subtasks are more complicated than others and take longer, we did not try to give each task exactly the same number of subtasks, but instead ensured that all tasks needed the same number of operations (e.g. menu item selections, button clicks, etc.) in order to be completed. Each subtask that was missing or completed differently than in the description shown in 'Materials' was counted as one error. Erroneous ways to complete subtasks included choosing a different menu item and adding information to the wrong object. For instance, a number of subjects, instead of specifying an interviewer for the interview, added a creator for the transcript; this was counted as one erroneously completed subtask, and therefore one error.

The list of subtasks above shows that some subtasks depend on the successful completion of other tasks; for instance, you cannot add an interviewer unless you have created an 'interview' object. We therefore analysed two error counts: the total number of errors, and the 'avoidable' errors. The 'avoidable' errors were the total number of errors minus those subtasks that depended on another subtask that was missing or had been completed incorrectly.

We analysed the mean completion times, number of operations used and the two error counts of the tasks that were completed first, second, third and last, using a repeated measures ANOVA (see Table 1 for the means and standard deviations). Mean completion times went down significantly (Huynh-Feldt p-value < 0.01). Tukey's HSD post-hoc (applied to a univariate ANOVA, with task order as the independent variable) test shows that both the third (p-value < 0.01) and the fourth (p-value 0.030) were completed significantly faster than the first task. However, no significant differences were found for the number of operations (Huynh-Feldt p-value 0.062), the total number of errors (Huynh-Feldt p-value .322) or the number of avoidable errors (Huynh-Feldt p-value .931).

Subject feedback on the tool was positive: it was perceived as useful (μ 3.94; 1='useless', 5='very useful'), and OK or easy to use (μ 2.69; 1='very easy', 5='very difficult'). Five subjects expressed a preference for a form-based interface, and five others for a NL-interface such as the one tested. In feedback, subjects indicated a desire for more form-based elements in the interface, to speed up the creation of the standard description elements (e.g. name/title, author), and complained that the environment was initially unfamiliar, with some menu items overlapping. This unfamiliarity meant that items that were necessary to complete the description were often overlooked; subjects often solved this by choosing the closest approximation they could find, e.g. 'creator' instead of 'interviewer'.

5 Discussion and Future Work

Although users quickly gained speed using the tool, and were positive in their feedback, the evaluation results are not nearly as positive as those found for CLEF (see section 4). The mean number of errors decreased, but this effect was not significant and only five out of sixteen subjects received a perfect score on the last task (four other subjects performed some earlier task(s) perfectly). Evidently there is a difference in usability of both tools - but what causes it? No doubt the difference can partly be ascribed to differences in the implementation of the interface. However, the most common feedback we received from the subjects was that they were overwhelmed by the large number of options available to them. Each class in the social science ontology has on average 30 properties, which means a description with three objects provides 90 options. In contrast, the number of available options in the CLEF system was deliberately kept small (max. three) for 'non-terminal anchors'. Especially in the first task, users had trouble finding the option they wanted, and although it became easier in the later tasks as they familiarised themselves with the system, the results indicate that it remained a problem. This was likely aggravated by our deliberate avoidance of subtask-repetition; more standard descriptions, which always involve titles and authors, might have produced a greater learning effect. CLEF was developed for a medical domain, which is well defined and understood by the experimental subjects. The social science domain encompasses many different theories and concepts, not just about what subjects are investigated, but also about how the research should be conducted. PolicyGrid has tried to develop an ontology that the different disciplines in social science could be satisfied with. As a result, it is quite large and complex, and most users will only recognise parts of it. Thus the number of available options in the tool driven by this ontology is large, and users have to explore the ontology and learn to navigate it where their domain knowledge does not suffice. This flattens the learning curve and decreases the usability of the tool.

Half the users preferred a form-based interface over an NLG interface. Although forms are an easily understood mechanism which are just as familiar to users as natural language, we have three reasons for preferring the WYSIWYM approach. First, the large number of options in the ontology means that a form would reach truly daunting proportions. Second, we want our resource descriptions to be connected through shared people, projects, institutions, etc; using the expressivity that RDF offers us. This would be more difficult to achieve in an interface where the user completes a form by providing each property with a free-text description. Thirdly, forms can be confusing for the user as well; the brief descriptions provided for each element are frequently ambiguous and therefore misunderstood. An NLG-interface, which provides feedback by presenting the property in a complete sentence, should help to clarify the meaning of the property name for the user.

As we discussed earlier, there are many constraints on the development of domain ontologies that can be accessed through NLG, and the evaluation indicates that the structure of the ontology is essential for the tool's usability. Still, the evaluation is sufficiently positive that we believe the WYSIWYM approach suitable for providing access to ontologies, especially for users who are unfamiliar with ontologies or their graphical representations. Navigation could be made easier by providing users with an overview of the underlying ontology, possibly presented as an index of objects, and the information that can be specified about each object. An online manual with some worked examples and screenshots might also help users get started on the more obvious parts of a description. We are currently attempting to adapt an ontology developed in another UK e-science project[8] for use in the WYSIWYM metadata elication tool. Instead of assuming the depositing of a resource, this ontology was developed to capture user-elicited metadata for video annotation. Part of this metadata is captured automatically, part of it is elicited from the user. We hope that the adaptation of an ontology that was originally developed for a different purpose for use in an NLG application will highlight other issues involved in the use of ontologies in NLG.

One way in which subjects did tasks erroneously was by using the 'hasComment' property when they could not find the option they wanted. This is not precisely *wrong*: the metadata it produces is correct and any human readers will understand the description. But it is not the best description for querying purposes. We think some subjects may have had trouble grasping the exact purpose of the produced descriptions. We hope that users who have used the query tool to find (the descriptions of) resources, will have a better understanding of what an effective metadata description is.

We intend to run more evaluation experiments, to assess the usability but also the usefulness of the combined toolset. Rather than asking subjects to copy descriptions or queries, we may ask them to find a particular resource, or to try to deposit and describe one of their own papers. If possible, it would also be interesting to see how they perform the same tasks using a different interface for metadata access, e.g. a graphical interface such as SHAKEN (Thoméré et al., 2002).

[8]http://www.ncess.ac.uk/research/digital_records/

6 Conclusion

We have presented a WYSIWYM interface for the creation of RDF metadata, which will be extended by the addition of querying and browsing tools. This tool is driven by an ontology that contains all domain-specific information needed to present it in natural language. We have highlighted a number of issues in ontology development for access through NLG. We have evaluated the tool's usability through an experiment with potential users. The results were encouraging, but indicate that the structure and familiarity of the underlying ontology strongly influence the usability of the interface.

Acknowledgments

Many thanks to Catalina Hallett and Richard Power from the CLEF project, for their help in comparing the two tools and their different evaluation results.

References

J.A. Bateman. 1990. Upper Modelling: A General Organisation of Knowledge for Natural Language Processing. In *Proceedings of the International Language Generation Workshop*, Pittsburgh, USA.

A. Bernstein and E. Kaufmann. 2006. GINO - A Guided Input Natural Language Ontology Editor. In *International Semantic Web Conference 2006*, pages 144–157.

K. Bontcheva and Y. Wills. 2004. Automatic Report Generation from Ontologies: the MIAKT approach. In *Nineth International Conference on Appli-*

cations of Natural Language to Information Systems (NLDB'2004)*, Manchester, UK.

T. Catarci, P. Dongilli, T. Di Mascio, E. Franconi, G. Santucci, and S. Tessaris. 2004. An Ontology-based Visual Tool for Query Formulation Support. In *Proceedings of the Sixteenth European Conference on Artificial Intelligence (ECAI 2004)*.

D. De Roure, N.R. Jennings, and N.R. Shadbolt. 2005. The Semantic Grid: Past, Present and Future. In *Proceedings of the IEEE 93(3)*, pages 669–681.

C. Hallett, D. Scott, and R. Power. 2007. Composing Questions through Conceptual Authoring. *Computational Linguistics*, 33(1):105–133.

C. Hallett. 2006. Generic Querying of Relational Databases using Natural Language Generation Techniques. In *Proceedings of the Fourth International Natural Language Generation Conference*, pages 88–95, Nottingham, UK.

S. Handschuh, S. Staab, and A. Maedche. 2001. CREAM: creating relational metadata with a component-based, ontology-driven annotation framework. In *K-CAP '01: Proceedings of the 1st international conference on Knowledge capture*, pages 76–83, New York, NY, USA. ACM Press.

F. Hielkema, P. Edwards, C. Mellish, and J. Farrington. 2007a. A Flexible Interface to Community-Driven Metadata. In *Proceedings of the Third International Conference on eSocial Science*.

F. Hielkema, C. Mellish, and P. Edwards. 2007b. Using WYSIWYM to Create an Open-ended Interface for the Semantic Grid. In S. Busemann, editor, *Proceedings of the 11th European Workshop on Natural Language Generation*.

I.A. Mel'cuk. 1988. *Dependency Syntax: Theory and Practice*. State University of New York.

P. Piwek, R. Evans, L. Cahil, and N. Tipper. 2000. Natural Language Generation in the MILE System. In *Proceedings of IMPACTS in NLG workshop*, pages 33–42, Schloss Dagstuhl, Germany.

P. Piwek. 2002. Requirements Definition, Validation, Verification and Evaluation of the CLIME Interface and Language Processing Technology. Technical Report ITRI-02-03, ITRI, University of Brighton.

R. Power, D. Scott, and R. Evans. 1998. What You See Is What You Meant: Direct Knowledge Editing with Natural Language Feedback. In *Proceedings of the Thirteenth European Conference on Artificial Intelligence*, Brighton, UK.

R. Schwitter and M. Tilbrook. 2004. Controlled Natural Language meets the Semantic Web. In *Proceedings of the Australasian Language Technology Workshop 2004*.

H.R. Tennant, K.M. Ross, R.M. Saenz, C.W.Thompson, and J.R. Miller. 1983. Menu-based Natural Language Understanding. In *Proceedings of the Twenty-first Annual Meetings on Association for Computational Linguistics*, pages 151–158, Cambridge, Massachusetts.

J. Thoméré, K. Barker, V. Chaudhri, P. Clark, M. Eriksen, S. Mishra, B. Porter, and A. Rodriguez. 2002. A Web-based Ontology Browsing and Editing System. In *Eighteenth National Conference on Artificial Intelligence*, pages 927–934, Menlo Park, CA, USA. American Association for Artificial Intelligence.

G. Wilcock. 2003. Talking OWLs: Towards an Ontology Verbalizer. In *Human Language Technology for the Semantic Web and Web Services (ISWC'03)*, pages 109–112, Sanibel Island, Florida.

The Importance of Narrative and Other Lessons from an Evaluation of an NLG System that Summarises Clinical Data

Ehud Reiter, Albert Gatt, François Portet
Dept of Computing Science
University of Aberdeen, UK
{e.reiter,a.gatt,fportet}@abdn.ac.uk

Marian van der Meulen*
Dept of Psychology
University of Edinburgh, UK
m.a.van-der-meulen@sms.ed.ac.uk

Abstract

The BABYTALK BT-45 system generates textual summaries of clinical data about babies in a neonatal intensive care unit. A recent task-based evaluation of the system suggested that these summaries are useful, but not as effective as they could be. In this paper we present a qualitative analysis of problems that the evaluation highlighted in BT-45 texts. Many of these problems are due to the fact that BT-45 does not generate good narrative texts; this is a topic which has not previously received much attention from the NLG research community, but seems to be quite important for creating good data-to-text systems.

1 Introduction

Data-to-text NLG systems produce textual output based on the analysis and interpretation of non-linguistic data (Reiter, 2007). Systems which produce short summaries of small amounts of data, such as weather-forecast generators (Reiter et al., 2005), have been one of the most successful applications of NLG, and there is growing interest in creating systems which produce longer summaries of larger data sets.

We have recently carried out an evaluation of one such system, BT-45 (Portet et al., 2007), which generates multi-paragraph summaries of clinical data from a Neonatal Intensive Care Unit (NICU). The summaries cover a period of roughly 45 minutes, and describe both sensor data (heart rate, blood oxygen saturation, etc, sampled at 1 sec intervals) as well as discrete events such as drug administration; they are intended to help medical staff make treatment decisions. This evaluation showed that from a decision-support perspective, the BT-45 texts were as effective as visualisations of the data, but less effective than human-written textual summaries.

In addition to quantitative performance data, which is presented elsewhere (van der Meulen et al., submitted), the evaluation also gave us valuable clues about what aspects of data-to-text technology need to be improved in order to make texts generated by such systems more effective as decision support aids; this is the subject of this paper. Somewhat to our surprise, many of the problems identified in the evaluation relate to the fact that BT-45 could not produce a good narrative describing the data. Generation of non-fictional narratives is not something which has been the focus of much NLG research in the past, but our results suggest it is important, at least in the context of producing texts which are effective decision-support aids.

1.1 Background: Data-to-Text

Data-to-text systems are motivated by the belief that (brief) linguistic summaries of datasets may in some cases be more effective than more traditional presentations of numeric data, such as tables, statistical analyses, and graphical visualisations (even simple visual/graphical displays require relatively complex cognitive processing (Carpenter and Shah, 1998)). Also linguistic summaries can be delivered in some contexts where visualisations are not possible, such as text messages on a mobile phone, or when the user is visually impaired (Ferres et al., 2006). In the NICU domain, Law et al. (2005) conducted an experiment which showed that medical professionals were more likely to make the correct treatment deci-

*Now at the Department of Clinical Neurosciences, University Hospital, Geneva, Switzerland

sion when shown a human-written textual summary of the data than when they were shown a graphical visualisation of the data.

A number of data-to-text systems have been developed and indeed fielded, especially in the domain of weather forecasts (Goldberg et al., 1994; Reiter et al., 2005). Most of these systems have generated short (paragraph-length or smaller) summaries of relatively small data sets (less than 1KB). Some research has been on systems that summarise larger data sets (Yu et al., 2007; Turner et al., 2008), but these systems have also generated paragraph-length summaries; we are not aware of any previous research on generating multi-paragraph summaries in a data-to-text system.

Data-to-texts systems have been evaluated in a number of ways, including human ratings (the most common technique) (Reiter et al., 2005), BLEU-like scores against human texts (Belz and Reiter, 2006), post-edit analyses (Sripada et al., 2005), and persuasive effectiveness (Carenini and Moore, 2006). However, again to the best of our knowledge no previous data-to-text system has been evaluated by asking users to make decisions based on the generated texts, and measuring the quality of these decisions.

2 BabyTalk and BT-45

Law et al. (2005) showed that human-written textual summaries were effective decision-support aids in NICU, but of course it is not practical to expect medical professionals to routinely write such summaries, especially considering that the summaries used by Law et al. in some cases took several hours to write. The goal of the BABYTALK research project is to use NLG and data-to-text technology to automatically generate textual summaries of NICU data, for a variety of audiences and purposes. The first system developed in BABYTALK, and the subject of this paper, is BT-45 (Portet et al., 2007), which generates summaries of 30-60 minute chunks of clinical data, for the purpose of helping nurses and doctors make appropriate treatment decisions.

An example of BABYTALK input data is shown in Figures 1 (sensor data) and 2 (selected event data). Figure 3 shows the human-written corpus text for this scenario, and Figure 4 shows the BT-45 text generated for this scenario. Note that for the purposes of

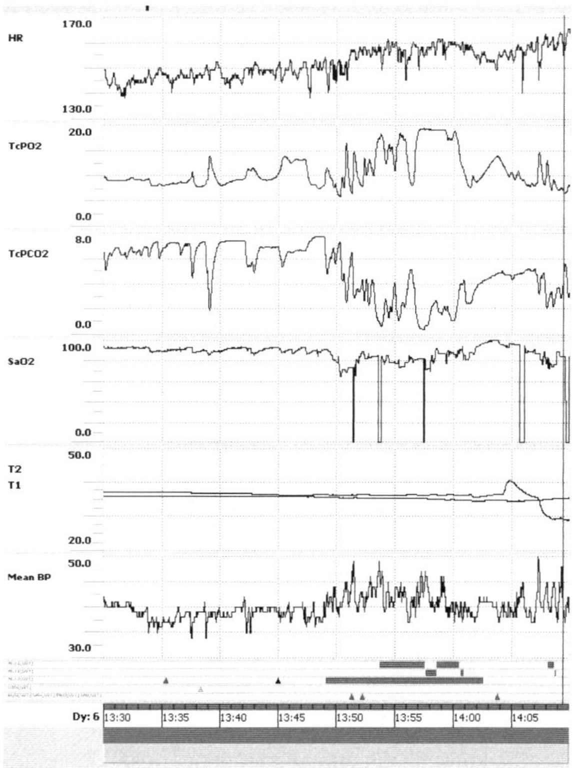

Figure 1: Example Babytalk Input Data: Sensors HR = Heart Rate; TcPO2 = blood O2 level; TCPCO2 = blood CO2 level; SaO2 = oxygen saturation; T1 = chest temperature; T2 = toe temperature; mean BP = blood pressure. The bars and triangles at the bottom show the time of discrete events (Figure 2).

event	*time*
Blood transfusion	13.35
Intermittent crying	13.38
FiO2 (oxygen level) changed to 50%	13.51
Incubator temperature changed to 36.4	13.52
Attempt to insert line	13.53
Line removed	13.57
Attempt to insert line	13.58
Line removed	14.00
FiO2 (oxygen level) changed to 45%	14.03
Attempt to insert line	14.08
Line removed	14.09

Figure 2: Example Babytalk Input Data: Selected Discrete Events

You saw the baby between 13:30 and 14:10.

Over the course of the monitoring period the HR increases steadily from 140 to 165; the BP varies between 41 and 49.

At the start of the period T1 is 37 and T2 is 35.8C.

During the first 15 minutes the pO2 is 7.8-9.2 and the pCO2 is 5.9-7.3.

At 13:35 a blood transfusion is commenced.

At 13:38 the baby is crying and there are a few upward spikes in the pO2 trace corresponding to downward spikes in the pCO2 trace. At 13.45 the humidity on the incubator walls is wiped away and T1 and T2 fall to 36.3 and 35.4 respectively

At 13:50 the baby is examined. There is a desaturation to 72% and the FiO2 is changed to 50%. Between now and 14.10 there are several attempts to site a peripheral cannula. The pO2 and pCO2 both have spikes in the traces, pO2 reaching 19.2 and pCO2 reaching 0.4. There are several episodes of artefact in the oxygen saturation trace.

T1 and T2 fall to 36.2 and 35.7 and the oxygen saturation falls to 65%. The FiO2 is adjusted to 50%. Also at this time the incubator temperature is adjusted to 36.4C.

At 14:03 with the pO2 at 13.9 and oxygen saturation at 100%, the FiO2 is reduced to 45

At 14:04 T1 rises sharply to 40, then drops fairly steeply to 28.5C. Between 14.06 and 14.10 there are several spikes in the pO2 and pCO2 traces but by 14.10 the pO2 is 8, pCO2 is 3.7, the oxygen saturation is 71%, the HR is 163, the BP 39, T1 29C and T2 35.4C.

Figure 3: Corpus Text for Fig 1, 2 data

You saw the baby between 13:30 and 14:10. Heart Rate (HR) = 149. Core Temperature (T1) = 37.0. Peripheral Temperature (T2) = 35.8. Transcutaneous Oxygen (TcPO2) = 9.5. Transcutaneous CO2 (TcPCO2) = 6.7. Mean Blood Pressure (mean BP) = 41. Oxygen Saturation (SaO2) = 94.

Over the next 39 minutes SaO2 decreased to 81, T2 decreased to 34.5, HR stayed at around 151, T1 decreased to 36.2 and mean BP stayed at around 40.

A blood transfusion was given to the baby at 13:35.

At 13:50 there was a desaturation down to 65. As a result, Fraction of Inspired Oxygen (FIO2) was set to 50

There were 3 failed attempts to insert a peripheral venous line at 13:53. TcPO2 suddenly decreased to 8.1. SaO2 suddenly increased to 92. TcPO2 suddenly decreased to 9.3. There was a spike in TcPO2 up to 14.8. There had been another spike in T1 up to 40.5. FIO2 had been lowered to 45%. Previously the baby had been examined.

Figure 4: BT-45 Text for Fig 1, 2 data

this paper, we have deliberately selected a relatively poor quality BT-45 output text.

The processing performed by BT-45 is described by Portet et al. (2007). Very briefly, BT-45 generates texts in four stages:

- *signal analysis*: for example, detecting spikes in the sensor channels; this is done using adaptations of standard pattern detection and recognition algorithms.

- *data abstraction*: for example, identifying three line-insertion-attempt and line-removal events within a short span of time and grouping these into the higher-level concept LINE-INSERTION-PROCESS-FAILED (BT-45 includes a domain ontology of such concepts); this is done using knowledge-based techniques.

- *document planning*: for example, deciding not to mention most of the spikes in O2 and CO2; this is primarily done in a bottom-up fashion, using information (computed by the data abstraction module) on the medical importance of events, and also on causal and other relationships between events.

- *microplanning and realisation:* producing the actual text shown in Figure 4; this is mostly done using relatively standard NLG techniques, although we have developed new techniques for communicating temporal information and relationships.

3 Evaluation of BT-45

BT-45 was evaluated by asking medical staff to make decisions about what actions they should take with regard to a baby, after viewing either a BT-45 text, a human-written textual summary, or a visualisation of the baby's data; this was similar in general terms to the experiment described by Law et al. (2005). van der Meulen et al. (submitted) gives details about the evaluation design and quantitative results of the evaluation; in this paper we just briefly summarise these aspects of the evaluation

Material: Our medical collaborators selected 24 scenarios (data sets), and defined 18 types of actions. For each of the data sets, they specified which of the 18 actions were appropriate, inappropriate, or neutral (neither appropriate nor inappropriate); one appropriate action was identified as the main target action. For the data set shown in Figures 1 and 2, for example:

- *Main target action*: Adjust monitoring equipment
- *Other appropriate actions*: calm/comfort baby, manage temperature, analyse blood sample
- *Neutral actions*: adjust CPAP (ventilation) settings, baby care (e.g., nappy change)
- *Inappropriate actions*: all other actions (e.g. blood transfusion, order X-Ray) (12 in all)

For each scenario, we created three presentations: a visualisation (similar to Figure 1), a human-written text summary written by our collaborators, and the summary produced by BT-45. Our collaborators were asked not to include any explicit medical interpretation of the data in their human-written summaries. For each scenario, our collaborators also prepared a text which gave background information about the baby.

When developing BT-45, we had access to the data collection that the scenario data sets were taken from (which includes several months of data), but did not know ahead of time which specific scenarios would be used in the experiment.

Subjects: 35 medical professionals, including junior nurses, senior nurses, junior doctors, and senior doctors.

Procedure: Each subject was shown 8 scenarios in each condition (visualisation, human text, BT-45 text) in a Latin Square design; all subjects were also shown the background texts. Subjects were asked to specify which actions should be taken for this baby, selecting actions from a fixed set of check-boxes; they were given three minutes to make this decision. Subjects were not explicitly asked for free-text comments, but any comments spontaneously made by subjects were recorded. Subject responses were scored by computing the percentage of appropriate actions they selected, and subtracting from this the percentage of inappropriate actions.

Results: The highest score was achieved by the human texts (mean score of 0.39); there was no significant difference between the BT-45 texts (mean score of 0.34) and the visualisations (mean score of 0.33). The largest differences occurred in the junior nurses group. van der Meulen et al. (submitted) present a detailed statistical analysis of the results.

Discussion: This shows that BT-45 texts were as effective as visualisation, but less effective than the human texts. This suggests that data-to-text technology as it stands could be useful as a supplement to visualisations (since some individuals do better with texts and some with graphics; also some data sets are visualised effectively and some are not), and in contexts where visualisation is not possible. But it also suggests that if we can improve the technology so that computer-generated texts are as effective as human texts, we should have a very effective decision-support technology.

4 Quantitative Comparison of BT-45 and Corpus Texts

In addition to the task-based evaluation described above, we also quantitatively compared the BT-45 and human texts, and qualitatively analysed problems in the BT-45 texts. Quantitative comparison was done by annotating the BT-45 and human texts to identify which events they mentioned. For each scenario, we computed the MASI coefficient (Passonneau, 2006) between the set of events mentioned in the BT-45 and human texts. The average MASI score was 0.21 ($SD = 0.13$), which is low; this suggests that BT-45 and the human writers choose different content. We also checked whether similar human and BT-45 texts (as judged by MASI score) obtained similar evaluation scores; in fact there was no significant correlation between MASI similarity of human and BT-45 texts and the difference between their evaluation scores.

We performed a second analysis based on comparing the structure (e.g., number and size of paragraphs) of the BT-45 and human texts, using a tree-edit-distance metric to compare text structures.

Again this showed that there were large differences between the structure of the BT-45 and human texts, and that these differences did correlate with differences in evaluation scores.

In other words, simple metrics of content and structural differences do not seem to be good predictors of text effectiveness; this is perhaps not surprising given the complexity of the texts and the information they are communicating.

5 Qualitative Analysis of Problems in BT-45 texts

The final step in our evaluation was to qualitatively analyse the BT-45 texts and the results of the task-based evaluation, in order to highlight problems in the BT-45 texts. Of course we were aware of numerous ways in which the software could be improved, but the evaluation gave us information about which of these mattered most in terms of overall effectiveness. We report this analysis below, including issues identified from subjects' comments, issues identified from scenarios where BT-45 texts did poorly, and problems identified via manual inspection of the texts. We do not distinguish between 'linguistic' and 'reasoning' problems, in part because it is usually difficult (and indeed somewhat artificial) to separate these aspects of BT-45.

5.1 Problems Identified by Subjects

Subjects made a number of comments during the experiment. Two aspects of BT-45 were repeatedly criticised in these comments.

5.1.1 Layout and bullet lists

Subjects wanted better layout and formatting, in the human texts as well as the BT-45 texts (BT-45 texts do not currently include any visual formatting). In particular, they wanted bullet lists to be used, especially for lab results. Such issues have been extensively discussed by other researchers (e.g., (Power et al., 2003)), we will not further discuss them here.

5.1.2 Continuity

BT-45 sometimes described changes in signals (or other events) which didn't make sense because they omitted intermediate events. For example, consider the last paragraph in the BT-45 text shown in Figure 4 (with italics added):

> There were 3 failed attempts to insert a peripheral venous line at 13:53. *TcPO2 suddenly decreased to 8.1.* SaO2 suddenly increased to 92. *TcPO2 suddenly decreased to 9.3.* There was a spike in TcPO2 up to 14.8. There had been another spike in T1 up to 40.5. FIO2 had been lowered to 45%. Previously the baby had been examined.

Subjects complained that it made no sense for TcPO2 to decrease to 9.3 when the last value mentioned for this parameter was 8.1

In this case (and in many others like it), BT-45 had identified the decrease events as being medically important, but had not assigned as much importance, and hence not mentioned, the increase event (TcPO2 went up to 19) between these decrease events. This is partially because BT-45 believed that a TcPO2 of 19 is a sensor artefact (not a real reading of blood oxygen), since 19kPa is a very high value for this channel. In fact this is a correct inference on BT-45's part, but the text is still confusing for readers.

We call this problem *continuity*, making an analogy to the problems that film-makers have in ensuring that scenes in a film (which maybe shot in very different times and locations) fit together in the eyes of the viewer. It is interesting to note that some of the human texts also seem to have continuity problems (for example, the text in Figure 3 says T2 falls to 35.4, and then says T2 falls to 35.7), but none of the subjects complained about continuity problems in the human texts. So some kinds of continuity violations seem more problematical to readers than others. Perhaps this depends on the proximity of the events both in the document structure and in time; we hope to empirically explore this hypothesis.

Continuity is just one aspect of the broader problem of deciding which events need to be explicitly mentioned in the text, and which can be omitted. Making such decisions is perhaps one of the hardest aspects of data-to-text.

5.2 Scenarios Where BT-45 did Badly

When analysing the results of the experiment, we noticed that BT-45 texts did as well as the human texts for scenarios based on five of the eight target actions; however they did significantly worse than

main target action	*human*	*BT-45*	*diff*
Adjust CPAP	0.37	0.37	0
Adjust monitoring equip	0.59	0.22	0.37
Adjust ventilation	0.22	0.23	-0.01
Extubate	0.14	0.12	0.02
Manage temperature	0.55	0.33	0.22
No action	0.61	0.43	0.18
Suction	0.34	0.42	-0.08
Support blood pressure	0.45	0.55	-0.10

Table 1: Average evaluation score by main target action

the human texts on the scenarios based on the other three actions (Adjust Monitoring Equipment, Manage Temperature, and No Action). Details are shown in Table 1; an ANOVA confirms that there is a significant effect of main target action on scores ($p < .001$). We have identified a number of reasons why we believe this is the case, which we discuss below.

5.2.1 Too much focus on medically important events

Content-selection in BT-45 is largely driven by rules that assess the medical importance of events and patterns. In particular, BT-45 tends to give low importance to events which it believes are due to sensor artefacts. While this strategy makes sense in many cases, it leads to poor performance in scenarios where the target action is Adjust Monitoring Equipment, when sensor problems need to be pointed out to the reader.

This can be seen in the example scenario used in this paper. The TcPO2 and TcPCO2 traces shown in Figure 1 are full of sensor artefacts (such as the implausibly high values of TcPO2 mentioned above). The human text shown in Figure 3 explicitly mentions these, for example (italics added)

> At 13:50 the baby is examined. There is a desaturation to 72% and the FiO2 is changed to 50%. Between now and 14.10 there are several attempts to site a peripheral cannula. *The pO2 and pCO2 both have spikes in the traces, pO2 reaching 19.2 and pCO2 reaching 0.4. There are several episodes of artefact in the oxygen saturation trace.*

The BT-45 text shown in Figure 4, in contrast, only mentions one spike in TcPO2, and does not mention any artefacts.

This is a difficult problem to solve, because in a context where medical intervention was needed, BT-45 would be correct to ignore the sensor problems. One solution would be for BT-45 to perform a top-level diagnosis itself, and adjust its texts based on whether it believed staff should focus on medical intervention or adjusting sensors. Whether this is desirable or even feasible is unclear; it relates to the more general issue of how a data-summarisation system such as BT-45 should be integrated with the kind of diagnosis systems developed by the AI/Medicine community.

5.2.2 Poor description of related channels

BT-45 essentially describes each channel independently. For temperature, however, it is often better to describe the two temperature channels together and even contrast them, which is what the human texts do; this contributes to BT-45's poor performance in Manage Temperature scenarios.

For example, in one of the Manage Temperature scenarios, the BT-45 text says

> Core Temperature (T1) = 36.4. Peripheral Temperature (T2) = 34.0. ...
> *(new paragraph)* Over the next 44 minutes T2 decreased to 33.4.

The human text says

> He is warm centrally but T2 drifts down over the 45 minutes from 34 to 33.3C.

The information content of the two texts is quite similar, but the human text describes temperature in an integrated fashion. Similar problems occur in other scenarios. In fact, over the 24 scenarios as a whole, the human texts include only three paragraphs which mention just one of the temperatures (T1 or T2, but not both), while the BT-45 texts include 18 such paragraphs.

BT-45's document planner is mostly driven by medical importance and causal relationships; although it does try to group together information about related channels, this is done as a secondary optimisation, not as a primary organising principle. The human texts place a much higher priority on grouping 'physiological systems' (to use NICU terminology) of related channels and events together, including the respiratory and cardiac systems as well as the temperature system. We suspect that BT-45 should place more emphasis on systems in its document planning.

5.2.3 Poor long-term overview

BT-45 does not do a good job of summarising a channel's behaviour over the entire scenario. This isn't a problem in eventful scenarios, where the key is to describe the events; but it does reduce the effectiveness of texts in uneventful scenarios where the main target action is No Action (i.e., do nothing).

This problem can be seen in the text extracts shown in the previous section. Even at the level of individual channels, *He is warm centrally* is a better overview than *Core Temperature (T1) = 36.4*; and *T2 drifts down over the 45 minutes from 34 to 33.3C* is better than *Peripheral Temperature (T2) = 34.0. ... Over the next 44 minutes T2 decreased to 33.4.*

At a signal analysis level, BT-45 also does not do a good job of detecting patterns (such as spikes) with a duration of minutes instead of seconds. This contributes to the system's poor performance in Manage Temperature scenarios, because temperature changes relatively slowly.

We believe these problems can be solved, by putting more emphasis on analysis and reporting of long time-scale events in the BT-45 modules.

5.3 Other Problems

We manually examined the texts, looking for cases where the BT-45 texts did not seem clear. This highlighted a number of additional issues.

5.3.1 Describing events at different temporal time-scales

BT-45 does not always do a good job of correctly identifying long-term trends in a context where there are also short-term patterns such as spikes. In fact accurately detecting simultaneous events at different time-scales is one of the major signal analysis challenges in BT-45. There are linguistic issues as well as signal analysis ones; for example, should long-duration and short-duration events be described in separate paragraphs?

5.3.2 Poor communication of time

BT-45 texts often did not communicate time well. This is for a number of reasons, of which the most fundamental is problems describing the time of long-duration events. For instance, in our example scenario, the sequence of insert/remove line events in Figure 2 is analysed by the data-abstraction module as the abstract event LINE-INSERTION-PROCESS-FAILED, with a start time of 13.53 (first insertion event) and an end time of 14.09 (last removal event). BT-45 expresses this as *There were 3 failed attempts to insert a peripheral venous line at 13:53*; the time given is the time the abstract event started, which is reasonable in this case. Now, if the final insertion attempt at 14.08 had been successful, the BT-45 data abstraction module would have instead produced the abstract event LINE-INSERTION-PROCESS-SUCCEEDED, with similar times, and BT-45 would have produced the text

> After three attempts, at 13.53 a peripheral venous line was inserted successfully.

In other words, the time given would still be the time that the abstract event started; but this is misleading, because readers of the above text expect that the stated time is the time of the successful insertion (14.08), not the time at which the sequence of insert/remove events started.

We need a much better model of how to communicate time, and how this communication depends on the semantics and linguistic expression of the events being described. An obvious first step, which we are currently working on, is to include a linguistically-motivated temporal ontology (Moens and Steedman, 1988), which will be separate from the existing domain ontology. We also need better techniques for communicating the temporal relationships between events in cases where they are not listed in chronological order (Oberlander and Lascarides, 1992).

6 Discussion

Two discourse analysts from Edinburgh University, Dr. Andy McKinlay and Dr Chris McVittie, kindly examined and compared some of the human and BT-45 texts. Their top-level comment was that the human texts had much better narrative structures than the BT-45 texts. They use the term 'narrative' in the sense of Labov (1972, Chapter 9); that is story-like structures which describe real experiences, and which go beyond just describing the events and include information that helps listeners make sense of what happened, such as abstracts, evaluatives, correlatives, and explicatives.

Dr McKinlay and Dr. McVittie pointed out many of the problems mentioned above, but they also pointed out a number of other narrative deficiencies in the BT-45 texts. The most fundamental was that the human texts did a much better job of linking related events into a coherent whole. Other deficiencies include the lack of any kind of conclusion in the BT-45 texts.

We agree with this analysis; it is striking that many of the specific problems identified are related to the problem of generating narratives. Continuity, description of related channels, overview of behaviour over time, and communication of time are all aspects of narrative in the broad sense; they are things we need to get right in order to turn a text into a story. This point is especially significant in light of the fact that many of our medical collaborators at Edinburgh have informally told us that they believe stories are valuable when presenting information about the babies, and indeed that a major problem with data visualisation systems compared to written notes (which they used many years ago) is that the visualisation systems do not tell stories.

Unfortunately, we are not aware of any previous research in the NLG community about these issues. Researchers in the creativity community have looked at issues such as plot and character development in systems that generate fictional stories (Perez y Perez and Sharples, 2004); but this is not relevant to our problem, which is presenting non-fictional events as a narrative. Callaway and Lester (2002) looked at microplanning issues in narrative generation, including reference, lexical variation, and aggregation; but none of these were identified in our evaluation as major problems in text quality.

7 Future Work

The BABYTALK project continues until August 2010, and during this period we hope to investigate most of the issues identified above, especially the ones related to narrative. We are currently conducting experiments to improve the way we communicate time, and we have started redoing the document planner to do a better job of describing systems of related channels in a unified manner. We are also investigating top-down data abstraction and document planning approaches which we hope will address continuity problems, and which may assist in better overviews and narrative structures. We are also working on many issues not directly related to narrative, such as reasoning about and communicating uncertainty, use of vague language, generation of texts for non-specialists (e.g., parents), and HCI issues.

We would welcome interest by other researchers in these topics (there is more that needs investigating than we can do on our own!), and we would be happy to assist such people, for example by sharing some of our code and data resources.

8 Conclusion

We believe that there is enormous potential in systems such as BABYTALK which generate textual summaries of data; the world desperately needs better techniques to help people understand data sets, and our experiments suggest that good textual summaries really can help communicate data sets, at least in some contexts. However, building good data summarisation systems requires the NLG research community to address a number of problems which it has not traditionally focused on, many of which have to do with generating good narratives. We intend to focus much of our energy on these issues, and would welcome research contributions from other members of the community.

Acknowledgements

Many thanks to our colleagues in the BabyTalk project, and to the doctors and nurses who participated in the evaluation; this work would not have been possible without them. Special thanks to Dr McKinlay and Dr McVittie for agreeing to analyse the texts for us. We are also grateful to our colleagues in the Aberdeen NLG group, and to the anonymous reviewers, for their helpful comments. This research was funded by the UK Engineering and Physical Sciences Research Council, under grant EP/D049520/1.

References

A Belz and E Reiter. 2006. Comparing automatic and human evaluation of NLG systems. In *Proceedings of EACL-2006*, pages 313–320.

C Callaway and J Lester. 2002. Narrative prose generation. *Artificial Intelligence*, 139:213–252.

G Carenini and J Moore. 2006. Generating and evaluating evaluative arguments. *Artificial Intelligence*, 170:925–952.

P Carpenter and P Shah. 1998. A model of the perceptual and conceptual processes in graph comprehension. *Journal of Experimental Psychology: Applied*, 4:74–100.

L Ferres, A Parush, S Roberts, and G Lindgaard. 2006. Helping people with visual impairments gain access to graphical information through natural language: The iGraph system. In *Proceedings of ICCHP-2008*.

E Goldberg, N Driedger, and R Kittredge. 1994. Using natural-language processing to produce weather forecasts. *IEEE Expert*, 9(2):45–53.

W Labov. 1972. *Language in the Inner City*. University of Pennsylvania Press.

A Law, Y Freer, J Hunter, R Logie, N McIntosh, and J Quinn. 2005. A comparison of graphical and textual presentations of time series data to support medical decision making in the neonatal intensive care unit. *Journal of Clinical Monitoring and Computing*, 19:183–194.

M Moens and M Steedman. 1988. Temporal ontology and temporal reference. *Computational Linguistics*, 14(2):15–28.

J Oberlander and A Lascarides. 1992. Preventing false temporal implicatures: Interactive defaults for text generation. In *Proceedings of COLING-1992*, pages 721–727.

R Passonneau. 2006. Measuring agreement on set-valued items (MASI) for semantic and pragmatic annotation. In *Proceedings of LREC-2006*.

R Perez y Perez and M Sharples. 2004. Three computer-based models of storytelling: Brutus, Minstrel, and Mexica. *Knowledge-Based Systems*, 17:15–29.

F Portet, E Reiter, J Hunter, and S Sripada. 2007. Automatic generation of textual summaries from neonatal intensive care data. In *Proceedings of AIME 2007*.

R Power, D Scott, and N Bouayad-Agha. 2003. Document structure. *Computational Linguistics*, 29:211–260.

E Reiter, S Sripada, J Hunter, J Yu, and I Davy. 2005. Choosing words in computer-generated weather forecasts. *Artificial Intelligence*, 167:137–169.

E Reiter. 2007. An architecture for Data-to-Text systems. In *Proceedings of ENLG-07*, pages 97–104.

S Sripada, E Reiter, and L Hawizy. 2005. Evaluation of an NLG system using post-edit data: Lessons learned. In *Proceedings of ENLG-2005*, pages 133–139.

R Turner, S Sripada, E Reiter, and I Davy. 2008. Using spatial reference frames to generate grounded textual summaries of georeferenced data. In *Proceedings of INLG-2008*.

M van der Meulen, R Logie, Y Freer, C Sykes, N McIntosh, and J Hunter. submitted. When a graph is poorer than 100 words: A comparison of computerised natural language generation, human generated descriptions and graphical displays in neonatal intensive care.

J Yu, E Reiter, J Hunter, and C Mellish. 2007. Choosing the content of textual summaries of large time-series data sets. *Natural Language Engineering*, 13:25–49.

Building a Large-scale Commercial NLG System for an EMR

Mary Dee Harris
Catalis, Inc.
7801 N. Capital of Texas Hwy., Ste. 260
Austin, TX 78731
mdharris@thecatalis.com

Abstract

Natural language generation technology is mature enough for implementing an NLG system in a commercial environment, but the circumstances differ significantly from building a research system. This paper describes the challenges and rewards of building a commercial NLG component for an electronic medical records system. While the resulting NLG system has been successfully completed, the path to that success could have been somewhat smoother knowing the issues in advance.

1 Introduction

In 2002 I was hired by a small start-up company to add narrative generation to their electronic medical records (EMR) system under development. After six months, we had a first-cut system producing narrative based on a doctor's selection of items from the graphical interface during an encounter with a patient. This paper describes the rewards and challenges of building such a system in a commercial environment, in hopes the lessons I learned can contribute to successful future commercial systems for natural language generation.

The company has always been funded by investment money with some recent revenue income. The founders were both medical doctors, with little corporate experience and even less knowledge of technology. They had the vision; the rest of us did the work. The company's product is a general-purpose EMR system on a tablet PC with handwriting recognition and extensive graphical representation of human anatomy. Its foundation is an elaborate database of medical content, outlining specific requirements for information collection. Much of this medical information is arranged in templates, one for each complaint. When a patient comes into the doctor's office complaining of chest pains, the template for Chest Pain provides the appropriate selections for the doctor to record pertinent information related to that condition. Other parts of the system deal with physical examinations, procedures, prescription of medication, orders for lab tests and procedures, and so on.

My mission was to implement a narrative generation system to record the doctor/patient encounter, following the traditional narrative created by the doctor's dictation, which is then transcribed into a narrative. These narratives serve as a legal record of the encounter and are used in court in malpractice suits. Thus the narrative is an extremely important part of the patient record and must be complete and accurate. Otherwise the doctor – and our company – could be liable for malpractice.

2 Challenges

The challenges of designing the narrative system were many. The narrative must be completely accurate to avoid liability. While the initial targets were small practices and clinics, the system would expand into larger clinics and hospitals. So the system had to be scalable. The scope of the project also had to be scalable. Beginning with hundreds of medical templates often with multiple names, there are now thousands for many specialties with different requirements for format and style.

Another challenge was the naïveté of the company and its staff. The CEO had a grand vision, but little concept of the technology for language generation. He believed the automated narrative was possible, but there was little understanding of the extent of commitment of staff, time, and money for building such a system.

One less obvious challenge is the difference between research and commercial applications. Our limited finances allowed us few available commercial products. However, the freely available resources that academics rely on were usually available *only* for research. In our field of health care technology, the UMLS was the primary resource available to us. The Unified Medical Library System[1] developed at the National Library of Medicine has resources which include a medically-oriented dictionary of English called SPECIALIST and tools to access it, a semantic network related to health care, and a Metathesaurus -- "a very large, multi-purpose, and multi-lingual vocabulary database that contains information about biomedical and health related concepts, their various names, and the relationships among them." This lack of resources was a mixed blessing: all our tools and program components belong to the company with no financial or licensing strings attached.

One usual way to start any NLP project is to acquire a large sample of the texts to be processed. However because of privacy issues, we had no "live" data representing medical narratives. The two doctors wrote some imaginary scenarios to serve as samples and provided feedback on our guesses of what the medical language should be. So the project started with no outside resources, little support, no samples, but a lot of enthusiasm.

3 Plan of Attack

Despite the challenges, I knew NLG technology would be able to fulfill the requirements for this application so the planning began. The original idea was to follow a standard development model: proof-of-concept (POC) system, prototype, and production system. The POC would have simple sentences and a restricted vocabulary, but enough to convince the company that the technology could provide a feasible solution. The prototype would extend the capability, adding a grammar and a more extensive vocabulary as well as being robust enough to handle more data. The POC was built in about six months with a Java developer assisting me with the design – it sounded like a second grader had written the narrative, but it was accurate and proved that we could do it.

The prototype never got built due to management decisions and some bad luck. We had no internal staff to devote to the task. To make matters more complicated, Steve Shipman, the original Java developer who knew some computational linguistics, was replaced by a developer with no real knack for linguistics whose English was a second language. I had to teach him the linguistic terminology and the language structures before he could write the code to handle them.

The next problem arose when the management saw the narrative output -- simple as it was -- and immediately started adding templates for us to handle. Despite my protests that it wasn't ready for deployment, we had to add additional features such as aggregation and negation to this simple-minded version. It took several years before we got the go-ahead to write the full-blown system, by which time we had several thousand templates in the system. We finally spent six months on the new system, followed by nearly a year of testing. Because the POC had been put into production, we had to establish a dual model that ran both old and new versions. We are still trying to get all the original parts converted to work on the full-blown production system so we can eliminate the POC section.

4 System Architecture

The architecture of the Narrative Engine followed the basic design described in Reiter and Dale (2000) for an NLG system, with adaptations to fit our data model. Because the narrative output had to be so accurate and the style so sophisticated to satisfy the physician client base, I doubted that completely automated generation would be suffi-

[1] http://www.nlm.nih.gov/research/umls/

cient. So following the lead of machine translation, I chose to implement human-assisted computer generation. That seemed the only appropriate approach, used similarly by CoGenTex in their Exemplars method (White and Caldwell, 1998). We considered using Exemplars, but they are Java-based which was not appropriate for our situation. Most of our NLG staff didn't know Java since we hired liberal arts and linguistics majors.

We developed a plan language called Linguo, after Lisa Simpson's robot by that name. Linguo helps us write plans to describe the translation from medical findings for a particular patient into appropriate medical language for an encounter. The plan writers select the predicate best suited for each finding in a template. That predicate then determines the semantic structure, following Jackendoff (1990; 1991). These plans are generalized to handle many similar findings, rather than being a one-to-one translation. The basic design for the Narrative Engine held up well through the various implementations, with only minor adjustments required. [2]

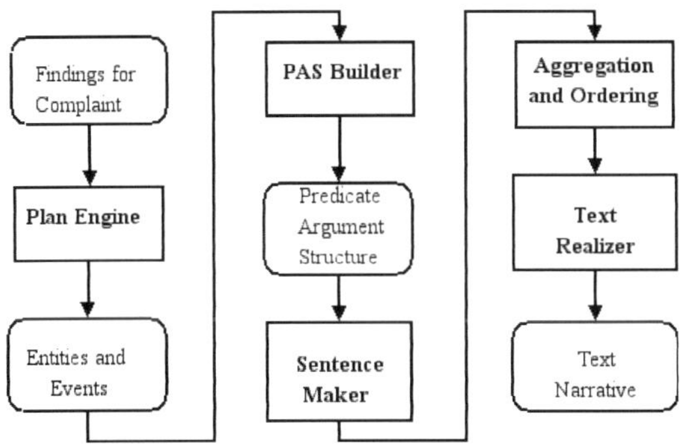

Figure 1 Architecture of Narrative Engine

5 Proof of Concept

The initial POC was string-based, for speed of development – a decision I would come to regret, but probably necessary to get the project underway. The POC system had no separate grammar, but handled syntactic and morphological issues in the code. We created two XML files for the translation into English: predicate templates and clause templates. The predicate templates define the semantic roles for each predicate in our restricted vocabulary, while the clause templates match the semantic forms to syntactic structures. The final stage of processing was the Sentence Realizer that converted the syntactic structures into English. The Narrative Engine was a separate module in the application that received medical findings (the individual items that the doctor selected) and that output English text to the application for the note.

5 Commercial Development

The commercial version of the Narrative Engine was called Component-Based Processing (CBP) to distinguish it from the string-based POC. We now had two lexicons: a semantic one containing the finding names for all the medical templates and the UMLS SPECIALIST syntactic lexicon. We added bracketed forms to specify language structures for each finding name, to go with the basic syntactic information. For example, the phrase "the right shoulder" would be represented as [np [det the][adj right][n shoulder]]. We hired a computational lexicographer, Ken Litkowski, to help produce the bracketed forms for the 60,000 plus entries. Creating these forms was not trivial since the finding phrases vary from a single word to a complex noun phrase to a complete clause.

Using the bracketed forms allowed us to extend our aggregation capability to a linguistically solid method of analyzing the component structure to identify corresponding parts to coordinate. We also added a means for asymmetric aggregation, known as *hypotactic aggregation* (Shaw, 2002). Besides being able to coordinate similar items, as

The patient described the pain as <u>sharp</u> and <u>throbbing</u>,

we can now combine dissimilar findings, as in

The skin was closed with <u>14</u> <u>2-0</u> <u>monofilament</u> sutures using <u>continuous stitch</u>.

One major addition to the Narrative Engine was the syntactic grammar set up as a properties file allowing modification of the grammar without code changes. We can test new features easily and

[2] This paper does not detail the technology specifically as it is proprietary. The company has patent applications pending for much of the design. This is another important contrast with the research community where sharing ideas is the norm.

try extensions to the language with no impact on the overall system. The clause templates used in the POC were replaced with verb templates since much of that work was now handled by the grammar. Verb templates describe the alternation patterns (Levin, 1993) and include the irregular forms.

Another change was the integration of the narrative process into the application more completely. This integration was not simply a code change, but a change in perception of the project as a whole. The company came to understand that adding the narrative capability had increased the value of the EMR in the marketplace. At this time, ours is the only EMR with real natural language generation, not handled by templates or canned text.

6 Recommendations

Many of the choices made during development of this system would be changed, if I had the luxury of starting over. I would like to offer up some suggestions for others to avoid the difficulties I faced. Consider these ideas before you start.

- Educate your clients. Your clients are mostly in your own company. Not everyone is going to understand the importance of the work and the need for resources or have the basic linguistic knowledge to comprehend the requirements. I gave many tutorials to help our staff understand what we were doing.
- Be clear about the costs of building the NLG system. Your estimates will be wrong, almost by definition, but you have to start somewhere. Since the uninitiated cannot imagine the potential until they see it, they will have many more ideas of how to apply the technology once they see it, thus extending the requirements. Here again, educate the company regarding the staff requirements (developers, linguists, quality assurance, marketing) and the training needed to make them productive. Consider the data development requirements as well as the coding.
- Be careful how you plan out the development stages. A proof-of-concept system is a great idea to demonstrate that the technology is feasible, but it is tempting to take it and run with it. You need to build the system in stages, but make sure the staging is spelled out in advance with an understanding from management of the process.
- Deployment and customer acceptance is the goal, not completion of the code. We found that the customers were gratified by the ability to eliminate the dictation and transcription process, but they do have opinions about the wording sometimes. We work with specialists to develop the medical templates and the narrative before we implement.
- Remember that a commercial system is not cutting-edge technology, no matter what management thinks. A commercial system should use time-proven, reliable methods robust enough for inevitable modifications. Some features will be untested, but the basic foundation of the system must be reliable.
- Make sure you have the funding to complete the project. A champion within the company can help fight your battles.

None of these recommendations should preclude anyone from trying to build a large-scale commercial product, but knowing in advance where the pitfalls lie can ease the process. It takes more than a good idea and a knowledge of the technology to make it work, but the effort can be worthwhile in the end. The language component of our EMR system has helped doctors increase their ability to see more patients by reducing the time required to take notes, dictate them, and pay for their transcription. So the doctors appreciate the automated narrative capability even though they have no idea how it is accomplished.

References

Ray Jackendoff. 1990. *Semantic Structures*. MIT Press.

Ray Jackendoff. 1991. Parts and Boundaries. *Lexical and Conceptual Structures*. Blackwell.

Beth Levin. 1993. *English Verb Classes and Alternations: A Preliminary Investigation*. University of Chicago Press.

Ehud Reiter and Robert Dale. 2000. *Building Natural Language Generation Systems*. Cambridge University Press.

James C. Shaw. *Clause Aggregation*. Dissertation, Columbia University. 2002.

Michael White and Ted Caldwell. 1998. Exemplars: Practical, Extensible Framework for Dynamic Text Generation. *Proceedings of the Ninth International Workshop on Natural Language Generation*.

Degree of Abstraction in Referring Expression Generation and its Relation with the Construction of the Contrast Set

Raquel Hervás
Facultad de Informática
Universidad Complutense de Madrid
Madrid, Spain
raquelhb@fdi.ucm.es

Pablo Gervás
Facultad de Informática
Universidad Complutense de Madrid
Madrid, Spain
pgervas@sip.ucm.es

Abstract

Referring Expression Generation (REG) is the task that deals with references to entities appearing in a spoken or written discourse. If these referents are organized in terms of a taxonomy, there are two problems when establishing a reference that would distinguish an intended referent from its possible distractors. The first one is the choice of the set of possible distractrors or *contrast set* in the given situation. The second is to identify at what level of the taxonomy to phrase the reference so that it unambiguously picks out only the intended referent, leaving all possible distractors in different branches of the taxonomy. We discuss the use of ontologies to deal with the REG task, paying special attention to the choice of the the contrast set and to the use of the information of the ontology to select the most appropriate type to be used for the referent.

1 Introduction

Referring Expression Generation (REG) is the task that deals with references of entities appearing in a discourse. In a context where possible referents are organized in terms of a taxonomy (or subsumption hierarchy) and may additionally be differentiated by their attributes, there are two possible ways of establishing a reference that will distinguish an intended referent from its possible distractors.

One is to identify at what level of the taxonomy to phrase the reference so that it unambiguously picks out only the intended referent, leaving all possible distractors in different branches of the taxonomy. Another, applied once a particular level of reference has been chosen, is to resort to mentioning additional attributes of the intended referents that distinguish it from any remaining distractors that share the same branch of the taxonomy.

While the second task has been addressed often in existing literature, the first one is often glossed over by requiring that the levels to be used for each element come specified in the input. However, if this task is to be considered as a specific problem to be solved computationally, it opens up an additional problem. If the elements in the universe are classified in a taxonomy with a single root and the reference was established at a high enough level in the taxonomy, potentially everything in the universe could be a distractor for any other element.

In this paper we will discuss the use of ontologies to deal with the referring expression generation task. We will pay special attention to the choice of the contrast set and the use of ontology information to select the most appropriate type to be used for the referent. This work has been centered in the generation of definite noun phrases where the type of an element and a set of its properties are given to distinguish it from the other elements in focus. We are also supposing that the situations in which the reference is produced are static, that is, the addressee's perception of the world does not change during the process of reference generation.

2 Related Work

The appropriate use of referring expressions to compete with human-generated texts involves a certain difficulty. According to Reiter and Dale (2000), a referring expression must communicate enough information to identify univocally the intended referent within the context of the current discourse, but always avoiding unnecessary or redundant modifiers.

Reiter and Dale (1992) describe a fast algorithm for generating referring expressions in the context of a natural language generation system. Their algorithm relies on the following set of assumptions about the underlying knowledge base that must be used: (1) every entity is characterized in terms of a collection of attributes and their values, (2) every entity has as one of its attributes a type, and (3) the knowledge base may organize some attribute values as a subsumption hierarchy. Additionally, each object represented in the system should have an associated *basic level value*, which corresponds to the concept which is preferred when referring to that object.

These assumptions are satisfied if a description logic ontology is used for this purpose. Entities would correspond to instances of concepts from the ontology, the attribute corresponding to the type would be the concept of which they are immediate instances, and the taxonomical structure of the ontology of concepts would provide the subsumption hierarchy. To construct a reference to a particular entity, the algorithm takes as input a symbol corresponding to the intended referent and a list of symbols corresponding to other entities in focus, known as the *contrast set*. The algorithm returns a list of attribute-value pairs that correspond to the semantic content of the referring expression.

3 Generating References Using Ontologies

A previously developed ontology about wines has been used to test the ideas presented in this work. This is a sample ontology implemented following a version published by Brachman and colleagues (Brachman et al., 1991) and distributed along with the CLASSIC knowledge representation system.

We have focused on the taxonomy of wines provided by the ontology. Wines are divided in three main categories: `Red_Wine`, `White_Wine` and `Rose_Wine`. Inside these main categories there is a complex taxonomy of different kinds of wines. In addition, the ontology also contains several instances of the different concepts. Each of these instances is described using features such as body, color, flavor, producer, and so on.

The aim is to generate references for different instances of wines which are together in a discourse. The first step is to select the set of distractors or contrast set for the specific referent. Then, an algorithm for deciding which is the best reference to use is applied. We have considered as the best reference possible the use of the type that distinguishes the referent from the distractors and at the same time is as general as possible. For example, if we are referring to an instance of `Chardonnay` wine (that is a white one) in a situation where the rest of wines are all red wines, the most suitable reference is *"the white wine"* and not *"the chardonnay"*. On the contrary, the more specific (but unnecessary) reference might lead the addressee to infer that this information is somehow relevant. If only white wines (as direct type of the referent) are considered for the contrast set, only the more specific (and inappropriate) reference may be generated. Therefore, a wide enough contrast set must be considered in each case.

Finally, if the type chosen is not enough to distinguish the referent from the contrast set, attribute selection is applied to select a subset of the element properties that distinguish it.

3.1 Composing the Contrast Set

Information about type is generally used to determine which elements of the world must be considered in the contrast set. In this work, all the information about the world is located in an ontology. Each instance of the world contained in it has a direct type (the most specific concept it belongs to) and a set of undirect types that are all the types between the direct type and the root of the ontology.

In the work developed we have used the whole ontology as contrast set. We have considered it as the most suitable option for most situations where the elements involved can belong to quite different types. As we will see later, this choice avoids the use of references more specific than desired while at the same time it allows the algorithm to choose the type that is more suitable in a given situation.

3.2 An Appropriate Type for the Referent

Our approach takes as initial distinguishing attribute the type of the elements appearing in the world. This kind of solution is enough when the types defined for each of the entities of the world are fixed and there is not a close relation for different types. For example, a solution that takes as type the strict one defined in an element would not consider a *doberman* and a *chihuahua* as being both of them *dogs*.

The algorithm we have implemented can be seen in Figure 1. Here, r is the intended referent, C is the contrast set, A is the list of attributes that the instances of the ontology hold, *typeValue* is the type that would be assigned to the referent by the algorithm, and L is the list of attribute-value pairs returned if the type is not enough to rule out all the distractors. The `rules-out` function works as the one used in the Incremental algorithm, and the function `incremental-algorithm` calls directly to the original algorithm by Reiter and Dale.

The function `find-best-value-type` is the one that delivers the most appropriate type for the intended referent r taking into account the information in the ontology. We have considered as basic level value for the type the most specific of the common types of the instances of the ontology. From this basic level type, the branch of concepts between it and the direct type of the intended referent r is visited. The type that will be used in the reference is the most general concept from this branch that discards a bigger number of distractors.

```
make-referring-expression ( r, C, A )

L ← {}
C ← instances-ontology()
typeValue ← find-best-value-type( r, C )
C ← C – rules-out( < type , typeValue > )
if C = {} then
   return < typeValue, {} >
else
   L ← incremental-algorithm( r , C , A )
   return < typeValue, L >
endif


find-best-value-type( r, C )

basic-level-type ← most-specific-common-type( r U C )
value ← basic-level-type
for v_i ∈ ontology-children(basic-level-type)
   if | rules-out( < type,v_i >) |
        > | rules-out( < type,value >) | then
        value ← v_i
   endif
next
return value
```

Figure 1: The Algorithm

3.3 Attribute Selection for Reference Completion

In some cases the type would not be enough to distinguish a referent from the other elements of the world. This situation is produced when they belong to the same type. In this situation it will be necessary to use their properties to distinguish between them. The attribute selection carried out in the Incremental algorithm from Reiter and Dale has been applied to these situations.

4 Some Examples

We have tested the implemented algorithm over different situations in which a set of wines is presented. For each of them, a distinguishing description is provided using the appropriate type found using the ontology and a set of attributes when they were required. The instances of the world we have considered are shown in Table 1 (the properties of the wines that have not been used by the algorithm are not shown). The references generated for each of the referents are (numbers correspond to examples in the table):

1. *"The Riesling"*. There is another white wine but not a `Dry_Riesling` one, so the most general type discarding all the distractors is `Riesling`.

2. *"The moderate Cabernet_Sauvignon"*. Here the type is not enough to distinguish this referent, so its attributes are used. The property that distinguish it from the other `Cabernet_Sauvignon` is the flavor.

3. *"The strong Cabernet_Sauvignon"*. As in the previous case the strong flavor is used to distinguish the wine from the other `Cabernet_Sauvignon`.

4. *"The Rose_Wine"*. In this case there are no more rose wines, so this generic type is enough to distinguish the referent.

<table>
<tr><th rowspan="2"></th><th rowspan="2">Name of the instance</th><th rowspan="2">Types</th><th colspan="4">Properties</th></tr>
<tr><th>Body</th><th>Color</th><th>Flavor</th><th>Sugar</th></tr>
<tr><td>1</td><td>Corban_Dry_White_Riesling</td><td rowspan="4">▼ ● Wine
▼ ● White_wine
▼ ● Riesling
● Dry_Riesling
◆ Corbans_Dry_White_Riesling
● Chardonnay
◆ Bancroft_Chardonnay
▼ ● Rose_wine
● White_Merlot
◆ Forest_Glen_White_Merlot_Rose
▼ ● Red_wine
● Cabernet_Sauvignon
◆ Marietta_Cabernet_Sauvignon
◆ Forman_Cabernet_Sauvignon</td><td></td><td></td><td></td><td></td></tr>
<tr><td>2</td><td>Marietta_Cabernet_Sauvignon</td><td>Medium</td><td>Red</td><td>Moderate</td><td>Dry</td></tr>
<tr><td>3</td><td>Forman_Cabernet_Sauvignon</td><td>Medium</td><td>Red</td><td>Strong</td><td>Dry</td></tr>
<tr><td>4</td><td>Forest_Glen_White_Merlot_Rose</td><td></td><td></td><td></td><td></td></tr>
</table>

Table 1: Examples

5 Conclusions and Future Work

The main advantage of this approach is that the algorithm always finds the most suitable value for the type, taking into account the other entities of the world. Since this solution is completely generic and domain-independent, the algorithm would work in the same way with more general ontologies. For example, if the considered ontology contains information not only about wines, but also about other kinds of drinks, the values to be used as types of the referents would also be chosen in the same way. In this situation the referent could be the only wine among other drinks, and the reference generated for it would be the most appropriate one: *"the wine"*.

In the Incremental algorithm, Reiter and Dale do not address the question of how the contrast set is constructed, stating that the contrast set is one of the inputs of their algorithm. In our work, we have chosen as contrast set all the instances that can be found in the ontology. This solution allows the algorithm to work with enough information to choose exactly at which level of the ontology the discourse is being displayed (more general or more specific). With this information the generated references are adapted to the level of specificity required in each case.

The Incremental algorithm also states that the basic level value is obtained from the knowledge base or the user model. In this paper we have implemented a dynamic way to obtain this value that only depends on the knowledge available about the world. However, the use of some kind of user model representing the expertise level of the addressee in a specific domain could be explored in the future.

Acknowledgments

This research is funded by the Spanish Ministry of Education and Science (TIN2006-14433-C02-01 project) and the UCM and the Dirección General de Universidades e Investigación of the CAM (CCG07-UCM/TIC-2803).

References

Brachman. Ronald J. and McGuiness, Deborah L. and Patel-Schneider, Peter F. and Resnick, Lori A. 1991. *Living with CLASSIC: when and how to use a KL-ONE-like language.* Principles in Semantic Networks: Explorations in the Representation of Knowledge, pages 401–456. Morgan Kaufmann, California.

Reiter, Ehud and Dale, Robert. 1992. A fast algorithm for the generation of referring expressions. *Proc. of the 14th conference on Computational Linguistics*, pp. 232-238. Association for Computational Linguistics.

Reiter, Ehud and Dale, Robert. 2000. *Building Natural Language Generation Systems.* Cambridge University Press.

Parser-Based Retraining for Domain Adaptation of Probabilistic Generators

Deirdre Hogan, Jennifer Foster, Joachim Wagner and Josef van Genabith
National Centre for Language Technology
School of Computing
Dublin City University
Ireland
{dhogan, jfoster, jwagner, josef}@computing.dcu.ie

Abstract

While the effect of domain variation on Penn-treebank-trained probabilistic parsers has been investigated in previous work, we study its effect on a Penn-Treebank-trained probabilistic generator. We show that applying the generator to data from the British National Corpus results in a performance drop (from a BLEU score of 0.66 on the standard WSJ test set to a BLEU score of 0.54 on our BNC test set). We develop a generator retraining method where the domain-specific training data is automatically produced using state-of-the-art parser output. The retraining method recovers a substantial portion of the performance drop, resulting in a generator which achieves a BLEU score of 0.61 on our BNC test data.

1 Introduction

Grammars extracted from the Wall Street Journal (WSJ) section of the Penn Treebank have been successfully applied to natural language parsing, and more recently, to natural language generation. It is clear that high-quality grammars can be extracted for the WSJ domain but it is not so clear how these grammars scale to other text genres. Gildea (2001), for example, has shown that WSJ-trained parsers suffer a drop in performance when applied to the more varied sentences of the Brown Corpus. We investigate the effect of domain variation in treebank-grammar-based generation by applying a WSJ-trained generator to sentences from the British National Corpus (BNC).

As with probabilistic parsing, probabilistic generation aims to produce the most likely output(s) given the input. We can distinguish three types of probabilistic generators, based on the type of probability model used to select the most likely sentence. The first type uses an n-gram language model, e.g. (Langkilde, 2000), the second type uses a probability model defined over trees or feature-structure-annotated trees, e.g. (Cahill and van Genabith, 2006), and the third type is a mixture of the first and second type, employing n-gram and grammar-based features, e.g. (Velldal and Oepen, 2005). The generator used in our experiments is an instance of the second type, using a probability model defined over Lexical Functional Grammar c-structure and f-structure annotations (Cahill and van Genabith, 2006; Hogan et al., 2007).

In an initial evaluation, we apply our probabilistic WSJ-trained generator to BNC material, and show that the generator suffers a substantial performance degradation, with a drop in BLEU score from 0.66 to 0.54. We then turn our attention to the problem of adapting the generator so that it can more accurately generate the 1,000 sentences in our BNC test set. The problem of adapting any NLP system to a domain different from the domain upon which it has been trained and for which no gold standard training material is available is a very real one, and one which has been the focus of much recent research in parsing. Some success has been achieved by training a parser, not on gold standard hand-corrected trees, but on parser output trees. These parser output trees can by produced by a second parser in a *co-training* scenario (Steedman et al., 2003), or by the same parser with a reranking component in a type of *self-training* scenario (McClosky et al., 2006). We tackle the problem of domain adaptation in generation in a similar way, by training the generator on domain specific *parser output* trees instead of manually corrected gold standard trees. This experiment achieves promising results, with an increase in BLEU score from 0.54 to 0.61. The method is generic and can be applied to other probabilistic generators (for which suitable training material can be automatically produced).

2 Background

The natural language generator used in our experiments is the WSJ-trained system described in Cahill and van Genabith (2006) and Hogan et al. (2007). Sentences are generated from Lexical Functional Grammar (LFG) f-structures (Kaplan and Bresnan, 1982). The f-structures are created automatically by annotating nodes in the gold standard WSJ trees with LFG functional equations and then passing these equations through a constraint solver (Cahill et al., 2004). The generation algorithm is a chart-based one which works by finding the most probable tree associated with the input f-structure. The yield of the most probable tree is the output sentence. An annotated PCFG, in which the non-terminal symbols are decorated with functional information, is used to generate the most probable tree from an f-structure. Cahill and van Genabith (2006) attain 98.2% coverage and a BLEU score of 0.6652 on the standard WSJ test set (Section 23). Hogan et al. (2007) describe an extension to the system which replaces the annotated PCFG selection model with a more sophisticated history-based probabilistic model. Instead of conditioning the righthand side of a rule on the lefthand non-terminal and its associated functional information alone, the new model includes non-local conditioning information in the form of functional information associated with ancestor nodes of the lefthand side category. This system achieves a BLEU score of 0.6724 and 99.9% coverage.

Other WSJ-trained generation systems include Nakanishi et al. (2005) and White et al. (2007). Nakanishi et al. (2005) describe a generator trained on a HPSG grammar derived from the WSJ Section of the Penn Treebank. On sentences of ≤ 20 words in length, their system attains coverage of 90.75% and a BLEU score of 0.7733. White et al. (2007) describe a CCG-based realisation system which has been trained on logical forms derived from CCG-Bank (Hockenmaier and Steedman, 2005), achieving 94.3% coverage and a BLEU score of 0.5768 on WSJ23 for all sentence lengths. The input structures upon which these systems are trained vary in form and specificity, but what the systems have in common is that their various input structures are derived from Penn Treebank trees.

3 The BNC Test Data

The new English test set consists of 1,000 sentences taken from the British National Corpus (Burnard, 2000). The BNC is a one hundred million word balanced corpus of British English from the late twentieth century. Ninety per cent of it is written text, and the remaining 10% consists of transcribed spontaneous and scripted spoken language. The BNC sentences in the test set are not chosen completely at random. Each sentence in the test set has the property of containing a word which appears as a verb in the BNC but not in the usual training sections of the Wall Street Journal section of the Penn Treebank (WSJ02-21). Sentences were chosen in this way so that the resulting test set would be a difficult one for WSJ-trained systems. In order to produce input f-structures for the generator, the test sentences were manually parsed by one annotator, using as references the Penn Treebank trees themselves and the Penn Treebank bracketing guidelines (Bies et al., 1995). When the two references did not agree, the guidelines took precedence over the Penn Treebank trees. Difficult parsing decisions were documented. Due to time constraints, the annotator did not mark functional tags or traces. The context-free gold standard parse trees were transformed into f-structures using the automatic procedure of Cahill et al. (2004).

4 Experiments

Experimental Setup In our first experiment, we apply the original WSJ-trained generator to our BNC test set. The gold standard trees for our BNC test set differ from the gold standard Wall Street Journal trees, in that they do not contain Penn-II traces or functional tags. The process which produces f-structures from trees makes use of trace and functional tag information, if available. Thus, to ensure that the training and test input f-structures are created in the same way, we use a version of the generator which is trained using gold standard WSJ trees *without* functional tag or trace information. When we test this system on the WSJ23 f-structures (produced in the same way as the WSJ training material), the BLEU score decreases slightly from 0.67 to 0.66. This is our baseline system.

In a further experiment, we attempt to adapt the generator to BNC data by using BNC trees as training material. Because we lack gold standard BNC trees (apart from those in our test set), we try instead to use parse trees produced by an accurate parser. We choose the Charniak and Johnson reranking parser because it is freely available and achieves state-of-the-art accuracy (a Parseval f-score of 91.3%) on the WSJ domain (Charniak and Johnson, 2005). It is, however, affected by domain variation — Foster et al. (2007) report that its f-score drops by approximately 8 percentage points when applied to the BNC domain. Our training size is 500,000 sentences. We conduct two experiments: the first, in which 500,000 sentences are extracted randomly from the BNC (minus the test set sentences), and the second in which only shorter sentences, of length ≤ 20 words, are chosen as training material. The rationale behind the second experiment is that shorter sentences are less likely to contain parser errors.

We use the BLEU evaluation metric for our experiments. We measure both coverage and full coverage. Coverage measures the number of cases for which the generator produced some kind of output. Full coverage measures the number of cases for which the generator produced a tree spanning all of the words in the input.

Results The results of our experiments are shown in Fig. 1. The first row shows the results we obtain when the baseline system is applied to the f-structures derived from the 1,000 BNC gold standard parse trees. The second row shows the results on the same test set for a system trained on Charniak and Johnson parser output trees for 500,000 BNC sentences. The results in the final row are obtained by training the generator on Charniak and Johnson parser output trees for 500,000 BNC sentences of length ≤ 20 words in length.

Discussion As expected, the performance of the baseline system degrades when faced with out-of-domain test data. The BLEU score drops from a 0.66 score for WSJ test data to a 0.54 score for the BNC test data, and full coverage drops from 85.97% to 68.77%. There is a substantial improvement, however, when the generator is trained on BNC data. The BLEU score jumps from 0.5358 to 0.6135. There are at least two possible reasons why a BLEU score of 0.66 is not obtained: The first is that the quality of the f-structure-annotated trees upon which the generator has been trained has degraded. For the baseline system, the generator is trained on f-structure-annotated trees derived from *gold* trees. The new system is trained on f-structure-annotated parser output trees, and the performance of Charniak and Johnson's parser degrades when applied to BNC data (Foster et al., 2007). The second reason has been suggested by Gildea (2001): WSJ data is easier to learn than the more varied data in the Brown Corpus or BNC. Perhaps even if gold standard BNC parse trees were available for training, the system would not behave as well as it does for WSJ material.

It is interesting to note that training on 500,000 shorter sentences does not appear to help. We hypothesized that it would improve results because shorter sentences are less likely to contain parser errors. The drop in full coverage from 86.69% to 79.58% suggests that the number of short sentences needs to be increased so that the size of the training material stays constant.

5 Conclusion

We have investigated the effect of domain variation on a LFG-based WSJ-trained generation system by testing the system's performance on 1,000 sentences from the British National Corpus. Performance drops from a BLEU score of 0.66 on WSJ test data to 0.54 on the BNC test set. Encouragingly, we have also shown that domain-specific training material produced by a parser can be used to claw back a significant portion of this performance degradation. Our method is general and could be applied to other WSJ-trained generators (e.g. (Nakanishi et

Train	BLEU	Coverage	Full Coverage
WSJ02-21	0.5358	99.1	68.77
BNC(500k)	0.6135	99.1	86.69
BNC(500k) $\leq$ *20 words*	0.5834	99.1	79.58

Figure 1: Results for 1,000 BNC Sentences

al., 2005; White et al., 2007)). We intend to continue this research by training our generator on parse trees produced by a BNC-self-trained version of the Charniak and Johnson reranking parser (Foster et al., 2007). We also hope to extend the evaluation beyond the BLEU metric by carrying out a human judgement evaluation.

Acknowledgments

This research has been supported by the Enterprise Ireland Commercialisation Fund (CFTD/2007/229), Science Foundation Ireland (04/IN/I527) and the IRCSET Embark Initative (P/04/232). We thank the Irish Centre for High End Computing for providing computing facilities.

References

Ann Bies, Mark Ferguson, Karen Katz, and Robert MacIntyre. 1995. Bracketing guidelines for treebank II style, Penn Treebank project. Technical Report Tech Report MS-CIS-95-06, University of Pennsylvania, Philadelphia, PA.

Lou Burnard. 2000. User reference guide for the British National Corpus. Technical report, Oxford University Computing Services.

Aoife Cahill and Josef van Genabith. 2006. Robust PCFG-based generation using automatically acquired lfg approximations. In *Proceedings of the 21st COLING and the 44th Annual Meeting of the ACL*, pages 1033–1040, Sydney.

Aoife Cahill, Michael Burke, Ruth O'Donovan, Josef van Genabith, and Andy Way. 2004. Long-Distance Dependency Resolution in Automatically Acquired Wide-Coverage PCFG-Based LFG Approximations. In *Proceedings of the 42nd Meeting of the ACL*, pages 320–327, Barcelona.

Eugene Charniak and Mark Johnson. 2005. Course-to-fine n-best-parsing and maxent discriminative reranking. In *Proceedings of the 43rd Annual Meeting of the ACL*, pages 173–180, Ann Arbor.

Jennifer Foster, Joachim Wagner, Djamé Seddah, and Josef van Genabith. 2007. Adapting WSJ-trained parsers to the British National Corpus using in-domain self-training. In *Proceedings of the Tenth IWPT*, pages 33–35, Prague.

Daniel Gildea. 2001. Corpus variation and parser performance. In *Proceedings of EMNLP*, Pittsburgh.

Julia Hockenmaier and Mark Steedman. 2005. Ccgbank: Users' manual. Technical report, Computer and Information Science, University of Pennsylvania.

Deirdre Hogan, Conor Cafferkey, Aoife Cahill, and Josef van Genabith. 2007. Exploiting multi-word units in history-based probabilistic generation. In *Proceedings of the joint EMNLP/CoNLL*, pages 267–276, Prague.

Ron Kaplan and Joan Bresnan. 1982. Lexical Functional Grammar: a Formal System for Grammatical Representation. In Joan Bresnan, editor, *The Mental Representation of Grammatical Relations*, pages 173–281. MIT Press.

Irene Langkilde. 2000. Forest-based statistical sentence generation. In *Proceedings of NAACL*, Seattle.

David McClosky, Eugene Charniak, and Mark Johnson. 2006. Effective self-training for parsing. In *Proceedings of the Human Language Technology Conference of the NAACL, Main Conference*, pages 152–159, New York City.

Hiroko Nakanishi, Yusuke Miyao, and Jun'ichi Tsujii. 2005. Probabilistic methods for disambiguation of an HPSG-based chart generator. In *Proceedings of the Ninth IWPT*, pages 93–102, Vancouver.

Mark Steedman, Miles Osbourne, Anoop Sarkar, Stephen Clark, Rebecca Hwa, Julia Hockenmaier, Paul Ruhlen, Steven Baker, and Jeremiah Crim. 2003. Bootstrapping statistical parsers from small datasets. In *Proceedings of EACL*, pages 331–338, Budapest.

Erik Velldal and Stephan Oepen. 2005. Maximum entropy models for realization ranking. In *Proceedings of the MT-Summit*, Phuket.

Michael White, Rajakrishnan Rajkumar, and Scott Martin. 2007. Towards broad coverage surface realization with CCG. In *Proceedings of the Workshop on Using Corpora for NLG: Language Generation and Machine Translation (UCNLG+MT)*, pages 267–276, Copenhagen.

Creation of a New Domain and Evaluation of Comparison Generation in a Natural Language Generation System

Matthew Marge
Language Technologies Institute
School of Computer Science
Carnegie Mellon University
mrmarge@cs.cmu.edu

Amy Isard
ICCS/HCRC
School of Informatics
University of Edinburgh
Amy.Isard@ed.ac.uk

Johanna Moore
ICCS/HCRC
School of Informatics
University of Edinburgh
J.Moore@ed.ac.uk

Abstract

We describe the creation of a new domain for the Methodius Natural Language Generation System, and an evaluation of Methodius' parameterized comparison generation algorithm. The new domain was based around music and performers, and texts about the domain were generated using Methodius. Our evaluation showed that test subjects learned more from texts that contained comparisons than from those that did not. We also established that the comparison generation algorithm could generalize to the music domain.

1 Introduction

There has been research into tailoring natural language to a user's previous browsing history in a variety of domains such as medicine, museum collections, and animal descriptions (McKeown, 1985; Milosavljevic, 1997; Dale et al., 1998; O'Donnell et al., 2001). Another domain in which this could be applied is automated disc jockeys (DJs) that accompany a music stream such as Pandora[1] and discuss interesting trivia or facts about music tracks recently played to the user. User modeling could make these texts much more natural and less repetitive, and comparisons and contrasts between music artists or tracks could also provide users with a novel way to explore their music collection.

The Methodius system (Isard, 2007) continues in a line of research which began with ILEX (O'Donnell et al., 2001) and continued with M-PIRO (Isard et al., 2003) and now also NaturalOWL (Galanis and Androutsopoulos, 2007). Like these other systems, Methodius creates customizable descriptions of objects from an database, but it features a novel algorithm for generating comparisons between a new object and objects that have previously been encountered, which stands out from previous research in this area because it uses several explicit parameters to choose the most relevant and interesting comparisons given the context (Isard, 2007).

There have been previous evaluations of some of these systems, including (Cox et al., 1999; Karasimos and Isard, 2004). Karasimos and Isard conducted an evaluation of comparisons and aggregation in the M-PIRO system. The results showed that participants learned more and perceived that they learned more from texts that contained comparisons and aggregations than they did from texts that did not. In this study, we investigate whether these results generalize to our new domain, and we isolate the effect of comparisons from that of aggregation.

2 Knowledge Base Construction

2.1 Corpus Collection

We collected a small corpus to investigate the type of facts disc jockeys tend to say about music. We selected two genres where music descriptions between pieces were common, jazz and classical music. The programmes we used were broadcast on BBC Radio Three[2]. We transcribed sixty-four discussions; to maintain uniformity, we followed the Linguistic Data Consortium's transcription guidelines[3]. This

[1] http://www.pandora.com

[2] http://www.bbc.co.uk/radio3

[3] http://projects.ldc.upenn.edu/Transcription/quick-trans

was not a thorough corpus collection; the purpose of collecting examples was to gain a sense of what disc jockeys tend to discuss and compare.

2.2 Ontology Design

Based on the transcribed examples, we selected and hand-wrote twelve database entries for music tracks, using the authoring tool developed by the M-PIRO project (Androutsopoulos et al., 2007). We transformed the output of this tool into files suitable for Methodius using an ad-hoc collection of Perl and XSLT scripts, which also added the necessary information to the OpenCCG grammars (White, 2006) used by Methodius. We discuss future plans in this area in Section 5.

We created a single-inheritance ontology for a knowledge base of music pieces. First, we listed the high-level entity types in the music domain, such as “person”, “instrument”, “classical music period”, and “jazz music period”. We then added attributes commonly found in our disc jockey transcriptions. For each entity type, we defined a set of fields. For example, the classical-period field must contain an entity which expresses a classical music piece's time period. We also specified a microplanning expression for each field, which provides detail on how the field's information should be generated at the sentence level. We then added all the lexical items necessary for the music domain.

2.3 Ontology Population

We populated our domain with six classical music pieces and six jazz music pieces from the allmusic.com database[4]. The songs were selected to yield at least two interesting comparisons when placed in a specific order. We also added entities linked to the twelve songs, for example, each song's album, performer, and composer, and information about these entities. One challenge inherent in selecting these entities from a publicly available database was to eliminate as much common knowledge as possible about the music. In order to decrease background knowledge as a potential factor in our experiment, we selected songs that primarily did not contain popular performers, composers, and conductors. We were able to gauge the popularity of artists by their “popularity rank” in the allmusic.com database. However, we had to maintain a careful balance between obscure artists and the ability to generate interesting comparisons. Obscure artists had less detailed information in the allmusic.com database than popular music artists, so were forced to select a few popular music artists for our experiment, as their music pieces had multiple possible interesting comparisons.

[4]http://www.allmusic.com

```
"Avatar" was written by Gary Husband and it was
performed by Billy Cobham, who was influenced
by Miles Davis.  Billy Cobham originated from
Panama City, Panama and he played the drums; he
was active from the 1970s to the 1990s and he
participated in the Mahavishnu Orchestra.  He
was influenced by Miles Davis.  "Avatar" was
written during the Fusion period.
```

Figure 1: A generated description without comparisons.

```
Unlike "Fracture" and "A Mystery in Town",
which were written by Eddie "Lockjaw" Davis and
were performed by Fats Navarro, "Avatar" was
written by Gary Husband and it was performed by
Billy Cobham.  Cobham originated from Panama
City, Panama and he played the drums; he was
active from the 1970s to the 1990s and he
participated in the Mahavishnu Orchestra.  He
was influenced by Miles Davis.  "Avatar" was
written during the Fusion period.
```

Figure 2: A generated description with comparisons to previously described songs.

3 Experiment

We tried to maintain as many conditions from the previous, similar study (Karasimos and Isard, 2004) as possible to allow us to directly compare our results to theirs. The previous study established that people learned more and perceived that they learned more from text enriched with comparisons and aggregations of facts than from texts that contained neither. Our experimental design was similar to theirs but all conditions of our experiment contained text generated with aggregations of facts; our aim was to isolate the effects of comparisons from those of sentence aggregation.

For jazz texts, comparisons between songs involving performers, albums, composers, and time periods were possible. Classical texts could produce all four of these types of comparisons. In addition, classical texts could also include comparisons of conductors. Although the potential similarities for classical and jazz texts were not equal, we decided to include the conductor as a potential comparison for classical music. This is because across both text types, we maintained the same number of generated comparisons for each text type by limiting Methodius to generating only one comparison or contrast per paragraph of text. We present examples of a paragraph of text generated by Methodius without (Figure 1) and with (Figure 2) comparisons. In both cases, we assume that the user has already seen texts about the songs "Fracture" and "A Mystery in Town", which expressed the facts about these previous songs which are used in the comparisons in Figure 2; the comparison text does not contain more new information.

3.1 Evaluation Design

For our user study, we created a web interface using WebExp2 Experiment Design software[5] that contained text generated by Methodius from our music fact knowledge base. Forty fluent English speakers were recruited and directed to a web page that gave detailed instructions. After providing some basic personal information including their name, age, gender, occupation and native languages, subjects started with a test page, where they read a sample paragraph and responded to one factual question, to make sure that they had understood the interface, and they then proceeded to the main experiment.

Participants read 6 paragraphs about either jazz or classical music, and answered 15 factual recall questions. They then read a further 6 paragraphs about the other type of music, followed by 15 factual recall questions on the second set of texts. Finally they completed a post-experimental survey of 12 Likert Scale questions (Likert, 1932). We used a within-subjects design, where each subject saw two sets of texts, one classical and one jazz, one with and one without comparisons, and the order in which text sets were presented was controlled. The multiple choice questions did not change given the condition; so every participant saw the same two sets of 15 multiple-choice questions in randomized orders. Seven multiple-choice questions of each fifteen-question set dealt with facts that may be reinforced by comparisons. The remaining eight questions in each section served as a control for this experiment.

[5]http://www.webexp.info

Group	Texts with comparisons	Texts without comparisons
A	**4.15** (1.814)	3.35 (1.872)
B	**4.45** (1.638)	3.10 (1.651)
All	**4.30** (1.713)	3.23 (1.747)

Table 1: Mean multiple choice scores with standard deviation in brackets.

On each page, the interface presented an image of a paragraph of text generated by Methodius. The users proceeded to the next paragraph when they were ready by pressing the "Next song" or "Next piece" button, depending on whether the music type was jazz or classical. The texts were presented as images for two reasons: so that the presentation of stimuli would remain consistent across the different computers and to prevent the text from being selected by the participant, thus discouraging them from copying the text and placing it into another window as a reference to answer the factual recall questions asked later.

4 Results

A summary of the participants' multiple choice scores are shown in Table 1. Group A read classical texts with comparisons and jazz texts without, and Group B read jazz texts with comparisons and classical texts without.

We performed a 2-way repeated measures ANOVA on our data and found that participants performed significantly better on questions about the texts which had comparisons (F (1, 36) = 11.131, $p < .01$). There were no ordering or grouping effects–the performance of participants did not depend on which type of texts they saw first, or on which type of texts contained comparisons.

In general, the Likert scores showed no significant differences between the texts which had comparisons and those which did not. Karasimos and Isard (2004) did find significant differences, but in their case, texts had either comparisons and sentence aggregations, or neither. In our study, all the texts had sentence aggregations, so it may be this factor which contributed to their higher Likert results on questions such as "I enjoyed reading about these songs" and the binary "Which text (quality, fluency) did you like more" question, for which we also found no significant difference. Details of results and statistics can be found in (Marge, 2007).

5 Conclusions and Future Work

We have shown that the Methodius comparison generation algorithm does generalize to new domains, and that it is possible to quickly author a new domain and generate fluent and readable text, using an appropriate authoring tool. We have also confirmed the findings of previous studies, and showed that the use of comparisons in texts does significantly improve participants' recall of the facts which they have read.

In future work, we would like to use the current text generation in an automatic DJ system with streaming music, and perform further user studies in order to make the texts as interesting and relevant as possible. We would also like to perform a study in which we compare the output of the comparison algorithm using different parameter settings, to see whether users express a preference.

Since this work was carried out, Methodius has been adapted to accept ontologies and sentence plans written in OWL/RDF. These can be created using the Protégé editor[6] with an NLG plugin developed at the Athens University of Economics and Business as part of the NaturalOWL generation system (Galanis and Androutsopoulos, 2007), which is available as an open source package[7]. A more principled method for the OpenCCG conversion process than the one described in Section 2.2 is in development, and we hope to publish a paper on this subject.

Acknowledgements

The authors would like to acknowledge the help and advice given by Colin Matheson, Ellen Bard, Keith Edwards, Ray Carrick, Frank Keller, and Neil Mayo and the comments of the anonymous reviewers. This work was funded in part by a grant from the Edinburgh-Stanford Link and by the Saint Andrew's Society of the State of New York. The music data in this study was used with the permission of the All Music Guide.

[6]http://www.protege.stanford.edu

[7]http://www.aueb.gr/users/ion/software/NaturalOWL.tar.gz

References

I. Androutsopoulos, J. Oberlander, and V. Karkaletsis. 2007. Source authoring for multilingual generation of personalised object descriptions. *Natural Language Engineering*, 13:191–233.

R. Cox, M. O'Donnell, and J. Oberlander. 1999. Dynamic versus static hypermedia in museum education: an evaluation of ILEX, the intelligent labelling explorer. In *Proceedings of the Artificial Intelligence in Education conference*, Le Mans.

R. Dale, J. Green, M. Milosavljevic, C. Paris, C. Verspoor, and S. Williams. 1998. The realities of generating natural language from databases. In *Proceedings of the 11th Australian Joint Conference on Artificial Intelligence*, Brisbane, Australia.

D. Galanis and I. Androutsopoulos. 2007. Generating multilingual descriptions from linguistically annotated OWL ontologies: the NaturalOWL system. In *Proceedings of ENLG 2007.*

A. Isard, J. Oberlander, I. Androutsopoulos, and C. Matheson. 2003. Speaking the users' languages. *IEEE Intelligent Systems*, 18(1):40–45. Special Issue on Advances in Natural Language Processing.

A. Isard. 2007. Choosing the best comparison under the circumstances. In *Proceedings of the International Workshop on Personalization Enhanced Access to Cultural Heritage*, Corfu, Greece.

A. Karasimos and A. Isard. 2004. Multi-lingual evaluation of a natural language generation system. In *Proceedings of the Fourth International Conference on Language Resources and Evaluation*, Lisbon, Portugal.

R. Likert. 1932. A technique for the measurement of attitudes. *Archives of Psychology*, 22(140):1–55.

M. Marge. 2007. An evaluation of comparison generation in the methodius natural language generation system. Master's thesis, University of Edinburgh.

K. McKeown. 1985. *Text Generation: Using Discourse Strategies and Focus Constraints to Generate Natural Language Text.* Cambridge University Press, New York, NY, USA.

M. Milosavljevic. 1997. Content selection in comparison generation. In *6th European Workshop on Natural Language Generation)*, Duisburg, Germany.

M. O'Donnell, C. Mellish, J. Oberlander, and A. Knott. 2001. ILEX: An architecture for a dynamic hypertext generation system. *Natural Language Engineering*, 7:225–250.

M. White. 2006. Efficient realization of coordinate structures in combinatory categorial grammar. *Research on Language and Computation*, 4(1):39–75.

Generating Baseball Summaries from Multiple Perspectives by Reordering Content

Alice Oh
MIT CSAIL
32 Vassar St.
Cambridge, MA 02139 USA
aoh@mit.edu

Howard Shrobe
MIT CSAIL
32 Vassar St.
Cambridge, MA 02139 USA
hes@csail.mit.edu

Abstract

This paper presents a reordering algorithm for generating multiple stories from different perspectives based on a single baseball game. We take a description of a game and a neutral summary, reorder the content of the neutral summary based on event features, and produce two summaries that the users rated as showing perspectives of each of the two teams. We describe the results from an initial user survey that revealed the power of reordering on the users' perception of perspective. Then we describe our reordering algorithm which was derived from analyzing the corpus of local newspaper articles of teams involved in the games as well as a neutral corpus for the respective games. The resulting reordering algorithm is successful at turning a neutral article into two different summary articles that express the two teams' perspectives.

1 Introduction

Stories about events are written in many different perspectives, or points-of-view. For example, following a baseball game, multiple articles are written that summarize the game from different perspectives. Although they are describing the same game, readers feel differently about the articles and may prefer to read a certain perspective over all the others. We have explored what factors contribute to the differences in perspective in these event summary stories and how we can automatically plan content to generate multiple summaries of a baseball game written from different perspectives. The end goal of this work is to build a system that takes as input a factual description of a baseball game and a neutral article about the game, then produces two other articles, each from a particular team's point of view. There is previous work such as (Robin and McKeown, 1996) on automatic summary generation of sports games, but our work goes further to generate multiple summaries.

It is first necessary to define what is meant by perspective and multiple perspectives. The definition of perspective in this work is somewhat different from a more traditional meaning of perspective in literature, such as the third-person perspective discussed in (Wiebe and Rapaport, 1988). Our definition is much closer to that used in (Lin and Hauptmann, 2006), where they look at ideological perspectives of online articles on political, social, and cultural issues. They look at the political domain of the issues between Israel and Palestine, and they try to infer, for each online article, whether it is written from the Israeli perspective or the Palestinian perspective. For our work, we are looking at the domain of baseball games, so we focus on the article's perspective in terms of the home team versus the visiting team. We first assume that the two opposing perspectives are expressed in the local newspaper articles of the two teams, and we assume that the neutral perspective is expressed in the Associated Press articles published on an ESPN website (www.espn.com). We confirmed these assumptions via a user study, then we identified some key factors contributing to an article having a certain perspective. The next section explains our corpus and user studies.

2 Corpus

The Major League Baseball (MLB) has 30 teams within the United States and Canada, and each team plays approximately 160 games per season. We have collected data for hundreds of games from the 2005 and 2006 MLB seasons. The corpus is divided into two sets. The first is factual descriptions of the games in quantitative form and simple natural language text, and the second is journalistic writings from online news sources.

2.1 Game Data

For every MLB game, the website of MLB (www.mlb.com) publishes game data consisting of two documents. The first is a game log (see figure 1) , which is a complete list of *at-bats* in the game, where each *at-bat* is a set of pitches thrown from a pitcher to a batter such that the batter either gets out or advances to a base at the completion of the *at-bat*. There are at least 3 *at-bats* per half of an inning (top or bottom), and there are at least 9 innings per game (except in extreme weather conditions), so there are at least 54 *at-bats*, but usually more. In our corpus, the average number of *at-bats* is 76.2 per game. The second is a boxscore, which is a list of each batter and pitcher's performance statistics for the game. Currently we do not use the boxscore documents.

The game log is parsed using simple regular expression type patterns to turn each *at-bat* into a feature vector. We have defined 22 features: *inningNumber, atBatNumber, pitchCount, homeScore, visitScore, team, pitcher, batter, onFirst, onSecond, onThird, outsAdded, baseHit, rbi, doubleplay, runnersStranded, homerun, strikeOut, extraBaseHit, walk, error, typeOfPlay*. Some of these features, such as *batter* and *typeOfPlay* are extracted directly from each line in the log that is being transformed into a feature vector. Some of the features, such as *inningNumber*, *team*, and *pitcher* are span multiple contiguous *at-bats* and are extracted from the current line or in one of the lines going back a few *at-bats*. The remaining features, such as *onFirst*, *outsAdded*, and *runnersStranded* are derived from looking at the feature vector of the previous *at-bat* and following simple rules of the baseball game. For example, *onSecond* is derived from looking at the previous feature vector's *onFirst* value, and if the current play is one that advances the runner one base, the previous feature vector's *onFirst* gets copied to the current *onSecond*. While we tried to identify features that are important for analyzing and generating multiple perspectives, later sections will show that some of them were not used, as they were not significant variables for our content ordering algorithm.

2.2 Online Articles

In addition to game logs and boxscores, we collected articles published on several online news sources. The MLB website (www.mlb.com) publishes two articles for every game, written for each of the two teams in the game. Each team has a unique sportswriter covering that team for the entire season, so we use the MLB articles as one of our sources with the home/visit team perspective. The ESPN website (www.espn.com) also has articles for every MLB game including the main summary articles from the Associated Press (AP). We use the AP articles as our neutral source. We also collected online local newspaper articles for MLB teams in the American League East Division: Boston Red Sox (The Boston Globe at www.boston.com), New York Yankees (The New York Times at www.nytimes.com), Baltimore Orioles (The Washington Post at www.washingtonpost.com), Toronto Blue Jays (The Toronto Star at torontostar.com), and Tampa Bay Devil Rays (The Tampa Tribune at tampatrib.com).

3 From Neutral to One-Sided Perspective

We are building a system that takes a neutral article and turns it into an article with a one-sided perspective, so we looked at whether we can use the same content of the neutral article and still produce a non-neutral perspective. Surprisingly, looking at the articles in terms of the game events, there were many games where the three articles overlap quite a bit in the (*at-bats*) that are mentioned in the articles. That is, the neutral and the home/visit team articles all describe the same set of game events, but they still manage to present them such that the readers notice the differences in perspective.

To compute the overlap of content, the articles were first tagged with player names and part-of-

Boston - Bottom of 2nd		SCORE	
Dan Haren pitching for Oakland		OAK	BOS
Manny Ramirez	Strike (looking), Strike (swinging), Ball, Ball, Ball, M **Ramirez doubled to deep right**	0	0
Trot Nixon	Strike (looking), Ball, Strike (foul), Ball, Strike (swinging), **T Nixon struck out swinging**	0	0
Mike Lovell	Ball, Ball, Strike (looking), M **Lowell doubled to deep left**, M Ramirez scored	0	1
Jason Varitek	Ball, Strike (looking), Ball, Ball, J **Varitek flied out to center**	0	1
Coco Crisp	Strike (looking), Strike (looking), C **Crisp flied out to left**	0	1
1 Runs, 2 Hits, 0 Errors			

Figure 1: Pitch by Pitch Log of a Baseball Game

Games	All	Home	Visit
41	215	23	21
Ave	5.24	0.56	0.51

Table 1: Number of at-bats described in all three articles, at-bats only in the home team articles, and at-bats only in the visit team articles for 41 games.

speech tags, and simple pattern matching heuristics were used to automatically align the sentences in the articles with game events. The player names were downloaded from the MLB team sites accessible from www.mlb.com, and the POS tagging was done with the Stanford POS tagger (Toutanova and Manninig, 2000). Pattern matching heuristics looked for co-occurrences of tags and words within a certain window (e.g., {player} AND "homerun" within 3 words), and the results from applying those heuristics were aligned with the *at-bat* feature vectors computed from the game log. Testing on 45 articles hand-annotated by the first author, we achieved a precision of 79.0% and recall of 79.2% for alignment. The average number of *at-bats* in those hand-annotated articles was 8. The percentage of overlapping content varies widely, mostly due to the way the games unfolded. For example, many games are one-sided where one team simply dominates, and there are just not enough events that are positive for one of the teams. For those games, the losing team's newspaper merely reports the result of the game without describing the events of the game in detail. However, games that are close in score and number of hits, we found a high overlap of content among all three articles. Table 1 lists the number of *at-bats* reported in common in all three articles.

Based on the corpus analyses we surveyed users to see whether we can identify the important factors that contribute to differences in perspective.

First, to confirm that the home team and the visit team perspectives of the local team articles are correctly perceived, we simply presented the AP and local newspaper articles to users and asked them to guess which team the articles were written for. As expected, users identified the local team perspective with ease and confidence. Then, we took out all sentences except ones that describe the the game events (*at-bats*). Player quotes, commentary about the team or players' historical performances, and financial and personal news were some of the content that were removed from the articles. Users were asked to guess which team the articles were written for, and again, they were able to identify the local team perspectives. We then removed sentences describing game events that did not overlap with the content in the neutral article, and again, users identified the local perspectives. Finally, we replaced all the sentences with canned surface forms, such that all the articles shared the same surface form of sentences and preserved only the ordering of the content. This last experiment, albeit with less confidence than the previous ones, still produced users' perception of local perspective for the non-neutral articles. 8 users participated in the study using 12 games, and table 2 summarizes the results of these user surveys. All 8 users rated all 36 articles, 3 articles for each game, but the ordering of the articles was randomized. For all four conditions, users were asked to rate each article on a scale of 1 to 5, where 1 is strongly home team perspective, 3 is neutral, and 5 is strongly visit team perspective.

4 Feature-based Ordering Strategies

Following the results from the user study, we used a corpus-driven approach to identify the ordering strategies that contribute to the different perspectives. We looked at the games for which the three

Condition	Home	AP	Visit
Original	1.75	2.75	4.06
Events Only	1.75	2.90	3.85
Overlapping	2.02	2.75	3.85
Ordering	2.18	2.83	3.83

Table 2: Users' ratings on how they perceived perspective. They rated using a 1 to 5 scale, where 1 is the home team perspective, 3 is neutral, and 5 is the visiting team perspective. For all lines, t-test for the users' ratings of home team articles and visit tema articles show a statistically significant difference at the level $p < 0.05$.

articles have highly overlapping content and studied how the content is organized differently. We segmented the articles into topic segments (e.g, paragraphs) and noticed that the three articles differ quite a bit in the topics that hold the content together. These topics can be expressed simply by the feature values that are shared among the *at-bats* that appear together in the same segment. Below is an example of two different orderings of *at-bats* based on feature values. The first segment (lines 1a, 2a) of the first ordering shares the same values for the features $pitcher$, $team$, $inning$, and R (score added by that play). The second segment (lines 3a, 4a) shares $pitcher$, $batter$, and $team$.

	Pitcher	Batter	Team	inn	type	R
1a	Johns	Damon	Bos	1	hr	1
2a	Johns	Ramir	Bos	1	dbl	1
3a	Schil	Jeter	Nyy	4	dbl	0
4a	Schil	Jeter	Nyy	6	hr	2

The second ordering shows the same content arranged in different segments, where both segments are organized based on the value of $type$ of play. This is a frequent pattern in our corpus that seems to be responsible for the different perspectives of the articles.

	Pitcher	Batter	Team	inn	type	R
1b	Johns	Damon	Bos	1	hr	1
2b	Schil	Jeter	Nyy	6	hr	2
3b	Johns	Ramir	Bos	1	dbl	1
4b	Schil	Jeter	Nyy	4	dbl	0

Since there are many features, we need to identify the features to use for assigning the *at-bats* to appear in the same segment. We used a simple counting of most frequent feature values of the corpus to derive these features. This comes from the intuition that the players whose names appear most frequently in the articles for a local newspaper tend to be important topics for those stories. So we aggregate all the local team articles and rank the feature values including pitcher and batter names and play types (e.g., homerun, single, strikeout). To turn a neutral article into a local perspective article, we take the *at-bats* that should appear in the article, look at the feature values that are shared among them, and find the highest-ranked feature value for that team. Any remaining *at-bats* are arranged in chronological order.

5 Conclusion

We presented a content ordering algorithm that takes a neutral article of baseball and produces two other articles from the two teams' perspectives. We showed that just by reordering, we can induce different perspectives, and we used a corpus for discovering the different ordering strategies. In the future, we will refine our reordering algorithm, carry out a full evaluation, and also look at other factors that contribute to perspective such as content selection and surface realization. We will also look at another domain, such as the socio-political conflict in the Middle East discussed in (Lin and Hauptmann, 2006), to see whether similar reordering patterns appear in those articles.

References

Wei-Hao Lin and Alexander Hauptmann. 2006. Are these documents written from different perspectives? A test of different perspectives based on statistical distribution divergence. *Proceedings of the 42th annual meeting on Association for Computational Linguistics*.

Jacques Robin and Kathleen McKeown. 1996. Empirically designing and evaluating a new revision-based model for summary generation. *Artificial Intelligence*.

Kristina Toutanova and Christopher D. Manning. 2000. Enriching the knowledge sources used in a maximum entropy part-of-speech tagger. *Proceedings of the Joint SIGDAT Conference on Empirical Methods in Natural Language Processing and Very Large Corpora (EMNLP/VLC-2000)*.

Janyce M. Wiebe and William J. Rapaport. 1988. A computational theory of perspective and reference in narrative. *Proceedings of the 26th annual meeting on Association for Computational Linguistics*, 131–138.

A Dynamic Programming Approach to Document Length Constraints

Keith Vander Linden
Department of Computer Science
Calvin College
Grand Rapids, MI 49546, USA
kvlinden@calvin.edu

Abstract

Natural language generation (NLG) applications must occasionally deliver rhetorically coherent output under length constraints. For example, certain types of documents must fit on a single webpage, on a cell phone screen, or into a fixed number of printed pages. To date, applications have achieved this goal by structuring their content as a rhetorical tree and using a greedy algorithm to pick the discourse elements to include in the final document. Greedy algorithms are known to pick sub-optimal solutions. This paper presents an alternate approach based on dynamic programming.

1 Document Length Constraints

A number of language engineering applications have addressed the issue of generating coherent documents under length constraints, including NLG applications, e.g., SciFly (Paris, *et al*, 2008), STOP (Reiter, 2000), ILEX (O'Donnell, 1997), and summarization applications, e.g., Daniel Marcu (1999). These applications all address the issue by representing the content to be delivered as a rhetorical tree and using some formulation of a greedy algorithm that satisfies the length constraints by either selecting the most important elements of the tree or pruning the least important elements.[1]

As an example, consider the two sample outputs shown in Figure 1. Both outputs were produced by a prototype that delivers information about a computer science department to prospective students via email; cf. (Paris, *et al*, 2008). The output is composed of coarse-grained elements (e.g., images, phrases and paragraphs) and is formatted in post-card size using HTML and includes hyperlinks to related pages on the main department website. The goal is to get the prospective student to visit the main website. The key difference between the two examples is their length. The one on the left, which is shorter, was generated using a greedy algorithm. The one on the right, which uses the space more fully, was generated using a dynamic programming algorithm. The greedy algorithm included the "FAQ" section because it fit at the time; the dynamic algorithm realized that waiting to include the "News" and the "Alumni" sections would be a more effective use of the space.

This paper discusses the mechanisms used to generate these two examples. It starts with a discussion of the rhetorical tree used as input for both sample outputs, and then details the algorithms used to satisfy the length constraint. The length constraint problem is viewed as a precedence-constrained 0-1 knapsack problem, and the algorithm is formulated using dynamic programming.

2 Rhetorical Structure Trees

Researchers have long viewed rhetorical trees as a means of structuring textual output and of distinguishing those elements that should be expressed (often called nuclei) from those that could be omitted (often called satellites) (Spark-Jones, 1993), and there is psycholinguistic evidence that this view is valid (Marcu, 1999). This paper will

[1] The STOP system identifies the problem as a bin-packing problem but then describes its mechanism using terms common to greedy algorithms (Reiter, 2000).

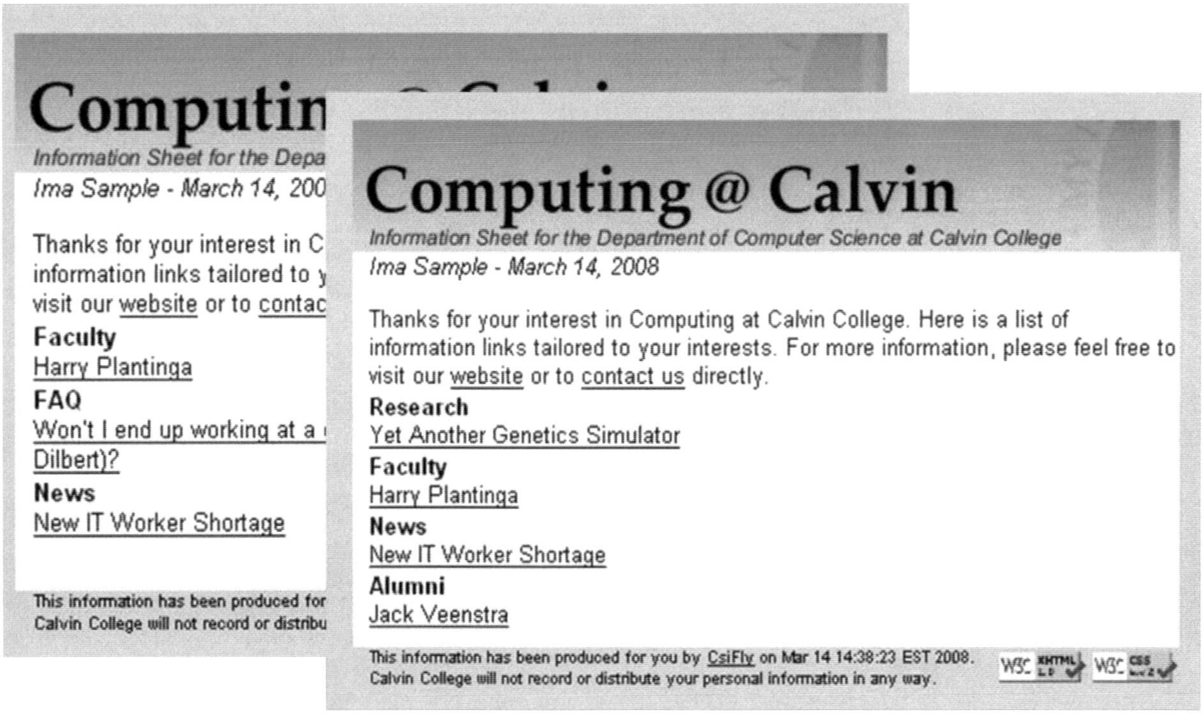

Figure 1. Two Sample Outputs – The greedy output is on the left, the dynamic is on the right.

build its trees using Rhetorical Structure Theory (RST), the most common of the theories deployed for rhetorical structuring (Mann & Thompson, 1988).

Figure 2 shows the annotated RST tree used as the basis for generating both of the sample outputs shown in Figure 1. The highest level of the tree shows a template that affixes the header image as a preparation satellite and the footer as a background satellite. The next level down shows the structure of the content of the email. Each node is associated with a block of text or an image in the output. The initial line (i.e., "Ima Sample…") is represented as a satellite setting the context for the main content in the nucleus (i.e., "Thanks for your interest…"). There then follows a set of six elaboration satellites, each with internal structures of its own (i.e., an image/caption pair, which is not realized in either sample output because of its cost, and a set of five topic/hyperlink pairs).

Each expressible node in the figure has an estimated length, denoted as a cost *c* measured in pixels, and an estimated importance, denoted as a benefit *b*. The cost of an expressible node is estimated based on the size of the text/image and specified format. Generally, the leaves are the expressible nodes, but in the case where multiple leaves should be expressed together, the RST tree places a combined cost value in the parent node (e.g., the header and footer should be expressed together or not at all, so their parent node shows their combined cost of 100 pixels).

The benefit setting, denoted *b(n,D)*, for a node *n* in a discourse tree *D* is formulated as follows:

$$b(n,D) = \begin{cases} 1.0 & n \text{ is the root} \\ b(P(n),D) & n \text{ is a nucleus} \\ b(P(n),D) \times W(r) & n \text{ is a satellite} \end{cases}$$

Here, *P(n)* denotes the parent of node *n* and *W(r)* denotes the weight of the satellite's rhetorical relation (e.g., in this paper, more important relations like context have weight 0.5 and less important relations like preparation, elaboration, background have weight 0.4). This formulation gives higher benefit values to nuclei. No penalty is placed on nodes lower in the tree. This formulation is implemented as a recursive decent algorithm whose values for the samples can be seen in Figure 2.

The tree is produced by a Moore and Paris-styled text planner (Moore & Paris, 1993). Selecting the appropriate content from a content management system, structuring it appropriately and estimating the cost/benefit of each node are interesting problems, but are not the focus of this paper.

In preparation for the length constraint algorithm, the system creates a queue of expressible nodes, each with its cost and benefit values. Nuclei are queued before satellites.

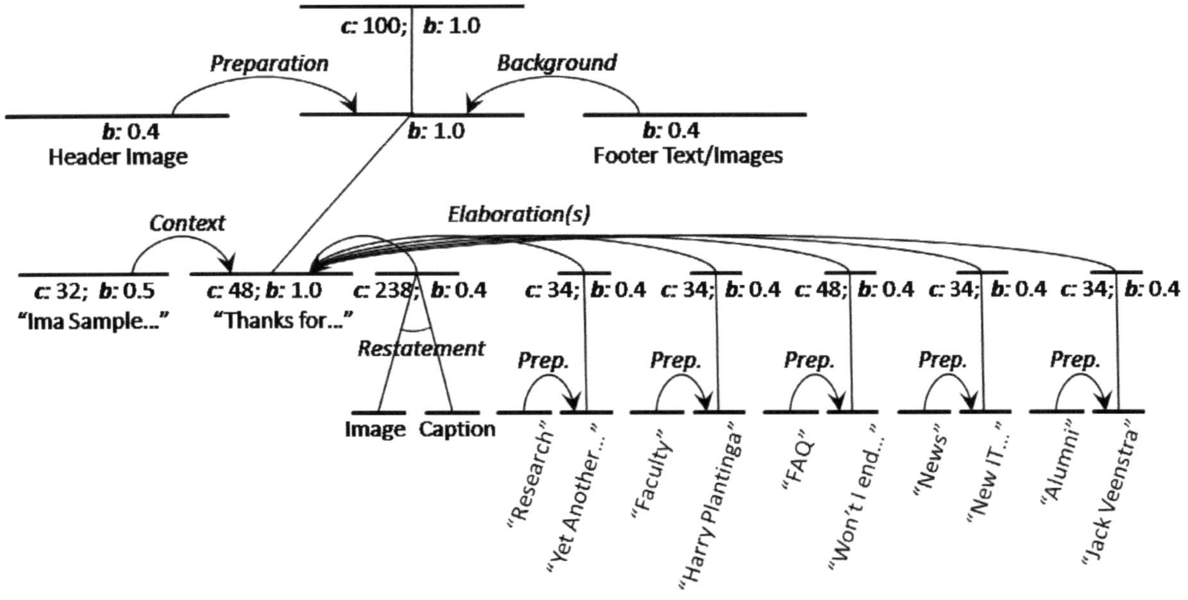

Figure 2. Sample Discourse Tree for the Output in Figure 1 with Cost/Benefit Settings

3 A Length Constraint Algorithm

This paper views the length constraint problem as a precedence-constrained 0-1 knapsack problem (Samphaiboon & Yamada, 2000); the output images/paragraphs are viewed as items for the knapsack, their length in pixels is viewed as their cost, and their rhetorical importance is viewed as their benefit. The prohibition against expressing a satellite without also expressing its governing nuclei is viewed as a precedence constraint on the items.

A common formulation for this problem is to define the solution in terms of the maximum benefit for a subset of the first k nodes given a maximum cost c as follows:

$$B(k,c) = \begin{cases} B(k-1,c) & c_k > c \\ \max\left(B(k-1,c),\; B(k-1,c-c_k)+b_k\right) & c_k \leq c \end{cases}$$

Here, b_k and c_k are the benefit and cost of node k respectively, and b_k is defined by $b(n, D)$ above. If the node k will fit within the maximum cost constraint c, then $B(k, c)$ is defined as the maximum of either the:

- previous solution for the first k-1 nodes not including node k; or
- previous solution with space for node k.

A dynamic programming algorithm that implements this formulation can be specified as follows:

Function: *format(C, Q, T)*
Input:

- A positive integer maximum cost limit C
- A queue Q of N nodes with positive integer cost (c_i) and real benefit (b_i) settings
- A tree T specifying rhetorical relationships

Output:

- A 2-D array $B[n+1, c+1]$ specifying the values for $B(k,c)$ as defined above

```
for c ← 0 to C
    B[0,c] ← 0
for k ← 1 to N
    for c ← 0 to C
        B[0,c] ← B[0,c-1]
    for c ← c_k to C
        if (not unexpressedNucleus(B,c,k,T) and
            B[k-1,c-c_i] + b_i > B[k-1,c])
            B[k,c] ← B[k-1,c-c_i] + b_i
```

The *format(C, Q, T)* algorithm declares a 2-D array of maximum benefit values and sets the first row to 0s. For each expressible node k in Q (rows *1* through N), it copies the previous row of benefit values and then, for each cost value above the cost of the current node (columns c_k through C), it either keeps the previous benefit value without node k or inserts the benefit that includes node k.

Given the array of maximal benefit values output by *format(C, Q, T)*, the following algorithm will compute set of nodes corresponding to a given benefit value:

Function: *output(B, k, c)*
Input:

- An array *B* of maximal benefit values
- A node number *k*
- *B*'s maximum cost value *c*.

Output:

- The set of nodes with total cost c and total benefit *B(k, c)*.

while k,c > 0
    if $B[k,c] \neq B[k\text{-}1,c]$
        include node_k
        $c \leftarrow c - c_k$
    $k \leftarrow k - 1$

The use of *unexpressedNucleus(B,c,k,T)* in the *format(C, Q, T)* if-condition is an extension of the standard algorithm for the 0-1 knapsack problem that addresses rhetorical precedence constraints. In RST-based NLG, satellites are not expressed without their nuclei. For example, we would not want to include the context expression (i.e., "Ima Sample…") without also including its nucleus (i.e., "Thanks for…"). Note that these "governing" nuclei are not always at the same level in the tree (e.g., the header image satellite is dependent upon the "Thanks for…" nucleus one level down).

The *unexpressedNucleus(B,c,k,T)* condition implements this constraint by requiring that $G(n,T) \subseteq output(B,k,d)$ before including any node *n*, where *G(n,T)* is the set of governing nuclei for *n* in tree *T* and is formulated as follows:

$$G(n,T) = \begin{cases} null & n \text{ is a root} \\ GN_+(P(n),T) \cup GN_-(P(n),T) - n & \end{cases}$$

$$G_+(n,T) = \begin{cases} null & n \text{ is not a root} \\ GN(P(n),T) & n \text{ is a root} \end{cases}$$

$$G_-(n,T) = \begin{cases} n & n \text{ is a leaf} \\ \displaystyle\bigcup_{c_i \in NC(n)} G_-(c_i,T) & n \text{ is not a leaf} \end{cases}$$

Here, $G_+()$ looks up the tree, $G_-()$ looks down the tree, *P(n)* is *n*'s parent node, and *NC(n)* is the set of *n*'s nucleus children. *G()* includes only expressible nodes. *G()* can be implemented by a set of three mutually recursive functions and can be memoized to improve efficiency.

The greedy algorithm used for the output in Figure 1 uses the same input and a precedence queue of expressible nodes ordered by decreasing benefit.

4 Analysis and Conclusions

The dynamic programming algorithm will always perform at least as well as the greedy algorithm, and sometimes better. For example, given a total cost maximum of 325, the greedy algorithm's output in Figure 1 has total cost/benefit: 297/3.7, while the dynamic algorithm's output has 316/4.1.

Dynamic programming algorithms are notoriously expensive in terms of space and time requirements. They are pseudo-polynomial time, O(NC), but if N and C are "small" they can work in practice. Typical document formatting problems with dozens of expressible nodes and hundreds of pixels of length are tractable.

Further work on this project will follow a number of directions, including: (1) doing a more complete quantitative analysis of the algorithm; (2) figuring out a more principled way to assign benefit values; (3) generalizing the problem to two dimensions and multiple pages; (4) drawing the content from a content management system.

References

Mann, W. C., & Thompson, S. A. (1988). Rhetorical structure theory: Toward a functional theory of text organization. Text , 8 (3), 243-281.

Marcu, D. (1999). Discourse trees are good indicators of importance in text. In I. Mani, & M. Maybury (Ed.), Advances in Automatic Text Summarization (pp. 123-136). MIT Press.

Moore, J. D., & Paris, C. L. (1993). Planning text for advisory dialogues: Capturing intentional and rhetorical information. *Computational Linguistics* , *19* (4), 651-694.

O'Donnell, M. (1997). Variable Length On-Line Document Generation. *Proceedings of the Sixth European Workshop on NLG.* Duisburg, Germany: Gehard Mercator University.

Paris, C. L., Colineau, N., Lampert, A., & Giralt Duran, J. (2008). *Generation under Space Constraints.* Sydney: CSIRO.

Reiter, E. (2000). Pipelines and Size Constraints. *Computational Linguistics* , *26* (2), 251-259.

Samphaiboon, N., & Yamada, T. (2000). Heuristic and Exact Algorithms for the Precedence-Constrained Knapsack Problem. *Journal of Optimization Theory and Applications* , *105* (3), 659-676.

Spark-Jones, K. (1993). What might be in a summary? In Knorz, Krause, & Womser-Hacker (Ed.), *Proceedings of Information Retrieval 93: Von der modellierung zur anwendung* (pp. 9-26). Universitatsverlag Konstanz.

Preface

Referring Expression Generation Challenges 2008 (REG'08) was the second shared-task evaluation challenge (STEC) in the field of Natural Language Generation (NLG) and took place between September 2007, when REG'08 was first announced, and May 2008, when the evaluation of the participating systems was completed.

REG'08 follows on from the Attribute Selection for Referring Expression Generation Challenge in 2007 (ASGRE'07) which was conceived as a pilot event for shared-task evaluation in NLG. Shared tasks in NLG are themselves a natural continuation of a growing interest in more comparative forms of evaluation among NLG researchers, and mirror trends in other HLT fields.

Since the foundational work of authors such as Appelt, Kronfeld, Grosz, Joshi, Dale and Reiter, Referring Expression Generation (REG) has been the subject of intensive research in NLG, and has — unusually for NLG — led to significant consensus on the REG problem definition, as well as the nature of the inputs and outputs of REG algorithms. This is particularly true of the attribute selection subtask, perhaps the most widely researched NLG subtask, which was the shared task in ASGRE'07. REG'08 included the same task (TUNA-AS), and added two more tasks based on the TUNA corpus: realisation (TUNA-R) and the complete referring expression generation task (TUNA-REG). REG'08 also introduced a new data set of short introductory sections from Wikipedia articles on geographic entities and people (the GREC corpus) and a new task based on it: generation of referring expressions for named entities in the context of a discourse longer than a sentence. The intended application context for this task is improvement of referential clarity in extractive summaries.

In addition to the four shared tasks, REG'08 offered, for each of the two datasets, (i) an open submission track in which participants could submit any work involving the data while opting out of the competetive element, and (ii) an evaluation track, in which proposals for new evaluation methods for the shared task could be submitted. We believe that these two types of open-access tracks are important because they allow the wider research community to shape the focus and methodologies of STECs directly.

We successfully applied (with the help of support letters from many of last year's participants and other HLT colleagues) for funding from the Engineering and Physical Sciences Research Council (EPSRC), the main funding body for HLT in the UK. This support enabled us to double the size of the GREC corpus and to carry out extensive human task performance evaluations, as well as employ a dedicated research fellow (Eric Kow) to help with all aspects of REG'08. It also enabled us to enlist the help of Jette Viethen from Macquarie University with the GREC evaluations.

REG'08 got underway with a first announcement in September 2007. We released samples for both datasets and invited preliminary registrations in January 2008, and released the full Participants' Pack including instructions and training/development data on 22nd February to registered participants. Twelve teams registered for one or more of the TUNA tasks, and five for the GREC Task. Among the participants were teams from Australia, Spain, Ireland, UK, USA, Brazil, Belgium, Netherlands, India and Germany.

By the deadline of 7th April (which was extended slightly), 8 teams submitted 13 systems for TUNA-AS, 4 teams submitted 5 systems for TUNA-R, and 6 teams submitted 15 systems for TUNA-REG. Three teams submitted 6 systems for the brand new GREC task, to which we added four baseline systems. We also received one submission in the TUNA Open Track which applies Portuguese surface realisation to TUNA attribute sets.

The submission process required participants to first submit a report describing their approach and reporting results on the development data for the task(s) they had participated in. For this purpose, they were supplied with programs to compute the relevant evaluation metrics. On submission of the report, they could download the test data, and had 48 hours to submit their outputs on the test set.

All submissions are described in the participants' reports in this volume. We are pleased to say that several of the contributions came from students, as well as from researchers entirely new to the field of NLG.

We had a total of 33 TUNA systems and 10 GREC systems to evaluate. We conducted task-performance experiments for all TUNA-REG systems and the 6 submitted GREC systems. We computed a range of automatic intrinsic measures for all task tracks. For the GREC task, we also tried out a new evaluation idea: automatic *ex*trinsic evaluation using coreference resolution tools. All these evaluation methods are described in detail in the two evaluation reports in this volume.

Preparations are already underway for a third NLG shared-task evaluation event in 2009, Generation Challenges 2009, which will include a TUNA-REG progress check task, a GREC task and a new task on instruction giving in virtual environments (the GIVE Challenge). Results will be presented at ENLG'09.

Like all STECs, REG'08 would not have been possible without the contributions of many different people. We would like to thank the faculty, staff and students of Brighton University and the friends who participated in the evaluation experiments; the INLG'08 organisers, in particular Mike White; the research support team at Brighton University and the EPSRC for help with obtaining funding; Jason Baldridge and Pascal Denis for assistance with the coreference resolvers; and last but not least, the REG'08 participants for making the most of the short available time to build their systems (and for never once complaining, even when they had good reason to). Special thanks are due to Eric Kow and Jette Viethen who worked extremely hard especially during the four weeks of the evaluation period.

Anja Belz and Albert Gatt

The GREC Challenge: Overview and Evaluation Results

Anja Belz **Eric Kow**
NLT Group
University of Brighton
Brighton BN2 4GJ, UK
{asb,eykk10}@bton.ac.uk

Jette Viethen
Centre for LT
Macquarie University
Sydney NSW 2109
jviethen@ics.mq.edu.au

Albert Gatt
Computing Science
University of Aberdeen
Aberdeen AB24 3UE, UK
a.gatt@abdn.ac.uk

Abstract

The GREC Task at REG'08 required participating systems to select coreference chains to the main subject of short encyclopaedic texts collected from Wikipedia. Three teams submitted a total of 6 systems, and we additionally created four baseline systems. Systems were tested automatically using a range of existing intrinsic metrics. We also evaluated systems extrinsically by applying coreference resolution tools to the outputs and measuring the success of the tools. In addition, systems were tested in a reading/comprehension experiment involving human subjects. This report describes the GREC Task and the evaluation methods, gives brief descriptions of the participating systems, and presents the evaluation results.

1 Introduction

The GREC task is about how to generate appropriate references to an entity in the context of a piece of discourse longer than a sentence. Rather than requiring participants to generate referring expressions from scratch, the GREC data provides sets of possible referring expressions for selection. As this is a new referring expression generation (REG) task, the shared task definition was kept fairly simple and the aim for participating systems was to select the appropriate *type* of referring expression (more specifically, its REG08-TYPE, full details below).

The immediate *motivating application context* for the GREC Task is the improvement of referential clarity and coherence in extractive summarisation by regenerating referring expressions in summaries. There has recently been a small flurry of work in this area (Steinberger et al., 2007; Nenkova, 2008). In the longer term, the GREC Task is intended to be a step in the direction of the more general task of generating referential expressions in discourse context.

The GREC Task Corpus is an extension of GREC 1.0 which had about 1,000 texts in the subdomains of cities, countries, rivers and people (Belz and Varges, 2007a). for the purpose of the REG'08 GREC Task, we obtained an additional 1,000 texts in the new subdomain of mountain texts and developed a new XML annotation scheme (Section 2.2).

Five teams from four countries registered for the GREC Task, of which three teams eventually submitted 6 systems. We also used the corpus texts themselves as 'system' outputs, and created four baseline systems. We evaluated the resulting 10 systems using a range of intrinsic and extrinsic evaluation methods. This report presents the results of all evaluations (Section 6), along with descriptions of the GREC data and task (Section 2), test sets (Section 3), evaluation methods (Section 4), and participating systems (Section 5).

2 Data and Task

The GREC Corpus (version 2.0) consists of about 2,000 texts in total, all collected from introductory sections in Wikipedia articles, in five different domains (cities, countries, rivers, people and mountains). In each text, three broad categories of Main Subject Reference (MSR)[1] have been annotated, re-

[1]The main subject of a Wikipedia article is simply taken to be given by its title, e.g. in the cities domain the main subject

sulting in a total of about 13,000 annotated REs.

The corpus was randomly divided into 90% training data (of which 10% were randomly selected as development data) and 10% test data. Participants used the training data in developing their systems, and (as a minimum requirement) reported results on the development data. Participants had 48 hours to submit outputs for the (previously unseen) test data.

2.1 Types of referential expression annotated

Three broad categories of main subject referring expression (MSREs) are annotated in the GREC corpus[2] — subject NPs, object NPs, and genitive NPs and pronouns which function as subject-determiners within their matrix NP. These categories of referring expression (RE) are relatively straightforward to identify and achieve high inter-annotator agreement on (complete agreement among four annotators in 86% of MSRs), and account for most cases of overt main subject reference (MSR) in the GREC texts. The annotators were asked to identify subject, object and genitive subject-determiners and decide whether or not they refer to the main subject of the text. More detail is provided in Belz and Varges (2007b).

In addition to the above, relative pronouns in supplementary relative clauses (as opposed to integrated relative clauses, Huddleston and Pullum, 2002, p. 1058) were annotated, e.g.:

(1) *Stoichkov is a football manager and former striker who was a member of the Bulgaria national team that finished fourth at the 1994 FIFA World Cup.*

We also annotated 'non-realised' subject MSREs in a restricted set of cases of VP coordination where an MSRE is the subject of the coordinated VPs, e.g.:

(2) *He stated the first version of the Law of conservation of mass, __ introduced the Metric system, and __ helped to reform chemical nomenclature.*

The motivation for annotating the approximate place where the subject NP would be if it were realised (the gap-like underscores above) is that from a generation perspective there is a choice to be made about whether to realise the subject NP in the second and third coordinates or not.

(and title) of one text is *London*.

[2]In terminology and view of grammar the annotations rely heavily on Huddleston and Pullum (2002).

2.2 XML format

Figure 1 is one of the texts distributed in the GREC data sample for the REG Challenge. The REF element indicates a reference, in the sense of 'an instance of referring' (which could, in principle, be realised by gesture or graphically, as well as by a string of words, or a combination of these). REFs have three attributes: ID, a unique reference identifier; SEMCAT, the semantic category of the referent, ranging over city, country, river, person, mountain; and SYNCAT, the syntactic category required of referential expressions for the referent in this discourse context (np-obj, np-subj, subj-det). A REF is composed of one REFEX element (the 'selected' referential expression for the given reference; in the corpus texts it is simply the referential expression found in the corpus) and one ALT-REFEX element which in turn is a list of REFEXs which are alternative referential expressions obtained by other means (see following section).

REFEX elements have four attributes. The HEAD attribute has the possible values nominal, pronoun, and rel-pron; the CASE attribute has the possible values nominative, accusative and genitive for pronouns, and plain and genitive for nominals. The binary-valued EMPHATIC attribute indicates whether the RE is emphatic; in the present version of the GREC corpus, the only type of RE that has this attribute is one which incorporates a reflexive pronoun used emphatically (e.g. *India itself*). The REG08-TYPE attribute indicates basic RE type as required for the REG'08 GREC task definition. The choice of types is motivated by the hypothesis that one of the most basic decisions to be taken in RE selection for named entities is whether to use an RE that includes a name, such as *Modern India* (the corresponding REG08-TYPE value is name); whether to go for a common-noun RE, i.e. with a category noun like *country* as the head (common); whether to pronominalise the RE (pronoun); or whether it can be left unrealised (empty).

2.3 The REG'08 GREC Task

The task for participating systems was to develop a method for selecting one of the REFEXs in the ALT-REFEX list, for each REF in each TEXT in the test sets. The test data inputs were identical to the

```xml
<?xml version="1.0" encoding="utf-8"?>
<!DOCTYPE TEXT SYSTEM "reg08-grec.dtd">
<TEXT ID="36">
<TITLE>Jean Baudrillard</TITLE>
<PARAGRAPH>
 <REF ID="36.1" SEMCAT="person" SYNCAT="np-subj">
  <REFEX REG08-TYPE="name" EMPHATIC="no" HEAD="nominal" CASE="plain">Jean Baudrillard</REFEX>
  <ALT-REFEX>
   <REFEX REG08-TYPE="name" EMPHATIC="no" HEAD="nominal" CASE="plain">Jean Baudrillard</REFEX>
   <REFEX REG08-TYPE="name" EMPHATIC="yes" HEAD="nominal" CASE="plain">Jean Baudrillard himself</REFEX>
   <REFEX REG08-TYPE="empty">_</REFEX>
   <REFEX REG08-TYPE="pronoun" EMPHATIC="no" HEAD="pronoun" CASE="nominative">he</REFEX>
   <REFEX REG08-TYPE="pronoun" EMPHATIC="yes" HEAD="pronoun" CASE="nominative">he himself</REFEX>
   <REFEX REG08-TYPE="pronoun" EMPHATIC="no" HEAD="rel-pron" CASE="nominative">who</REFEX>
   <REFEX REG08-TYPE="pronoun" EMPHATIC="yes" HEAD="rel-pron" CASE="nominative">who himself</REFEX>
  </ALT-REFEX>
 </REF>
 (born June 20, 1929) is a cultural theorist, philosopher, political commentator,
 sociologist, and photographer.
 <REF ID="36.2" SEMCAT="person" SYNCAT="subj-det">
  <REFEX REG08-TYPE="pronoun" EMPHATIC="no" HEAD="pronoun" CASE="genitive">His</REFEX>
  <ALT-REFEX>
   <REFEX REG08-TYPE="name" EMPHATIC="no" HEAD="nominal" CASE="genitive">Jean Baudrillard's</REFEX>
   <REFEX REG08-TYPE="pronoun" EMPHATIC="no" HEAD="pronoun" CASE="genitive">his</REFEX>
   <REFEX REG08-TYPE="pronoun" EMPHATIC="no" HEAD="rel-pron" CASE="genitive">whose</REFEX>
  </ALT-REFEX>
 </REF>
 work is frequently associated with postmodernism and post-structuralism.
</PARAGRAPH>
</TEXT>
```

Figure 1: Example text from REG'08 Training Data.

training/development data, except that REF elements contained only an ALT-REFEX list, not the preceding 'selected' REFEX. ALT-REFEX lists are generated for each text by an automatic method which collects all the (manually annotated) MSREs in a text including the title and adds several defaults: pronouns and reflexive pronouns in all subdomains; and category nouns (e.g. *the river*), in all subdomains except people. The main objective in the REG'08 GREC Task was to get the REG08-TYPE attribute of REFEXs right.

3 Test Data

1. GREC Test Set C-1: a randomly selected 10% subset (183 texts) of the GREC corpus (with the same proportions of texts in the 5 subdomains as in the training/testing data).

2. GREC Test Set C-2: the same subset of texts as in C-1; however, for C-2 we did not use the MSREs in the corpus, but replaced each of them with three human-selected alternatives. These were obtained in an online experiment as described in Belz & Varges (2007a) where subjects selected MSREs in a setting that duplicated the conditions in which the participating systems in the REG'08 GREC Task made selections.[3] We obtained three versions of each text, where in each version all MSREs were selected by the same person. The motivation for creating this version of Test Set C was firstly that having several human-produced chains of MSREs to compare the outputs of participating ('peer') systems against is more reliable than having one only; and secondly that Wikipedia texts are edited by multiple authors and so MSR chains may sometimes be adversely affected by this; we wanted to have additional reference texts without this characteristic.

3. GREC Test Set L: 74 Wikipedia introductory texts from the subdomain of lakes; participants did not know what this subdomain was until they received the test data (there were no lake texts in the training/development set).

4. GREC Test Set P: 31 short encyclopaedic texts in the same 5 subdomains as in the GREC corpus, in approximately the same proportions as in the training/testing data, but from a source other than

[3]The experiment can be tried out here: http://www.nltg.brighton.ac.uk/home/Anja.Belz/TESTDRIVE/

Wikipedia. We transcribed these texts from printed encyclopaedias published in the 1980s which are not available in electronic form, and this provenance was not revealed to participants. The texts in this set are much shorter and more homogeneous than the Wikipedia texts, and the sequences of MSRs follow very similar patterns. It seems likely that it is these properties that have resulted in better scores overall for Test Set P (see Section 6).

Each test set was designed to test peer systems for a different aspect of generalisation. Test Set C tests for generalisation to unseen material from the same corpus and the same subdomains as the training set; Test Set L tests for generalisation to unseen material from the same corpus but different subdomain; and Test Set P tests generalisation to a different corpus but same subdomains.

4 Evaluation methods

4.1 Automatic intrinsic evaluations

Accuracy of REG08-Type: when computed against the single-RE test sets (C-1, L and P), REG08-Type Accuracy is the proportion of REFEXs selected by a participating system that have a REG08-TYPE value identical to the one in the corpus.

When computed against the triple-RE test set (C-2), first the number of correct REG08-Types is computed at the text level for each of the three versions of a corpus text and the maximum of these is determined; then the maximum text-level numbers are summed and divided by the total number of REFs in all the texts, which gives the global REG08-Type Accuracy score. The rationale behind computing the REG08-Type Accuracy scores in this way for multiple-RE test sets (maximising scores on RE chains rather than individual REs) is that an RE is not good or bad in its own right, but depends on the other MSRs in the same text.[4]

String Accuracy: This is defined just like REG08-Type Accuracy, except here what is determined is identity between REFEX word strings (the MSREs themselves), not between REG08-Types.

String-edit distance metrics: String-edit distance (SE) is straightforward Levenshtein distance with a substitution cost of 2 and insertion/deletion cost of 1. We also used the version of string-edit distance described by Bangalore et al. (2000) which normalises for length. This version is denoted 'SEB' below. For the single-RE test sets, the global score is simply the average of all RE-level scores. For Test Set C-2, we used an approach analogous to that described above for REG08-Type Accuracy. We first computed the best string-edit distance at the text level (here, just the sum of RE-level distances) and then obtained the global distance by dividing the sum of best text-level distances by the number of REFs in all the texts.

Other metrics: BLEU is a precision metric from MT that assesses the quality of a peer translation in terms of the proportion of its word n-grams ($n \leq 4$ is standard) that it shares with several reference translations. We used BLEU-3 rather than the more standard BLEU-4 because most REs in the corpus are less than 4 tokens long. We also used the NIST version of BLEU which weights in favour of less frequent n-grams, as well as ROUGE-2 and ROUGE-SU4 (the two official automatic scores from the DUC summarisation competitions). In all cases, we assessed just the MSREs selected by peer systems (leaving out the surrounding text), and computed scores globally (rather than averaging over RE-level scores), as this is standard for these metrics.

BLEU, NIST and ROUGE are designed to work with either one or multiple reference texts, so we did not need to use a different method for Test Set C-2.

4.2 Human extrinsic evaluation

We designed a reading/comprehension experiment in which the task for subjects was to read texts one sentence at a time and then to answer three brief multiple-choice comprehension questions after reading each text. The basic idea was that it seemed likely that badly chosen MSR reference chains would adversely affect ease of comprehension, and that this might in turn affect reading speed and accuracy in answering comprehension questions.

We used a randomly selected subset of 21 texts from Test Set C, and recruited 21 subjects from among the staff, faculty and students of Brighton and Sussex universities. We used a Repeated Latin Squares design in which each combination of text and system was allocated three trials. During the experiment we recorded *SRTime*, the time subjects

[4]This definition is also slightly different from the one given in the Participants' Pack.

took to read sentences (from the point when the sentence appeared on the screen to the point at which the subject requested the next sentence).

We also recorded the speed and accuracy with which subjects answered the questions at the end (*Q-Time* and *Q-Acc*). The role of the comprehension questions was to encourage subjects to read the texts properly, rather than skimming through them, and we did not necessarily expect any significant results from the associated measures.

The questions were designed to be of varying degrees of difficulty and predictability. There was one set of three questions (each with five possible answers) associated with each text, and questions followed the same pattern across the texts: the first question was always about the subdomain of a text; the second about the location of the main subject; the third question was designed not to be predictable.

The order of the answers was randomised for each question and each subject. The order of texts (with associated questions) was randomised for each subject. We used the DMDX package for presentation of sentences and measuring reading times and question answering accuracy (Forster and Forster, 2003). Subjects did the experiment in a quiet room, under supervision.

4.3 Automatic extrinsic evaluation

As a new and highly experimental method, we tried out an automatic approach to extrinsic evaluation. The basic idea was similar to that in the human-based experiments described above: badly chosen reference chains seem likely to affect the reader's ability to resolve REs. In the automatic version, the role of the reader is played by an automatic coreference resolution tool and the expectation is that the tool performs worse (are less able to identify coreference chains correctly) with worse MSR reference chains.

To counteract the potential problem of results being a function of a specific coreference resolution algorithm or tool, we decided to use three different resolvers—those included in LingPipe,[5] JavaRap (Qiu et al., 2004) and OpenNLP (Morton, 2005)—and to average results.

There does not appear to be a single standard evaluation metric in the coreference resolution community, so we opted to use three: MUC-6 (Vilain et al., 1995), CEAF (Luo, 2005), and B-CUBED (Bagga and Baldwin, 1998), which seem to be the most widely accepted metrics.

All three metrics compute Recall, Precision and F-Scores on aligned gold-standard and resolver-tool coreference chains. They differ in how the alignment is obtained and what components of coreference chains are counted for calculating scores. Results for the automatic extrinsic evaluations are reported below in terms of the F-Scores from these three metrics, as well as in terms of their average.

5 Systems

Base-rand, Base-freq, Base-1st, Base-name: We created four baseline systems. *Base-rand* selects one of the REFEXs at random. *Base-freq* selects the REFEX that is the overall most frequent given the SYNCAT and SEMCAT of the reference. *Base-1st* always selects the REFEX which appears first in the list of REFEXs; and *Base-name* selects the shortest REFEX with attributes REG08-TYPE=name, HEAD=nominal and EMPHATIC=no.[6]

CNTS-Type-g, CNTS-Prop-s: The CNTS systems are trained using memory-based learning with automatic parameter optimisation. They use a set of 14 features obtained by various kinds of syntactic preprocessing and named-entity recognition as well as from the corpus annotations: SEMCAT, SYNCAT, position of RE in text, neighbouring words and POS-tags, distance to previous mention, SYNCATs of three preceding REFEXs, binary feature indicating whether the most recent named entity was the main subject (MS), main verb of the sentence. For *Type-g*, a single classifier was trained to predict just the REG08-TYPE property of REFEXs. For *Prop-s*, four classifiers were trained, one for each subdomain, to predict all four properties of REFEXs (rather than just REG08-TYPE).

OSU-b-all, OSU-b-nonRE, OSU-n-nonRE: The OSU-2 systems are maximum-entropy classifiers trained on a range of features obtained by prepro-

[5] http://alias-i.com/lingpipe/

[6] Attributes are tried in this order. If for one attribute, the right value is not found, the process ignores that attribute and moves on the next one.

System	REG08-Type Accuracy for Development Set					
	All	Cities	Coun	Riv	Peop	Moun
CNTS-Type-g	76.52	64.65	75	65	85.37	75.42
CNTS-Prop-s	73.93	65.66	69.57	70	79.51	74.58
IS-G	66	54.5	64	80	66.8	65
OSU-n-nonRE	62.50	53.54	63.04	65	67.32	61.67
OSU-b-all	58.54	53.54	57.61	75	65.85	49.58
OSU-b-nonRE	51.07	51.52	53.26	40	57.07	45.83

Table 1: Self-reported REG08-Type Accuracy scores for development set.

cessing the text, as well as from the corpus annotations: SEMCAT, SYNCAT, position of RE in text, presence of contrasting discourse entity, distance between current and preceding reference to the MS, string similarity measures between REFEXs and title of text. *OSU-b-all* and *OSU-b-nonRE* are binary classifiers which give the likelihood of selecting a given REFEX vs. not selecting it, whereas *OSU-n-nonRE* is a 4-class classifier giving the likelihoods of selecting each of the four REG08-TYPEs. *OSU-b-all* also uses the REFEX attributes as features.

IS-G: The IS-G system is a multi-layer perceptron which uses four features obtained by preprocessing texts as well as from the corpus annotations: SYNCAT, distance between current and preceding reference to the MS, position of RE in text, REG08-TYPE of preceding reference to the MS, feature indicating whether the preceding MSR is in the same sentence.

6 Results

This section presents the results of all the evaluation methods described in Section 4. We start with REG08-Type Accuracy, an intrinsic automatic metric which participating teams were told was going to be the chief evaluation method, followed by other intrinsic automatic metrics (Section 6.2), the extrinsic human evaluation (Section 6.3) and the extrinsic automatic evaluation (Section 6.4).

6.1 REG08-Type Accuracy

Participants computed REG08-Type Accuracy for the development set (97 texts) themselves, using a tool provided by us. These scores are shown in Table 1, and are also included in the participants' reports elsewhere in this volume. Systems are ordered in terms of their overall REG08-Type Accuracy (column 1), and scores for each subdomain are also shown. Scores are highly consistent across the subdomains, except for the river subdomain which was the smallest set (containing only 4 texts), and results for it may be idiosyncratic for this reason.

Corresponding results for the (unseen) test set C-1 are shown in column 2 of Table 2. As would be expected, results are slightly worse than for the (seen) development set (although some systems managed to improve over their development set scores). Also included in this table are results for the four baseline systems, and it is clear that selecting the most frequent REG08-Type given SEMCAT and SYNCAT (as done by the Base-freq system) provides a strong baseline.

Other columns in Table 2 contain results for test sets L and P. Again as expected, results for Test Set L are lower than for Test Set C-1, because in addition to consisting of unseen texts (like C-1), Test Set L is also from an unseen subdomain (unlike C-1). The results for Test Set P are higher and on a par with those for the development set, probably for the reasons discussed at the end of Section 3.

For each test set in Table 2 we carried out a univariate ANOVA with System as the fixed factor. We found significant main effects at $p < .001$ in all three cases (C-1: $F = 95.426$; L: $F = 63.758$; P: $F = 21.188$). The columns containing capital letters in Table 2 show the homogeneous subsets of systems as determined by post-hoc Tukey HSD comparisons of means. Systems whose REG08-Type Accuracy scores are not significantly different (at the .05 level) share a letter.

The results for REG08-Type Accuracy computed against the triple-RE Test Set C-2 are shown in Table 3. These should be considered as the chief results of the GREC Task evaluations, as stated in the guidelines. Here too we performed a univariate ANOVA with System as the fixed factor and REG08-Type as the dependent variable. Having established by ANOVA that there was a significant main effect of System ($F = 86.946$, $p < .001$), we compared the mean scores with Tukey's HSD. As can be seen from the resulting homogeneous subsets, there is no significant difference between the corpus texts (C-1) and system CNTS-Type-g, but also there is no sig-

single-RE Test Set C-1						Test Set L						Test Set P						
CNTS-Type-g	68.15	A				CNTS-Type-g	62.06	A				CNTS-Type-g	75.31	A				
CNTS-Prop-s	67.04	A				CNTS-Prop-s	62.06	A				CNTS-Prop-s	72.84	A	B			
IS-G	66.48	A				IS-G	60.93	A				IS-G	67.90	A	B	C		
OSU-n-nonRE	63.69	A				OSU-n-nonRE	41.80		B			OSU-n-nonRE	66.67	A	B	C		
OSU-b-nonRE	53.11		B			OSU-b-nonRE	39.23		B			OSU-b-all	57.41		B	C	D	
OSU-b-all	52.39		B			OSU-b-all	37.62		B	C		OSU-b-nonRE	56.17			C	D	
Base-freq	43.47			C		Base-freq	35.53		B	C		Base-freq	44.44				D	F
Base-name	39.49			C		Base-rand	23.63			C	D	Base-rand	33.95					F
Base-1st	39.17			C		Base-name	23.63				D	Base-name	32.10					F
Base-rand	32.72				D	Base-1st	29.74				D	Base-rand	32.10					F

Table 2: REG08-Type Accuracy scores and homogeneous subsets (Tukey HSD, alpha = .05) for single-RE test sets. Systems that do not share a letter are significantly different.

System	REG08-Type Accuracy for multiple-RE Test Set C-2										
	All						Cities	Countries	Rivers	People	Mountains
Corpus	*78.58*	*A*					*70.92*	*77.49*	*85.29*	*84.67*	*75.81*
CNTS-Type-g	72.61	A	B				65.96	71.73	73.53	77.64	70.73
CNTS-Prop-s	71.34		B				64.54	67.02	70.59	75.38	71.75
IS-G	70.78		B				69.50	65.45	76.47	76.88	67.89
OSU-n-nonRE	69.82		B				65.25	64.92	79.41	78.14	65.65
OSU-b-nonRE	58.76			C			52.48	60.73	50.00	59.80	59.55
OSU-b-all	57.48			C			53.90	58.64	47.06	59.05	57.52
Base-name	50.00				D		53.19	54.45	35.29	43.22	53.86
Base-1st	49.28				D		53.19	49.21	38.24	43.22	53.86
Base-freq	48.17				D		43.97	42.41	55.88	56.78	44.11
Base-rand	41.24					E	41.84	36.13	32.35	44.47	41.06

Table 3: REG08-Type Accuracy scores against Test Set C-2 for complete set and for subdomains; homogeneous subsets (Tukey HSD, alpha = .05) for complete set only (systems that do not share a letter are significantly different).

nificant difference between the latter and systems CNTS-Prop-s, IS-G and OSU-n-nonRE. In this analysis, all systems outperform the random baseline; all peer systems outperform all of the baselines; and the four best peer systems outperform the remaining two.

6.2 Other automatic intrinsic metrics

In addition to the chief evaluation measure reported on in the preceding section, we computed the string similarity metrics described in Section 4.1 for all four test sets. Results were very similar to those for REG08-Type Accuracy, so we are reporting only scores for Test Set C-2 (Table 4). The corpus texts again receive the best scores across the board (SE is the odd one out, because here lower scores are better). Ranks for peer systems are very similar to the results reported in the last section.

We performed an ANOVA ($F = 138.159$, $p < .001$) and Tukey HSD post-hoc analysis for String Accuracy. The resulting homogeneous subsets (Table 4, columns 3–8) reveal significant differences similar to those for REG08-Type Accuracy. We also computed Pearson product-moment correlation coefficients between all automatic intrinsic evaluation measures we used. All pairwise correlations were significant at the .01 level (using a two-tailed test). One of the strongest correlations (.961) was between REG08-Type Accuracy and String Accuracy, implying that getting REG08-Type right gets you some way towards getting the actual RE right.

6.3 Human-based extrinsic measures

As a result of the experiment described in Section 4.2 we had SRTime measures (sentence reading times) for each sentence in each of the 21 texts that were included in the experiment. Table 5 shows the resulting SRTimes in milliseconds averaged per system. None of the differences were statistically significant. We also analysed SRTimes normalised by sentence length; SRTimes only from sentences that contained MRSs; and SRTimes normalised for subject reading speed. There were no significant differences under any of these analyses.

Much of the variance in SRTimes was due to subjects' very different average reading speeds: means of SRTime normalised for sentence length ranged from 188.45ms to 426.10ms for individual subjects.

System	Word string similarity for Triple-RE Test Set C-2												
	String Accuracy							BLEU-3	NIST	ROUGE-2	ROUGE-SU4	SE	SEB
Corpus	*71.18*	*A*						*0.7792*	*7.5080*	*0.66102*	*0.70991*	*0.7229*	*0.5136*
CNTS-Type-g	65.61	A	B					0.7377	6.1288	0.60280	0.64998	0.8838	0.3627
CNTS-Prop-s	65.29	A	B					0.6760	5.9338	0.60103	0.64963	0.9068	0.3835
OSU-n-nonRE	63.85		B	C				0.6715	5.7745	0.53395	0.57459	0.9666	0.0164
IS-G	58.20			C				0.5107	5.6102	0.50270	0.57052	1.1616	0.1818
OSU-b-nonRE	51.11				D			0.4964	5.5363	0.38255	0.42969	1.2834	0.0247
OSU-b-all	50.72				D			0.5050	5.6058	0.35133	0.39570	1.2994	0.3402
Base-freq	41.32					E		0.2684	3.0155	0.27727	0.33007	1.54299	-0.3250
Base-name	39.41					E		0.4641	5.9372	0.20730	0.25379	1.5175	-0.1912
Base-1st	39.09					E		0.3932	5.1597	0.21443	0.24037	1.6449	-0.0751
Base-rand	17.99						F	0.2182	2.9327	0.36056	0.41847	2.3217	-0.7937

Table 4: String Accuracy, BLEU, NIST, ROUGE and string-edit scores, computed on single-RE and triple-RE test sets (systems in order of String Accuracy); homogeneous subsets (Tukey HSD, alpha = .05) for String Accuracy only (systems that do not share a letter are significantly different).

	Mean SRTime (msecs)
CNTS-Prop-s	6305.8551
IS-G	6340.5131
OSU-n-nonRE	6422.5073
CNTS-Type-g	6435.6574
OSU-b-all	6451.7624
OSU-b-nonRE	6454.6749
Corpus	*6548.2734*

Table 5: Mean SRTimes for each system.

Question 1				Q2	Q3
Corpus	*1.00*	*A*		*.78*	*.63*
CNTS-Type-g	1.00	A	B	.83	.71
CNTS-Prop-s	.98	A	B	.86	.75
OSU-b-nonRE	.97	A	B	.83	.67
OSU-b-all	.95	A	B	.75	.62
IS-G	.95	A	B	.81	.63
OSU-n-nonRE	.90		B	.76	.76

Table 6: Question types 1–3, proportions correct; homogeneous subsets for Q1 (Tukey HSD, alpha = .05).

There was also variance from Text, i.e. some of the texts appear to be harder to read than others.

The other two measures from the task-performance experiment were Q-Acc (question answering accuracy) and Q-Time (question answering speed). ANOVAs revealed no significant main effect of System on Q-Time. For Q-Acc, we looked at each of the three question types Q1, Q2, Q3 (see Section 4.2) separately. ANOVAs showed no significant effect of System on Q-Acc for Q2 and Q3; there was a slight effect ($F = 2.193, p < .05$) of System on Q-Acc for Q1 (the easiest of the questions which simply asked for the subdomain of a text). Table 6 shows Q-Acc for Q1 and Q2, and the results of a post-hoc analysis (Tukey HSD) which revealed two homogeneous subsets with a lot of overlap (columns 2 and 3).

Table 6 shows the results of this analysis: there was

6.4 Automatic extrinsic measures

We used the same 21 texts as in the human extrinsic experiments, fed the outputs of each peer system as well as the corpus texts through the three coreference resolvers, and computed average MUC, CEAF and B-CUBED F-Scores as described in Section 4.3. The second column Table 7 shows the average of these three F-Scores, to give a single overall result for this evaluation method. A univariate ANOVA with the average F-Score (column 2) as the dependent variable and System as the single fixed factor revealed a significant main effect of System on average F-Score ($F = 5.051, p < .001$). A post-hoc comparison of the means (Tukey HSD, alpha = .05) found the significant differences indicated by the homogeneous subsets in columns 3–5 (Table 7). The numbers shown in the last three columns are the separate MUC, CEAF and B-CUBED F-Scores for each system, averaged over the three resolver tools. ANOVAs revealed the following effects of System: on CEAF $F = 9.984, p < .001$; on MUC: $F = 10.07, p < .001$; on B-CUBED: $F = 8.446, p < .001$.

The three F-Score measures (MUC, CEAF and B-CUBED) are all strongly and highly significantly correlated: Pearson's correlation coefficient is .947 for B-CUBED and CEAF, .917 for B-CUBED and MUC, and .951 for CEAF and MUC ($p < .01$, 2-tailed).

System	(MUC+CEAF+B3)/3				MUC	CEAF	B3
Base-1st	53.50	A			47.59	52.64	60.28
Base-name	52.84	A			45.99	51.73	60.81
OSU-n-nonRE	51.39	A			46.92	49.8	57.45
OSU-b-nonRE	51.27	A			47.68	48.62	57.50
OSU-b-all	50.87	A			47.06	48.40	57.14
CNTS-Type-g	48.64	A	B		43.77	46.32	55.82
IS-G	48.05	A	B		43.25	46.24	54.66
CNTS-Prop-s	46.35	A	B		42.82	43.36	52.88
Corpus	*43.32*	*A*	*B*		*37.89*	*41.6*	*50.47*
Base-freq	41.41		B	C	34.48	40.28	49.46
Base-rand	35.13			C	21.24	35.60	48.55

Table 7: MUC, CEAF and B-CUBED F-Scores for all systems; homogeneous subsets (Tukey HSD), alpha = .05, for average of F-Scores.

7 Concluding Remarks

The GREC Task is a new task not only for an NLG shared-task challenge, but also as a research task in general (improving referential clarity in extractive summaries seems to be just taking off as a research subfield). It was therefore not unexpected that only three teams were able to participate in this task.

We continued the traditions of the ASGRE'07 Challenge in that we used a wide range of evaluation metrics to obtain a well-rounded view of the quality of the participating systems. It had been our intention to use evaluation methods in all four possible extrinsic/intrinsic and automatic/human combinations. However, the combination intrinsic/human is missing from this report and will have to be left to future research.

There was no indication in the human task performance experiment that the different reference chains selected by different systems had any impact on subjects' reading speeds, and the evidence that there is an effect on comprehension was scant. This means that we will need to investigate alternative task-performance measures. Because of the lack of significant results from the human extrinsic experiment, we were also unable to validate the automatic extrinsic experiment against it, and so at this point we do not really know how useful it is (despite some correlation with intrinsic measures), something we will seek to establish in future research.

Acknowledgments

Many thanks to Jason Baldridge and Pascal Denis for help with selecting coreference resolution tools and metrics, and to the colleagues and students who helped with the task-performance experiment. Thanks are also due to the members of the Corpora and SIGGEN mailing lists, colleagues, friends and friends of friends who helped with the online MSRE selection experiment.

References

A. Bagga and B. Baldwin. 1998. Algorithms for scoring coreference chains. In *Proceedings of the Linguistic Coreference Workshop at LREC'98*, pages 563–566.

S. Bangalore, O. Rambow, and S. Whittaker. 2000. Evaluation metrics for generation. In *Proceedings of INLG'00*, pages 1–8.

A. Belz and S. Varges. 2007a. Generation of repeated references to discourse entities. In *Proceedings of ENLG'07*, pages 9–16.

A. Belz and S. Varges. 2007b. The GREC corpus: Main subject reference in context. Technical Report NLTG-07-01, University of Brighton.

K. I. Forster and J. C. Forster. 2003. DMDX: A windows display program with millisecond accuracy. *Behavior Research Methods, Instruments, & Computers*, 35(1):116–124.

R. Huddleston and G. Pullum. 2002. *The Cambridge Grammar of the English Language*. Cambridge University Press.

X. Luo. 2005. On coreference resolution performance metrics. *Proc. of HLT-EMNLP*, pages 25–32.

T. Morton. 2005. *Using Semantic Relations to Improve Information Retrieval*. Ph.D. thesis, University of Pensylvania.

A. Nenkova. 2008. Entity-driven rewrite for multi-document summarization. In *Proceedings of IJCNLP'08*.

L. Qiu, M. Kan, and T.-S. Chua. 2004. A public reference implementation of the rap anaphora resolution algorithm. In *Proceedings of LREC'04*, pages 291–294.

J. Steinberger, M. Poesio, M. Kabadjov, and K. Jezek. 2007. Two uses of anaphora resolution in summarization. *Information Processing and Management: Special issue on Summarization*, 43(6):1663–1680.

M. Vilain, J. Burger, J. Aberdeen, D. Connolly, and L. Hirschman. 1995. A model-theoretic coreference scoring scheme. *Proceedings of MUC-6*, pages 45–52.

IS-G: The Comparison of Different Learning Techniques for the Selection of the Main Subject References

Bernd Bohnet
University of Stuttgart
Visualization and Interactive Systems Group
Universitätstr. 58, 70569 Stuttgart, Germany
bohnet@informatik.uni-stuttgart.de

Abstract

The GREC task of the Referring Expression Generation Challenge 2008 is to select appropriate references to the main subject in given texts. This means to select the correct type of the referring expressions such as *name*, *pronoun*, *common*, or *elision (empty)*. We employ for the selection different learning techniques with the aim to find the most appropriate one for the task and the used attributes. As training data, we use the syntactic category of the searched referring expressions and additionally gathered data from the text itself.

1 Introduction

The training data of the GREC task consists of Wikipedia articles from five domains. The articles are about People, Cities, Countries, Rivers, and Mountains. An XML annotation replaces the original referring expressions in the articles with a set of alternative experssions which could be inserted in the empty space in order to complete the text. The training data additionally consists of the original referring expressions. From the annotations, we use for the training the *syntactic category* (SYNCAT) for the searched referring expression.

The annotation allows us easily to access additional data. One of the values that we calculate is the *distance* (DIST) to the last referring expression. The idea behind this value is that the references becomes with increasing *distance* unclear because of other content in the text and therefore, to provide a short form such as a pronoun is not enough or would be even misleading. Of cause there might be other reasons to use the name too. The next information, we use is the *count* (POS) of the referring expression in the text. Because we expect that the first referring expression is in most cases the name of the main subject and at the end of a text, it might be used less frequent. Then we use the type of the *last* (LAST) used referring expression in the text. This might be a good candidate because people want to avoid consecutive repetitions of the same word. The disadvantage of this attribute is that it is based itself on the classification of its predecessor and therefore, on insecure information. Finally, we use a second distance measure which provides the information if the last referring expression was in the same sentence (SENT).

2 Comparison of Learning Techniques

We tried several machine learning techniques and selected among them the three bests that are Bayesian Networks with the attribute selection method K2 (Cooper and Herskovits, 1992), decision trees C4.5 (Quinlan, 1993), and Multi Layer Perceptrons with a sigmoid function (Minsky and Papert, 1969). For the comparison with the three machine learning techniques, we provide in Table 1 a base line where we chose the type with the most occurrences in the training data of the domain.

Table 2 shows the results for the Bayesian Network. The results are significant better then the base line results. Table 3 shows the results of C4.5. The results are close to the results of the Bayesian Network. An advantage of decision trees is that they provide some explanation. A part of the decision tree is shown in Figure 1. The part selects a refer-

Set	Most frequent type	Accuracy
Cities	name	0.47
Countries	name	0.45
Mountains	name	0.39
People	pronoun	0.61
Rivers	name	0.43
Total	–	0.47

Table 1: Base Line

Set	Cities	Cou.	Mount.	Peo.	Ri.	Total
Acc	0.48	0.62	0.63	0.673	0.7	0.62

Table 2: Results for Bayesian Networks (K2)

ring expression in the case that the last expression was already within the same sentences.

Set	Cities	Cou.	Mount.	Peo.	Ri.	Total
Acc	0.545	0.63	0.641	0.673	0.7	0.638

Table 3: Results for C4.5

The uppercase words are the attributes followed by the value for the branch. If the value of a distinct instance is in the range of the value then the algorithms chooses the branch until it reaches a leaf. The leafs are labelled with the result of the decision and with information of an evaluation that provides the information how many training instances (cases) are classified correct / wrong. Interesting for the case are the following observations:

- The text writers chose nearly always (>99%) an other referring expression than the name.
- They select more frequent pronouns and an elisions (empty) compared to common names.
- The writers select common names in case of a high distance to the last referring expression.

Table 4 shows the results for the Multi Layer Perceptron, which performed best compared to the other learning techniques.

3 Conclusion

We calculated the information gain of each attribute to get an overview of the relevance of the attributes. The most releveant attribute is DIST (0.32) followed by POS (0.24), LAST (0.239), SENT (0.227), and SYNCAT (0.19).

```
SENT = true
— SYNCAT = subj-det
—— DIST <= 158: pronoun (103.0/8.0)
—— DIST > 158: common (4.0/1.0)
— SYNCAT = np-subj
—— DIST <= 33: pronoun (32.0/15.0)
—— DIST > 33
——— LAST = common
———— DIST <= 123: empty (25.0/5.0)
———— DIST > 123: common (2.0/1.0)
——— LAST = pronoun: empty (69.0/22.0)
——— LAST = name
———— POS <= 2: empty (17.0/2.0)
———— POS > 2
————— POS <= 15
—————— DIST <= 79
——————— DIST <= 39: pronoun (3.0)
——————— DIST > 39: empty (46.0/15.0)
—————— DIST > 79
——————— POS <= 5: pronoun (3.0)
——————— POS > 5
———————— POS <= 11
————————— DIST <= 113: common (4.0/1.0)
————————— DIST > 113: name (2.0/1.0)
———————— POS > 11: pronoun (2.0)
————— POS > 15: common (2.0)
——— LAST = empty: pronoun (5.0/1.0)
— SYNCAT = np-obj
—— DIST <= 109
——— POS <= 9: pronoun (23.0/12.0)
——— POS > 9: common (10.0/4.0)
—— DIST > 109: common (17.0/3.0)
SENT = false
...
```

Figure 1: Part of the decision tree

The results of all three learning techniques are significant better than the base line which has in average an accuracy of 0.47. The multi layer perceptron provides the best results with an average accuracy of 0.66.

References

G. F. Cooper and E. Herskovits. 1992. A Bayesian Method for the Induction of Probabilistic Networks from Data. In *Machine Learning 9*.

M. Minsky and S. Papert. 1969. *Perceptrons*. MIT Press.

J. R. Quinlan. 1993. *C4.5 Programs for Machine Learning*. Morgan Kaufmann, California.

Set	Cities	Cou.	Mount.	Peo.	Ri.	Total
Acc	0.545	0.64	0.65	0.668	0.8	0.66

Table 4: IS-G: Multi Layer Perceptron

CNTS: Memory-Based Learning of Generating Repeated References

Iris Hendrickx, Walter Daelemans, Kim Luyckx, Roser Morante, Vincent Van Asch
CNTS, Department of Linguistics
University of Antwerp
Prinsstraat 13, 2000, Antwerp, Belgium
firstname.lastname@ua.ac.be

Abstract

In this paper we describe our machine learning approach to the generation of referring expressions. As our algorithm we use memory-based learning. Our results show that in case of predicting the TYPE of the expression, having one general classifier gives the best results. On the contrary, when predicting the full set of properties of an expression, a combined set of specialized classifiers for each subdomain gives the best performance.

1 Introduction

In this paper we describe the systems with which we participated in the GREC task of the REG 2008 challenge (Belz and Varges, 2007). The GREC task concerns predicting which expression is appropriate to refer to a particular discourse referent in a certain position in a text, given a set of alternative referring expressions for selection. The organizers provided the GREC corpus that consists of 2000 texts collected from Wikipedia, from 5 different subdomains (people, cities, countries, mountains and rivers) .

One of the main goals of the task is to discover what kind of information is useful in the input to make the decision between candidate referring expressions. We experimented with a pool of features and several machine learning algorithms in order to achieve this goal.

2 Method

We apply a standard machine learning approach to the task. We train a classifier to predict the correct label for each mention. As our machine learning algorithm we use memory-based learning as implemented in the Timbl package (Daelemans et al., 2007). To select the optimal algorithmic parameter setting for each classifier we used a heuristic optimization method called paramsearch (Van den Bosch, 2004). We also tried several other machine learning algorithms implemented in the Weka package (Witten and Frank, 2005), but these experiments did not lead to better results and are not further discussed here.

We developed four systems: a system that only predicts the TYPE of each expression (Type), so it predicts four class labels; and a system that predicts the four properties (TYPE, EMPATHIC, HEAD, CASE) of each expression simultaneously (Prop). The class labels predicted by this system are concatenated strings: 'common_no_nominal_plain', and these concatenations lead to 14 classes, which means that not all combinations appear in the training set. For both Type an Prop we created two variants: one general classifer (g) that is trained on all subdomains, and a set of combined specialized classifiers (s) that are optimized for each domain separately.

3 System description

To build the feature representations, we first preprocessed the texts performing the following actions: rule-based tokenization, memory-based part-of-speech tagging, NP-chunking, Named entity recognition, and grammatical relation finding (Daelemans and van den Bosch, 2005). We create an instance for each mention, using the following features to represent each instance:

- Positional features: the sentence number, the NP number, a boolean feature that indicates if the mention appears in the first sentence.
- Syntactic and semantic category given of the entity (SEMCAT, SYNCAT).
- Local context of 3 words and POS tags left and right of the entity.
- Distance to the previous mention measured in sentences and in NPs.
- Trigram pattern of the given syntactic categories of 3 previous mentions.
- Boolean feature indicating if the previous sentence contains another named entity than the entity in focus.
- the main verb of the sentence.

We do not use any information about the given set of alternative expressions except for post processing. In a few cases our classifier predicts a label that is not present in the set of alternatives. For those cases we choose the most frequent class label (as estimated on the training set).

We experimented with predicting all subdomains with the same classifier and with creating separate classifiers for each subdomains. We expected that semantically different domains would have different preferences for expressions.

4 Results

We provide results for the four systems Type-g, Type-s, Prop-g and Prop-s in Table 1. The evaluation script was provided by the organisers. The variant Type-g performs best with a score of 76.52% on the development set.

5 Conclusions

In this paper we described our machine learning approach to the generation of referring expressions. We reported results of four memory-based systems. Predicting all subdomains with the same classifier is more efficient when predicting the coarse-grained TYPE class. On the contrary, training specialized classifiers for each subdomain works better for the more fine-grained prediction of all properties simulaneously. For the test set we will present results the two best systems: CNTS-Type-g and CNTS-Prop-s.

Data	Type-g	Type-s
Cities	64.65	60.61
Countries	75.00	71.74
Mountains	75.42	77.07
People	85.37	72.50
Rivers	65.00	80.00
All	**76.52**	72.26
Data	**Prop-g**	**Prop-s**
Cities	63.64	65.66
Countries	72.83	69.57
Mountains	72.08	74.58
People	79.51	79.51
Rivers	65.00	70.00
All	73.02	**73.93**

Table 1: Accuracy on GREC development set.

Acknowledgments

This research is funded by FWO, IWT, GOA BOF UA, and the STEVIN programme funded by the Dutch and Flemish Governments.

References

A. Belz and S. Varges. 2007. Generation of repeated references to discourse entities. In *In Proceedings of the 11th European Workshop on Natural Language Generation (ENLG'07)*, pages 9–16.

W. Daelemans and A. van den Bosch. 2005. *Memory-based language processing*. Cambridge University Press, Cambridge, UK.

W. Daelemans, J. Zavrel, K. Van der Sloot, and A. Van den Bosch. 2007. TiMBL: Tilburg Memory Based Learner, version 6.1, reference manual. Technical Report 07-07, ILK, Tilburg University.

A. Van den Bosch. 2004. Wrapped progressive sampling search for optimizing learning algorithm parameters. In *Proceedings of the 16th Belgian-Dutch Conference on Artificial Intelligence*, pages 219–226.

I. H. Witten and E. Frank. 2005. *Data Mining: Practical machine learning tools and techniques, second edition*. Morgan Kaufmann, San Francisco.

OSU-2: Generating Referring Expressions with a Maximum Entropy Classifier

Emily Jamison
Department of Linguistics
The Ohio State University
Columbus, OH 43210, USA
jamison@ling.osu.edu

Dennis Mehay
Department of Linguistics
The Ohio State University
Columbus, OH 43210, USA
mehay@ling.osu.edu

Abstract

Selection of natural-sounding referring expressions is useful in text generation and information summarization (Kan et al., 2001). We use discourse-level feature predicates in a maximum entropy classifier (Berger et al., 1996) with binary and n-class classification to select referring expressions from a list. We find that while mention-type n-class classification produces higher accuracy of type, binary classification of individual referring expressions helps to avoid use of awkward referring expressions.

1 Introduction

Referring expression generation is the task of inserting noun phrases that refer to a mentioned extra-linguistic entity into a text. REG is helpful for tasks such as text generation and information summarization (Kan et al., 2001).

2 Task Description

The Referring Expressions Generation Challenge (Belz and Gatt, 2008) includes a task based on the GREC corpus, a collection of introductory texts from Wikipedia that includes articles about cities, countries, rivers, people, and mountains. In this corpus, the main topic of each text (MSR) has been replaced with a list of possible referring expressions (REs). The objective of the task is to identify the most appropriate referring expression from the list for each mention of the MSR, given the surrounding text and annotated syntactic and semantic information.

3 Predicates

We created 13 predicates, in addition to the six predicates available with the corpus. All predicates can be used with the binary classification method; only non-RE-level predicates can be used with the n-class classification method. Predicates describe: string similarity of the RE and the title of the article, the mention's order in the article, distance between previous mention and current mention, and detection of a contrastive discourse entity in the text.[1]

4 Maximum Entropy Classifier

We defined indicator feature functions for a number of contextual predicates, each describing a pairing of some potential property of the syntactico-semantic and discourse context of a RE (a 'predicate') and a label. These feature functions f_i were used to train a maximum entropy classifier (Berger et al., 1996) (Le, 2004) that assigns a probability to a RE re given context c_x as follows:

$$p(re \mid c_x) = Z(c_x) \exp \sum_{i=1}^{n} \lambda_i f_i(c_x, re)$$

where $Z(c_x)$ is a normalizing sum and the λ_i are the parameters (feature weights) learned. Two classification systems were used: binary and n-class. With the binary method, the classifier estimates the likelihood of a possible referring expression's correct insertion into the text, and inserts the RE with the highest 'yes' probability. With the n-class method,

[1] More details at http://www.ling.ohio-state.edu/~jamison

Predicates Used	Single	Combinations
GREC predicates	40.40%	50.91%
all predicates	50.30%	58.54%
no contrasting entities	50.30%	59.30%
all non-RE-level preds	44.82%	51.07%

Table 1: Results with binary classification.

Predicates Used	Single	Combinations
all non-RE-level preds	61.13%	62.50%

Table 2: Results with n-class classification.

the mention is classified according to type of referring expression (proper name, common noun, pronoun, empty) and a RE of the proper type is chosen.

A predicate combinator was implemented to create pairs of predicates for the classifier.

5 Results

Our results are shown in tables 1 and 2; table 3 shows further per-category results. N-class classification has a higher type accuracy than the binary method(single: 61.13% versus 44.82%). Added predicates made a notable difference (single, original predicates: 40.40%; with added predicates: 50.30%). However, the predicates that detected contrasting discourse entities proved not to be helpful (combinations: 59.30% declined to 58.54%). Finally, the predicate combinator improved all results (binary, all predicates: 50.30% to 58.54%).

6 Discussion

The n-class method does not evaluate characteristics of each individual referring expression. However, the accuracy measure is designed to judge appropriateness of a referring expression based only on whether its type is correct. A typical high-accuracy n-class result is shown in example 1.

System	City	Ctry	Mnt	River	Pple
b-all	53.54	57.61	49.58	75.00	65.85
b-nonRE	51.52	53.26	45.83	40.00	57.07
n-nonRE	53.54	63.04	61.67	65.00	67.32

Table 3: Challenge-submitted results by category.

Example 1: Albania
The Republic of Albania itself is a Balkan country in Southeastern Europe. **Which itself** borders Montenegro to the north, the Serbian province of Kosovo to the northeast, the Republic of Macedonia in the east, and Greece in the south.

In example 1, both mentions are matched with an RE that is the proper type (proper name and pronoun, respectively), yet the result is undesireable.

A different example typical of the binary classification method is shown in example 2.

Example 2: Alfred Nobel
Alfred Nobel was a Swedish chemist, engineer, innovator, armaments manufacturer and the inventor of dynamite. [...] In **his** last will, **Alfred Nobel** used **his** enormous fortune to institute the Nobel Prizes.

In example 2, the use of predicates specific to each RE besides the type causes use of the RE "Alfred Nobel" as a subject, and the RE "his" as a possessive pronoun. The text, if mildly repetitive, is still comprehensible.

7 Conclusion

In this study, we used discourse-level predicates and binary and n-class maximum entropy classifiers to select referring expressions. Eventually, we plan to combine these two approaches, first selecting all REs of the appropriate type and then ranking them.

References

Anya Belz and Albert Gatt. 2008. *REG Challenge 2008: Participants Pack.* http://www.nltg.brighton.ac.uk/research/reg08/.

A. L. Berger, S. D. Pietra, and V. D. Pietra. 1996. A maximum entropy approach to natural language processing. *Computational Linguistcs*, 22(1):39–71.

Min-Yen Kan, Kathleen R. McKeown, and Judith L. Klavans. 2001. Applying natural language generation to indicative summarization. *EWNLG '01: Proceedings of the 8th European workshop on Natural Language Generation.*

Zhang Le. 2004. *Maximum Entropy Modeling Toolkit for Python and C++.* http://homepages.inf.ed.ac.uk/s0450736/maxent_toolkit.html.

The TUNA Challenge 2008: Overview and Evaluation Results

Albert Gatt
Department of Computing Science
University of Aberdeen
Aberdeen AB24 3UE, UK
a.gatt@abdn.ac.uk

Anja Belz **Eric Kow**
Natural Language Technology Group
University of Brighton
Brighton BN2 4GJ, UK
{asb, eykk10}@brighton.ac.uk

Abstract

The TUNA Challenge was a set of three shared tasks at REG'08, all of which used data from the TUNA Corpus. The three tasks covered attribute selection for referring expressions (TUNA-AS), realisation (TUNA-R) and end-to-end referring expression generation (TUNA-REG). 8 teams submitted a total of 33 systems to the three tasks, with an additional submission to the Open Track. The evaluation used a range of automatically computed measures. In addition, an evaluation experiment was carried out using the peer outputs for the TUNA-REG task. This report describes each task and the evaluation methods used, and presents the evaluation results.

1 Introduction

The TUNA Challenge 2008 built on the foundations laid in the ASGRE 2007 Challenge (Belz and Gatt, 2007), which consisted of a single shared task, based on a subset of the TUNA Corpus (Gatt et al., 2007). The TUNA Corpus is a collection of human-authored descriptions of a referent, paired with a representation of the *domain* in which that description was elicited.

The 2008 Challenge expanded the scope of the previous edition in a variety of ways. This year, there were three shared tasks. TUNA-AS is the Attribute Selection task piloted in the 2007 ASGRE Challenge, which involves the selection of a set of attributes which are true of a target referent, and help to distinguish it from its distractors in a domain. TUNA-R is a realisation task, involving the mapping from attribute sets to linguistic descriptions. TUNA-REG is an 'end to end' referring expression generation task, involving a mapping from an input domain to a linguistic description of a target referent. In addition, there was an Open Submission Track, where participants were invited to submit a report on any interesting research that involved the shared task data, and an Evaluation Track, for which submissions were invited on proposals for evaluation methods. This year's TUNA Challenge also expanded considerably on the evaluation methods used in the various tasks. The measures can be divided into *intrinsic*, automatically computed methods, and *extrinsic* measures obtained through a task-oriented experiment involving human participants.

The training and development data for the Challenge included the full dataset used in the ASGRE Challenge, that is, all of the 2007 training, development and test data. For the 2008 edition, two new test sets were constructed. Test Set 1 was used for TUNA-R, Test Set 2 was used for both TUNA-AS and TUNA-REG.

1.1 Overview of submissions

Overall, 8 research groups submitted 33 systems by the deadline. Table 1 provides a summary of the submissions. The extrinsic evaluation experiment was carried out on peer outputs in the TUNA-REG task only, using outputs from at most 4 systems per participating group. The 10 systems included are indicated in boldface in the table. An additional submission was made by the USP team to the Open Track. No submissions were made to the Evaluation Track. Given the number of submissions, space restrictions do not permit us to give an overview of the characteristics of the various systems; these can be found in the reports authored by each participating group, which are included in this volume.

Group	Organisation	TUNA-AS	TUNA-R	TUNA-REG
ATT	AT&T Labs Research Inc.	ATT-DR-b ATT-DR-sf ATT-FB-f ATT-FB-m ATT-FB-sf ATT-FB-sr	ATT-R	ATT-TemplateS-ws **ATT-TemplateS-drws** ATT-Template-ws ATT-Template-drws **ATT-PermuteRank-ws** **ATT-PermuteRank-drws** **ATT-Dependency-drws** ATT-Dependency-ws
DIT	Dublin Institute of Technology	DIT-FBI DIT-TVAS	DIT-CBSR DIT-RBR	**DIT-FBI-CBSR** **DIT-TVAS-RBR**
GRAPH	University of Tilbug etc	GRAPH-FP		**GRAPH-4+B***
IS	University of Stuttgart	IS-FP	IS-GT	**IS-FP-GT**
JUCSENLP	Jadavpur University	JU-PTBSGRE		
NIL-UCM	Universidad Complutense de Madrid	NIL-UCM-MFVF	NIL-UCM-BSC	**NIL-UCM-FVBS**
OSU	Ohio State University	OSU-GP		**OSU-GP***
USP	University of Sao Paolo	USP-EACH-FREQ		

Table 1: Overview of participating teams and systems, by task. TUNA-REG peer systems whose outputs were included in the extrinsic, task-based evaluation are shown in boldface. Systems marked * were submissions to TUNA-AS which made use of the off-the-shelf ASGRE realiser for their entries to TUNA-REG.

Participants in TUNA-AS and TUNA-R were also given the opportunity to submit peer outputs for TUNA-REG, and having them included in the extrinsic evaluation, by making the use of off-the-shelf modules. For systems in TUNA-AS, we made available a template-based realiser, written by Irene Langkilde-Geary at the University of Brighton. Originally used in the 2007 ASGRE Challenge, this was re-used by some TUNA-AS participants to realise their outputs. Systems which made use of this facility are marked by a (*) in Table 1.

In the rest of this report, we first give an overview of the tasks and the data used for the Challenge (Section 2), followed by a description of the evaluation methods (Section 3). Section 4 gives the comparative evaluation results for each task, followed by a few concluding remarks in Section 5. In what follows, we will use the following terminology, in keeping with their usage in Belz and Gatt (2007): a *peer system* is a system submitted to the shared-task challenge, while *peer output* is an attribute set or a description (in the form of a word string) produced by a peer system. We will refer to a description in the TUNA corpus as a *reference output*.

2 Data and task overview

2.1 The TUNA Data

The TUNA corpus was constructed via an elicitation experiment as part of the TUNA project[1]. Each file in the data consists of a single pairing of a domain (representation of entities and their attributes) and a human-authored description (reference output) which is intended to describe the target referent in the domain. Only the singular descriptions in the corpus were used for the TUNA Challenge.

[1] http://www.csd.abdn.ac.uk/research/tuna/

```
<TRIAL CONDITION="+/-LOC" ID="...">

    <DOMAIN>
        <ENTITY ID="..." TYPE="target" IMAGE="...">
            <ATTRIBUTE NAME="..." VALUE="..." />
            ...
        </ENTITY>
        <ENTITY ID="..." TYPE="distractor" IMAGE="...">
            <ATTRIBUTE NAME="..." VALUE="..." />
            ...
        </ENTITY>
        ...
    </DOMAIN>

    <WORD-STRING>
        the string describing the target referent
    </WORD-STRING>

    <ANNOTATED-WORD-STRING>
        the string in WORD-STRING annotated
        with attributes in ATTRIBUTE-SET
    </ANNOTATED-WORD-STRING>

    <ATTRIBUTE-SET>
        the set of domain attributes in the description
    </ATTRIBUTE-SET>

</TRIAL>
```

Figure 1: Format of corpus items

The descriptions in the corpus are subdivided by *entity type*: there are references to people, and references to furniture items. In addition, the elicitation experiment manipulated a single condition, ±LOC. In the +LOC condition, experimental participants were told that they could refer to entities using any of their properties, including their location. In the −LOC condition, they were *discouraged* from doing so, though not prevented.

Figure 1 is an outline of the XML format used in the Challenge. Each file has a root TRIAL node with a unique ID and an indication of the experimental condition. The DOMAIN node subsumes 7

ENTITY nodes, which themselves subsume a number of ATTRIBUTE nodes defining the properties of an entity in attribute-value notation. The attributes include properties such as an object's colour or a person's clothing, and the location of the image in the visual display which the DOMAIN represents. Each ENTITY node indicates whether it is the target referent or one of the six distractors, and also has a pointer to the image that it represents. Images were made available to the TUNA Challenge participants.

The WORD-STRING is the actual description typed by a human author, and the ATTRIBUTE-SET is the set of attributes belonging to the referent that the description includes. The ANNOTATED-WORD-STRING node was only provided in the training and development data, to display how substrings of a human-authored description were mapped to attributes to determine the ATTRIBUTE-SET.

Training and development data: For the TUNA Challenge, the 780 singular corpus instances were divided into 80% training data and 20% development data. This data consists of all the training, development and test data used in the 2007 ASGRE Challenge.

Test data: Two new test sets were constructed by replicating the original TUNA elicitation experiment. The new experiment was designed to ensure that each DOMAIN in the new test sets had two reference outputs. Thus, this year's corpus-based evaluations are conducted against multiple instances of each input DOMAIN. Both sets consisted of 112 items, divided equally into furniture and people descriptions, sampled from both experimental conditions (±LOC). Test Set 1 was used for the TUNA-R Task. Participants in this task received a version of the test set whose items consisted of a DOMAIN node and an ATTRIBUTE-SET node. There were 56 unique DOMAINs, each represented twice in the test set, with two attribute sets from two different human authors. Because each DOMAIN and ATTRIBUTE-SET combination in this test set is unique, the results for this task are reported below over the whole of Test Set 1. Test Set 2 was used for the TUNA-AS and TUNA-REG Tasks. For these tasks, the test items given to participants consisted of a DOMAIN node only. There were 112 unique DOMAINs; the evaluations on these tasks were conducted by comparing each peer output to two different reference outputs for each of these domains. Therefore, in the TUNA-AS and TUNA-REG tasks, the data presented here averages over the two outputs per DOMAIN.

2.2 The tasks

Task 1: Attribute Selection (TUNA-AS): The TUNA-AS task focused on *content determination* for referring expressions, and follows the basic problem definition used in much previous work in the area: given a domain and a target referent, select a subset of the attributes of that referent which will help to distinguish it from its distractors. The inputs for this task consisted of a TRIAL node enclosing a DOMAIN node (a representation of entities and properties). A peer output was a TRIAL node enclosing just an ATTRIBUTE-SET node whose children were the attributes selected by a peer system for the target entity.

Task 2: Realisation (TUNA-R): The TUNA-R task focussed on *realisation*. The aim was to map an ATTRIBUTE-SET node to a word string which describes the ENTITY that is marked as the *target* such that the entity can be identified in the domain. The inputs for this task consisted of a TRIAL node enclosing a DOMAIN and an ATTRIBUTE-SET node. A peer output for this task consisted of a TRIAL node enclosing just a WORD-STRING node.

Task 3: 'End-to-end' Referring Expression Generation (TUNA-REG): For the TUNA-REG task, the input consisted of a DOMAIN, and a peer output was a word string which described the entity marked as the *target* such that the entity could be identified in the domain. The input for this task was identical to that for TUNA-AS, i.e. a TRIAL node enclosing just a DOMAIN node. A peer output for this task was identical in format to that for the TUNA-R task, i.e. a TRIAL enclosing just a WORD-STRING node.

3 Evaluation methods

The evaluation methods used in each task, and the quality criteria that they assess, are summarised in Table 2. Peer outputs from all tasks were evaluated using intrinsic methods. All of these were automatically computed, and are subdivided into (a)

Task	Criterion	Type	Methods
TUNA-AS	Humanlikeness	Intrinsic	Accuracy, Dice, MASI
	Minimality	Intrinsic	Proportion of minimal outputs
	Uniqueness	Intrinsic	Proportion of unique outputs
TUNA-R	Humanlikeness	Intrinsic	Accuracy, BLEU, NIST, string-edit distance
TUNA-REG	Humanlikeness	Intrinsic	Accuracy, BLEU, NIST string-edit distance
	Ease of comprehension	Extrinsic	Self-paced reading in identification experiment
	Referential Clarity	Extrinsic	Speed and accuracy in identification experiment

Table 2: Evaluation methods used per task

those measures that assess humanlikeness, i.e. the degree of similarity between a peer output and a reference output; and (b) measures that assess intrinsic properties of peer outputs. Peer outputs from the TUNA-REG task were also included in a human, task-oriented evaluation, which is extrinsic insofar as it measures the adequacy of a peer output in terms of its utility in an externally defined task. In the remainder of this section, we summarise the properties of the intrinsic methods. Section 3.1 describes the experiment conducted for the extrinsic evaluation.

Dice coefficient (TUNA-AS): This is a set-comparison metric, ranging between 0 and 1, where 1 indicates a perfect match between sets. For two attribute sets A and B, Dice is computed as follows:

$$Dice(A, B) = \frac{2 \times |A \cap B|}{|A| + |B|} \quad (1)$$

MASI (TUNA-AS): The MASI score (Passonneau, 2006) is an adaptation of the Jaccard coefficient which biases it in favour of similarity where one set is a subset of the other. Like Dice, it ranges between 0 and 1, where 1 indicates a perfect match. It is computed as follows:

$$MASI(A, B) = \delta \times \frac{|A \cap B|}{|A \cup B|} \quad (2)$$

where δ is a *monotonicity coefficient* defined as follows:

$$\delta = \begin{cases} 0 & \text{if } A \cap B = \emptyset \\ 1 & \text{if } A = B \\ \frac{2}{3} & \text{if } A \subset B \text{ or } B \subset A \\ \frac{1}{3} & \text{otherwise} \end{cases} \quad (3)$$

Accuracy (all tasks): This is computed as the proportion of the peer outputs of a system which have an exact match to a reference output. In TUNA-AS, Accuracy was computed as the proportion of times a system returned an ATTRIBUTE-SET identical to the reference ATTRIBUTE-SET produced by a human author for the same DOMAIN. In TUNA-R and TUNA-REG, Accuracy was computed as the proportion of times a peer WORD-STRING was identical to the reference WORD-STRING produced by an author for the same DOMAIN.

String-edit distance (TUNA-R, TUNA-REG): This is the classic Levenshtein distance measure, used to compare the difference between a peer output and a reference output in the corpus, as the minimal number of insertions, deletions and/or substitutions of words required to transform one string into another. The cost for insertions and deletions was set to 1, that for substitutions to 2. Edit distance is an integer bounded by the length of the longest description in the pair being compared.

BLEU (TUNA-R, TUNA-REG): This is an n-gram based string comparison measure, originally proposed by Papineni et al. (2002) for evaluation of Machine Translation systems. It evaluates a system based on the proportion of word n-grams (considering all n-grams of length $n \leq 4$ is standard) that it shares with several reference translations. Unlike Dice, MASI and String-edit, BLEU is by definition an aggregate measure (i.e. a single BLEU score is obtained for a system based on the entire set of items to be compared, and this is generally not equal to the average of BLEU scores for individual items). BLEU ranges between 0 and 1.

NIST (TUNA-R, TUNA-REG): This is a version of BLEU, which gives more importance to less frequent (hence more informative) n-grams. The range of NIST scores depends on the size of the test set. Like BLEU, this is an aggregate measure.

Uniqueness (TUNA-AS): This measure was included for backwards comparability with the ASGRE Challenge 2007. It is defined as the proportion of peer ATTRIBUTE-SETs which identify the target referent uniquely, i.e. whose (logical conjunction of) attributes are true of the target, and of no other entity in the DOMAIN.

Minimality (TUNA-AS): This measure was defined as the proportion of peer ATTRIBUTE-SETs which are *minimal*, where 'minimal' means that there is no attribute-set which uniquely identifies the target referent in the domain which is smaller. Note that this definition includes Uniqueness as a prerequisite, since the description must identify the target entity uniquely in order to qualify for Minimality.

All intrinsic evaluation methods except for BLEU and NIST were computed (a) overall, using the entire test data set (i.e. Test Set 1 or 2 as appropriate); and (b) by object type, that is, computing separate values for outputs referring to targets of type *furniture* and *people*.

3.1 Extrinsic evaluation in TUNA-REG

The experiment for the extrinsic evaluation of TUNA-REG peer outputs combined a self-paced reading and identification paradigm, comparing the peer outputs from 10 of the TUNA-REG systems shown in Table 1, as well as the two sets of human-authored reference outputs for Test Set 2. We refer to the latter as HUMAN-1 and HUMAN-2 in what follows[2].

In the task given to experimental subjects, a trial consisted of a description paired with a visual domain representation corresponding to an item in Test Set 2. Each trial was split into two phases: (a) in an initial reading phase, subjects were presented with the description only. This phase was terminated by subjects once they had read the description. (b) In the second, identification phase, subjects saw the visual domain in which the description had been produced, consisting of images of the domain entities in the same spatial configuration as that in the test set DOMAIN. They clicked on the object that they thought was the intended referent of the description they had read.

The experiment yielded three dependent measures: (a) reading time (RT), measured from the point at which the description was presented, to the point at which a participant called up the next screen via mouse click; (b) identification time (IT), measured from the point at which pictures (the visual domain) were presented on the screen to the point where a participant identified a referent by clicking on it; (c) error rate (ER), the proportion of times the wrong referent was identified.

This design differs from that used in the 2007 ASGRE Challenge, in which descriptions and visual domains were presented in a single phase (on the same screen), so that RT and IT were conflated. The new experiment replicates the methodology reported in Gatt and Belz (2008), in a follow-up study on the ASGRE 2007 data. Another difference between the two experiments is that the current one is based on peer outputs which are themselves realisations, whereas the ASGRE experiment involved attribute sets which had to be realised before they could be used.

Design: We used a Repeated Latin Squares design, in which each combination of SYSTEM[3] and test set item is allocated one trial. Since there were 12 levels of SYSTEM, but 112 test set items, 8 randomly selected items (4 furniture and 4 people) were duplicated, yielding 120 items and 10 12×12 latin squares. The items were divided into two sets of 60. Half of the participants did the first 60 items (the first 5 latin squares), and the other half the second 60.

Participants and procedure: The experiment was carried out by 24 participants recruited from among the faculty and administrative staff of the University of Brighton, as well as from among the authors' acquaintances. Participants carried out the experiment under supervision in a quiet room on a laptop. Stimulus presentation was carried out using DMDX, a Win-32 software package for psycholinguistic experiments involving time measurements (Forster and Forster, 2003). Participants initiated each trial, which consisted of an initial warning bell and a fixation point flashed on the screen for 1000ms. They then read the description and called up the visual domain to identify the referent. Trials timed out after 15000ms.

Treatment of outliers and timeouts: Trials which

[2]Note that HUMAN-1 and HUMAN-2 were both sets of descriptions randomly sampled from the data collected in the experiment. Each set of human descriptions contains output from different human authors.

[3]The SYSTEM independent variable in this experiment includes HUMAN-1 and HUMAN-2.

timed out with no response were discounted from the analysis. Out of a total of ($24 \times 60 =$) 1440 trials, there were 4 reading timeouts (0.3%) and 7 identification timeouts (0.5%). Outliers for RT and IT were defined as those exceeding a threshold of mean $\pm 2SD$. There were 64 outliers on RT (4.4%) and 191 on IT (13.3%). Outliers were replaced by the overall mean for RT and IT (see Ratliff (1993) for discussion of this method).

4 Evaluation results

This section presents results for each of the tasks. For all measures, except BLEU and NIST, we present separate descriptive statistics by entity type (people vs. furniture subsets of the relevant test set), and overall.

4.1 Results for TUNA-AS

Descriptive statistics are displayed for all systems in Table 3. This includes the Accuracy and Minimality scores (proportions), and mean MASI and Dice scores. Values are displayed by entity type and overall. The standard deviation for Dice and MASI is displayed overall. Scores average over both sets of reference outputs in Test Set 2. All systems scored 100% on Uniqueness, and either 0 or 100% on Minimality. These measures are therefore not included in the significance testing, though Minimality is included in the correlations reported below.

Two 15 (SYSTEM) $\times$ 2 (ENTITY TYPE) univariate ANOVAs were conducted on the Dice and MASI scores. We report significant effects at $p \leq .001$. There were main effects of SYSTEM (Dice: $F(13, 1540) = 193.08$; MASI: $F(13, 1540) = 93.45$) and ENTITY TYPE (Dice: $F(1, 1540) = 91.75$; MASI: $F(1, 1540) = 168.12$), as well as a significant interaction between the two (Dice: $F(13, 1540) = 7.45$, MASI: $F(13, 1540) = 7.35$). Post-hoc Tukey's comparisons on both Dice and MASI yielded the homogeneous subsets displayed in Table 4.

Differences among systems on Accuracy were analysed by coding this as an indicator variable: for each peer output, the variable indicated whether it achieved perfect match with *at least one* of the two reference outputs on the same DOMAIN. A Kruskall-Wallis test showed that the difference between systems was significant ($\chi^2 = 275.01, p < .001$).

	Minimality	Accuracy	Dice	MASI
Minimality		-0.877	-0.959	-0.901
Accuracy	-0.877		0.973	0.998
Dice	-0.959	0.973		0.985
MASI	-0.901	0.998	0.985	

Table 5: Correlations for TUNA-AS; all values are significant at $p \leq .05$

Pairwise correlations using Pearson's r are shown in Table 5, for all measures except Uniqueness. All correlations are positive and significant, with the exception of those involving Minimality, which correlates negatively with all other measures (i.e. the higher the proportion of minimal descriptions of a system, the lower its score on humanlikeness, as measured by Dice, MASI and Accuracy). This result corroborates a similar finding in the 2007 ASGRE Challenge.

4.2 Results for TUNA-R

Table 6 shows descriptives for the 5 participating systems in TUNA-R. Once again, mean Edit scores and Accuracy proportions are shown both overall and by entity type, while BLEU and NIST are overall aggregate scores.

A 15 (SYSTEM) $\times$ 2 (ENTITY TYPE) univariate ANOVA was conducted on the Edit Distance scores. There was no main effect of SYSTEM, and no interaction, but ENTITY TYPE exhibited a main effect ($F(1, 550) = 19.99, p < .001$). Given the lack of a main effect, no post-hoc comparisons between systems were conducted. A Kruskall-Wallis test also showed no difference between systems on Accuracy. Pairwise correlations between all measures are shown in Table 7; this time, the only significant correlation is between NIST and BLEU.

	Edit	Accuracy	NIST	BLEU
Edit		0.195	-0.095	0.099
Accuracy	0.195		0.837	0.701
NIST	-0.095	0.837		0.900*
BLEU	0.099	0.701	0.900*	

Table 7: Correlations for the TUNA-R task (* indicates $p \leq .05$).

4.3 Results for TUNA-REG

4.3.1 Tests on the intrinsic measures

Results for the intrinsic measures on the TUNA-REG task are shown in Table 8. As in Section 4.1,

	Dice				MASI				Accuracy			Minimality
	furniture	*people*	*both*	SD	*furniture*	*people*	*both*	SD	*furniture*	*people*	*both*	*both*
GRAPH	0.858	0.729	0.794	0.160	0.705	0.465	0.585	0.272	0.53	0.56	0.40	0.00
JU-PTBSGRE	0.858	0.762	0.810	0.152	0.705	0.501	0.603	0.251	0.55	0.58	0.41	0.00
ATT-DR-b	0.852	0.722	0.787	0.154	0.663	0.441	0.552	0.283	0.52	0.54	0.36	0.00
ATT-DR-sf	0.852	0.722	0.787	0.154	0.663	0.441	0.552	0.283	0.50	0.52	0.36	0.00
DIT-FBI	0.850	0.731	0.791	0.153	0.661	0.451	0.556	0.280	0.50	0.53	0.36	0.00
IS-FP	0.828	0.723	0.776	0.165	0.641	0.475	0.558	0.278	0.52	0.54	0.37	0.00
NIL-UCM-MFVF	0.821	0.684	0.753	0.169	0.601	0.383	0.492	0.290	0.44	0.46	0.31	0.00
USP-EACH-FREQ	0.820	0.663	0.742	0.176	0.616	0.404	0.510	0.291	0.46	0.48	0.33	0.00
DIT-TVAS	0.814	0.684	0.749	0.166	0.580	0.383	0.482	0.285	0.43	0.46	0.29	0.00
OSU-GP	0.640	0.443	0.541	0.226	0.352	0.114	0.233	0.227	0.17	0.20	0.06	0.00
ATT-FB-m	0.357	0.263	0.310	0.245	0.164	0.119	0.141	0.125	0.13	0.14	0.00	1.00
ATT-FB-f	0.231	0.307	0.269	0.215	0.093	0.138	0.116	0.104	0.13	0.12	0.00	1.00
ATT-FB-sf	0.231	0.307	0.269	0.215	0.093	0.138	0.116	0.104	0.13	0.12	0.00	1.00
ATT-FB-sr	0.231	0.307	0.269	0.215	0.093	0.138	0.116	0.104	0.13	0.12	0.00	1.00

Table 3: Descriptives for the TUNA-AS task. All means are shown by entity type; standard deviations are displayed overall.

Dice				MASI					
ATT-FB-f	A			ATT-FB-f	A				
ATT-FB-sf	A			ATT-FB-sf	A				
ATT-FB-sr	A			ATT-FB-sr	A				
ATT-FB-m	A			ATT-FB-m	A	B			
OSU-GP		B		OSU-GP		B			
USP-EACH-FREQ			C	DIT-TVAS			C		
DIT-TVAS			C	NIL-UCM-MFVF			C	D	
NIL-UCM-MFVF			C	USP-EACH-FREQ			C	D	E
IS-FP			C	ATT-DR-b			C	D	E
ATT-DR-b			C	ATT-DR-sf			C	D	E
ATT-DR-sf			C	DIT-FBI			C	D	E
DIT-FBI			C	IS-FP			C	D	E
GRAPH			C	GRAPH				D	E
JU-PTBSGRE			C	JU-PTBSGRE					E

Table 4: Homogeneous subsets for systems in TUNA-AS. Systems which do not share a common letter are significantly different at $p \leq .05$

	Edit				Accuracy			NIST	BLEU
	furniture	*people*	*both*	SD	*furniture*	*people*	*both*	*both*	*both*
IS-GT	7.750	9.768	8.759	6.319	0.02	0.00	0.01	0.4526	0.0415
NIL-UCM-BSC	7.411	9.143	8.277	6.276	0.05	0.04	0.04	1.7034	0.0784
ATT-1-R	7.143	9.268	8.205	6.140	0.02	0.00	0.01	0.1249	0
DIT-CBSR	7.054	10.286	8.670	6.873	0.09	0.02	0.05	1.1623	0.0686
DIT-RBR	6.929	9.857	8.393	6.668	0.04	0.00	0.02	0.9151	0.0694

Table 6: Descriptives for the TUNA-R task.

	Edit				Accuracy			BLEU	NIST
	furniture	*people*	*both*	SD	*furniture*	*people*	*both*	*both*	*both*
ATT-PermuteRank-ws	8.339	8.304	8.321	3.283	0.00	0	0	0.007	0.0288
ATT-Template-ws	8.304	8.161	8.232	3.030	0.00	0	0	0	0.0059
ATT-Dependency-ws	8.232	8.000	8.116	3.023	0.00	0	0	0.0001	0.0139
ATT-TemplateS-ws	8.214	8.161	8.188	3.063	0.00	0	0	0	0.0057
OSU-GP	7.964	13.232	10.598	4.223	0.00	0	0	1.976	0.0236
ATT-PermuteRank-drws	7.464	8.411	7.938	3.431	0.02	0.04	0.03	0.603	0.0571
DIT-TVAS-RBR	6.893	8.161	7.527	3.358	0.05	0	0.03	1.0233	0.0659
ATT-TemplateS-drws	6.786	7.679	7.232	3.745	0.07	0.02	0.04	0.6786	0.0958
ATT-Template-drws	6.768	7.696	7.232	3.757	0.07	0.02	0.04	0.6083	0.0929
NIL-UCM-FVBS	6.643	8.411	7.527	3.618	0.07	0.04	0.05	1.8277	0.0684
IS-FP-GT	6.607	7.304	6.955	3.225	0.05	0.02	0.04	0.8708	0.1086
DIT-FBI-CBSR	6.536	7.643	7.089	3.889	0.16	0.05	0.11	0.8804	0.1259
ATT-Dependency-drws	6.482	7.446	6.964	3.349	0.07	0	0.04	0.3427	0.0477
GRAPH	5.946	9.018	7.482	3.541	0.18	0	0.09	1.141	0.0696

Table 8: Descriptives for TUNA-REG on the intrinsic measures.

means for the intrinsic measures average over both sets of reference outputs in Test Set 2.

A 15 (SYSTEM) $\times 2$ (ENTITY TYPE) univariate ANOVA was conducted on the Edit Distance scores. There were significant main effects of SYSTEM ($F(13, 1540) = 8.6, p < .001$) and ENTITY TYPE ($F(1, 1540) = 47.5, p < .001$), as well as a significant interaction ($F(13, 1540) = 5.77, p < .001$). A Kruskall-Wallis test on Accuracy, coded as an indicator variable (see Section 4.2), showed that systems differed significantly on this measure as well ($\chi^2 = 26.27, p < .05$).

Post-hoc Tukey's comparisons were conducted on Edit Distance; the homogeneous subsets are shown in Table 9. The table suggests that the main effect of Edit Distance may largely have been due to the difference between OSU-GP and all other systems.

Correlations between these measures are shown in Table 10. Contrary to the results in Section 4.2, the correlation between BLEU and NIST does not reach significance. The negative correlations between Edit distance and Accuracy, and between Edit and BLEU are as expected, since higher Edit cost implies greater distance from a reference output.

IS-FP-GT	A	
ATT-Dependency-drws	A	
DIT-FBI-CBSR	A	
ATT-Template-drws	A	
ATT-TemplateS-drws	A	
GRAPH-4+B	A	
DIT-TVAS-RBR	A	
NIL-UCM-FVBS	A	
ATT-PermuteRank-drws	A	
ATT-Dependency-ws	A	
ATT-TemplateS-ws	A	
ATT-Template-ws	A	
ATT-PermuteRank-ws	A	
OSU-GP		B

Table 9: Homogeneous subsets for systems in TUNA-REG, Edit Distance measure. Systems which do not share a common letter are significantly different at $p \leq .05$

	Edit	Accuracy	NIST	BLEU
Edit		-0.584*	0.250	-0.636*
Accuracy	-0.584*		0.383	0.807**
NIST	0.250	0.383		0.371
BLEU	-0.636*	0.807**	0.371	

Table 10: Correlations for TUNA-REG (* indicates $p \leq .05$; ** indicates $p \leq .01$).

4.3.2 Tests on the extrinsic measures

Table 11 displays the results for the extrinsic measures. Reading time (RT), identification time (IT) and error rate (ER), are displayed only for the systems that participated in the evaluation experiment, as well as for the two sets of reference outputs HUMAN-1 and HUMAN-2.

Separate univariate ANOVAs were conducted testing the effect of SYSTEM and ENTITY TYPE on IT and RT. For IT, there was a significant main effect of SYSTEM ($F(11, 1409) = 5.66, p < .001$) and ENTITY TYPE ($F(1, 1409) = 23.507, p < .001$), as well as a significant interaction ($F(11, 1409) = 2.378, p < .05$). The same pattern held for RT, with a main effect of SYSTEM ($F(11, 1412) = 9.95, p < .001$) and ENTITY TYPE ($F(1, 1412) = 9.74, p < .05$) and a significant interaction ($F(11, 1412) = 2.064, p < .05$). A Kruskall-Wallis test conducted on ER showed a significant impact of SYSTEM on the extent to which experimental participants identified the wrong referents ($\chi^2 = 35.45, p < .001$). The homogeneous subsets yielded by post-hoc Tukey's comparisons among systems, on both RT and IT, are displayed in Table 12.

Finally, pairwise correlations were estimated between all three extrinsic measures. The only significant correlation was between RT and IT ($r = .784, p < .05$), suggesting that the longer experimental subjects took to read a description, the longer they also took to identify the target referent.

5 Conclusion

The first ASGRE Challenge, held in 2007, was regarded and presented as a pilot event, for a research community in which there was growing interest in comparative evaluation on shared datasets. Referring Expression Generation was an ideal starting point, because of its relatively long history within the NLG community, and the widespread agreement on inputs, outputs and task definitions.

The tasks described and evaluated in this report constitute a broadening of scope over the 2007 Challenge. Like the previous Challenge, the 2008 edition emphasised diversity in terms of the measures of quality used. This year, there was also an increased emphasis on broadening the range of tasks, with the inclusion of realisation and end-to-end referring expressions generation. This extends the scope of the REG problem, which has traditionally been focussed on content determination (attribute selection) for the most part. As for evaluation, the diversity of measures can shed light on different aspects of quality in these tasks. The fact that the correlation among measures based on different quality criteria is not straightforward is in itself an argument for maintaining this diversity, particularly as comparative evaluation exercises such as this one provide the opportunity for further investigation of the nature of these relationships.

Another indicator of the growing diversity in this year's Challenge is the range of algorithmic solutions in the three tasks, ranging from new models based on classical algorithms, to data-driven methods, evolutionary algorithms, and graph- and tree-based frameworks. The body of work represented by submissions to the TUNA-R and TUNA-REG tasks is also interesting for its exploration of how to apply

	RT				IT				ER		
	furniture	*people*	*both*	SD	*furniture*	*people*	*both*	SD	*furniture*	*people*	*both*
HUMAN-1	2155.376	2187.737	2171.693	2036.462	1973.369	1911.742	1942.297	809.5139	11.864	6.780	9.322
OSU-GP	2080.532	3204.198	2637.644	1555.003	2063.441	2274.690	2167.275	682.8325	6.667	18.966	12.712
HUMAN-2	1823.553	2298.467	2061.010	1475.005	1873.621	1945.880	1909.750	761.3386	16.667	5.000	10.833
ATT-PremuteRank-drws	1664.911	1420.087	1543.528	1392.729	1765.731	1719.456	1742.788	675.3462	10.000	8.475	9.244
DIT-FBI-CBSR	1581.535	1521.799	1551.667	1170.031	1528.119	1932.806	1732.163	694.9878	10.169	10.000	10.084
NIL-UCM-FVBS	1561.291	1933.833	1747.562	1428.490	1531.378	1723.148	1627.263	672.9894	6.667	3.333	5.000
GRAPH	1499.582	1516.804	1508.193	952.158	1706.153	2026.268	1866.211	704.0210	5.000	5.000	5.000
DIT-TVAS-RBR	1485.149	1442.573	1463.861	998.332	1559.953	1734.853	1647.403	588.4615	8.333	13.333	10.833
ATT-Dependency-drws	1460.152	1583.887	1522.019	1177.817	1505.059	2078.336	1791.697	725.9459	1.667	18.333	10.000
ATT-TemplateS-drws	1341.245	1641.539	1490.130	1098.304	1656.401	1720.365	1687.841	650.8357	3.333	10.345	6.780
IS-FT-GT	1292.754	1614.712	1453.733	1374.652	1616.855	1884.557	1750.706	732.4362	6.667	1.667	4.167
ATT-PermuteRank-ws	1218.136	1450.603	1334.369	1203.975	1876.680	1831.485	1854.082	688.3493	31.667	13.333	22.500

Table 11: Descriptives for the extrinsic measures in TUNA-REG.

IT				RT				
NIL-UCM-FVBS	A			ATT-PermuteRank-ws	A			
DIT-TVAS-RBR	A			IS-FT-GT	A			
ATT-TemplateS-drws	A	B		DIT-TVAS-RBR	A			
DIT-FBI-CBSR	A	B		ATT-TemplateS-drws	A			
ATT-PremuteRank-drws	A	B		GRAPH-4+B	A	B		
IS-FT-GT	A	B		ATT-Dependency-drws	A	B		
ATT-Dependency-drws	A	B		ATT-PremuteRank-drws	A	B		
ATT-PermuteRank-ws	A	B		DIT-FBI-CBSR	A	B		
GRAPH-4+B	A	B		NIL-UCM-FVBS	A	B	C	
HUMAN-2	A	B	C	HUMAN-2		B	C	
HUMAN-1		B	C	HUMAN-1			C	D
OSU-GP			C	OSU-GP				D

Table 12: Homogeneous subsets for systems in TUNA-REG, extrinsic time measures. Systems which do not share a common letter are significantly different at $p \leq .05$

realisation techniques to the specific problem posed by referring expressions.

The outcomes of this evaluation exercise are obviously not intended to be a 'final word' on the right way to carry out evaluation in referring expressions generation. Rather, comparative results open up the possibility of improvement and change. Another important aspect of a shared task of this nature is that it results in an archive of data that can be further exploited, either through follow-up studies, or for the provision of baselines against which to compare novel approaches. We have already used the data from ASGRE 2007 for further investigation, particularly in the area of extrinsic evaluation. We plan to carry out more such studies in the future.

Acknowledgements

Our heartfelt thanks to the participants who helped to make this event a success. Thanks to Advaith Siddharthan, who proposed MASI for TUNA-AS.

References

A. Belz and A. Gatt. 2007. The attribute selection for gre challenge: Overview and evaluation results. In *Proc. UCNLG+MT: Language Generation and Machine Translation.*

K. I. Forster and J. C. Forster. 2003. DMDX: A windows display program with millisecond accuracy. *Behavior Research Methods, Instruments, & Computers*, 35(1):116–124.

A. Gatt and A. Belz. 2008. Attribute selection for referring expression generation: New algorithms and evaluation methods. In *Proceedings of the 5th International Conference on Natural Language Generation (INLG-08).*

A. Gatt, I. van der Sluis, and K. van Deemter. 2007. Evaluating algorithms for the generation of referring expressions using a balanced corpus. In *Proc. 11th European Workshop on Natural Language Generation (ENLG-07).*

S. Papineni, T. Roukos, W. Ward, and W. Zhu. 2002. Bleu: a. method for automatic evaluation of machine translation. In *Proc. 40th Annual Meeting of the Association for Computational Linguistics (ACL-02)*, pages 311–318.

R. Passonneau. 2006. Measuring agreement on set-valued items (MASI) for semantic and pragmatic annotation. In *Proc. 5th International Conference on Language Resources and Evaluation (LREC-06).*

R. Ratliff. 1993. Methods for dealing with reaction time outliers. *Psychological Bulletin*, 114(3):510–532.

The Fingerprint of Human Referring Expressions and their Surface Realization with Graph Transducers

Bernd Bohnet
University of Stuttgart
Visualization and Interactive Systems Group
Universitätstr. 58, 70569 Stuttgart, Germany
bohnet@informatik.uni-stuttgart.de

Abstract

The algorithm IS-FP takes up the idea from the IS-FBN algorithm developed for the shared task 2007. Both algorithms learn the individual attribute selection style for each human that provided referring expressions to the corpus. The IS-FP algorithm was developed with two additional goals (1) to improve the indentification time that was poor for the FBN algorithm and (2) to push the dice score even higher. In order to generate a word string for the selected attributes, we build based on individual preferences a surface syntactic dependency tree as input. We derive the individual preferences from the training set. Finally, a graph transducer maps the input strucutre to a deep morphologic structure.

1 IS-FP: Generating Referring Expression with a Human Imprint

A review of the referring expressions shows that humans prefer frequently distinct attributes and attribute combination such as in the following examples.

grey desk (30t1), a red chair (30t2), red sofa (30t3), blue chair (30t5), a small green desk (30t6)

the one in the top left corner (31t1), the one to the left in the middle row (31t2), the bottom right most one (31t3), the blue chair at the bottom center (31t5), etc.

The first individual (#30) seems to prefer colour and size while the second one (#31) seems to prefer the relative position (*to the left*) and places (*the top left corner*). Because of the review, we checked, if the Incremental Algorithm (Dale and Reiter, 1995) using the order for the attributes due to the frequency calculated for each individual can outperform the algorithm using the order for the attributes due to the frequency of the complete training set. This was the case. Table 1 shows the results. Using the individual attribute order, the IA performed as good as the FBN algorithm, cf. Table 1.

Algorithm	Furniture	People	Avg.
IA (complete)	0.796	0.710	0.753
IA (individual)	0.835	0.736	0.7855
FBN	0.810	0.762	0.786

Table 1: Incremental algorithm and FBN

However, the FBN algorithm generates all possible referring expressions and selects based on the dice metric the most similar expressions of the same human. Since there is usually a set of equal good referring expressions, it is possible to select a referring expression among these results due to another metric. That this would improve the results shows the experiment to selected among these results the referring expression that is closest to the correct result. The outcome was that the FBN algorithm has still about 9% room for improvements. The following sections investigates possibilities to use this chance.

1.1 Identification Time

An important metric is the identification time that is the time which is used by a human to identify an entity due to a given referring expression. The identification time is very loosely related with the number of minimal referring expressions and therefore likely with the length of a referring expression. The best identification times had a system with 74% minimal referring expressions and the second and third best systems had about 41%. Good identification times had nearly all systems with only a maximum difference of 0.38 seconds except FBN and FBS which are about 1.05 and 1.49 seconds behind the best one. This is a huge difference compared to all other systems. What could be the reason for that? We know of two differences of FBN to all other systems: **(1)** the lowest portion of minimal referring expressions of all systems and **(2)** the nearest neighbour learning technique. The number of minimal referring expressions is also different to the number of expressions found in the training set. Table 2 shows in the columns *human* the average length and portion of minimal human referring expressions. Because of the different length of the human and the generated expressions, we conducted the experiment to chose always the shortest. Table 2 shows the change between the random selection (FBN) and the selection of the shortest (FP). The experiment leads to a result that have a length and percentage of minimal referring expressions in average similar to the humans ones, cf. columns of *human* and *shortest*.

selection	human		random (FBM)		shortest (FP)	
RE	Len.	Min.	Len.	Min.	Len.	Min.
Furniture	3.1	26.3	3.5	9.4	3.1	15.9
People	3.0	30.9	2.8	28.8	2.8	30.8

Table 2: Length and portion of min. RE

The second difference is the use of the nearest neighbour technique. Could the poor identification time be caused by the nearest neighbour technique? How does it influence referring expressions? – The referring expressions are generated in all the different styles like the human expressions of the corpus. Do humans learn the style of referring expressions and expect then the next expression in the same style? And are we confused when we don't get what we expact? Or does FBN look too much on the expressions of the humans and too less on the domain? We hope to get answers for these questions from the shared task evaluation of IS-FP.

1.2 The IS-FP Algorithm

The basis for the IS-FP algorithm is an extended full brevity implementation in terms of problem solving by search which computes all referring expression, cf. (Bohnet and Dale, 2005). IS-FP uses also the nearest neighbour technique like the IS-FBN algorithm that was introduced by Bohnet (2007). With the nearest neighbour technique, IS-FP selects the expressions which are most similar to the referring expressions of the same human and a human that builds referring expressions similar. The similarity is computed as the average of all dice values between all combinations of the available trails for two humans. From the result of the nearest neighbour evaluation, FP selects the shortest and if still more than one expressions remain then it computes the similarity among them and chooses the most typical and finally, if still alternatives remain, it selects one with the attributes having the highest frequency. Table 3 shows the results for IS-FP trained on the training set and applied to the development set.

Set	Dice	MASI	Accuracy	Uniq.	Min.
Furniture	0.881	0.691	51.25%	100%	1.25%
People	0.790	0.558	36.8%	100%	0%
Total	0.836	0.625	44%	100%	0.62%

Table 3: Results for the IS-FP algorithm

2 IS-GT: Realization with Graph Transducers

We build the input depedency tree for the text generator due to the statistical information that we collect from the training data for each person. This procedure is consistent with our referring expression generator IS-FP that reproduces the individual imprint in a referring expression for the target person. We start with the realization of the referring expressions from a surface syntactic dependency tree, cf. (Mel'čuk, 1988). For the realization of the text, we use the Text Generator and Linguistic Environment MATE, cf. (Bohnet, 2006). We reportet the first time about MATE on the first International Natural Language Generation Conference, cf. (Bohnet et al., 2000). It was since then continuously enhanced and in the last years, large grammars for several languages such as Catalan, English, Finnish, French, German, Polish, Portougees have been developed within the European Project MARQUIS and PatExpert, cf. (Wanner et al., 2007), (Lareau and Wanner, 2007) and (Mille and Wanner, 2008).

2.1 The Referring Expression Models

A learning program builds a Referring Expression Model for each person that contributed referring expression to the corpus. The model contains the following information: (1) The lexicalization for the values of a attribute such as couch for the value sofa, man for value person, etc. (2) The prefered usage of determiners for the type that can be definite (*the*), indefinite (*a*), no article. (3) The syntactic preferences such as *the top left chair*, *the chair at the bottom to the left*, etc.

The information about the determiner and the lexicalization is collected from the annotated word string and the word string itself. We collect the most frequent usage for each person in the coprpus. In order to collect the prefered syntax, we annotated the word strings with syntactic dependency trees. Each of the dependency tress contains additional attributes, which describe the information content of a branch outgoing from the root as well as the possible value of the attriube at the nodes which carry the information. The learning program cuts the syntactic tree at edges starting at the root node and stores the branches in the referring expression model for the person. For instance, the complete referring expression model of a person would contain due to the training data the following information:

article: definite
lexicalization: person → man, light → white
syntax:
t21a: wearing glasses {t:hasGlasses a1:1 v1:glasses}
t21b: with *compl* → beard {t:hasBeard a1:1 v1:beard} *det* → a beard *compl* → white {t:hairColour a1:light v1:white a2:dark v2:dark}
t22: with *compl* → beard {t:hasBeard a1:1 v1:beard} beard *det* → a
t23: wearing *obj* →glasses {t:hasGlasses a1:1 v1:glasses}
t26: with *compl* → glasses {t:hasGlasses a1:1 v1:glasses} glasses *coord* → and *compl* → heair *mod* → dark{t:hairColour a1:dark v1:dark}

2.2 Setting up the Input for the Generator

One of the input attribute sets of the people domain looks like the following one:

```
<TRIAL CONDITION="-LOC" ID="s81t25">
  ...
    <ATTRIBUTE-SET>
    <ATTRIBUTE ID="a4" NAME="hasBeard" VALUE="1"/ >
    <ATTRIBUTE ID="a3" NAME="hairColour" VALUE="light"/ >
    <ATTRIBUTE ID="a2" NAME="hasGlasses" VALUE="1"/ >
    <ATTRIBUTE ID="a1" NAME="type" VALUE="person"/ >
  < /ATTRIBUTE-SET>
< /TRIAL>
```

We start to set up the input structure with the top node which is labeled with the lexicalization of the type or in seldom cases with *elision*, when the type is not in the attribute set. Then we look up in the referring expression model which determiner the per-

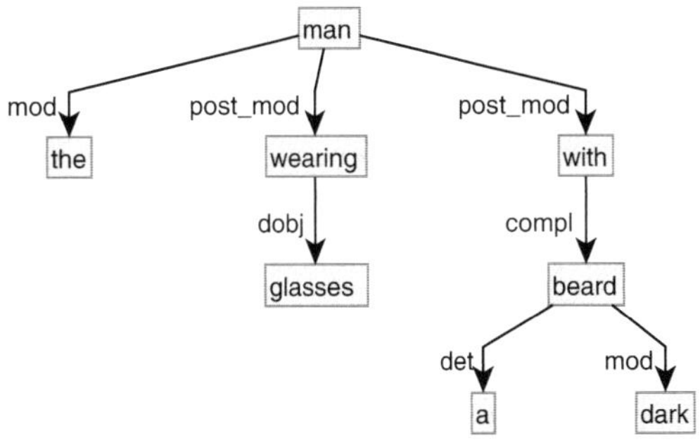

Figure 1: The input to the graph transducer

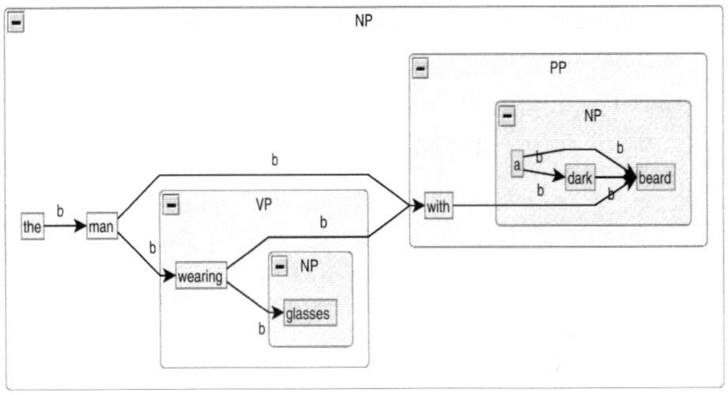

Figure 2: The output of the graph transducer

son prefers. If she prefers any then a node is build, labeled with the determiner and connected with an edge to the type node. After that we add the lexicalized values of that attributes which are nearly always directly attached to the type node such as age in the people domain or colour and size in the furniture domain. Then the program searches in the model the syntactic annotations of attribute combinations. If IS-FP has build the referring expression then it starts to search in the trail selected by the nearest neighbour algorithm otherwise it calculates the closest due to the dice metric. In our example IS-FP might have build as well the given combination since it is equal to the attribute set of trail *s81t21*. Then the program would select the syntactic part t21b first and adapt the value of the node label *white* to *dark*. After that the the syntactic part t21a would be selected since the attribute *hasGlasses* is still not covered in the structure. This part does not need any adaption. Figure 1 shows the result of the process.

2.3 Realization of the Word String

For the realization, we use a handcrafted grammar that generates out of the dependency trees roughly deep morphologic structure / topologic graph. The main task of the grammar is to determine the word order. The grammar contains four main rule groups. The vertical rules order the parent in relation to one of its dependent. The horizontal rules oder two childs. The constituent creation rules build constituents and the constituent adjoin rules adjoins constituents with constituents. Special consideration needed the order of prepositional constituents after the type and the adjective before the type. The prepostional constituents are order because of the order of the prepostions in the corpus. In order to be able to derive the order of the adjective, we used the functional class of the adjectives. Halliday (1994) proposes for English, the classes deictic (this, those, ...), numerative (many, second, , ...), epithet (old, blue, ...), and classifier (vegetarian, Spanish, ...). The order of the adjectives in a noun phrase is in the given order of the classes. In the lexicon entry of the adjectives, we store only a number between one and four which refers to the adjective class.

Table 5 shows the result for the TUNA-R task. The system was developed only by looking on the training data without any consideration of the development data as well without any annotation of the syntax of the development data. We used as guide for the optimization cross validation of training data.

Set	Accuracy	String-Edit Distance
Furniture	35 %	3,163
People	22,06 %	3,647
Total	28,53	3,405

Table 4: Results for the TUNA-R Task

3 IS-FP-GT: The Combination of Attribute Selection and Realization

The only change, we made in compare to IS-FP is that we switched off the feature to add the most similar referring expressions of another human from the training set for the nearest neighbour evaluation since the results have been lower. The reason for this is that other human preferes similar attributes but the individual preferences such as the chosen words and syntax of the other human is different. Table 5 shows the results.

4 Conclusion

The IS-FP algorithm reproduces the imprint of human referring expressions. It generates combinations such as the x-dimension and y-dimension. Elements of a combination have not to occur always together, however they tent to occur together. This is an advantage over incremental algorithms which might have to include other attributes ordered between elements of a combination. FP has the advantage over its predecessor FBN to generate expressions which are additionally mostly equal in respect to the length to human referring expressions, it enlarges automatically the training set for an individual human and it takes into account properties of the domain like the frequency of the attributes.

Set	Accuracy	String-Edit Distance
Furniture	15 %	3,8625
People	8,82 %	4,764
Total	11,91	4,313

Table 5: Results for the TUNA-REG Task

References

B. Bohnet and R. Dale. 2005. Viewing referring expression generation as search. In *IJCAI*, pages 1004–1009.

B. Bohnet, A. Langjahr, and L. Wanner. 2000. A Development Environment for an MTT-Based Sentence Generator. In *Proceedings of the First International Natural Language Generation Conference*.

B. Bohnet. 2006. *Textgenerierung durch Transduktion linguistischer Strukturen.* Ph.D. thesis, University Stuttgart.

B. Bohnet. 2007. IS-FBN, IS-FBS, IS-IAC: The Adaptation of Two Classic Algorithms for the Generation of Referring Expressions in order to Produce Expressions like Humans Do. In *MT Summit XI, UCNLG+MT*, pages 84–86.

R. Dale and E. Reiter. 1995. Computational Interpretations of the Gricean Maxims in the Generation of Referring Expressions. *Cognitive Science*, 19:233–263.

M. A. K. Halliday. 1994. *An Introduction to Functional Grammar*. Edward Arnold, London.

F. Lareau and L. Wanner. 2007. Towards a Generic Multilingual Dependency Grammar for Text Generation. In *GEAF-07*, Palo Alto.

I.A. Mel'čuk. 1988. *Dependency Syntax: Theory and Practice.* State University of New York Press, Albany.

S. Mille and L. Wanner. 2008. Making Text Resources Available to the Reader: The Case of Patent Claims. In *LREC*, Morocco, Marrakech.

L. Wanner, B. Bohnet, N. Bouayad-Agha, F. Lareau, A. Lohmeyer, and D. Nickla. 2007. On the Challenge of Creating and Communicating Air Quality Information. In *In: Swayne A., Hrebicek J.(Eds.): Environmental Software Systems Dimensions of Environmental Informatics. Vol.7.*

Referring Expression Generation Using Speaker-based Attribute Selection and Trainable Realization (ATTR)

Giuseppe Di Fabbrizio and **Amanda J. Stent** and **Srinivas Bangalore**
AT&T Labs - Research, Inc.
180 Park Avenue
Florham Park, NJ 07932, USA
{pino,stent,srini}@research.att.com

Abstract

In the first REG competition, researchers proposed several general-purpose algorithms for attribute selection for referring expression generation. However, most of this work did not take into account: a) stylistic differences between speakers; or b) trainable surface realization approaches that combine semantic and word order information. In this paper we describe and evaluate several end-to-end referring expression generation algorithms that take into consideration speaker style and use data-driven surface realization techniques.

1 Introduction

There now exist numerous general-purpose algorithms for attribute selection used in referring expression generation (e.g., (Dale and Reiter, 1995; Krahmer et al., 2003; Belz and Gatt, 2007)). However, these algorithms by-and-large focus on the algorithmic aspects of referring expression generation rather than on psycholinguistic factors that influence language production. For example, we know that humans exhibit individual style differences during language production that can be quite pronounced (e.g. (Belz, 2007)). We also know that the language production process is subject to *lexical priming*, which means that words and concepts that have been used recently are likely to appear again (Levelt, 1989).

In this paper, we first explore the impact of individual style and priming on attribute selection for referring expression generation. To get an idea of the potential improvement when modeling these factors, we implemented a version of full brevity search (Dale, 1992) that uses speaker-specific constraints, and another version that also uses recency constraints. We found that using speaker-specific constraints led to big performance gains for both TUNA domains, while the use of recency constraints was not as effective for TUNA-style tasks. We then modified Dale and Reiter's classic attribute selection algorithm (Dale and Reiter, 1995) to model speaker-specific constraints, and found performance gains in this more greedy approach as well.

Then we looked at surface realization for referring expression generation. There are several approaches to surface realization described in the literature (Reiter and Dale, 2000) ranging from hand-crafted template-based realizers to data-driven syntax-based realizers (Langkilde and Knight, 2000; Bangalore and Rambow, 2000). Template-based realization involves the insertion of attribute values into predetermined templates. Data-driven syntax-based methods use syntactic relations between words (including long-distance relations) for word ordering. Other data-driven techniques exhaustively generate possible realizations with recourse to syntax in as much as it is reflected in local n-grams. Such techniques have the advantage of being robust although they are inadequate to capture long-range dependencies. In this paper, we explore three techniques for the task of referring expression generation that are different hybrids of hand-crafted and data-driven methods.

The remainder of this paper is organized as follows: In Section 2, we present the algorithms for attribute selection. The different methods for surface realizers are presented in Section 3. The experiments concerning the attribute selection and surface realization are presented in Section 4 and Section 5. The final remarks are discussed in Section 6.

2 Attribute Selection Algorithms

Full Brevity (FB) We implemented a version of full brevity search (Dale, 1992). It does the following: first, it constructs $\mathcal{AS}$, the set of attribute sets that uniquely identify the referent given the distractors. Then, it selects an attribute set $AS_u \in \mathcal{AS}$ based on a selection criterion. The **minimality (FB-m)** criterion selects from among the smallest elements of $\mathcal{AS}$ at random. The **frequency (FB-f)** criterion selects from among the elements of $\mathcal{AS}$ the one that occurred most often in the training data. The **speaker frequency (FB-sf)** criterion selects from among the elements of $\mathcal{AS}$ the one used most often by this speaker in the training data, backing off to FB-f if necessary. This criterion models speaker-specific constraints. Finally, the **speaker recency (FB-sr)** criterion selects from among the elements of $\mathcal{AS}$ the one used most recently by this speaker in the training data, backing off to FB-sf if necessary. This criterion models priming and speaker-specific constraints.

Dale and Reiter We implemented two variants of the classic Dale & Reiter attribute selection (Dale and Reiter, 1995) algorithm. For **Dale & Reiter basic (DR-b)**, we first build the preferred list of attributes by sorting the most frequently used attributes in the training set. We keep separate lists based upon the "+LOC" and "-LOC" conditions and backoff to a global preferred frequency list in case the attributes are not covered in the current list (merge and sort by frequency). Next, we iterate over the list of preferred attributes and select the next one that rules out at least one entity in the contrast set until no distractors are left. The **Dale & Reiter speaker frequency (DR-sf)** uses a speaker-specific preferred list, backing off to the DR-b preferred list if an attribute is not in the current speaker's preferred list. For this task, we ignored any further attribute knowledge base or taxonomy abstraction.

3 Surface Realization Approaches

We summarize our approaches to surface realization in this section. All three surface realizers have the same four stages: (a) lexical choice of words and phrases for the attribute values; (b) generation of a space of surface realizations (T); (c) ranking the set of realizations using a language model (LM); (d) selecting the best scoring realization.

$$T^* = BestPath(Rank(T, LM)) \quad (1)$$

Template-Based Realizer To construct our template-based realizer, we extract the annotated word string from each trial in the training data and replace each annotated text segment with the attribute type with which it is annotated. The key for each template is the lexicographically sorted list of attribute types it contains. Consequently, any attribute lists not found in the training data cannot be realized by the template-based realizer; however, if there is a template for an input attribute list it is quite likely to be coherent.

At generation time, we find all possible realizations of each attribute in the input attribute set, and fill in each possible template with each combination of the attribute realizations. We report results for two versions of this realizer: one with speaker-specific lexicon and templates (**Template-S**), and one without (**Template**).

Dependency-Based Realizer To construct our dependency-based realizer, we first parse all the word strings from the training data using the dependency parser described in (Bangalore et al., 2005; Nasr and Rambow, 2004). Then, for every pair of words w_i, w_j that occur in the same referring expression (RE) in the training data, we compute: $freq(i < j)$, the frequency with which w_i precedes w_j in any RE; $freq(i = j - 1)$, the frequency with which w_i immediately precedes w_j in any RE; $freq(dep(w_i, w_j) \wedge i < j)$, the frequency with which w_i depends on and precedes w_j in any RE, and $freq(dep(w_i, w_j) \wedge j < i)$, the frequency with which w_i depends on and follows w_j in any RE.

At generation time, we find all possible realizations of each attribute in the input attribute set, and for each combination of attribute realizations, we find the most likely set of dependencies and precedences given the training data.

Permute and Rank In this method, the lexical items associated with each of the attribute value to be realized are treated as a disjunctive set of tokens. This disjunctive set is represented as a finite-state automaton with two states and transitions between them labeled with the tokens of the set. The transitions are weighted by the negative logarithm of the probability of the lexical token (w) being associated with that attribute value ($attr$): $(-log(P(w|attr)))$. These sets are treated as unordered bags of tokens; we create permutations of these bags of tokens to represent the set of possible surface realizations. We then use the language model to rank this set of possible realizations and recover the highest scoring RE.

	DICE	MASI	Acc.	Uniq.	Min.
	Furniture				
FB-m	.36	.16	0	1	1
FB-f	.81	.58	.40	1	0
FB-sf	.95	.87	.79	1	0
FB-sr	.93	.81	.71	1	0
DR-b	.81	.60	.45	1	0
DR-sf	.86	.64	.45	1	.04
	People				
FB-m	.26	.12	0	1	1
FB-f	.58	.37	.28	1	0
FB-sf	.94	.88	.84	1	.01
FB-sr	.93	.85	.79	1	.01
DR-b	.70	.45	.25	1	0
DR-sf	.78	.55	.35	1	0
	Overall				
FB-m	.32	.14	0	1	1
FB-f	.70	.48	.34	1	0
FB-sf	.95	.87	.81	1	.01
FB-sr	.93	.83	.75	1	.01
DR-b	.76	.53	.36	1	0
DR-sf	.82	.60	.41	1	.02

Table 1: Results for attribute selection

Unfortunately, the number of states of the minimal permutation automaton of even a linear automata (finite-state machine representation of a string) grows exponentially with the number of words of the string. So, instead of creating a full permutation automaton, we choose to constrain permutations to be within a local window of adjustable size (also see (Kanthak et al., 2005)).

4 Attribute Selection Experiments

Data Preparation The training data were used to build the models outlined above. The development data were then processed one-by-one. For our final submissions, we use training and development data to build our models.

Results Table 1 shows the results for variations of full brevity. As we would expect, all approaches achieve a perfect score on uniqueness. For both corpora, we see a large performance jump when we use speaker constraints. However, when we incorporate recency constraints as well performance declines slightly. We think this is due to two factors: first, the speakers are not in a conversation, and self-priming may have less impact; and second, we do not always have the most recent prior utterance for a given speaker in the training data.

Table 1 also shows the results for variations of Dale and Reiter's algorithm. When we incorporate speaker constraints, we again see a performance jump, although compared to the best possible case (full brevity) there is still room for improvement.

	String-Edit Dist.			Accuracy		
	Furniture					
	DEV	FB-sf	DR-sf	DEV	FB-sf	DR-sf
Permute&Rank	4.39	4.60	4.74	0.07	0.04	0.03
Dependency	3.90	4.25	5.50	0.14	0.06	0.03
Template	4.36	4.33	5.39	0.07	0.05	0.03
Template-S	3.52	3.81	5.16	0.28	0.20	0.04
	People					
Permute&Rank	6.26	6.46	7.01	0.01	0.01	0.00
Dependency	3.96	4.32	7.03	0.06	0.06	0.00
Template	5.16	4.62	7.26	0.03	0.06	0.00
Template-S	4.25	4.31	7.04	0.18	0.13	0.00
	Overall					
Permute&Rank	5.25	5.45	5.78	0.05	0.03	0.01
Dependency	3.93	4.28	6.20	0.07	0.06	0.01
Template	4.73	4.46	6.25	0.05	0.05	0.01
Template-S	3.86	4.04	6.03	0.23	0.17	0.02

Table 2: Results for realization

Discussion We have shown that by using speaker and recency constraints in standard algorithms, it is possible to achieve performance gains on the attribute selection task.

The most relevant previous research is the work of (Gupta and Stent, 2005), who modified Dale and Reiter's algorithm to model speaker adaptation in dialog. However, this corpus does not involve dialog so there are no cross-speaker constraints, only within-speaker constraints (style and priming).

5 Surface Realization Experiments

Data Preparation We first normalize the training data to correct misspellings and remove punctuation and capitalization. We then extract a phrasal lexicon. For each attribute value we extract the count of all realizations of that value in the training data. We treat locations as a special case, storing separately the realizations of x-y coordinate pairs and single x- or y-coordinates. We add a small number of realizations to the lexicon by hand to cover possible attribute values not seen in the training data.

Results Table 2 shows the evaluation results for string-edit distance and string accuracy on the development set with three different attributes sets: **DEV** – attributes selected by the human test; **FB-sf** – attributes generated by the full brevity algorithm with speaker frequency; and **DR-sf** – attributes selected by the Dale & Reiter algorithm with speaker frequency.

For the TUNA realization task (**DEV** attributes), our approaches work better for the furniture domain, where there are fewer attributes, than for the people domain. For the furniture domain, the **Template-S** approach achieves lowest string-edit distance, while for the people domain, the **Dependency** approach achieves lowest string-edit distance. The latter method was submitted for human evaluation.

When we consider the "end-to-end" referring expression generation task (**FB-sf** and **DR-sf** attributes), the best overall performing system is the speaker-based template generator with full-brevity and speaker frequency attribute selection. In terms of generated sentence quality, a preliminary and qualitative analysis shows that the combination **Permute & Rank** and **DR-sf** produces more naturalistic phrases.

Discussion Although the Template-S approach achieves the best string edit distance scores overall, it is not very robust. If no examples were found in the training data neither Template approach will produce no output. (This happens twice for each of the domains on the development data.) The Dependency approach achieves good overall performance with more robustness.

The biggest cause of errors for the Permute and Reorder approach was missing determiners and missing modifiers. The biggest cause of errors for the Dependency approach was missing determiners and reordered words. The Template approach sometimes had repeated words (e.g. "middle", where "middle" referred to both x- and y-coordinates).

6 Conclusions

When building computational models of language, knowledge about the factors that influence human language production can prove very helpful. This knowledge can be incorporated in frequentist and heuristic approaches as constraints or features. In the experiments described in this paper, we used data-driven, speaker-aware approaches to attribute selection and referring expression realization. We showed that individual speaking style can be usefully modeled even for quite 'small' generation tasks, and confirmed that data-driven approaches to surface realization can work well using a range of lexical, syntactic and semantic information.

In addition to individual style and priming, another potentially fruitful area for exploration with TUNA-style tasks is human visual search strategies (Rayner, 1998). We leave this idea for future work.

Acknowledgments

We thank Anja Belz, Albert Gatt, and Eric Kow for organizing the REG competition and providing data, and Gregory Zelinsky for discussions about visually-based constraints.

References

S. Bangalore and O. Rambow. 2000. Exploiting a probabilistic hierarchical model for generation. In *Proc. COLING*.

S. Bangalore, A. Emami, and P. Haffner. 2005. Factoring global inference by enriching local representations. Technical report, AT&T Labs-Research.

A. Belz and A. Gatt. 2007. The attribute selection for GRE challenge: Overview and evaluation results. In *Proceedings of UCNLG+MT at MT Summit XI*.

A. Belz. 2007. Probabilistic generation of weather forecast texts. In *Proceedings of NAACL/HLT*.

R. Dale and E. Reiter. 1995. Computational interpretations of the Gricean maxims in the generation of referring expressions. *Cognitive Science*, 19(2).

Robert Dale. 1992. *Generating Referring Expressions: Constructing Descriptions in a Domain of Objects and Processes*. MIT Press, Cambridge, MA.

S. Gupta and A. Stent. 2005. Automatic evaluation of referring expression generation using corpora. In *Proceedings of UCNLG*.

S. Kanthak, D. Vilar, E. Matusov, R. Zens, and H. Ney. 2005. Novel reordering approaches in phrase-based statistical machine translation. In *Proc. ACL Workshop on Building and Using Parallel Texts*.

E. Krahmer, S. van Erk, and A. Verleg. 2003. Graph-based generation of referring expressions. *Computational Linguistics*, 29(1).

I. Langkilde and K. Knight. 2000. Forest-based statistical sentence generation. In *Proc. NAACL*.

W. Levelt, 1989. *Speaking: From intention to articulation*, pages 222–226. MIT Press.

A. Nasr and O. Rambow. 2004. Supertagging and full parsing. In *Proc. 7th International Workshop on Tree Adjoining Grammar and Related Formalisms (TAG+7)*.

K. Rayner. 1998. Eye movements in reading and information processing: 20 years of research. *Psychological Bulletin*, 124(3).

E. Reiter and R. Dale. 2000. *Building Natural Language Generation Systems*. Cambridge University Press.

NIL-UCM: Most-Frequent-Value-First Attribute Selection and Best-Scoring-Choice Realization

Pablo Gervás, Raquel Hervás, Carlos León
Natural Interaction based on Language (NIL)
Universidad Complutense de Madrid
c/ Profesor José García Santesmases s/n, 28040 Madrid, Spain
`pgervas@sip.ucm.es`, `raquelhb@fdi.ucm.es`, `cleon@fdi.ucm.es`

1 Introduction

The NIL entry for the challenge has been constructed upon the general architecture for developing Natural Language Generation systems provided by the TAP project (Gervás, 2007). TAP (Text Arranging Pipeline) is a set of interfaces that define generic functionality for a pipeline of tasks oriented toward natural language generation, from an initial conceptual input to surface realization as a string, with intervening stages of content planning and sentence planning.

The TAP architecture considers three basic stages: content planning, sentence planning and surface realization. Of these, the first stage is not relevant to the challenge tasks. The configuration choices applied to the other two stages to adapt them to the challenge tasks are described below.

2 NIL-UCM-MFVF Entry for Task 1

The NIL-UCM-MFVF for Task 1 applies a Most-Frequent-Value-First method for Attribute Selection. Of the five evaluation dimensions considered in this challenge (Dice, MASI, accuracy, minimality and uniqueness), this method has been designed to address explicitly only three: Dice, MASI and uniqueness. Minimality was abandoned in view of results in previous challenges (Hervás and Gervás, 2007) that showed good minimality results tended to produce low Dice scores. We have also opted for not using *accuracy* evaluation to fit the performance of our system, since the corpus contains a wide range of style of reference and we are interested in providing our system with only a subset of these that ensure correct identification.

2.1 Most-Frequent-Value-First Attribute Selection

The selection algorithm employed is an adaptation of the algorithm described in (Reiter and Dale, 1992). The original algorithm has been modified to allow for a dynamically changing *list of preferred attributes*, which determine the particular order in which attributes are considered to generate the distinguishing expression. This list is constructed dynamically for each reference by computing the probability of occurrence in the corpus of the particular attribute-value pairs associated with the referent, and using those probabilities to rank them into a specific list of preferred attributes. The idea is that attributes should be considered in a particular order depending highly on their values. For example, in the people domain we have observed that almost the 100% of the target entities that have beard (attribute has value `1`) are referred using the attribute `hasBeard`, but when this attribute has value `0` it is never used. For the `hasHair` attribute, the opposite seems to be the case (mentioned only when lacking).

The training data was studied to obtain the probability of occurrence of an attribute given a certain value for it. This probability was calculated using Formula 1:

$$prob_{val_i} = \frac{\sum appsValueInAttSet}{\sum appsValueInTarget} \tag{1}$$

For each possible value of each of the attributes of the domains, the sum of the appearances of this value in the `ATTRIBUTE-SET` elements (*appsValueInAttSet*) and the sum of the appearances of this value in the attributes of all targets (*appsValueInTarget*) are calculated. The division of these two values is the probability of mentioning an attribute when it has a specific value.

		Dice	MASI	Accuracy	Uniqueness	Minimality
Train.	**Furniture**	79,18%	56,95%	41,69%	100%	0%
	People	69,71%	42,41%	22,99%	100%	0%
	Both	74,80%	50,23%	34,81%	100%	0%
Dev.	**Furniture**	77,55%	53,97%	41,25%	100%	0%
	People	70,86%	42,59%	22,06%	100%	0%
	Both	74,48%	48,75%	32,43%	100%	0%

Table 1:Task 1 results for training and development data

Some examples of the results obtained are that the attribute `hasGlasses` is mentioned in the 60% of the situations when its value is `1`, and in the 0% of the situations when its value is `0`. On the contrary, the attribute `hasShirt` is almost never mentioned (0.8% when its value is `1` and 0% with value `0`).

The only exception in the algorithm is the `type` attribute for the people domain. As every entity in this domain is of type `person`, the attribute selector does not choose this attribute because no distractor is discarded by it. However, the experiments have shown us that in the corpus a lot of descriptions include the type `person` even when it is redundant. Following this idea, our algorithm always includes the `type` in the list of chosen attributes for the people domain.[1]

2.2 Obtained Results

Results obtained over the training and development data are shown in Table 1. As can be seen comparing both tables there are no surprises in the final results: the system gets similar results with both domains and with both the training and development data. These results confirm that the probability of appearance of an attribute depending on its value is more or less the same in the whole corpus.

3 NIL-UCM-BSC Entry for Task 2

The NIL-UCM-BSC for Task 2 applies a Best-Scoring-Choice approach to Realization.

The realization tasks of the 2008 GRE challenge required specific instantiations of the Referring Expression Generation, Syntactic Choice, and Lexicalization stages of the Sentence Planning module of TAP, and it draws on the SurReal (Gervás, 2006) surface realization module. SurReal provides a Java implementation of the surface realization mechanisms of FUF described in Elhadad (Elhadad, 1993), operating over a grammar which follows the notational conventions of the SURGE grammar in Elhadad (Elhadad and Robin, 1996), but it is not systemic in nature. It currently has much smaller coverage than the original, but quite sufficient to deal with the kind of realizations required for the challenge tasks.

3.1 Realization Choices in the Corpus

An analysis of the domain was carried out to ascertain what the various alternatives required for realization were for the given corpus, both in terms of how to realize syntactically the different concepts and what alternative lexicalizations should be considered. With respect to linguistic variation in the form of expression we have distinguished between choices that give rise to different syntactic structures (which we consider as syntactic choices) and choices which give rise to the same syntactic structures but with different lexical items (which we consider as lexical choices).

With respect to the *Referring Expression Generation* stage, the following issues required specific decisions. The use of **determiners** is erratic. Some examples in the corpus use indefinite article, some use definite articles, and some omit the determiners altogether. The corpus shows many cases where **spatial expressions** describing the location of referents are used, many using different systems of reference (north-south vs. top-bottom). The use of **particular features of the object** in its description, as in "the desk with the drawers facing the viewer" or "the chair with the seat facing away". **Comparison**

[1]We have only recently discovered that the surprising difference between NIL-UCM results for the *people* and the *furniture* domains in the 2007 GRE challenge was the mostly due to our not having taken this issue into account at the time. The effect is noticeable only when the type attribute is redundant, as it is in the *people* domain.

with all or some of the distractors are also used, either as adjuncts describing their position relative to other distractors, as in "the blue fan next to the green fan", or as comparative adjectives used for particular attributes, as in "the largest red couch" (and even combinations of the two as in "the smaller of the two blue fans"). Finally, there are samples in the corpus of use of **ellipsis and ungrammatical expressions**. The mention of particular features and the use of comparison would involve operating on more data than are generated in task 1, and the current submission is aimed to interconnection with task 2 for addressing task 3. The issue of ungrammaticality is important since it implies that there is an upper limit to the possible scores that the system may achieve over the corpus under the circumstances, totally unrelated with the correctness of the generated expressions.

With respect to *Syntactic Choice*, some attributes show **more than one possible option** for syntactic realization. The number of alternatives varies from color ("grey chair - chair that is gray"), through beards ("with beard - with the beard - with whiskers - the bearded man - with a beard - with facial hair") to orientation (12 different syntactic alternatives for expressing orientation: back).

There are slight **variations** of *Lexical Choice* over the corpus, as in "sofa - couch - settee - loveseat", "ventilator - fan - windmill" or "man - guy - bloke" (for nouns) and "large - big" or "small - little" (for adjectives). Because it has a significant impact on the edit distance measure, it is also important to consider the existence of a large number of **misspellings** in the corpus. Finally, there are some **conceptual mismatches in annotation**, between the attribute set and the given realization in some cases ("purple - blue", "black and white - grey",...).

3.2 Best Scoring Choice Solution

The solution employed in the present submission for selecting among the features described above implements straight forward realization rather than choice, in the sense in which (Cahill, 1998) uses the terms for lexicalization. To implement real choice the system would have to consider more than one alternative for a specific feature and to select one of them based on some criteria. This has not been done in the present submission. Instead, a single alternative has been implemented for each feature, using it consistently across all samples. The selection of which particular alternative to implement has been done empirically to ensure the best possible score over the training corpus.

3.3 Results and Discussion

Results obtained over the training and development data are shown in Table 2.

		SE distance	Accuracy
Train.	**Furniture**	4,26	14,15%
	People	5,43	9,12%
	Both	4,8	11,82%
Dev.	**Furniture**	4,21	15%
	People	4,94	7,35%
	Both	4,54	11,48%

Table 2:Task 2 results for training and development data

An important point to consider with respect to the current submission is whether a solution implementing real choice would have obtained better results. Such a solution might have benefited from the information that can be extracted from the `ANNOTATED-WORD-STRING` to train a decision procedure on the various features. This has not been addressed in the present submission more for lack of time than lack of conviction on its merit.

Addressing explicitly some of the possible constructions that are described in section 3.1 may also have a positive effect on the results.

4 NIL-UCM-FVBS Entry for Task 3

The NIL-UCM-FVBS entry for Task 3 applies a combination of the Most-Frequent-Value-First method for Attribute Selection and the Best-Scoring-Choice approach to Realization.

The modular architecture of TAP has allowed easy integration for Task 3 of the solution for attribute selection described in section 2, and the solution for realization described in section 3.

4.1 Results and Discussion

Results obtained over the training and development data are shown in Table 3. Comparing both sets of results there are no surprises in the final results: the system gets similar results with both domains and with both the training and development data. These results confirm that the probability of appearance of an attribute depending on its value is more or less the same in the whole corpus.

		SE distance	Accuracy
Train.	**Furniture**	5,03	5,03%
	People	6,11	5,47%
	Both	5,53	5,24%
Dev.	**Furniture**	5,06	3,75%
	People	6,24	1,47%
	Both	5,60	2,70%

Table 3:Task 3 results for training and development data

The results obtained are a bit lower than the ones obtained by both the attribute selection and realization submodules separately. This is not an unexpected result. Bad choices produced in the attribute selection are propagated through the realization, resulting in accumulated errors in the final evaluation.

However, there are additional shortcomings that arise from considering the general goal of task 3 as a composition of task 2 over task 1. The reduction of the types of expression produced by human subjects to a set of attributes involves in some cases a certain loss of information. This is particularly the case when the human-produced expressions involve attributes for which additional information is provided. This can be seen if the `ANNOTATED-WORD-STRING` is compared with the actual attribute set generated for some of the human-produced expressions. For instance, the corpus contains examples in which the `hasBeard` attribute has a nested attribute that indicates the beard is white. Other examples provide color information on pieces of clothing worn. This information is lost to the realization stage if the data have to go through task 1, which reduces the available format to a set of individual unstructured attributes.

Considering a version of task 3 that allowed full realization directly from input data as considered for task 1, with no requirements on the stages of intermediate representation to be employed in the process, may result in a richer range of realizations, and possibly in improved performance with respect to human evaluation.

In more general terms, it seems that the corpus does contain adequate data for informing system performance at the level of sentence planning subtasks such as lexical choice or syntactic choice. Nevertheless, some of the variations in the corpus, such as the free use of determiners or the flexibility that subjects exhibit in the way they refer to the images do introduce a certain "noise". Instances of these occur when human-produced descriptions involve intense forms of ellipsis, and agrammatical ordering of attributes. Some of these might be reduced if a refined version of the corpus were produced with more control on the experimental settings, to ensure that subjects either described the elements as images or as the things represented in the images, for instance.

Acknowledgments

This research is funded by the Spanish Ministry of Education and Science (TIN2006-14433-C02-01 project) and the UCM and the Dirección General de Universidades e Investigación of the CAM (CCG07-UCM/TIC-2803).

References

Cahill, Lyne. 1998. Lexicalisation in applied NLG systems. *Technical Report* ITRI-99-04.

Elhadad, Michael. 1993. Technical Report CUCS-038-91. Columbia University.

Elhadad, Michael and Robin, Jacques. 1996. Technical Report 96-03. Department of Computer Science, Ben Gurion University.

Gervás, Pablo. 2006. SurReal: a Surface Realization module. *Natural Interaction based on Language Group Technical Report*, Universidad Complutense de Madrid, Spain.

Gervás, Pablo. 2007. TAP: a Text Arranging Pipeline. *Natural Interaction based on Language Group Technical Report*, Universidad Complutense de Madrid, Spain.

Hervás, Raquel and Gervás, Pablo. 2007. NIL: Attribute Selection for Matching the Task Corpus Using Relative Attribute Groupings Obtained from the Test Data. *First NLG Challenge on Attribute Selection for Generating Referring Expressions (ASGRE)*, UCNLG+MT Workshop, Machine Translation Summit XI, Copenhagen.

Reiter, Ehud and Dale, Robert. 1992. A fast algorithm for the generation of referring expressions. *Proceedings of the 14th conference on Computational Linguistics*, pp. 232-238. Association for Computational Linguistics.

USP-EACH Frequency-based Greedy Attribute Selection for Referring Expressions Generation

Diego Jesus de Lucena
Escola de Artes, Ciências e Humanidades
University of São Paulo – USP
Av. Arlindo Bettio, 1000 - São Paulo, Brazil
diego.si@usp.br

Ivandré Paraboni
Escola de Artes, Ciências e Humanidades
University of São Paulo – USP
Av. Arlindo Bettio, 1000 - São Paulo, Brazil
ivandre@usp.br

Abstract

Both greedy and domain-oriented REG algorithms have significant strengths but tend to perform poorly according to humanlikeness criteria as measured by, e.g., Dice scores. In this work we describe an attempt to combine both perspectives into a single attribute selection strategy to be used as part of the Dale & Reiter Incremental algorithm in the REG Challenge 2008, and the results in both Furniture and People domains.

1 Introduction

Minimality and Humanlikeness in REG are often conflicting goals. Greedy algorithms tend to favour shorter descriptions, but in doing so their output may look unnatural. On the other hand, domain-oriented algorithms that arguably favour more "human-like" strategies (e.g., selecting the most typical attributes first) pay little or no attention to minimality, and as a result the generated descriptions may become overly long or clumsy.

Which strategy might a human speaker favour? In this work we describe an algorithm that disregards minimality entirely and attempts to select 'typical' attributes based on two simple assumptions: first, when facing a complex context with a large number of objects, an attempt to compute the precise attribute capable of ruling out the largest possible number of distractors is not only hard (from the computational point of view), but also less natural than simply using typical (e.g., frequent) attributes. On the other hand, as the number of distractors decreases, it may become gradually clearer for the speaker which attributes are most helpful to achieve uniqueness, up to the point in which she may naturally switch to a 'greedy' strategy and finalize the description. These assumptions are implemented as an attribute selection strategy to be used with the Incremental algorithm (Dale & Reiter, 1995) described below.

2 System Description

We take a simple view of humanlikeness in which the list of preferred attributes is sorted by relative frequency[1] as seen in the training data. The resulting list P is the centre piece of the following attribute selection strategy:

(1) select all attributes whose relative frequency falls above a trainable threshold value t (in our experiments t is estimated to be 0.8 for both Furniture and People domains.)

(2) if the resulting description uniquely describes the target object, then finalizes.

(3) if not, starting from the most frequent attribute in P, search exhaustively for an attribute g such that g, if selected, would rule out *all* remaining distractors in the context.

[1] This contrasts the work in Kelleher (2007), which takes into account *absolute* counts seen in the training data.

(4) if such attribute *g* exists, then *g* is selected and the algorithm finalizes.

(5) if not, select the most frequent attribute *f* that can rule out at least one distractor, and repeat steps (3-5).

The selection of attribute *g* stands for the greedy component of our approach, whilst the initial attributes in step 1 and the attribute *f* account for our 'humanlikeness as frequency' assumption. The overall effect attempted is the following:

- Highly frequent attributes are always selected. In our tests this means that the attributes *type* and *colour* were always included in Furniture descriptions, and *type* was always included in People descriptions (in both cases this is so regardless of discriminatory power.) As a result, we can only produce minimal descriptions by chance.
- In a complex situation of reference (in which many attributes may rule out many distractors, but more than one will be required to achieve uniqueness) the algorithm simply selects the most frequent attributes, perhaps not unlike a human speaker who has to single out the target object but who does not have the time or resources to come up with the 'best' attribute straight away.
- As the number of distractors decreases, a single attribute capable of ruling out all distractors will eventually emerge, forcing the algorithm to switch to a greedy strategy and finalize. Once again, this might be just what humans do when a suitable (i.e., economical) attribute becomes sufficiently salient and all distractors in the context can be ruled out at once.

3 Results

Below we summarize our results for Task 1 (Attribute Selection) and also for Task 3 (Attribute Selection and Surface Realisation combined) for the REG 2008 development data set (80 instances for Furniture and 68 instances for People.) As expected, our algorithm is heavily penalized in the Minimality criteria but performs reasonably well in Humanlikeness (Dice and MASI.) if compared to the systems presented in the previous GRE Challenge.

	Overall		Furniture		People	
	Mean	SD	Mean	SD	Mean	SD
Dice	0.75	0.25	0.82	0.22	0.66	0.26
MASI	0.53	0.39	0.62	0.39	0.42	0.35
Accuracy	0.37	0.48	0.49	0.50	0.24	0.43
Uniqueness	1.00	-	1.00	-	1.00	-
Minimality	-	-	-	-	-	-
String-edit distance	6.70	3.09	6.13	3.28	7.38	2.72
String-accuracy	0.02	0.14	0.04	0.19	-	-

Figure 1. Attribute Selection and Surface Realisation results

Acknowledgments

This work has been supported by CNPq-Brazil (484015/2007-9) and FAPESP (2006/03941-7).

References

Dale, Robert and Ehud Reiter. 1995. *Computational interpretations of the Gricean maxims in the generation of referring expressions*. Cognitive Science (19).

Kelleher, J.D. (2007) *DIT - Frequency Based Incremental Attribute Selection for GRE*. MT Summit XI Workshop Using Corpora for Natural Language Generation: Language Generation and Machine Translation, pp. 90-91.

Referring Expression Generation Challenge 2008 DIT System Descriptions

J.D. Kelleher
School of Computing
Dublin Institute of Technology
john.kelleher@comp.dit.ie

B. Mac Namee
School of Computing
Dublin Institute of Technology
brian.macnamee@comp.dit.ie

1 Task 1: Attribute Selection

This section describes the two systems developed at DIT for the attribute selection track of the REG 2008 challenge. Both of theses systems use an incremental greedy search to generate descriptions, similar to the incremental algorithm described in (Dale and Reiter, 1995). The output of these incremental algorithms are, to a large extent, determined by the order in which the algorithm tests the target object's attributes for inclusion in the description. Indeed, the major difference between the two systems described in this section is the mechanism used to order the attributes for inclusion.

1.1 DIT-FBI System

The DIT-FBI system selects the next attribute to be tested for inclusion in the description by ordering each attribute based on its frequency in the subset of the training corpus that is defined by the test trial's domain (i.e., furniture versus people) and condition (+LOC versus -LOC). Attributes are selected in descending order of frequency (i.e. the attribute that occurred most frequently in the relevant subset of the training corpus is selected first). Where two or more attributes have the same frequency of occurrence the first attribute found with that frequency is selected. The *type* attribute is always included in the description. Other attributes are included in the description if they exclude at least 1 distractor from the set of distractors that fulfil the description generated prior to that attribute's selection.

The mapping from qualitative linguistics descriptions, such as middle or centre, to the TUNA corpus' quantitative location attribute values, i.e, *x-dimension* and *y-dimension*, can result in both the *x-dimension* and *y-dimension* attributes being included in the target set. These cases, where both the dimensional attributes are required, are difficult to capture because each of the dimensional attributes would be sufficiently discriminative to result in a distinguishing description simply by their lone inclusion. As a result, a rule was put in place whereby if we have included either of the dimensional attributes we include the other dimensional attribute if the included one refers to the center of the display (i.e., x=3, y=2).

The algorithm terminates when a distinguishing description has been generated (i.e., all the distractors have been excluded) or when all of the target's attributes have been tested for inclusion in the description. Table 1 lists the results for the system.

	Furniture	People	Both
Dice	0.816	0.702	0.763
MASI	0.606	.452	0.535
Accuracy	37	17	54
Minimality	80	68	148
Uniqueness	0	0	0

Table 1: Results for furniture, people and both domains.

1.2 DIT-TVAS System

In the DIT-TVAS system the selection of the next target attribute to test for inclusion in the description is based on the prior probability of a target's attribute *with a particular value* being used to describe the target, given that the target has a particular attribute with that particular value. This prior is computed by counting the number of trials in the training corpus where the *target description* included a particular attribute-value pair and dividing this count by the number of trials in the training corpus where the target's properties listed a particular attribute-value pair.

For example, there are *143* trials in the Reg-08-Challenge training corpus where the target's type attribute had the value *chair*, and in *134* of these trials the description of the target included the attribute value pair *type-chair*. As a result, the atribute-value pair *type-chair* has a prior probability of being used to describe the target, given that the target properties contain this attribute-value combination, of $\frac{134}{143} \approx 0.937$. Table 2 lists the priors for each attribute-value combination in the furniture corpus and Table 3 lists the priors for each attribute-value combination in the people corpus (for space reasons these tables do not include the priors for the *x-dimension*, *y-dimension* and *other* attributes-value pairs). Given these tables and a test trial, the next attribute-value pair to be tested for inclusion in the description of the test target is the attibute-value with the highest prior that has not already been tested for inclusion and that the target object fulfils.

As is evident from Table 2 and Table 3, there is no significant difference between the priors of some attribute-value pairs. For example, in the furniture domain *orientation=left* and *hasShirt=true* have priors of 0.023 and 0.022 respectively. In order to avoid situations where a non-significant difference in priors unduly biases the system toward the inclusion of a particular attribute-value pair, each time an attribute-vaule pair has been selected for testing the DIT-TVAS system checks whether there are any other attribute-value pairs that have not been previously tested for inclusion in the description of the target and whose prior is within 5% of the prior of the attribute-value that has been selected for testing. In cases where this test returns one or more attribute-value pairs, the system uses the attribute-value pair whose inclusion would exclude the most amount of distractors. Finally, if there is a tie between one or more attribute-value pairs with respect to distractor exclusion this is resolved by slecting the attribute-value pair with the highest prior. Table 4 lists the results for the system.

Attribute	VALUE	Sel	Occur	Prior
TYPE	fan	41	42	0.976
TYPE	chair	134	143	0.937
TYPE	sofa	43	48	0.896
COLOUR	green	35	40	0.875
COLOUR	blue	75	86	0.872
COLOUR	red	82	96	0.854
TYPE	desk	73	86	0.849
COLOUR	grey	81	97	0.835
ORIENTATION	back	25	51	0.490
SIZE	small	56	130	0.431
ORIENTATION	front	31	86	0.360
SIZE	large	61	189	0.324
ORIENTATION	left	22	86	0.256
ORIENTATION	right	28	96	0.292

Table 2: Prior's for each attribute-value pair in the furniture domain. Sel: how often an attribute-value pair was included in a description; Occur: how often an attribute-vaule pair appeared in targets in the training corpus. Prior's listed to three decimal places.

Attribute	VALUE	Sel	Occur	Prior
TYPE	person	225	274	0.821
hasBeard	true	123	181	0.680
hasGlasses	true	117	184	0.636
hasSuit	true	4	94	0.43
hasHair	true	36	233	0.155
hasHair	false	6	41	0.146
AGE	old	15	132	0.114
ORIENTATION	right	2	44	0.045
ORIENTATION	front	4	143	0.028
ORIENTATION	left	2	87	0.023
hasShirt	true	3	136	0.022
hasTie	true	2	94	0.021
AGE	young	2	142	0.014
hasShirt	false	0	138	0
hasBeard	false	0	93	0
hasGlasses	false	0	90	0
hasTie	false	0	180	0
hasSuit	false	0	180	0

Table 3: Prior's for each attribute-value pair in the furniture domain. Sel: how often an attribute-value pair was included in a description; Occur: how often an attribute-vaule pair appeared in targets in the training corpus. Prior's listed to three decimal places.

	Furniture	People	Both
Dice	0.778	0.709	0.746
MASI	0.540	.426	0.488
Accuracy	33	15	48
Uniqueness	80	68	148
Minimality	0	0	0

Table 4: Results for furniture, people and both domains.

2 Task 2: Realisation

This section describes the two systems developed at DIT for the realisation track of the REG 2008 challenge. The DIT-CBSR system, Section 2.1, uses a case-based reasoning approach to realization, which (Daelemans and van den Bosch, 2005) have recently argued is an appropriate machine learning approach to natural language processing. The DIT-RBR system, Section 2.2, uses a set of hand-crafted domain-specific rules to generate descriptions.

2.1 DIT-CBSR System

Cased-Based Reasoning attempts to use a history of past problems and their solutions to solve newly arising problems. The solution to a new problem is generated by finding the problem in the set of training problems the system has previously seen (i.e. the *case base*) which most closely matches it and adapting its solution.

The DIT-CBSR system uses a relatively simple case matching algorithm. When a new trial requires sentence generation it's attribute set is matched against all of the cases in the training set to determine which cases is matches most closely. This matching firstly considers only attributes and their values. There are three kinds of matches that can arise from this process:

- **Perfect match:** the attributes used in both the query case and the case from the case-base match perfectly as do their values.
- **Partial match:** the attribute used by both the query case and the case from the case-base match perfectly, but the attribute values do not match.
- **No match:** no member of the case-base has a list of attributes used that match those required by the query case.

Slightly different actions are taken depending on the type of match achieved. These are as follows.

Perfect Match Perfect matches are the easiest to deal with as little effort is required in order to produce a useful sentence. In fact, if only one perfect match is found then that trial's word string is used, unedited, as the generated sentence. However, things become a little more interesting if more than one case in the case-base matches the query case perfectly (remembering that the match is only based on the attributes used and their values). In this case, the list of matches is first trimmed of any cases that are not based on the same image as the query case, as long as this does not remove all cases. If this does remove all cases we revert to the original set of matching cases. In either instance, the word strings in the set of remaining matching cases are considered to determine if there are any duplicates. If there are, the word string that appears most frequently is used as the generated sentence. If there are no duplicates, the shortest word string in the set is chosen.

Partial Match Partial matches occur when there is no example in the case-base for which all of the attribute values are the same as those of the query case. However, there are some case whose attributes match the query, but whose attribute values are different. This set of cases is sub-divided based on the number of attribute values in each case that match those in the query case. This results in a set of cases that share the highest match score. From this set all of those cases that are not based on the same image as the query case are removed, as long as this does not completely empty the set. If this trimming would completely empty the set it is not performed. The trial with the shortest word string from the set of remaining candidate matches is selected. The word string associated with the selected trial needs to be modified to account for the disparity between its attribute values and those of the query case. This modification is done by replacing all substrings in the selected case's word string that arise from attribute values not matching those in the query case with the substring that is most commonly associated in the training corpus with the query case's attribute value. All of these substrings are identified using the annotated word string element present in each trial.

No Match When no match is found a simple rule-based realiser is used to construct a sentence matching the attribute value set of the query case. The rules used by the realiser are based on the most common strings found in the corpus for each attribute value pair.

Table 5 lists the results for the system.

	Furniture	People	Both
String-edit distance	3.95	4.81	4.34
Accuracy score	12	6	18

Table 5: Results for furniture, people and both domains.

2.2 DIT-RBR System

In Section 2.1 we noted that if no match was found in the case-base a simple rule-based realiser was used. This rule-based realiser, the DIT-RBR system, uses a sequence of `IF-THEN` rules based on a study of the frequencies and order of the phrases used to realise specific attribute-value pairs in the training corpus. Theses phrase are easily extracted from the annotated word-string xml element. The great advantage of this algorithm is that it always able to return a string given an input. However, the rule-set is specific to the task and would not generalise as well as the DIT-CBSR system. Due to space restrictions we do not list the rules used by the system. Table 6 lists the results for the system.

	Furniture	People	Both
String edit distance	3.613	4.132	3.851
Accuracy	11	3	14

Table 6: Results for furniture, people and both domains.

3 Task 3: Referring Expression Generation

This section describes describes our approach to task 3 of REG Challenge 2008. Each of the systems described in this section simply chains together DIT solutions to task 1 and task 2.

3.1 DIT-FBI-CBSR System

The DIT-FBI-CBSR system chains together the DIT-FBI attribute selection system, described in 1.1, and the DIT-CBSR system, described in Section 2.1. Table 7 lists the results for the system.

	Furniture	People	Both
String-edit distance	4.45	5.162	4.777
Accuracy score	7	1	8

Table 7: Results for furniture, people and both domains.

3.2 DIT-TVAS-RBR Task 3 System

The DIT-TVAS-RBR system chains together the DIT-TVAS attribute selection system, described in Section 1.2, and the DIT-RBR realiser, described in Section 2.2. Table 8 lists the results for the system.

	Furniture	People	Both
String-edit distance	4.725	5.178	4.905
Accuracy score	4	0	4

Table 8: Results for furniture, people and both domains.

References

Walter Daelemans and Antal van den Bosch. 2005. *Memory-Based Language Processing*. Cambridge University Press.

R. Dale and E. Reiter. 1995. Computatinal interpretations of the gricean maxims in the generation of referring expressions. *Cognitive Science*, 18:233–263.

OSU-GP: Attribute Selection using Genetic Programming

Josh King
Department of Computer Science and Engineering
The Ohio State University
Columbus, OH 43210, USA
kingjo@cse.ohio-state.edu

Abstract

This system's approach to the attribute selection task was to use a genetic programming algorithm to search for a solution to the task. The evolved programs for the furniture and people domain exhibit quite naive behavior, and the DICE and MASI scores on the training sets reflect the poor humanlikeness of the programs.

valueIn	{variables}
target	sequence
distractors	canUseLoc
eqA	ifte
set_empty	for
set_add	and, or, not
set_remove	{attributeERC}
add	{attributeListERC}
remove	

Table 1: Functions supplied to the GP algorithm

1 Genetic Programming

Genetic programming is a form of evolutionary computing in which a meta program evolves another program to solve a problem. Creating by hand a program which solves the problem may be possible, but if the problem has many parameters which contribute to a solution's quality, the program designer may miss some subtle interplay in favor of an expected solution. Genetic programming evolves a pool of programs to optimize a user supplied fitness function which gives some indication of how well a program performs on the problem.

This report in no way attempt to fully explain genetic programming. See, *e.g.*, (Koza, 1992) for a better understanding of genetic programming. The evolutionary computation toolkit ECJ available from `http://www.cs.gmu.edu/~eclab/projects/ecj/` was used for the genetic programming algorithm.

2 Functions

The genetic programming algoritm had at its disposal the functions listed in Table 1. The function eqA tests whether two attribute *values* are equal. The functions add and remove operate on attribute lists, whereas the similarly named set_add and set_remove operate on entity sets. The function ifte is an if-then-else construct, and the function for is a foreach operator on sets of entities or lists of attributes and requires both a variable to change the value of (the iterating variable) and the set or list to operate over. The functions surrounded by braces represent various things: for {variables}, various variables of the different types were globally accessible. {attributeERC} and {attributeListERC} represent random variables that take on attributes from the trial set and lists of those attributes. A mutation of an ERC (ephemeral random constant) simply sets it to a different random value from the random constant's domain.

The functions supplied to the genetic programming method were more than expressive enough to formulate, *e.g.*, Dale and Reiter's Incremental Algorithm (Dale and Reiter, 1995), a well known standard algorithm for doing this task. During the run of the genetic programming algorithm, every function shown in Table 1 was explored in the search, even though many of them are not used in the solutions found.

diceDist	locationUse
masiDist	inappropriate
noHit	length
bloat	empty
similar	excessive

Table 2: The costs GP should minimize

3 Fitness Function

The genetic programming algorithm must be supplied with a fitness function which judges how well a program performs on the problem. For this task of attribute selection, there are multiple dimensions to optimize in. For simplicity, a linear combination of the various dimensions was used for the fitness function. The dimensions to optimize on were represented as costs or penalties that the genetic programming algorithm sought to minimize. The various costs are listed in Table 2. The costs were devised with an eye towards optimizing quantities that existing algorithms for this task also attempt to optimize.

DICE and MASI scores on the training data were converted to costs by subtracting from one. The noHit cost is for not forming a distinguishing collection of attributes and was given a high weight. The bloat penalty penalizes long programs (to make interpreting the result easier).

The fitness function is a weighted sum of these costs. A fitness of zero would mean that each dimension is optimized fully. This is not possible, as some of the costs conflict with each other: for example, length and empty. The weights for the fitness function were hand tuned, which is counter to the desire to use genetic programming rather than hand tune an algorithm. The use of evolutionary computing to tune these weights may produce better results, but was not tried here.

4 Resulting System

The program which evolved for the training trials of the furniture domain is shown here:

```
(ifte canUseLoc
 (var_aList_set al0
  (add [ orientation size ]
      colour))
 (var_aList_set al0
  (add (add [ orientation size ]
      colour) type)))
```

The program found for the people domain is shown here:

```
(ifte canUseLoc
 (var_aList_set al0 (add
  (add [ hairColour hasGlasses ]
      hasBeard) hasSuit))
 (var_aList_set al0
  (add [ hairColour hasGlasses ]
      hasBeard)))
```

Both of these programs seem quite unintelligent in their behavior. They only ever set the attribute list to one of two lists, depending only on whether the location condition is flagged or not, and don't even make use of the location information. Further tweaking of the fitness function or using different schemes for evolution may improve the performance of an evolved solution.

	DICE	MASI
Furniture	0.61	0.30
People	0.35	0.10
Average	0.49	0.21

Table 3: DICE and MASI scores on training set

The performance metrics of DICE score and MASI score on the training set are shown in Table 3. The accuracy of the realization[1] of the attributes is both zero. The scores reflect the obvious point that the evolved programs have plenty of room for improvement. A fitness function which is less reliant on the user to specify weightings for optimization may be necessary, or an evaluation which tests the program's ability to generalize may catalyze program evolution into less naive directions than those programs shown here.

References

Robert Dale and Ehud Reiter. 1995. Computational interpretations of the gricean maxims in the generation of referring expressions. *Cognitive Science*, 19(2):233–263.

John R. Koza. 1992. *Genetic Programming: on the Programming of Computers by Means of Natural Selection*. The MIT Press.

[1]The realizer was the simple template-based realizer written by Irene Langkilde-Geary, Brighton University for the ASGRE 2007 challenge.

GRAPH: The Costs of Redundancy in Referring Expressions

Emiel Krahmer
Tilburg University
The Netherlands
e.j.krahmer@uvt.nl

Mariët Theune
University of Twente
The Netherlands
m.theune@utwente.nl

Jette Viethen
Macquarie University
Australia
jviethen@ics.mq.edu.au

Iris Hendrickx
University of Antwerp
Belgium
iris.hendrickx@ua.ac.be

Abstract

We describe a graph-based generation system that participated in the TUNA attribute selection and realisation task of the REG 2008 Challenge. Using a stochastic cost function (with certain properties for free), and trying attributes from cheapest to more expensive, the system achieves overall .76 DICE and .54 MASI scores for attribute selection on the development set. For realisation, it turns out that in some cases higher attribute selection accuracy leads to larger differences between system-generated and human descriptions.

1 Introduction

Referring Expression Generation (REG) is a key-task in NLG, and the topic of the REG 2008 Challenge.[1] In this context, referring expressions are understood as *distinguishing descriptions*: descriptions that uniquely characterize a target object in a visual scene (e.g., "the red sofa"), and do not apply to any of the other objects in the scene (the distractors). Generating such descriptions is usually assumed to be a two-step procedure: first, it has to be decided which attributes of the target suffice to characterize it uniquely, and then the selected set of attributes should be converted into natural language.

For the first step, attribute selection, we use a version of the Graph-based REG algorithm of Krahmer et al. (2003). In this approach, a visual scene is represented as a directed labelled graph, where vertices represent the objects in the scene and edges their attributes. A key ingredient of the approach is that costs can be assigned to attributes; the generation of referring expressions can then be defined as a graph search problem, which outputs the cheapest distinguishing graph (if one exists) given a particular cost function. For the second step, realisation, we use a simple template-based realiser written by Irene Langkilde-Geary from Brighton University that was made available to all REG 2008 participants.

A version of the Graph-based algorithm was submitted for the ASGRE 2007 Challenge (Theune et al. 2007). For us, one of the most striking, general outcomes was the observed "trend for the mean DICE score obtained by a system to decrease as the proportion of minimal descriptions increases" (Belz and Gatt 2007).[2] Thus, while REG systems have a tendency to produce minimal descriptions, human speakers tend to include redundant properties in their descriptions, which is in line with recent findings in psycholinguistics on the production of referring expressions (e.g., Engelhardt et al. 2006).

In principle, the graph-based approach has the potential to deal with redundancy by allowing some attributes to have zero costs. Viethen et al. (2008), however, show that merely assigning zero costs to an attribute is not a sufficient condition for inclusion; if the search terminates before the free properties are tried, they will not be included. In other words: the order in which attributes are tried should be explicitly controlled as well. In the experiment we describe here, we consider both these factors and their interplay.

[1] See http://www.itri.brighton.ac.uk/research/reg08/.

[2] DICE (like MASI) is a measure for similarity between a predicted attribute set and a (human produced) reference set.

2 Method

We experimentally combine four cost functions and two search orders (Table 1). (1) **Simple** simply assigns each edge a 1-point cost. (2) **Stochastic** associates each edge with a frequency-based cost, based on both the 2008 training and development sets (assuming that a larger data set allows for more accurate frequency estimates). (3) **Free-Stochastic** is like the previous cost function, except that highly frequent attributes are assigned 0 costs. For the Furniture domain, this applies to "colour"; for People to "hasBeard = 1" and "hasGlasses = 1." (4) **Free-Naive**, finally, reduces the relatively fine-grained costs of Free-Stochastic to three values (0 = free, 1 = cheap, 2 = expensive). In addition, we compare results for two property orderings: (A) Properties are tried in a **Random** order. (B) **Cost-based**, where properties are tried (in stochastic order) from cheapest to most expensive. Finally, since human speakers nearly always include the "type" property, we decided to simply always include it. Tables 2 to 4 summarize the evaluation results for all combinations of cost functions and search orders.

3 Attribute Selection Results

The measures used to evaluate attribute selection are DICE, MASI, attribute accuracy (A-A, the proportion of times the generated attribute set was identical to the reference set), and minimality (MIN).

Notice first that the order in which attributes are tried in the search process matters; the B-systems nearly always outperform their A-counterparts. Second, assigning varying costs also helps; both 1-variants (**Simple** costs) perform worse than the systems building on **Stochastic** cost functions (2, 3 and 4). Third, adding free properties is also beneficial; the 3 and 4 variants clearly outperform the 1 and 2 variants. It is interesting to observe that the **Free-naive** cost function (4) performs equally well as the more principled **Free-stochastic** (3), but only in combination with the **Cost-based** order (B). To the extent that it is possible to compare the results, the submitted GRAPH 4+B outperforms our best 2007 variant (GRAPH FP in Table 2). This suggests that the interplay between property ordering and cost function is a flexible and efficient approach to attribute selection.

Table 1: Overview of cost functions and search orders. The GRAPH 4+B settings were submitted to the REG 2008 Challenge.

Costs		**Orders**	
1	Simple	A	Random
2	Stochastic	B	Cost-based
3	Free-stochastic		
4	Free-naive		

Table 2: Furniture development set results (80 trials).

GRAPH	DICE	MASI	A-A	MIN	EDIT	S-A
1+A	.61	.32	.12	.29	5.90	.04
1+B	.61	.31	.12	.29	5.89	.04
2+A	.71	.47	.31	.11	5.06	.05
2+B	.69	.44	.28	.16	5.19	.05
3+A	.80	.58	.45	.00	4.90	.05
3+B	.80	.58	.45	.00	4.90	.05
4+A	.80	.59	.48	.00	4.61	.05
4+B	.80	.59	.48	.00	4.61	.05
FP 2007	.71	–	–	–	–	–

Table 3: People development set results (68 trials).

GRAPH	DICE	MASI	A-A	MIN	EDIT	S-A
1+A	.59	.36	.24	.00	6.54	.00
1+B	.66	.42	.24	.00	6.78	.00
2+A	.66	.42	.24	.00	6.78	.00
2+B	.66	.42	.24	.00	6.78	.00
3+A	.68	.41	.19	.00	6.79	.00
3+B	.72	.48	.28	.00	6.96	.00
4+A	.59	.34	.18	.00	6.56	.00
4+B	.72	.48	.28	.00	6.96	.00
FP 2007	.67	–	–	–	–	–

Table 4: Combined Furniture and People development set results.

GRAPH	DICE	MASI	A-A	MIN	EDIT	S-A
1+A	.60	.34	.18	.16	6.20	.02
1+B	.63	.36	.18	.16	6.30	.02
2+A	.69	.45	.28	.06	5.85	.03
2+B	.68	.43	.26	.09	5.92	.03
3+A	.74	.51	.33	.00	5.77	.03
3+B	.76	.54	.37	.00	5.84	.03
4+A	.70	.48	.34	.00	5.51	.03
4+B	.76	.54	.39	.00	5.69	.03
FP 2007	.69	–	–	–	–	–

4 Realization Results

To evaluate realisation, the following two word-string comparison measures were used: string-edit distance (EDIT), which is the Levenshtein distance between generated word string and human reference output, and string accuracy (S-A), which is the proportion of times the word string was identical to the reference string.

For all settings of the algorithm, we see that S-A is much lower than A-A. This is as expected, since any set of attributes can be expressed in many different ways, and the chance that the realizer produces exactly the same string as the human reference is quite small. For the furniture domain, we see that S-A has a fairly constant low score, while EDIT follows the same pattern as A-A: including redundant (free) properties leads to better results. For the people domain, S-A is always 0, and surprisingly EDIT gets worse as A-A gets better.

To explain these results, we inspect those descriptions where A-A = 1 but S-A = 0, i.e., the attribute set is identical to the human reference but the word string is not. In setting 4+B (submitted to REG 2008) this is the case for 34 furniture and 19 people descriptions. For furniture, we see that the low S-A score can be largely explained by the fact that in 23 of the 34 descriptions the human reference either included no determiner or an indefinite one, whereas the system always included a definite determiner. This also explains why S-A hardly improves with higher A-A scores, since determiner choice is independent from attribute selection.

In the people domain, the zero scores for S-A can be explained by the fact that the realizer always uses "person" to express the type attribute, where the human references have either "man" or "guy" (in line with the human preference for *basic level* values; cf. Krahmer et al. 2003). We also encounter the determiner problem again, aggravated by the fact that many person descriptions include embedded noun phrases (e.g., "man with beard").

To find out why EDIT gets worse as A-A increases for different system settings in the people domain, we look at the six descriptions that have A-A = 1 for setting 4+B but not for 4+A. It turns out that five of these descriptions are realized as "the light-haired person with a beard", while the human reference strings are variations of "the man with a white beard", resulting in a relatively high EDIT value. The problem here is that the link between beard and hair colour has been lost in the data annotation process.

In general, we can conclude that simply combining more or less human-like attribute selection with an off-the-shelf surface realiser is not sufficient to produce human-like referring expressions.

Acknowledgements We thank the REG 2008 organizers for making the realiser available, and Hendri Hondorp for his help with installing and using it.

References

Belz, A. and A. Gatt 2007. The attribute selection for GRE challenge: Overview and evaluation results *Proceedings of UCNLG+MT* 75-83

Engelhardt, P., K. Bailey and F. Ferreira 2006. Do speakers and listeners observe the Gricean Maxim of Quantity? *Journal of Memory and Language, 54*, 554-573.

Krahmer, E., S. van Erk and A. Verleg 2003. Graph-based generation of referring expressions. *Computational Linguistics, 29(1)*, 5372.

Theune, M., P. Touset, J. Viethen, and E. Krahmer. 2007. Cost-based attribute selection for generating referring expressions (GRAPH-FP and GRAPH-SC). *Proceedings of the* ASGRE *Challenge 2007*, Copenhagen, Denmark

Viethen, J., R. Dale, E. Krahmer, M. Theune and P. Touset. 2008. Controlling redundancy in referring expressions. *Proceedings LREC 08*, Marrakech, Morroco.

JU-PTBSGRE: GRE Using Prefix Tree Based Structure

Sibabrata Paladhi
Department of Computer Sc. & Engg.
Jadavpur University, India
sibabrata_paladhi@yahoo.com

Sivaji Bandyopadhyay
Department of Computer Sc. & Engg.
Jadavpur University, India
sivaji_cse_ju@yahoo.com

Abstract

This paper presents a Prefix Tree based model of Generation of Referring Expression (RE). Our algorithm PTBSGRE works in two phases. First, an encoded prefix tree is constructed describing the domain structure. Subsequently, RE is generated using that structure. We evaluated our system using Dice, MASI, Accuracy, Minimality and Uniqueness scoring method using standard TEVAl tool and the result is encouraging.

1 Introduction

Generation of referring expression (GRE) is an important task in the field of Natural Language Generation (NLG) systems. The existing algorithms in GRE lie in two extremities. Incremental Algorithm is simple and speedy but less expressive in nature whereas others are complex and exhaustive but more expressive in nature. We propose a new Prefix Tree (Trie) based framework for modeling GRE problems. It incorporates intricate features of GRE (like set and boolean descriptions, context sensitivity, relational description etc.) while achieving attractive properties of Incremental algorithm (simplicity, speed etc.). The prefix tree based algorithm works in two phases. First, it encodes the description, stored in the knowledge base, in the form of prefix tree structure. Secondly, it generates the referring expression identifying the target object, which is basically a node search problem in the tree. The edges in our encoded trie structure are labeled and the path from root to that node forms the distinguishing description for the target object.

Let **D** be the Domain, **r** be the target object and **P** be the **'PreferredAttributes'** List.The Trie constructionn algorithm **ConstructTrie(D,P,T)** is shown in figure 1, Referring expression generation algorithm **MakeRefExpr(r,p,T,L) is** shown in figure 2, where **T** is a node pointer and **p** is pointer to parent of that node. Our algorithm **MakeRefExpr** returns set of attribute-values **L** to identify **r** in the domain. **[[Ni]]**= {**d** |**d**∈**D** and **d** is stored at node **Ni** where **Ni** is an i-th level node}. **Card(N)** is cardinality of set of objects in node **N**.

```
ConstructTrie(D, P, T) {
 If (D = ∅ ∨ P = ∅)
 Then Stop
 Else
   Create a node N at T
   Set ⟦ N ⟧ = D
   Extract front attribute A_i from list P
   P′ = P – { A_i }
   For each value V_j of attribute A_i do
      Create Edge E_j with label V_j as T→Next_j
      D_j′ = D ∩ ⟦ Val(E_j) ⟧
      ConstructTrie(D_j′ , P′, T→Next_j)
   End For
  End If
}
```

Figure 1. Prefix Tree Generation Algorithm

```
MakeRefExpr(r, P, T, L) {
  If ( r ∉ ⟦ T→N ⟧ )
        Then L ← ∅
         Return L
   Else If ({r} = ⟦ T→N ⟧)
        L = L ∪ Val(P→E_j )
        Return L
  Else If (isLeaf (T) ∧ {r} ⊂ ⟦ N ⟧)
         Then L ← ∅
         Return L
  Else {
     If (Card(P→N) > Card (T→N))
       Then L = L ∪ Val(P→E_j )
     P = T
     For each outgoing edge T→ Next_j (E_j) do
       L′ = MakeRefExpr(r, P,T→ Child_j, L)
         If (L′ ≠ ∅ )
         Then Return L′
   }}
```

Figure 2. Expression Generation Algorithm

The significant achievement is that incompleteness of previous algorithms can be tackled in this model in a straightforward way. For example, in case of vague descriptions (overlapping properties), Incremental and other algorithms are unable to find unambiguous description even if it exists but our prefix tree model takes into account hearer model and generate description for identifying the target object. Besides, in case of Boolean, plural, context sensitive and relational description generation our model provides a simple and linguistically rich approach to GRE.

2 Evaluation Results

In Table 1 and 2 the evaluation results for Furniture and People data has been shown.

TRIAL	DICE	MASI	A_A CCU RAC Y	UNI QUE NES S	MIN IMA LIT Y
s101t4	1.0	1.0	1.0	1.0	0.0
s101t6	0.75	0.2	0.0	1.0	0.0
s101t7	1.0	1.0	1.0	1.0	0.0
s108t5	0.85714	0.5	0.0	1.0	0.0
s114t1	1.0	1.0	1.0	1.0	0.0
s114t6	1.0	1.0	1.0	1.0	0.0
s120t4	0.57142	0.13333	0.0	1.0	0.0
s120t6	0.57142	0.13333	0.0	1.0	0.0
s123t1	0.0	0.0	0.0	1.0	0.0
s131t5	1.0	1.0	1.0	1.0	0.0
s169t1	0.8	0.44444	0.0	1.0	0.0
s169t3	1.0	1.0	1.0	1.0	0.0
s18t1	1.0	1.0	1.0	1.0	0.0
s191t3	0.66666	0.16667	0.0	1.0	0.0
s191t4	1.0	1.0	1.0	1.0	0.0
s191t6	0.57142	0.13333	0.0	1.0	0.0
s195t1	0.4	0.08333	0.0	1.0	0.0
s197t1	1.0	1.0	1.0	1.0	0.0
s197t3	0.85714	0.5	0.0	1.0	0.0
s197t4	1.0	1.0	1.0	1.0	0.0
s197t6	0.75	0.2	0.0	1.0	0.0
s19t5	0.57142	0.13333	0.0	1.0	0.0
s19t7	0.5	0.11111	0.0	1.0	0.0
s20t5	1.0	1.0	1.0	1.0	0.0
s20t6	0.66666	0.33333	0.0	1.0	0.0
s22t3	0.85714	0.5	0.0	1.0	0.0
s22t4	0.85714	0.5	0.0	1.0	0.0
s28t6	0.57142	0.13333	0.0	1.0	0.0
s307t3	0.8	0.44444	0.0	1.0	0.0
s30t4	1.0	1.0	1.0	1.0	0.0
s310t3	0.57142	0.13333	0.0	1.0	0.0
s312t5	1.0	1.0	1.0	1.0	0.0
s313t2	1.0	1.0	1.0	1.0	0.0
s315t2	0.8	0.44444	0.0	1.0	0.0
s31t4	0.33333	0.06667	0.0	1.0	0.0
s31t6	0.28571	0.05555	0.0	1.0	0.0
s320t2	0.66666	0.16667	0.0	1.0	0.0
s320t4	1.0	1.0	1.0	1.0	0.0
s320t7	0.57142	0.13333	0.0	1.0	0.0
s323t1	1.0	1.0	1.0	1.0	0.0
s323t3	1.0	1.0	1.0	1.0	0.0
s326t2	0.5	0.22222	0.0	1.0	0.0
s326t6	1.0	1.0	1.0	1.0	0.0
s329t5	0.8	0.44444	0.0	1.0	0.0
s331t6	0.57142	0.13333	0.0	1.0	0.0
s346t2	0.33333	0.06667	0.0	1.0	0.0
s367t4	1.0	1.0	1.0	1.0	0.0
s367t5	1.0	1.0	1.0	1.0	0.0
s373t5	1.0	1.0	1.0	1.0	0.0
s373t6	0.66666	0.33333	0.0	1.0	0.0
s374t4	1.0	1.0	1.0	1.0	0.0
s374t5	0.57142	0.13333	0.0	1.0	0.0
s41t2	1.0	1.0	1.0	1.0	0.0
s41t5	1.0	1.0	1.0	1.0	0.0
s48t4	0.66666	0.16667	0.0	1.0	0.0
s49t4	1.0	1.0	1.0	1.0	0.0
s49t6	0.5	0.11111	0.0	1.0	0.0
s50t6	0.85714	0.5	0.0	1.0	0.0
s53t1	1.0	1.0	1.0	1.0	0.0
s53t2	1.0	1.0	1.0	1.0	0.0
s53t4	1.0	1.0	1.0	1.0	0.0
s57t5	0.57142	0.13333	0.0	1.0	0.0
s57t6	0.66666	0.16667	0.0	1.0	0.0
s59t3	1.0	1.0	1.0	1.0	0.0
s60t2	0.8	0.44444	0.0	1.0	0.0
s62t1	1.0	1.0	1.0	1.0	0.0
s62t5	0.33333	0.06667	0.0	1.0	0.0
s62t6	0.5	0.11111	0.0	1.0	0.0
s73t1	1.0	1.0	1.0	1.0	0.0
s73t3	1.0	1.0	1.0	1.0	0.0
s73t6	1.0	1.0	1.0	1.0	0.0
s73t7	0.57142	0.13333	0.0	1.0	0.0
s78t4	0.66666	0.33333	0.0	1.0	0.0
s78t7	0.57142	0.13333	0.0	1.0	0.0
s81t2	1.0	1.0	1.0	1.0	0.0
s81t4	1.0	1.0	1.0	1.0	0.0
s84t1	1.0	1.0	1.0	1.0	0.0
s84t6	0.66666	0.33333	0.0	1.0	0.0
s98t5	1.0	1.0	1.0	1.0	0.0
s98t7	1.0	1.0	1.0	1.0	0.0

Table1: Evaluation Result of Furniture data

TRIAL	DICE	MASI	A_A CCU RAC Y	UNI QUE NES S	MIN IMA LIT Y
s101t24	1.0	1.0	1.0	1.0	0.0
s102t23	1.0	1.0	1.0	1.0	0.0
s106t23	0.0	0.0	0.0	1.0	0.0
s114t21	0.85714	0.5	0.0	1.0	0.0
s114t23	0.66667	0.33333	0.0	1.0	0.0
s123t25	0.28577	0.05556	0.0	1.0	0.0
s131t21	1.0	1.0	1.0	1.0	0.0
s131t22	1.0	1.0	1.0	1.0	0.0
s132t24	0.4	0.08333	0.0	1.0	0.0
s132t25	0.28571	0.05556	0.0	1.0	0.0
s169t26	0.85714	0.5	0.0	1.0	0.0
s177t22	0.8	0.44444	0.0	1.0	0.0
s181t24	1.0	1.0	1.0	1.0	0.0
s18t25	0.85714	0.5	0.0	1.0	0.0
s191t22	0.4	0.08333	0.0	1.0	0.0
s191t24	1.0	1.0	1.0	1.0	0.0
s192t25	0.66667	0.16667	0.0	1.0	0.0
s197t22	0.85714	0.5	0.0	1.0	0.0
s197t23	0.33333	0.06667	0.0	1.0	0.0
s197t26	0.33333	0.06667	0.0	1.0	0.0
s19t25	0.28571	0.05556	0.0	1.0	0.0
s20t22	0.8	0.44444	0.0	1.0	0.0
s20t26	0.85714	0.5	0.0	1.0	0.0
s22t25	0.85714	0.5	0.0	1.0	0.0
s307t22	0.66667	0.16667	0.0	1.0	0.0
s30t25	1.0	1.0	1.0	1.0	0.0
s310t25	0.57143	0.13333	0.0	1.0	0.0
s312t25	0.85714	0.5	0.0	1.0	0.0
s315t21	0.66667	0.33333	0.0	1.0	0.0
s315t24	1.0	1.0	1.0	1.0	0.0
s31t24	0.4	0.08333	0.0	1.0	0.0
s31t26	0.33333	0.06667	0.0	1.0	0.0
s320t23	1.0	1.0	1.0	1.0	0.0
s323t23	1.0	1.0	1.0	1.0	0.0
s323t26	0.66667	0.16667	0.0	1.0	0.0
s331t23	1.0	1.0	1.0	1.0	0.0
s332t26	0.85714	0.5	0.0	1.0	0.0
s373t23	1.0	1.0	1.0	1.0	0.0
s373t26	0.85714	0.5	0.0	1.0	0.0
s374t21	1.0	1.0	1.0	1.0	0.0
s374t22	0.85714	0.5	0.0	1.0	0.0
s374t23	0.66667	0.33333	0.0	1.0	0.0
s40t26	0.4	0.08333	0.0	1.0	0.0
s41t23	0.4	0.08333	0.0	1.0	0.0
s48t21	0.75	0.2	0.0	1.0	0.0
s49t21	0.28571	0.05556	0.0	1.0	0.0
s49t22	0.4	0.08333	0.0	1.0	0.0
s49t23	0.8	0.44444	0.0	1.0	0.0
s50t24	1.0	1.0	1.0	1.0	0.0
s50t25	0.85714	0.5	0.0	1.0	0.0
s50t26	0.85714	0.5	0.0	1.0	0.0
s53t21	1.0	1.0	1.0	1.0	0.0
s53t23	0.66667	0.33333	0.0	1.0	0.0
s53t26	0.85714	0.5	0.0	1.0	0.0
s57t23	0.4	0.08333	0.0	1.0	0.0
s57t24	0.4	0.08333	0.0	1.0	0.0
s57t25	0.28571	0.05556	0.0	1.0	0.0
s59t21	0.66667	0.33333	0.0	1.0	0.0
s59t24	1.0	1.0	1.0	1.0	0.0
s59t25	0.85714	0.5	0.0	1.0	0.0
s60t24	0.57143	0.26667	0.0	1.0	0.0
s62t21	0.0	0.0	0.0	1.0	0.0
s69t25	0.0	0.0	0.0	1.0	0.0
s73t25	0.85714	0.5	0.0	1.0	0.0
s78t21	0.85714	0.5	0.0	1.0	0.0
s78t25	0.88889	0.53333	0.0	1.0	0.0
s81t24	1.0	1.0	1.0	1.0	0.0
s81t25	0.85714	0.5	0.0	1.0	0.0

Table2: Evaluation Result of People data

References

R. Dale and E. Reiter. 1995. Computational Interpretations of the Gricean Maxims in the generation of Referring Expressions. *Cognitive Science* (18): 233 –263

S. Paladhi and S. Bandyopadhyay. 2008. Generation of Referring Expression Using Prefix Tree Structure. Proceedings of IJCNLP: 697-702

van Deemter. 2002. Boolean Extensions of Incremental Algorithm. *Computational Linguistics* 28(1): 37-52

From TUNA Attribute Sets to Portuguese Text: a First Report

Daniel Bastos Pereira
Escola de Artes, Ciências e Humanidades
University of São Paulo – USP
Av. Arlindo Bettio, 1000 - São Paulo, Brazil
daniel.bastos@usp.br

Ivandré Paraboni
Escola de Artes, Ciências e Humanidades
University of São Paulo - USP
Av. Arlindo Bettio, 1000 - São Paulo, Brazil
ivandre@usp.br

Abstract

This document describes the development of a surface realisation component for the Portuguese language that takes advantage of the data and evaluation tools provided by the REG-2008 team. At this initial stage, our work uses simple n-gram statistics to produce descriptions in the Furniture domain, with little or no linguistic variation. Preliminary results suggest that, unlike the generation of English descriptions, contextual information may be required to account for Portuguese word order.

1 Introduction

In this work we describe a surface realisation component for Portuguese definite descriptions using the data and evaluation tool provided as part of the REG-2008 Challenge. However, given the differences between language and a number of project decisions discussed below, the present results are not suitable for comparison with the work done by the actual task participants, and it should be regarded simply as an ongoing effort to generate and evaluate Portuguese descriptions using similar standards.

2 System Description

Our work is a simple application of n-gram statistics to surface realisation. Two independent annotators started by producing individual lists of the most likely phrases that could possibly be associated with every attribute–value pair in the corpus. Since at this initial stage we are only considering 1-to-n relations (i.e., each phrase is the realisation of exactly one attribute-value pair) the mapping annotation was straightforward. More complex (m-to-n) cases – those in which two or more properties may combine to form a single text unit (e.g., the properties of being human, young and male may be realised simply as "a young man" or even as "a boy") – will be discussed elsewhere.

Given a TUNA attribute set as an input, we compute all (unordered) sets of phrases that correspond to a possible description, including gender variations. Next, we compute all possible permutations of each phrase set that matched a pre-defined description template suitable to Portuguese phrase order, once again with gender variation. As a result, even a simple attribute set as in "the large red table" would have at least eight possible realisations in Portuguese, although only a few can be considered well-formed and likely to be uttered for the purpose of identification. The final task of selecting the most likely output string is left to a simple bigram language model built from a 40-million words corpus of Brazilian Portuguese newspaper articles.

3 Preliminary Evaluation

We produced a surface realisation form for each of the 80 instances of Portuguese descriptions in the REG-2008 development data. Overall, 32 instances (40%) of descriptions were incorrectly generated. The major source of errors was the lack of complete gender agreement, since our simple bigram-based model cannot handle long-distance dependencies appropriately, as in "o sofá grande vermelha", in which the gender agreement between "sofá" (masculine) and "vermelha" (feminine) could not be established. We believe that this could be easily fixed had we used a more expressive language model instead.

Two independent annotators built a Portuguese reference set by manually translating each of the 80 descriptions in the development data set and taking into account the possible phrase realisations defined earlier. More specifically, we produced a 'normalized' reference set, removing much of the noise that naturally occurs in the raw data. This included a number of likely errors (e.g., "red chair in center red"), meta-attributes (e.g., "first picture on third row"), illegal attributes (e.g.., "the grey desk with drawers"), differences in specificity (e.g., "shown from the side" as a less specific alternative to both "facing left" and "facing right" values) and synonymy (e.g., "facing the viewer" as an alternative to "facing forward"). Moreover, given that definiteness cannot be worked out from the attribute set alone, all indefinite descriptions were changed to definite.

Regarding the usefulness of this modified reference set, there are a number of due observations: firstly, given the differences between languages, our reference data set is not to be regarded as a resource for investigating language use as the original TUNA data set is intended to be, but rather as a standard of acceptable performance for a practical Portuguese NLG system. Moreover, since the translated descriptions were not produced in real situations of reference, we are aware that our results are not directly comparable to, e.g., the work carried out in the REG-2008 challenge for evaluating English descriptions, and that would remain the case even without normalization.

On the other hand, although the result of both translation and normalization tasks is a somewhat simplified set of Portuguese descriptions, this is not to say that these descriptions are tailored to match those that we intend to generate. In fact, one of the goals in the normalization task was to retain the most appropriate instances of reference, which included a large number of cases that we are not presently able to produce, e.g., those combining the *x-dimension* and *y-dimension* attributes in single references to corners, as in "in the upper right corner". Figure 1 summarizes our findings for the 80 instances of descriptions in the Furniture domain.

	Furniture
String Accuracy	0.26
String-edit dist.	3.26

Figure 1. Portuguese descriptions (Furniture domain)

4 Final Remarks

One striking difference between system descriptions and the reference set was the word order of Portuguese adjectives. To our surprise, it is not clear in which order attributes such as *colour* and *size* should be combined in Portuguese definite descriptions. For example, "*a large red table*" could be realised either as *type* + *colour* + *size* (e.g., "a mesa vermelha, grande") or as *type* + *size* + *colour* (e.g., "a mesa grande, vermelha"). As both alternatives seem equally acceptable, the choice may depend on which property contrasts each of the distractors in the situation of reference. Whilst the present ambiguity reveals a weakness in our artificially-built reference set, it may also suggest that a much more sophisticated approach to Portuguese realisation is called-for, especially if compared to the generation of English descriptions whose word order seems fairly standard. We believe that further investigation on this issue is still required

Acknowledgments

This work has been partially supported by CNPq-Brazil (484015/2007-9), FAPESP (2006/03941-7) and Ensinar com Pesquisa / USP.

References

Gatt, A.; I. van der Sluis, and K. van Deemter (2007) Evaluating algorithms for the generation of referring expressions using a balanced corpus. 11th European Workshop on Natural Language Generation 49–56.

van Deemter, K.; I. van der Sluis and A. Gatt (2006) Building a semantically transparent corpus for the generation of referring expressions. 4th International Conference on Natural Language Generation.

Author Index